THE SUMMER THAT DIDN'T END

by the same author

AN ACT OF CONSCIENCE

THE SUMMER THAT DIDN'T END

THE STORY OF THE MISSISSIPPI CIVIL RIGHTS PROJECT OF 1964

Len Holt

New Preface by Julian Bond

DA CAPO PRESS • NEW YORK

Library of Congress Cataloging in Publication Data

Holt, Len.
    The summer that didn't end / Len Holt. — 1st Da Capo Press ed.
        p.   cm.
    Originally published: New York: Morrow, 1965. With new pref.
    ISBN 0-306-80469-7
    1. Afro-Americans—Civil rights—Mississippi. 2. Civil rights move-
ments—Mississippi—History—20th century. 3. Murder—Mississippi—
Meshoga County—History—20th century. 4. Neshoba County
(Miss.)—Race relations. I. Title.
E185.615.H6   1992   91-43866
323.1 1960730762685—dc20   CIP

First Da Capo Press edition 1992

This Da Capo Press paperback edition of *The Summer That Didn't
End* is an unabridged republication of the edition published in New
York in 1965, with the addition of a new preface by Julian Bond. It is
reprinted by arrangement with William Morrow and Company.

Published by Da Capo Press, Inc.
A Subsidiary of Plenum Publishing Corporation
233 Spring Street, New York, N.Y. 10013

to the two greatest Freedom Soldiers I've met:

JOSEPH A. JORDAN of Norfolk, Virginia
and
NEWTON HUSTEAD of Lakewood, New Jersey

Acknowledgment

To those *Freedom Soldiers*—black and white, southern-born or northern-bred—who are even of this day existing on peanut-butter sandwiches and sardines in Alabama, Arkansas, Georgia and Mississippi, without whom this book could not have been written.

To Arlene Wilgoren, Karen Treusch, Mary McGrory and Joel Dressler for helping with the gathering and sorting of information.

To William Mahoney for wisdom and technical suggestions.

To the efficient and analytical Dawn Landers for editorial evaluations and production helps.

To Adele Dogan Horwitz, my editor at Morrow.

CONTENTS

Preface to the Da Capo Edition

Len Holt's *The Summer that Didn't End* is a forgotten and ignored classic. This personal and candid account of the 1964 Mississippi Freedom Summer, first issued in 1965, met the fate of many books written about civil rights in the middle sixties—events moved quickly then, and were presented to the public as brief flashes in headlines and television bites, so that Holt's book was doomed to be overlooked as history—and the movement—rolled quickly on.

The movement's character changed too. The interracial corps of youthful idealists, led by the stalwart Martin Luther King, were replaced in the public mind by posturing and threatening black militants. King seemed to turn away from summoning America to repudiate its racist past and present, and to many he became an annoying scold, condemning America for tolerating poverty and for criminally visiting death and destruction on Vietnam.

A quarter of a century later, time and distance allow us to look at Holt's account of the civil rights movement's assault on Mississippi—and Mississippi's assault on the movement—with a fresh vision informed by the traumas of the years since 1964.

For movement scholars, the story of the 1964 summer is well known. But Holt's account is accessible to the general reader, and is one of a precious few first hand reports of civil rights activism. It reads as well today as it did when it first appeared.

The 1964 Mississippi Freedom Summer was an attempt to see whether the Southern civil rights movement could, in three months, dent a century's domination of black Southerners by their white neighbors. Choosing Mississippi as the state where white resistance was the greatest, and where any small victories would have their greatest effect, the beleaguered Mississippi movement planned to bring 1000 Northern white college students to register voters, run Freedom Schools, and build an independent political party that would challenge the all-white state Democratic party—whose ties to national power guaranteed that the virtual peonage suffered by most of Mississippi's blacks would continue without challenge.

Holt was an unapologetic advocate of and a participant in the movement he recorded. Like the planners of the Freedom Summer, he believed that Mississippi was America written large, the ultimate end of racial policies practiced with lesser intensity in every American state. Like the architects of the Freedom Summer, he believed that if Mississippi could be cracked, America's racial stranglehold could be loosened too.

By 1964, workers from the Student Nonviolent Coordinating Committee (SNCC) had bloodied their heads for three years against Mississippi's sometimes brutal refusal to permit blacks to register to vote. Mississippi was infamous among the Southern states for its treatment of its black citizens. It had a long history of black activism met by harsh repression, of bravery answered by bestiality. A series of celebrated racial crimes—the lynchings of the Rev. George Lee in 1954, Emmett Till in 1955, Mack Parker in 1959, Herbert Lee in 1961—were more than mob punishment for individual transgressions of the state's racial mores; they were also warnings to the state's large black population that this fate could be—would be—theirs too if they dared breach the wall of white supremacy. SNCC's Bob Moses, joined by former Freedom Riders fresh from thirty days in the state's notorious Parchman State Penitentiary, had begun a registration project in Southwest Mississippi in 1961, assured by Attorney General Robert Kennedy that the federal government would provide protection. Kennedy had argued—and SNCC had reluctantly agreed—that registration work would prove more productive than the confrontational tactics of the Freedom Rides. Privately Kennedy hoped that abandoning headline-grabbing activity would permit continuation of a benign relationship between his brother, the President, and Southern congressional barons whose votes he needed for his legislative program. The newly registered black voters would be Democrats, he assumed. They would help insure President Kennedy's re-election in 1964. But a combination of state oppression and private terror—and the Justice Department's inaction—forced a relocation of SNCC's efforts to Jackson, the state capitol, and the majority-black Delta Counties in the state's central Northwest. Moses had recruited a staff composed largely of native black Mississippians, believing they would fit into the communities they sought to organize more easily than would imported workers from outside the Magnolia Curtain. From the beginning they were joined by local stalwarts, frequently activists in local NAACP chapters, and then by a small corps of workers from the Congress of Racial Equality (CORE); together they formed the Council of Federated Organizations (COFO) to serve as umbrella and protective local cover for their work.

In 1962, COFO encouraged the Rev. R. L. T. Smith of Jackson to run for Congress in a hopeless race against entrenched Democratic Congressman John Bell Williams. But Smith ran in order to win hearts and minds as much as an election; his platform called for expanded education, health insurance, and industrial training for all Mississippians—notions Williams had never dreamt of mentioning, and ideas Mississippians had never heard from a political candidate.

In November, 1963, COFO sponsored a "Freedom Vote" campaign to give the lie to white arguments that Mississippi blacks did not want to vote. Over 80,000 blacks cast "Freedom Votes" for Governor and Lieutenant Governor. Over 100 white college students, most from Yale and Stanford, worked in the closing weeks of the "Freedom Vote" campaign. Their presence in the state attracted attention from the national media and the Department of Justice. Black registration workers had seldom been able to engage media interest in their work, or to get the Federal government to provide the promised protection. But when the sons of America's elite were harassed, arrested, and beaten by Mississippi whites, the nation's newspapers reported it and the nation's federal apparatus moved swiftly to protect them.

The lesson learned in the Freedom Vote campaign created the Freedom Summer of 1964. Len Holt documents what happened—with the summer volunteers, the largely black COFO staff, and the local black population which risked life and limb to house and befriend them. If for no other reason, the summer was remarkable because the poorest people in America opened their homes and shared their daily grits and fatback with the children of America's most powerful families.

The effect on both groups was long-lasting. Recent scholarship has shown how much the volunteers' future lives were shaped by their three months in Mississippi. Twenty years later, many continued doing "good works" as teachers, union organizers, and community activists, and most credit the summer of 1964 for the direction their lives have taken since then. The families who opened doors and shared beds with students from Harvard, Berkeley, and Wisconsin were changed too; if nothing else, many later reported seeing whites for the first time as individuals who could be either friend or foe.

The summer changed SNCC and CORE too. Long-simmering racial and sexual tensions erupted during the Freedom Summer and in the summer's aftermath. Neither organization would be the same even after most volunteers returned to their homes.

Most of all, Mississippi changed. Mississippi blacks had begun to move the mountain of white racism years before, and organizations like the NAACP had long histories of organized resistance across the state. But the Freedom Summer helped to spread Freedom's message in towns and homes where it had never been before.

Len Holt tells about the volunteers and the workers and families who welcomed them and what they accomplished—the Freedom Schools, the strengthening of the Mississippi Freedom Democratic Party (MFDP), and largely fruitless voter registration work.

The MFDP would become one of the summer's most important legacies. It lost attempts to unseat the state's delegation to the 1964 Democratic Convention and its all-white delegation to the Congress in 1965, but both these efforts—and their graphic documentation of Mississippi terror aimed at keeping blacks from voting—laid important groundwork for passage of the Voting Rights Act of 1965.

The MFDP's lawsuits, especially *Allen v. State Board of Elections* (393 U.S. 544 [1969]), helped define for the nation what an unfettered vote really was—decisions which reverberate in racially free elections in locations as far from Mississippi as New York and Los Angeles.

The Freedom Schools were pioneers in successful curriculum diversity—a topic much debated everywhere today. They showed black Mississippi schoolchildren a world outside their impoverished classrooms, and taught them things about themselves and their history Mississippi's schools had never dared to teach.

Holt's greatest contribution may be in his detailed description of one of the Freedom Summer's least known efforts, the "White Folks" Project. Run by the Southern Students Organizing Conference (SSOC)—"the white SNCC"—the "White Folks" Project involved 25 volunteers who worked in white neighborhoods in four communities, voluntarily segregated for their own protection from the overt "civil rights" activity of the COFO staff. The Project's success rate was hardly encouraging, but Holt rightly argues that it held the key to overcoming the racial barrier the South had successfully raised for a century—and Presidents and other politicians everywhere raise successfully today—that kept white Mississippians in 1964 and white Americans in 1992 from coming to grips with economic and class questions that transcend race. Had it been more successful, SNCC and CORE might not have been subjected to the racial tensions which helped to tear them apart.

Holt provides a useful appendix of documents that are as much a gold mine as his narrative; these pages literally do speak volumes.

The Summer That Didn't End is a necessary look into the machinery and personalities of the Southern civil rights movement's largest attempt to break racism at its strongest point. The summer broke lives: Holt reminds us that more deaths were recorded than the celebrated kidnapping of Cheney, Goodman, and Schwerner. Len Holt's story is, however, the story of a success whose victories are still being recorded daily. For the white volunteers, it was the Freedom Summer; for black Americans, in Mississippi and elsewhere, almost two decades later it is still The Summer That Didn't End.

—Julian Bond
Washington, D.C.
November, 1991

Julian Bond has been an active participant in the movements for civil rights, economic justice, and peace, as well as an aggressive spokesman for the disinherited, for over thirty years. As an activist who has faced jail for his convictions, as a veteran of more than twenty years of service in the Georgia General Assembly, as a writer, teacher, and lecturer, Bond has been in the forefront of social change since he was a college student leading sit-in demonstrations in Atlanta in 1960.

Bond is currently a Distinguished Scholar in Residence at the American University in Washington, D.C., and a Vis-

iting Professor at Harvard University. He is the host of "America's Black Forum," the oldest Black-owned show in television syndication. And he is the author of two books, A Time to Speak, A Time to Act, *a collection of essays; and* Black Candidates: Southern Campaign Experiences.

Introduction

A long look at Mississippi can help us understand our own communities and our neighboring communities, north and south, because Mississippi is not another country. Neither passports nor visas are needed to travel between it and other parts of the United States. There's no need to exchange currency and no necessity to submit helpless arms to needles full of immunization serum to obtain "re-entry."

For the worse, not the better, Mississippi is America.

Whatever corruption, vice, evil, pettiness, tyranny, callousness may exist in this nation flourishes *best* in the Magnolia State . . . and in its purest forms. These conditions lend themselves to study and analysis and possibly a discovery of cures for problems national in scope. Literally, Mississippi is an exaggerated New York, Illinois or California.

The delegates to the 1964 Democratic National Convention from the Mississippi Freedom Democratic Party discovered this in Atlantic City when they found themselves being treated in the "North" as they are mistreated at home. Howard Zinn, historian, recognized this and described this phenomenon beautifully in his recent book, *The Southern Mystique*.

I, too, recognized it.

I am a Negro lawyer.

Almost a decade has passed since graduation from law school (Howard University/'56), during which time the bulk of my professional life has been spent handling what are known as "civil rights" matters in most of the states of the Confederacy—usually as attorney for others, but on occasions as the arrested defendant, victim of an injunction, or plaintiff in an integration suit.

Recently home base was shifted to Washington, D.C., where I rest better at night. For years prior to coming to Washington, the base was in Norfolk, Virginia, as a member of the firm of Jordan, Dawley and Holt.

Such well-ordered plans as my life may have are arranged by unexpected (collect) long-distance calls' arriving at those hours of the morning when sleep is best. During 1964 several such calls caused me to sojourn in Mississippi for short periods during the months of April, May, June, July and September.

While in Mississippi in June, as the world became aware of the Mississippi Freedom Summer Project of 1964, several of us expressed concern about the obsession of the newsmen with the hundreds of beatings, shootings and jailings and the more than a dozen murders—including those of the three civil rights workers in Philadelphia, Mississippi. (By October, 1964, there were 15 murders, 4 woundings, 37 churches bombed or burned to the ground and more than 1,000 arrests.)

Our concern was that the violence would be dwelt upon to the exclusion of the positive achievements of the Summer Project and the message of Mississippi that needs to be heard everywhere—those matters which prevented the horrors from being in vain.

Staughton Lynd (coordinator of the freedom schools during their first two months of existence and professor of history at Yale) suggested that I act as a "wastepaper basket," i.e., historian.

With misgivings I accepted the *ordination* and began to collect clippings and memos, to take pictures and to tape interviews with persons engulfed in the task of not letting the work of the summer end. Out of this collection and my own experiences of pitching in every once in a while came this book.

Violence and death are not strangers to Mississippi: they were intimate fibers of life there before the summer of 1964; they are imminent and unforeseeable parts of every breath drawn in that state today. Tomorrow will be no different. It is the concern of this book that there be an awareness of the "strangers": the achievements of the Summer Project. It is a further concern that there be an awareness that the septic conditions of Mississippi are not localized—that the state is a mirror.

Imperativeness surrounds the two concerns, because the Summer Project of 1964 is continuing; in fact, it is spreading to at least three more states (Alabama, Arkansas and Georgia) during the summer of 1965.

In a narrow sense, some aspects of the Summer Project failed. Take the voter registration program as an example. For the registration of Negroes in the state to be meaningful, new voters should flow from the clerk's office in the 82 counties of Mississippi like the "waters of a mighty river." Before the summer of 1964 the new voters being registered were but a weak trickle. In spite of Herculean efforts during the summer, that trickle remained a trickle.

But, in reality, nothing about the Summer Project could fail.

It was impossible for things to have grown worse.

As for specific achievements of the Summer Project, the four most impelling ones are these: the freedom schools, the white community project, the Mississippi Freedom Democratic Party, and the *focus*. For the first time in a century, the state became a part of the national consciousness. World attention was riveted on it. As a nation we looked at it and examined it, although it was in much the same fashion as a physician studies human excrement to discover hidden diseases within the body.

So large and diverse was the Summer Project that it doesn't lend itself to discussion in pure chronological sequences. However, as far as possible, the organization of this book is chronological. It was the lynching of the three civil rights workers in Philadelphia which exploded the Summer Project into the world's awareness. The background of those murders is discussed in the first chapter. This is followed by chapters that discuss the preparation for the summer and how the Project nearly ended before it began, the training and arrival of the summer volunteers, and the role and nature of the federal government.

Subsequent chapters describe the freedom schools, the "White

Folks" Project, the Mississippi Freedom Democratic Party, and the National Democratic Convention and the Congressional challenge.

The purpose of the book as a whole is to anatomize the work of one summer, showing what a living thing it became and how it shall go on living.

PART ONE

I

Philadelphia Lynching

Marvel not at Mississippi
For Hitler had a Mother—
Distant victories are proximate defeats.
'Cause the bitch that spawned him
Is in heat
Again.

—The Wisdom of Dawley

THE DRIVE WAS LONG from Oxford, Ohio: sixteen hours. They had left yesterday in the afternoon—James Chaney, Louise Hermey, Michael Schwerner, Andy Goodman and other volunteers on the Mississippi Project. James Chaney glanced at the speedometer, which showed that he was propelling the station wagon along at a safe 50 miles per hour, headed West on U.S. Highway 11 in Alabama. Ahead was the green sign they had been looking for, with its white letters. Someone read it aloud as they passed by:

"Welcome to Mississippi . . .
The Magnolia State"

The station wagon drove into Mississippi with its cargo of young people—all younger than Mickey Schwerner's 24 years—who were destined to man the projects of the Mississippi Freedom Summer of 1964, centered around Meridian, Mississippi. Louise Hermey marveled at the lush green countryside, hardly touched by the ravages of civilization. Everything looked so peaceful and calm. She later related that she wondered how this could be the Mississippi that was described as being heinous. She challenged the characterization in her mind even though she recalled the parting scenes the day before, June 20, 1964, in Oxford.

Everyone had shaken hands so warmly and meaningfully and had drunk so deeply of each other's face and eyes. The parting of Mickey Schwerner and his wife Rita had been especially emotional and yet somber.

The blue 1964 Ford station wagon then turned on to Interstate Highway 59, where the speed-limit signs said that one could go 70 miles per hour. Yet Chaney increased the speed to only 55. This was Mississippi. A station wagon with whites and Negroes had to set its own speed limits—and set them somewhere below those given by the signs.

By the time the station wagon reached Meridian, the sun had risen higher. A sprinkling of neon signs gaudily flashed, and the buzz of the signs coming on and going off pierced the Sunday-morning quiet of vacant Meridian Streets.

At approximately 5:10 A.M., Sunday, June 21, 1964, the blue Ford station wagon drove down Twenty-fifth Street past the E. F. Young Hotel; made a right turn onto the one-way street, Fifth Avenue; and parked in front of the door of 2505½ in the space reserved for the Service Cab Company (for colored).

"Hey, Baby, welcome home," one of the taxi drivers waiting idly for his next run called out as he recognized Chaney and the station wagon. Soon the taxicab-stand folks emptied their small office and came out to the station wagon to introduce themselves, welcome Chaney and Mickey back, and assist the summer volunteers in carrying their belongings up the 31 stairs to the Movement office. (This office served many functions, including that of hotel when civil rights workers hit Meridian at ungodly hours.)

While Chaney checked the box marked "important," which contained urgent messages and matters needing attention, Mickey gave Andy, Louise and the others a quick tour of the five-room office, showing the 9,000 books, allocation of space, and private areas open only to staff working on the project. Mickey then explained the special uses of the several phones in the office, the necessity for maintenance of a phone log of calls, and how that log was to be kept. He also pointed out the list of jails and police stations for all the counties around, including Meridian, with their phone numbers; a list of all the law enforcement officers; and the State Highway Patrol and the FBI numbers. One phone, 482-6103, was to be used primarily for outgoing calls. Another phone, 485-9286, was to be used for incoming calls. An important thing to remember was that every hour of the day, on the half hour, they had to check with the Jackson office to let them know that "all is well."

Louise Hermey was in charge of Meridian communications, see-ing to the proper flow of messages into and out of the Meridian Project headquarters for an area that included Kemper, Clarke, Newton, Jasper, Lauderdale and Neshoba counties, all close to Meridian, which is located on the eastern border of Mississippi, half-way between the top and bottom of the state.

While the others claimed their luggage and got ready for rides to the private homes where they would stay, Chaney motioned to Mickey to come into the little inner office, where there was a small sink, the mimeograph machine and office supplies. There they talked quietly about Philadelphia and Neshoba. The church where the community center and freedom school were to have been operated during the summer of 1964 had been burned down, and three of the people who were the Movement's strongest supporters had been beaten.

This was serious. Something had to be done. The people in Neshoba had to get reassurance that the program could go on and should go on . . . or things never would get any better and the kill-ings would never stop. The two men decided that they would go to Neshoba as soon as they had a few hours' rest. Because Andy Goodman had shown signs of being able to handle himself and to lead others effectively, he was put in charge of the freedom school to be operated in Neshoba if the Negroes there would still have one. In addition to acquainting Andy with the people with whom he would work, the trip would also provide the two veterans, Chaney and Schwerner, with an opportunity for another intense private session with Andy.

Chaney went to the outgoing-call phone and dialed a Meridian number, 482-2327, the weather bureau: "Temperatures in the high nineties, clear skies, no rain, sunset at 7:05 P.M." The trip could be made, Chaney informed Mickey.

Orientation of the 750 summer volunteers had taken place at the Western College for Women in Oxford, Ohio. Mickey (who had been working in Meridian since January, 1964), Chaney (who had been working with the Movement for nearly a year), and Preston Ponder (who had been working with the Meridian Project for several months) had joined the nearly 100 other Mississippi staff members at the Oxford, Ohio, campus on June 15, 1964, to meet and help orient the hundreds of college students who had volunteered for eight weeks of service in the Summer Project of 1964.

When Chaney and Mickey had left Meridian to drive to Oxford, Ohio, the Mt. Zion Methodist Church of Neshoba had been standing intact and committed to use as a freedom school. On June 16 it had been burned.

The trip taken on Sunday, June 21, 1964, had several purposes. First, the volunteers hoped to bolster any sagging spirits of those who might have faltered as a result of the recent burning of the church and beatings. Second, there was hope that some information could be gained as to who was responsible for the burning, in order that the FBI might be involved. There was hope that some sort of plan could be worked out whereby a national appeal could be made to raise funds to rebuild the church. Finally there was the hope that the program planned for the summer could continue in spite of the burning and beatings.

After approximately two hours' sleep, Chaney roused himself and drove to the Phillips 66 station on the block over from Fifth Avenue, where the Movement's Meridian office was. In addition to watching the Negro proprietor check the battery, radiator and oil, Chaney inspected the white-walled, heavy-duty, oversized Firestone tires on the rear wheels. This type of tire was vital to effective movement on the soft dirt roads so common throughout the Longdale section of Neshoba County. The inspection was visual and manual. Chaney's eyes and hands searched for sharp rocks and metal objects. A similar inspection was given to the front tires.

Around 9:30 A.M., Mickey Schwerner explained to Louise Hermey where they were going and what procedures she was to follow during the day: "There's an immutable rule here: no one is to remain in Neshoba after four P.M. If for any reason we aren't back by four P.M., you should alert Jackson and begin checking every city jail, county jail, sheriff's office, police station and hospital between Meridian and Neshoba. O.K.?"

"It will be done," she answered.

With a sense of urgency, Louise worked on convincing herself that these precautions about being back, regular checks, and arms over back seats and lookout positions when driving in cars were more or less routinized acts against dangers that were *possible* but not *probable*. It wasn't good for one to live full of the tensions that characterized persons who sleep cradled in a guillotine.

The Longdale community is unusual in Mississippi. Only Negroes live in it, and all own their own land. Of the more than 50 persons in the section, 3 are registered voters. In Neshoba County there are 5,000 Negroes, 10 of whom are voters.

Neshoba is a square-shaped county of approximately 568 square miles. Of the total population of 20,927, 28 per cent, or 5,901, are what the census calls "non-white." The county has but two law enforcement officers: Sheriff Lawrence Rainey and his deputy, Cecil Price. A sheriff and his deputy are particularly close in Mississippi; neither is salaried. Sheriffs get their income from a fee system and themselves hire, fire and pay such deputies as they may have.

Sheriff Rainey is a powerful figure with torso and limbs like a rhinoceros: he's 41, six foot two, 250 pounds and barrel-chested. His reddish, crackly skin hangs in pouches on his face from the constant carrying of oversized wads of chewing tobacco. Two Negroes have been killed by him in "self-defense." Prior to the assumption of the lawman's role, he was a mechanic.

Rainey's only deputy, Cecil Price, is a younger, less awesome replica of the sheriff.

With the aid of two State Highway patrolmen who live in the Philadelphia area, Cecil Price arrested Chaney, Mickey and Andy and caused them and their well-known blue Ford station wagon, Mississippi license H-25503, to be transported into the populous area of Philadelphia, where the county jail and city jail are located.

Shortly after the arrest, a phone call was made to Meridian, where Sheriff Rainey was at a hospital with his wife.

When Deputy Price and the Mississippi State Highway patrolmen confronted the three young men, they were helpless. There are few phones in the county and no roadside telephone booths. The persons with phones would not have let them be used by a "nigger" or a "nigger lover." Some would have refused because of hate; others would have refused because of fear—fear that somebody might learn that they had been human to the enemy. The three young men had no radio to alert others of their danger. When they were arrested, Cecil Price was their god and they were his creation. Only he, Cecil Price, could have mercy on their souls.

Not only was Price god, but he was also the United States of America, the President, the Supreme Court, the Constitution and all the high-sounding principles and mouthings of a nation that is the wealthiest and most powerful country in the history of mankind. Mickey, Chaney and Andy knew this at the moment of arrest, when they stood at the gates of eternity. They had been told in unmistakable terms by the United States that their rights to freedom of speech, freedom of association, safety of their persons—and all the other rights—would be *protected* by local law enforcement agencies, which have the primary responsibility. "There is no federal police force," John Doar of the Justice Department had announced in Oxford, Ohio, at the orientation session.

When they were arrested, what rights they had by reasons of the laws and the Constitution were in the hands of Deputy Price. In accordance with his power and duty of being the United States Constitution, he then dispensed those rights.

Sometime around 4 P.M. on June 21, 1964, screams were heard in the area of where the jail is located. A passer-by described them as like those of "a baby caught in a fire," according to unofficial sources.

On June 21, 1964, the sun set at 7:05 P.M. in Philadelphia, Mississippi.

According to Deputy Price, at 9 P.M., 10 P.M. or perhaps 10:30 P.M. —his versions differed—on a steamy, moonlit night, he, the Constitution of the United States, turned the three men loose after collecting a $20 fine.

They were never seen alive again.

The will of *god* was done.

When the clock showed 3:30 P.M. on June 21, 1964, Louise Hermey became concerned, but she said little to the other summer volunteers. Between 3:30 P.M. and 4:00 P.M. she walked repeatedly from the inner office, where the phones were, to the window of the room 21 steps away and peered out on the street past the Joe Louis Café on Fifth Avenue and down past the E. F. Young Hotel on Twenty-fifth Street. Her fingers, usually adorned with average-length fingernails, were shorn by her teeth so that pink flesh showed.

4 P.M.: Louise called the state headquarters of the Mississippi Summer Project at Jackson and reported the lack of contact with the three. Jackson called back immediately on the Wide Area Telephone Service (WATS line), which enables the state headquarters to call directly all over the state (cost, $500 plus, monthly). Jackson confirmed the emergency procedures given and asked that Louise not begin them until 5 P.M., because the trio would have to walk for hours to get to a phone if there had been a mechanical failure of the car.

5 P.M.: Louise in Meridian and the WATS line operators in Jackson began calling methodically, one by one, every jail from Meridian to Philadelphia: Philadelphia city jail, Neshoba County jail, Decatur city jail, Suqualena city jail, Collinsville jail, Lauderdale County jail, Meridian city jail. The response was negative. No one knew anything about the three: "Ain't here." "That nigger and his nigger lover ain't here."

Just as methodically, hospitals along the same route were called. The result was also negative. Samuel Block was dispatched to make a personal inquiry at the Meridian jail.

6 P.M.: Jackson and Meridian began calling the FBI and State Highway Patrol, asking for help in finding the missing three. Both agencies expressed indifference. Methodical checks began again of the jails and hospitals along the route.

7 P.M.: Charles Young, owner of the Young Hotel, made calls to people he knew in the Philadelphia area. No results.

8 P.M.: Meridian reported in to Jackson on efforts and lack of results.

9 P.M.: After making the same checks of hospitals and jails, Louise called Jackson. Jackson reported that the Atlanta office of the Student Nonviolent Coordinating Committee (SNCC) had been alerted and had joined the pressuring of the Justice Department and the FBI to give some help at once.

9:05 P.M.: Cars full of white males circled the Meridian office.

9:06 P.M.: Meridian police called about the cars circling.

The phone log in Meridian indicates more checks of the hospitals and jails at 11 P.M. and 12 midnight and at 1 A.M. on June 22, 1964— all with negative results. As the hour grew later, calls were made to the nearest kin of the three missing persons, while both SNCC in Atlanta and the Jackson headquarters called, fought, and harassed the FBI, the Justice Department and the Mississippi State Highway Patrol to help find the missing trio. The response by these three law enforcement agencies was less than heartening. (The phone log of the Jackson headquarters for the Summer Project as it attempted to get help is set forth in the appendix.)

The first break occurred the following day, June 22, 1964, at 7:30 A.M., when Mrs. Herring, wife of the Neshoba County jailer, stated that the three boys had been arrested the day before, Sunday June 21, *and released at 6 P.M. the same day, June 21.*

Three days later, Thursday, June 25, 1964, the three were still *missing* (a status they would have for another 41 days) when I and several other volunteers went into Neshoba and talked with the people in the Longdale section who were the last friendly persons to see the trio alive.

To our chagrin, we learned that these persons had not yet been interviewed by the FBI. Our group waited at the sight of the burned-out Mt. Zion Methodist Church while Matteo S. Suarez, "Flukey," a CORE field secretary, conducted a private interview with a person whose identity has to be concealed. So hot and muggy was the day that I contented myself to sit on one of the blackened cinder blocks from the foundation of the church. Three of the other fellows began an odd pursuit: they began tinkering around with the bell from the church.

For more than a half hour, while awaiting Flukey's return, they tinkered and failed, tinkered some more and failed some more, as they tried to assemble the bell on its iron cradle so that it could ring. Again and again the makeshift repair would fall apart as one rusty piece of wire would break or a screw would fall out of the hook that was supposed to hold the clapper.

Sam Block, SNCC field secretary, turned on a transistor radio just as news was coming forth: "We, the parents of the summer volunteers, demand that the President and the federal government protect those working in Mississippi to implement the ideals of our Constitution—and the people who live there the year round."

The announcer indicated that the lady speaking was Mrs. Marcia Rabinowitz.

"That's Joni's Mother," Sam screamed. Words can't describe the feeling that surged over us as the radio let us know that someone did care, that somebody was not blandly accepting the postulations of the federal government that our protection had to come from sheriffs like Lawrence Rainey. Almost simultaneously the fellows working on the bell got it together and began to ring it:

"Freedom! Freedom!" The shout rose between rings of the bell. We were swept up out of our fears and began to cry and shout: "Freedom! Freedom!" And louder: "Freedom!"

"Freedom!"

The bell clanged.

"Freedom—from all the sheriffs, governors and governments who would sacrifice us to prove the lies that make their truths," Sam Block shouted.

"Freedom!" The shout came again, and there was more clanging of the sweet tone of a bell that wasn't supposed to ring any more. The woods reverberated with excited and defiant shouts of men who were crying for Chaney, Mickey and Andy and for themselves —men who, through no virtue of their own, had been spared.

Willie Blue, SNCC staff motion-picture cameraman, approached

Sam Block: "You know they're dead. Why did they have to kill 'em? Why did they have to kill 'em?"

If you lived in Mississippi, in Neshoba or some other county, there are several reasons—other than your own sick mind—why you might have felt it necessary to take your service .38 revolver and kill three young men involved in the Mississippi Freedom Summer of 1964.

A study of Neshoba County and its county seat, Philadelphia, suggests some of those reasons.

Neshoba is a virgin land with hundreds of thousands of acres of valuable pine-timber country, through which run more than 80 miles of the Pearl River, which can supply the water needed and the disposal system for hundreds of manufacturing plants that might be attracted to the area by tax-free land that the county might care to donate. It's located in a state that is dry—hard beverages are prohibited—and has adults, with a yearning for the forbidden liquor, who will pay $5 for a pint of Four Roses whisky.

One of the important crops of the county is cotton, which is grown on strict allotment of acreages parceled out to farmers by a three-man white committee elected by the white farmers of the county—free of any interference from those farmers who are colored. It's a county where you can find thousands of able-bodied Negro males and females willing to work from "kin to kaint," as sunrise to sunset is colloquially described, for a mere $3 a day or less.

As a resident of Neshoba County, you would proudly point to two very fine manufacturing plants, which are the largest employers in the county, U.S. Motor Division of Emerson Electric and Wells-Lamont Glove Factory—which either have or are trying to get contracts with the federal government—and to your proximity to the Naval Aviation Air Station nearby, which buys thousands of gallons of milk from your cows along with other food products. With pride you could point to the number of country residents who work at the Meridian Naval Air Station without fear of some Negro's successfully asserting that he ought to be entitled to a *white man's job*.

In describing the county, you would not forget such things as the rural and city postal system with star routes efficiently served because the personnel is white. As a Neshobian you could take comfort in the fact that there are only 10 Negro voters and that all of the white voters have long since learned that communism, integration, sex and sin are synonymous. No trouble would be had in reaching the conclusion that you are doing right well because you are better off than the Negro—your standard, as well as the enemy when he seeks to move out of the order of things.

More than a quarter of a million dollars in liquor is sold in the county annually at various joints and dives. The person who permits this continued operation can expect to be handsomely favored with appreciation. In addition to the legal liquor sold "illegally" (whisky made with the federal alcoholic tax paid on it), there is considerable moonshining.

Under the provisions of recent federal enactments, companies in Neshoba County such as Emerson's U.S. Motor Division, serving the government through contracts, cannot easily refuse to hire a Negro if he presses his case. By reason of location and wages, the local Negroes are the ones most likely to be attracted to the jobs; but, alone, few Negroes would venture such a step. However, with an organized community of Negroes, aided by civil rights workers, the story could be very different. Therefore, organization which could lead to integration is "bad."

The farm income of the county is closely related to the support programs of the federal government which allocate acreage to the white farmers through a three-man committee elected by the farmers of the county. Unlike political elections, to vote for this three-man county committee, one need be only a farmer or sharecropper. No literacy tests, poll taxes or what have you are required to vote. Pressure for integration would stir up the farmers and sharecroppers who are Negroes, and this convenient arrangement would be in trouble.

Regardless of whether you employed Negroes for $3 or less per day, ran the cotton gin where you put the short weight on the Negro farmers in addition to commandeering the valuable cotton seeds from the ginning, sold butane gas for the thousands of rural homes at excessive prices, or dealt in "illegal" liquor, integration in your mind would represent a threat.

In Neshoba County James Chaney, Mickey Schwerner and Andy Goodman would have represented that threat if you had become a part of things as they were—and this consideration was, and is, not limited to white people. In a showdown the Negro bootleggers, moonshiners and schoolteachers might find something within them tugging them to uncoil the rope or pull the trigger. In September, 1964, proof of this fact was offered when Negro Prof. Moore, principal of the Neshoba Negro High School, expelled 40 students for wearing SNCC "one-man, one-vote" buttons to school. Many of these students had attended the freedom school in Neshoba in July and August, 1964—the project that the burning of the Mt. Zion Methodist Church and the killing of the three civil rights workers was supposed to end.

The threat would have been heightened when the rights workers consistently involved themselves with those "Longdale niggers" who had a reputation for being "arrogant and independent."

The county citizens may never forget four years ago, when it was reported that 13 Longdale Negroes came into Philadelphia wearing their Sunday best to register to vote: neat suits and bright print dresses, shiny shoes—and polished shotguns.

Or June 22, 1964, 29 hours after the first call to the federal government for help, four of the nation's 6,140 FBI agents arrived in Philadelphia. On June 25, 1964, 100 sailors from the nearby Meridian Naval Air Station were involved; on June 27 the number was increased to 200 sailors and on June 29 to 400—for a search that was to last 44 days, until the three bodies were unearthed on an informer's tip.

The shock of the triple lynching festered itself into a double bitterness among the SNCC and CORE staff, who had dreaded this summer program even as they had prepared for its beginning. It became apparent that a phone call to the Neshoba jail by a federal agent before 9:30 P.M. could have done much to preserve the three lives.

Adams Bootleggers Forced To Retreat

Cross River To Louisiana, Insist Governor's Doing

NATCHEZ, Miss. (Special)—"We don't know why Gov. Johnson is shutting off liquor here," said a Natchez bootlegger, "We think he must be very ungrateful to previous contributions we have made to his campaigns while running."

In Natchez and throughout Adams County today bootleggers were taking inventory and moving stock across the Mississippi River bridge to Vidalia, La. Sale of all intoxicating liquor and gambling in Adams County was ordered ended by midnight tonight in a joint order from the sheriff and chief of police.

The governor's offices today claimed the governor issued no order for the Natchez shutdown but the bootlegger said, "When we were told we must close, we were told that the governor was definitely behind it. He must really be ungrateful."

A spokesman in the governor's office said today that the local authorities initiated the action "but as always the state stands ready to back up local authorities on any law enforcement whene requested to do so."

The spokesman said the state is willing to cooperate in any way as requested by local authorities.

Sheriff Odell Anders and Police Chief J. T. Robinson said the closedown came after Gov. Johnson told them by telephone if they did not close the places he would use the newly-enlarged highway patrol to close them.

The sheriff said the order included all clubs both public and private. The order also placed a midnight curfew on the sale of beer and wine. Both are legal in Adams County.

Liquor has been sold openly in the county for many years and the city of Natchez has collected a black market tax on sales since 1948. The state also collects a black market tax on all lquor sales in the state.

Mayor John Nosser and Anders said the crackdown was designed to aid an investigation by the FBI and state officers into racial violence here. The Mississippi Highway Patrol has been under heavy criticism in the area for some of the methods used in its search for weapons.

It was reported that liquor sales in the county had been under "strict control" for several weeks and that liquor drinking was not being allowed in any of the bootleg establishments.

At least for a time, Adams County residents will be forced to drive all the way to Louisiana for their liquor—about five minutes from any part of Natchez.

The *Jackson* (Miss.) *Daily News,* Thursday, October 29, 1964, p. 10.

"We cannot protect. We can only investigate." Those are infamous phrases of the Mississippi summer that began in death on June 21, 1964.

The second aspect of the bitterness was the search. Rita Schwerner, Mickey's widow, stated it well: "We all know that this search with hundreds of sailors is because Andrew Goodman and my husband are white. If only Chaney was involved, nothing would've been done." Her lips spoke a deadly truth; the 80 SNCC and 20 CORE members who had been preparing for the coming of the summer volunteers knew it. Five Negroes are *known* to have been killed in Mississippi between January and May, 1964, with indifferent silence given to pleas for help.

The kind of white "troops" volunteering for the Mississippi Summer Project of 1964 made the difference—those northern students who were to staff freedom schools and community centers and to engage in voter registration. Preparations made in the spring of 1964 for the Summer Project had also helped make that difference.

II

COFO and the Summer Project

> In my Father's house are many mansions:
> if it were not so, I would have told you.
> I go to prepare a place for you.
> . . . that where I am, there ye may be also
> And whither I go ye know, and the way ye know.
>   —St. John 14:2

IN NOVEMBER, 1963, Governor Ross Barnett and the other reigning lords of a private enclave called Mississippi had long since developed a loathing for chiggers, weevils and "Snickites." And in November, 1963, the SNCC personnel added a new cuss word to the racist vocabulary: "COFO."

COFO, or the Council of Federated Organizations, is a composite of the civil rights organizations functioning in Mississippi . . . SNCC (Student Nonviolent Coordinating Committee), The Congress of Racial Equality (CORE), The National Association for the Advancement of Colored People (NAACP), The Southern Christian Leadership Conference (SCLC), and smaller groups, such as the Holmes County Voters League and the Ruleville citizenship organization.

At the formation of COFO it was expected that the expenses of the state's civil rights activities would be borne by direct grants from the national civil rights groups.* In keeping with the unity concept

* The name COFO goes back to the spring of 1961, when such persons as Medgar Evers, the slain NAACP field secretary; Aaron Henry; Carsie Hall, who is

for forming COFO, the officers elected for the organization reflected the broad membership. Dr. Aaron Henry (a Clarksdale druggist and president of the state NAACP) was elected president. Bob Moses (field secretary and Mississippi project director for SNCC) became COFO's program director. Dave Dennis (CORE field secretary) was elected the COFO assistant program director.

As beautiful as the idea of unity was, one cannot say that the idea ever succeeded or failed; from the beginning it wasn't tried. CORE said it could not participate unless it was given some special area of the state in which to work, so that it could get "projection" (image in news releases about Mississippi that would assist in CORE fund raising). As a result, agreement was reached to allow such emphasis by assigning to CORE the Fourth Mississippi Congressional District (counties which include the cities of Canton, Meridian and Philadelphia). Into this area CORE placed 20 field secretaries; it paid their salaries but, otherwise, made only minor contributions to the over-all budget of COFO.

Tension increased between CORE and COFO when, inadvertently or otherwise, the national office of CORE repeatedly issued news releases and made comments to the contributing public in the North that implied that CORE was *the* organization planning, directing and staffing the voter registration, civil rights activities and political education program of the entire state, to the detriment of the organization really pulling the financial load.

Similar claims were made by the NAACP's New York Office on occasions. In actuality the NAACP contributes neither staff nor money to COFO programs. The NAACP claims to be participating in the state through its direct contributions of money to the NAACP chapters of the state. Examination shows that these NAACP chapters are, for the most part, programmatically dead. The NAACP members desirous of activity find it outside of the "let's hold a

---

one of the state's three civil rights lawyers; and others formed the group in order to have a meeting with Governor Ross Barnett to secure the release of the Freedom Riders. It was felt that the Governor would not meet with older, established civil rights organizations. After the Barnett meeting, COFO became inactive. It was revitalized in January, 1962, by Bob Moses of SNCC, whose experience at that time had shown him that discrimination in Mississippi would yield only to a unified attack by as strong a force as possible.

meeting" postulating of the state chapters; they work with COFO. The NAACP "big gun" in Mississippi is Charles Evers, whose only apparent skill lies in having the same last name as his martyred brother, Medgar.

SCLC makes no claim regarding itself in Mississippi, contributes two staff persons to the COFO program and has made nominal financial contributions to the heavy financial burden of COFO's effort to create "The Beloved Community."

SNCC supplies the personnel in four of the five Congressional districts of the state, 95 per cent of the staff in the state headquarters in Jackson, and 90 to 95 per cent of the money for operating the civil rights program and facilities throughout the entire state.

Civil Rights in Mississippi is COFO.

SNCC for all practical purposes, is COFO.

And SNCC is people.

SNCC is in reality a 48-year-old Mississippi field secretary named Mrs. Fannie Lou Hamer, whose ample matronly frame dragged a long picking sack down thousands of rows of somebody else's cotton, snatching bolls, while she projected her deep powerful voice in the "Lord's songs," shaking the air to the outermost corners of the fields. One day she tried to register for the vote. Swiftly she became unemployable. She was shot at. On one occasion she was beaten until the drawing of a breath shot rivulets of pain throughout her.

SNCC is the gaunt frame of 25-year-old Jesse Harris, towering above the six-foot mark and crowned by a slender, high-cheekboned face in burnished brown—and refusing to let the words "yes, sir" flow through his goateed lips to placate an angry Mississippi State Highway patrolman alarmed by a racially mixed car driving to the McComb Freedom House.

SNCC is Bob Moses, the 30-year-old director of SNCC's Mississippi Project, who arrived in the state in the fall of 1961—a date which the subsequent crowded, terror-filled, often foodless days have made seem a million years ago. Moses is a medium-built young man with a romantically alive tan face. Ever so slightly his hair is thining at the front. His clothes are almost always casual.

Feverishly he drinks in the contents of books as if they were a

rare wine. Equally well he gulps in meaningful conversations that
bear upon his interests. When he does speak, it's in a soft, low,
languid voice laden with sincerity. But he doesn't speak often or at
great length. Because of his relation to the Movement and the importance of his ideas, his silences have become a form of eloquence.
In many ways Bob Moses is ascetic.

By virtue of his innate abilities and good fortune, he has obtained formal education at Hamilton College and Harvard University—advantages obtained in spite of his low-income Harlem background.

Moses was one of the prime authors of the idea of year-round
day-to-day living among those whom you would purport to lead
into advanced positions of protest in the civil rights effort. This
approach was a major factor in establishing SNCC in Mississippi,
because one of the biggest fears of Negro Mississippians was that
"civil rights workers will come, stir up trouble and then leave."

Moses was one of the major guiding spirits of the Mississippi Summer Project of 1964—albeit a troubled one. He was, and is, troubled
because of the constant decision-making that he must do—which has
appended to each decision the specter of death. In Mississippi the
innocent dispatching of a person on a five-mile journey can result
in the ultimate.

And death has clung close to Bob on too many occasions. On
February 28, 1963, just outside of Greenwood, Mississippi, Moses
was riding in a car which was splattered with 14 bullets, 3 of
which went into the upper part of the body of James Travis, who
sat next to Moses on the front seat. By one of those mystiques of the
Movement, Travis was not killed. But there were deaths. They
occurred in McComb, Mississippi.

For years the McComb area has been infested with scores of white
men with the unshakable belief that the pathway to sainthood while
alive, and perhaps deification when dead, comes when one's aim is
good, the squeeze of the trigger is steady and the target is a "nigger"
or "nigger lover."

When Moses arrived in McComb in 1961, there were neither
candles nor matches—nor hands that believed that the matches could

light the candles. In this environment Bob Moses and the first of the now 80 SNCC field secretaries began canvassing to get people to vote.

Finally one Negro, Herbert Lee, agreed to go down to register. This struck a match. The candle was lighted. And then it was snuffed out precipitously as the blood oozed through Lee's clothes and stickily clung to the blackness of his death-cold skin.

Louis Allen witnessed the killing of Lee by a Mississippi legislator, E. H. Hurst. The coroner's jury of the county termed the killing as being justified and in self-defense.

Bob Moses encouraged Allen to give the facts to the FBI, which he did.

Moses sought to get the FBI to protect Allen, which it didn't.

After a series of harassments, arrests on trumped-up charges, beatings and surveillance, the misery ended for Louis Allen. Three days before Allen was to leave McComb—January 31, 1964—he was found dead with half of his face scattered several feet away from his head.

Events such as this shaped the thinking and concern that made a Freedom Summer in Mississippi in 1964 an extraordinary undertaking.

The event that probably concretized the idea of having thousands of summer volunteers in Mississippi was the Freedom Vote Campaign for Governor in 1963. In this mock election, COFO attempted to enroll all the Negroes of Mississippi in freedom registration books. After registration, a Freedom Vote was cast by the registrants. On the Freedom Ballot were the names of Paul Johnson (Democrat) and Rubel Phillips (Republican)—who were vying with each other for the title of the greatest "nigger hater"—and Aaron Henry of the Freedom Democratic Party. Henry received 70,000 votes to swamp his opposition in the freedom election.

Amidst the jubilation of the successful mock election, pause was taken to evaluate how the large freedom registration was attained. Much of the credit had to be given to the 100 volunteers who had come into the state for two weeks from Yale and Stanford universities. It became apparent that the same job done by these volunteers in the freedom election working under the direction of the veteran staff could be done on a larger scale during the summer of 1964. An idea was impregnated in the minds of some of the SNCC staff members working with COFO.

But giving birth to the idea was not done without pain and travail.

In the week that followed the successful Freedom Vote Campaign for Governor, SNCC staff members in Mississippi met in Greenville, Mississippi, to answer this question: "Where do we go from here?"

On Friday, the first day, the staff meeting began with a discussion of the white man's role in the Movement. The interracial staff of SNCC approached the topic at first with caution, then with intensity.

In almost undisguised expressions of "black nationalism," four or five of the Negro SNCC staff members at first urged that the role of the white students be severely limited if they decided to ask thousands of northern white students to come and help roll the stone away from the tomb. The idea of restrictions based on race was immediately pounced upon.

Mrs. Fannie Lou Hamer said: "If we're trying to break down segregation, we can't segregate ourselves." Bob Moses said that it was much more important that the "right type of persons be brought into Mississippi" and that for such an evaluation skin pigmentation was irrelevant.

Gradually, as thoughts and counterthoughts were exchanged, the SNCC staffers began reaching their consensus and ideas emerged: Mississippi and the Movement had to move away from the viewpoint that the struggle was "black versus white"; there was no better way to make that departure than to have more white people in Mississippi working alongside black people so that the articulation and thinking could become one of "rational people against irrational people."

Having wrestled with its own being until it came up with a blessing, as Jacob once had done with the angel, the SNCC staffers were able to get the leadership of COFO to reach a similar consensus.

The summer of 1964 was on.

The SNCC Mississippi and national staff began at once to work for the solution of major obstacles, such as securing a site for the basic training of the summer volunteers, recruiting volunteers, securing contingents of lawyers, getting federal protection, completing 10,008 administrative tasks, and finding $200,000 or more to begin the project.

By May, 1964, with the gigantic Summer Project only weeks away, things were very good and very bad.

The National Council of Churches had agreed to provide a site for the basic training of the volunteers and to donate $50,000 to a Delta Project in Mississippi.

Friends of SNCC groups and ex-SNCC staff members were screening thousands of applicants in northern cities and at major recruiting centers at Howard, Yale, Harvard, the University of Illinois, Oberlin College, the University of Oregon, Stanford University and the University of North Carolina.

The National Lawyers Guild Committee for Legal Assistance to the South (CLAS) and the NAACP Legal Defense and Educational Fund, Inc., along with lesser legal groups, had pledged scores of lawyers for the Project.

SNCC had fund-raising drives at a number of colleges. (Yale, for example, was trying to raise $15,000.) Appeals were being made to the Field, New World and Taconic Foundations, which had donated in the past.

In April and May, though, the "good" seemed to be smothered by the "bad."

The same news stories in national magazines and newspapers which were attracting hundreds of students as volunteers simultaneously signaled an unleashing of more of the police-state nature of Mississippi. Governor Paul Johnson had worked to unite the racists, as well as those considered "moderates" by Mississippi standards, behind him. In March Johnson had asked for and received legislative approval of an increase in the number of State Highway patrolmen from 275 to 475. (In addition, legislation was passed which allowed the Highway patrolmen to make arrests within the limits of a city and to go into a city or county and act as policemen without first getting a request from local officials. This legislation was passed reluctantly after assurance was had that the state police would not interfere with the lush "illegal" liquor hustle of the counties.)

Legislation was passed allowing counties and cities to borrow policemen from each other. One law provided for massive quarantine (house arrest) "where there is imminent danger to public safety"; another made it a felony to circulate material that encouraged boycotts; and another bill made it a crime to operate a school without the permission of the county clerk.

The Jackson *Daily News* and other news media had characterized the coming of the summer volunteers as an invasion. The city of Jackson, Mississippi, took this literally: the police force was expanded from 200 to 390; Mayor Allen Thompson bought 250 shotguns, and mounts for them were installed in squad cars and on motorcycles; three flat-bed trailer trucks were converted into paddy wagons; and a mammoth "Thompson tank" was secured—which had 12-gauge steel walls and bulletproof windows.

Jackson police began in May to arrest, without provocation, anyone seen on the streets who appeared to be connected with COFO. The SNCC field secretary serving as COFO's legal coordinator, Hunter Morey, had the "distinction" of being arrested three times in less than four hours. After leaving the police station for one arrest where he had put up bond, he was arrested again before he could go the few blocks between the police station and the COFO headquarters.

Twice within a three-day period the windows of the COFO headquarters were broken. On the second occasion Nedra Winan, SNCC field secretary from San Francisco, was hit in the head with the brick. Panic gripped the office personnel. It became difficult to concentrate on processing the applications, preparing curriculum materials, answering correspondence and performing the other administrative tasks needed to bring to fruition the Summer Project.

Three-fourths of the persons who were in the Jackson headquarters were Negro and white girls; most of them—ten—lived in the Freedom House located nine blocks from the office.

There was constant police surveillance from dusk until daybreak, including the shining of spotlights and the blaring noise of police radios turned to highest volume, interspersed with cynical laughs of the officers. The intent of Mississippi appeared to be to run the staff which was processing the applicants and preparing the materials for the summer out of the state.

The officials almost succeeded.

The girls became desperate for peace that would allow them to sleep. They became willing to do almost anything to buy that peace. One young lady proposed to buy the peace by "enforcing strict segregation"—only to be embarrassed when she realized what she'd proposed.

At the office the people were more likely to snap or snarl at each other rather than speak—and this was May, with the beginning of the Summer Project only days away.

The most damaging aspect of May was the poverty of the staff; SNCC workers had not received their subsistence-level salaries ($10, minus 36 cents for Social Security) for three weeks. For a week, the ten girls living in the Freedom House had no toilet. The plumbing was stopped up. The plumber wanted $5—$5 more than anyone had. Food was a communal effort of chipping in to buy sardines, "because they have a lot of vitamins," and peanut butter and bread, "because it fills and sticks to your ribs." All this occurred in May, with the Mississippi Summer Project beginning in but a few days.

One would think that the pressures would have turned the staff preparing for the Summer Project into animals—jackals. But one would have found that they were still humans . . . if perchance one could have looked in on a meeting, one of the hundreds held in April and May of 1964 in the Jackson headquarters.

Headquarters on Lynch Street consists of a storefront in the 1000 block that was formerly used as a Negro radio station and has five rooms, of varying sizes, located behind boarded windows covered with dullish-blue drapes of thin, tired cotton.

The five rooms are lined with little stalls made of half-inch plywood attached to the many walls created by short partitions or formed by the building itself. All in all, the storefront is about 40 feet wide and 100 feet long with finger-smudged, foot-smudged, emerald-green walls in spots. In the connecting corridor, as one comes in, there are usually fresh boxes of clothing or books awaiting distribution throughout the state. The facility is always crowded, the floors have papers on them, ash trays are always overflowing, and things are cluttered from having too many bees in a small hive.

Though the hour is late, say 11 P.M., there is still the sound of business. The typewriters hammer out a dull and incessant pecking that provides background "music" for a serious discussion that filters from a table in the center of the large middle room. It's getting awfully late. The topic is the Summer Project which will bring thousands into Mississippi: all young, some black, some white . . . and most inexperienced.

The discussants are Mendy Samstein, soft-sell, dedicated, and a veteran of more unpleasantness crowded into the past nine months (arrests, jails, beatings, and even murders) than the average American is exposed to in a lifetime.

Next to Mendy is Nedra Winan of San Francisco, who will in a few days "celebrate" two weeks of Mississippi life. She puffs casually on a Marlboro cigarette and fits well into this pattern of life; she seemingly brought few illusions with her and a lot of political savvy from working with student groups in California.

Beside Nedra is Donna Moses. Her short brown-skinned frame is accentuated by well-developed arms and legs from more than average physical activity all her life—so much that her parents must have feared she would never stop being a tomboy. Her shoulders are slightly broad. Five months ago the charismatic symbol of the Movement in Mississippi, Bob Moses, married her. As befits the human qualities of the Movement at this stage, all pay a little more than ordinary attention to her waistline: the slightest bulge will be quickly interpreted as a new recruit for the "Freedom Army."

At the other end of the small, tan, cigarette-burned table is Margaret Burnham, who is soon to pass her second month in the state. She's from New York City. Margaret is catching it hard. Simultaneously she is learning to adjust to the South, to Mississippi and to the rigors of a "soldier's life." This is her first extended stay in an earthly hell. Though she tries to conceal her apprehensions, she fails; she has her father's expressive eyes.

To Margaret Burnham's right is Betty Garman from SNCC's Atlanta office. Betty has savvy and confidence. Her comments flow freely interspersed with a "damn" or "hell!" As she rhythmically moves her bare legs, which are crossed at the knees and encased in strap sandals, she gesticulates with a green ball-point pen and explains the problems of money, transportation, orientation and logistics for moving 1,000 volunteers safely into and out of Mississippi during the summer of 1964. In spite of the fact that the Summer Project will cost nearly $800,000 and even though there is not now even enough money for those at the discussion table to eat, the planning is positive. Crisis is new neither to her nor to SNCC. SNCC has lived for four years from one miracle to the next, and another miracle will happen. One can sense confidence in the coming of another miracle in Betty's handsome face, with eyes that are set back a little deeper than most people's. "What do you say is the absolute essential to running the freedom schools?" she asks Mendy Samstein.

"This is all new. Your ideas are as good as the next person's," Mendy replies.

For reasons unknown, the real old veteran of this gathering seems fresh, although she has gotten barely six hours' sleep in the last few days. Her face gleams. Her personality, like her face, is soft. Like the other girls, she wears no lipstick to accent her small oval mouth. Her ideas roll forth in a logical and systematic order. This is Penny Patch. Barely over 20 years old, she's a veteran of Southwest Georgia, Atlanta and other protest centers. For nearly three years she's been jabbing her body and intellect into the jaws of predicaments created by the power structure of a racist South. She has scars—some in her mind, others perhaps concealed by the black sweater and gaudy orangish-print dress she wears—from filthy jails and brutish policemen.

The next member of the conference around the small table is Margaret Cunningham. She does not talk; she just listens and gulps into her soul the new and strange words and ideas of the prepara-

tion for the summer that threatens not to begin. Relatively fresh
from Chicago's West Side, she seems intent on learning everything
that will help her do her tasks better and survive. Her natural
beauty is enhanced by the plain, olive-green dress she wears and by
her long brunette hair, parted down the middle, which frames a
delicately molded face that silently communicates a love and kindness not expressible in words. She is the sort of girl you'd cast
in the role of Mary in a play about the birth of Christ.

Also participating in the conference is Robert Weil, who defies
the laws of Mississippi and nature by constantly rousting himself
at full speed at least 16 hours of each day. Bob's the communications
man for headquarters—a position he seems ideally suited for: he
loves details and is happiest while typing, clipping, pasting excerpts
from newspapers and generally providing anybody and everybody
with little-known facts about Mississippi from files and folders concealed in hidden and out-of-the-way places. At this conference he
now looks as he has always looked since arriving in Mississippi:
bushy hair, denim pants, white shirt, horn-rimmed glasses and the
shadow of a beard, which leaves no doubt that every inch of his
five-foot-seven-inch, 155-pound being is totally dedicated to helping
explode a crack in the iceberg of despotism.

And then there's John O'Neal. He's a story unto himself—slender
and a thing of beauty in his manly blackness. His hands and face
are expressive to the point of naturally becoming an extension of his
voice and its modulated southern Illinois accent.

"At any rate, we should not limit ourselves to an academic program," John urges. "Freedom schools should be merged with the
concepts of the community centers."

And on and on and on the conferees talk and plan for the coming
of the troops for the Summer Project.

III

The Troops

Rendezvous with Life
Assign me restless souls with a sense of destiny
to be met at the disputed barricade
When Summer comes with rustling shade
And vultures' screeches fill the air.
Let us stand tall in spite of epithet, political taunt,
To forge a people who care.
We have a rendezvous with life.
                              —The Wisdom of Dawley

On June 15, 1964, the "luck of the Africans" held up. The miracle prayed for by Mrs. Fannie Lou Hamer, hoped for by Betty Garman and demanded by Jesse Morris (the get-it-done SNCC field secretary in the Jackson headquarters) occurred.

The Mississippi Summer Project began—though the combined moneys in the Jackson and Atlanta offices of SNCC didn't amount to $500.

Gathered and gathering in Oxford, Ohio, at the Western College for Women on June 15, 1964, were the first 300 of the more than 800 volunteers to serve in the Mississippi Summer Project of 1964, along with a score of psychiatrists and psychologists, three lawyers, and almost all of the veteran Mississippi staff, known as the "jungle fighters."

Early in the year Mississippi's ruling clique had begun referring to the Summer Project as the *invasion*. If the Summer Project was an invasion, then these young volunteers were the *troops* and this orientation session in the quiet little college town of 8,000 people was the basic training center or "boot camp."

From the applications and interviews, SNCC knew the group of green troops to be seriously motivated, emotionally stable individuals, intent on making social change and American history, as opposed to just reading about it. Many of the volunteers were from prominent and influential families in New York, Illinois, California and New Jersey—the 20- through 25-year-old children of psychiatrists, physicists, lawyers and physicians—and one was the son of a Congressman (W. Donlan Edwards, Dem., Calif.).

Most generalizations about the summer volunteers, beyond the fact of their dedication, would be inaccurate. It is doubtful that one could willfully arrange a more diverse assortment of racial, social, cultural and economic backgrounds.

One example was Stokely Carmichael, an ex-SNCC staff member who had withdrawn from the Movement to attend school at Howard University in Washington. To volunteer for the project, Stokely had to borrow a dime for a phone call to Mike Thelwell, director of the Washington SNCC office.

Stokely was born in Trinidad. He is proportioned well, with longer-than-average arms, which can encircle with ease a 100-gallon gasoline container, and a head whose roundness is easily seen because of Stokely's custom of wearing his hair cut close—close enough to reveal several scars presented to him in nonviolent demonstrations: his burning pearllike eyes had silently asserted "Kiss my black ass!" to a cop who was determined that not a whit of segregation would change. Stokely is the person sculptors would seek as a model for a statue of a Nubian god.

His spirit is characterized by a disciplined wildness: he would study around the clock for several days for exams—and then miss them because of impetuous participation in a racial protest in nearby Cambridge, Maryland. Freedom rides, sit-ins, stall-ins, rent strikes—you name it; Stokely Carmichael has done it. Protest is part of the fiber of his being.

Stokely was project director in the Greenwood, Mississippi, area during the summer of 1964. Though there was a great deal of harassment and jailing and some beating, he was tempted to cry only once. Shortly before the 1964 civil rights bill became the law of the land, Stokely found himself sternly pleading with a group of local Greenwood Negro students not to get involved in public accommodations testing. For the summer, SNCC had decided to forgo public accommodations testing in Mississippi. Stokely wept . . . inwardly.

In sharp contrast to the appearance of Stokely, the magnificent barbarian, was another summer volunteer, Mrs. Ruth Schine.

Mrs. Schine is a handsome, matronly New Yorker with stark black hair bobbed around the neckline. Her bearing is faintly military because of her erect posture and her sense of orderliness, which she is secure enough not to flaunt. Although she is in her forties and has a grown daughter, it seemed to be of little concern to either Ruth or her fellow summer volunteers, many of whom were half her age. What did give her status as a "curiosity" for a day or so was a rumor that she could type 125 words per minute and take shorthand at 180 words per minute as a result of years of experience as a legal secretary. The heat, tension, chaos, hurry and desperateness of the Summer Project bothered her little, if at all. She worked in the Jackson headquarters. Her only two demands were quickly met: first, that the trash and dust be swept up at least once a day to make way for new trash and dust; second, that whatever tired soul passed through Jackson in the wee hours of the morning and was unable to find lodging and stretched out on top of her desk in exhaustion be off that desk by 9:30 A.M.

Regrettably, more of the summer volunteers were not Negroes. The ratio of white to Negro among the volunteers was about five to one. Historians report that Lincoln was extremely reluctant to allow Negroes in the Union Army but that necessity forced a waiving of this opposition. In 1964, a hundred years later, in its summer army SNCC would have preferred a more proportional representation of Negroes. But the money wasn't available. "Support promised by important people and institutions didn't materialize," James

Forman, SNCC's executive secretary, said. President Johnson didn't want the Summer Project to happen, and his influence was felt widely in the circles of the foundations when SNCC's requests for subsidies were considered.

The fact of the matter is that one needed money to be a volunteer. A volunteer had to be able to forgo earning income during the summer, have at least a source of getting a $500 bond when arrested, pay his transportation to the training session in Ohio and to Mississippi, pay his living and eating expenses in Mississippi, take care of medical and hopitalization bills if they arose, and pay his way back home at the summer's end.

How vastly different were the conditions under which this army would exist in Mississippi from the conditions for those who serve in the vaunted United States Peace Corps!

If, instead of volunteering for Mississippi, they had volunteered for Morocco, the United States would have provided all of this:

1. Subsidized studies for weeks of the language, history, geography, economy and traditions of the host country.
2. Draft deferment.
3. Food, clothing, shelter, incidental expenses and $75 monthly deposited in a savings account.
4. Transportation to and from Morocco.
5. 45 days of vacation at $7.50 a day.
6. Some $10,000 in insurance.
7. Complete medical care, civil service credit and other benefits.
8. Protection of their lives.

All these benefits—and more—would have been received, because we Americans have concluded that the activities of the Peace Corps are *"activities in the national health, safety or interest."*

The Mississippi summer volunteers were going to teach freedom schools, get people registered to vote, open community centers, organize the poor of both races and challenge racial segregation, and they would enter Mississippi with all the protection, concern and benefits that the veteran SNCC and CORE staff members have had for years . . .

Nothing!

If a summer volunteer had not already received a "Prospectus for the Mississippi Freedom Summer" before his arrival at the orientation, he could get his copy there. This prospectus, by use of rhetorical questions, "told it like it is":

A program is planned for this summer which will involve the massive participation of Americans dedicated to the elimination of racial oppression. Scores of college students, law students, medical students, teachers, professors, ministers, technicians, folk artists and lawyers from all over the country have already volunteered to work in Mississippi this summer—and hundreds more are being recruited.

Why a project of this size?

1. Projects of the size of those of the last three summers (100 to 150 workers) are rendered ineffective quickly by police threats and detention of members.
2. Previous projects have gotten no national publicity on the crucial issue of voting rights and, hence, have little national support either from public opinion or from the federal government. A large number of students from the North making the necessary sacrifices to go South would make abundantly clear to the government and the public that this is not a situation which can be ignored any longer, and would project an image of cooperation between Northern and white people and Southern Negro people to the nation which will reduce fears of an impending race war.
3. Because of the lack of numbers in the past, all workers in Mississippi have had to devote themselves to voter registration, leaving no manpower for stopgap community education projects which can reduce illiteracy as well as raise the level of education of Negroes. Both of these activities are, naturally, essential to the project's emphasis on voting.
4. Bail money cannot be provided for jailed workers; hence, a large number of people going South would prevent the project from being halted in its initial stages by immediate arrests. Indeed, what will probably happen in some communities is the filling of jails with civil rights workers to overflowing, forcing the community to realize that it cannot dispense with the problem of Negroes' attempting to register simply by jailing "outsiders."

Authorship of the prospectus was not credited on the document, but there was the unmistakable ring in the writing of the vocal cadence and logical sequences so characteristic of the SNCC director of the Mississippi Project, Bob Moses.

The other important question raised and answered by the prospectus was *Why this summer?*

Mississippi at this juncture in the movement has received too little attention—that is, attention to what the state's attitude really is—and has presented COFO with a major policy decision. Either the civil rights struggle has to continue, as it has for the past few years, with small projects in selected communities with no real progress on any fronts, or there must be a task force of such a size as to force either the state and the municipal governments to change their social and legal structures, or the federal government to intervene on behalf of the constitutional rights of its citizens.

Since 1964 is an election year, the clear-cut issue of voting rights should be brought out in the open. Many SNCC and CORE workers in Mississippi hold the view that Negroes will never vote in large numbers until federal marshals intervene. At any rate, many Americans must be made to realize that the voting rights they so often take for granted involve considerable risks for Negroes in the South. In the larger context of the national civil rights movement, enough progress has been made during the last year that there can be no turning back. *Major victories in Mississippi, recognized as the stronghold of racial intolerance in the South, would speed immeasurably the breaking down of legal and social discrimination in both North and South.* (Emphasis supplied.)

The project is seen as a response to the Washington March and an attempt to assure that in the Presidential election year of 1964 all American citizens are given the franchise. The people at work on the project are neither working at odds with the federal government nor at war with the State of Mississippi The impetus is *not against* Mississippi, but for the right to vote, the ability to read, the aspirations and the training to work.

The orientation meetings were staggered with an average of more than 250 volunteers at each of the one-week sessions. I attended the first one.

The week was crowded. In charge of the training was a cadre of 80 Mississippi veterans, who had the task of making Freedom Fighters out of the eager, naïve and frightened students from the bowels of suburbia and some of the best schools in the country:

Howard, Yale, Cornell, Harvard, Princeton, Bryn Mawr, Skidmore, Antioch.

The veterans pushed, pulled, prodded, lectured, questioned and studied the new recruits. The volunteers were photographed, catalogued, assigned, tested and given forms to fill out. The long schedule of the day was divided between sectional meetings (more than 20 of them, geographically designated) and general assemblies in one of the small auditoriums of the women's college. There instructions were given in how to protect vital organs when attacked, answer questions when arrested and develop friendly relations when greeted by a suspicious Negro community. The volunteers were subjected to a cram course in the ways of life—and death—in Mississippi. When the volunteers arrived in Oxford, Ohio, they were merely scared. Before they left, they were terrified. Speakers informed the volunteers: "There's not even a sharp line between living and dying; it is just a thin fuzz."

Within six days the volunteers must have heard 600 statements of warning similar to the one made by Jim Forman: "I may be killed and you may be killed."

The volunteers were informed at every possible turn that they had no rights worth mentioning. Particularly vivid were the instructions of R. Jess Brown, a practical lawyer from Jackson, Mississippi, and one of the only four Mississippi attorneys who will accept civil rights cases. Pointing a slender finger like a sword, Brown said: "If you're riding down somewhere and a cop stops you and starts to put you under arrest even though you haven't committed any crime—go on to jail. Mississippi is not the place to start conducting Constitutional law classes for policemen, many of whom don't have a fifth-grade education."

The remarks were greeted with laughter, the kind one blurts out when the real reaction is to cry. Jess Brown had related the instructions with a smile on his face and presented the remarks in a light vein, but the message got across.

On a few occasions the volunteers found themselves being rebuffed by the veterans who walked out of an assembly. The volunteers had chuckled at a film on voter canvassing when the aged

Negro spoke in a dialect that most of the volunteers had heard only over the "Amos and Andy" program. No matter. These petty conflicts—inevitable whenever green troops join battle-tested veterans—were soon forgotten.

For the volunteers, the most crushing experience was the assembly meeting with John Doar, representative of the Department of Justice of the United States of America.

Doar spoke for 15 minutes, reading a prepared statement setting forth the accomplishments of the Kennedy-Johnson administration that made nothing seem everything: where no voting case had been filed in a certain state in 100 years, the Kennedy-Johnson administration had filed one, making for a 100 per cent increase. Casually Doar mentioned the absence of legislation to enable the federal government to protect anyone, added that the FBI was *only* an investigative agency, and opened the floor to questions.

A spectacled, overalled Negro screamed at Doar: "What are you going to do to enable us to see the fall?"

The room was hushed.

Matter-of-factly, Doar replied, "Nothing. There is no federal police force. The responsibility for protection is that of the local police. We can only investigate."

Bedlam broke loose.

Questions were hurtled in anger and fright from all corners of the large assembly room. Invectives and even denunciations came forth. Nobody was angry with Doar—the man. In this situation he was more than a man; he was the symbol of the United States government and all the fine things that the volunteers believed about the federal government and its ability and willingness to protect the lives of citizens. The blow was cruel.

For a week the volunteers had been taught to view Mississippians—in and out of police uniforms—as the persons ready, willing and able to find a warm spot for a "nigger lover" on the cool bottom of the Pearl River.

Now there was nothing.

Later, in the privacy of rooms, many cried unashamedly. There were reappraisals by all as they asked themselves: "What is there in Mississippi that I'm willing to die for?"

"We can only investigate. We can only investigate!"

Even the veterans were edgy. Supper was served in a large modern cafeteria with a circular opening in the middle which opened to a floor below, where there was a recreational area. Ostensibly it was a time for eating; in fact, it became a theater, where each person performed within himself for his captive audience of one. Some told each other joke after joke, and their continuous laughter scattered across the dining hall, where others talked about nothing and everything just so long as they didn't have to think about the helplessness in the horror to the South. Others merely brooded: "The government can 'only investigate'!"

Departure was to take place on Saturday morning, June 20, 1964. On the night of Friday, June 19, a soul-singing session began shortly after supper was over. Leading it was Matthew Jones of the SNCC Freedom Singers. Everyone was intense. Pete Smollett from New York, on hand for a final session with several of the SNCC field secretaries trained in his studio in the use of motion-picture cameras, knew the score and "told it like it was." He saw the fear: "It hangs in this air like a stale blanket."

Song after song poured into the moonlit night. Old verses were remembered; new verses were created. They sang of triumphs, of defeats, of fallen martyrs and rising heroes. They sang of jails, of picket lines. While groups with arms across each other's shoulders in the wide circle tried to remember a song that hadn't already been sung, there were just hums and moans like those found in little country churches. But the dawn, which they tried to stop with the anguish of their hearts transposed into the wails of their vocal cords, came anyway. Saturday, June 20, 1964, was a bright sunny day. Everything was perfect about the weather from Oxford, Ohio, to Biloxi, Mississippi, on the Gulf Coast and from Natchez, Mississippi, on the river to Meridian near the Alabama-Mississippi line.

A handful went north. We could only be amazed that there weren't more.

The rest headed south to the smell of magnolias and fetid

swamp waters—James Chaney, Charles Cobb, Mickey Schwerner, Andrew Goodman, Mary Lovelace, Ruth Schine, Stokely Carmichael and all the others.

The summer had begun.

For Mississippi, the South and the nation, this invasion by this strangely concocted army was the most devastating assault on things as they are since Sherman's march to the sea. It opened the eyes of a lot of smug people—within and without the Movement.

There were many of us since 1960 who had chauvinistically concluded that courage was a black monopoly, though a few had ever articulated the idea. There were the few exceptions like Robert Zellner, Zev Avelony and Mickey Schwerner; but these were exceptions that proved the rule.

It appeared that the black college student came closest to fulfilling the role of catalyst for meaningful social reform (and sometimes revolution) that is played by students in Africa, Europe, Asia and Latin America. The best that the "infantile" minds of the white college students could conceive of appeared to be "panty raids," beer-can stacking and telephone-booth packing. The white college student had such a stake in "things as they are" in American suburbia that in his whiteness he couldn't afford to become concerned about the sickness; so he merely added to it. Things had to be played safe—so much so that even if he were standing in a torrential downpour he couldn't afford to say that "it's raining" unless he could first check the pages of a soaked *New York Times*.

These troops had proven these fantasies to be lies. They had pressed onward to Mississippi in the face of deliberate and repeated intimidation from those whom they trusted, the Mississippi veterans, who had said as cruelly as they could, "If you go, you can die." The troops went because they had to.

They went for the same reasons that Bob Moses had gone to McComb, Mississippi, in 1961; for the same reasons that Charley Cobb, Jesse Morris and Stokely Carmichael went; and for the same reasons that brought the Rev. Edwin King (a white Methodist minister) and his wife Jeanette back to Mississippi to fight the thing they had almost decided to run away from.

Ole Miss Panty Raid Turns Into Rioting; Five Arrested

UNIVERSITY, Miss. (Special) — At least five Ole Miss students were arrested early this morning after a mass panty raid erupted into violence.

Officers said about a dozen students' identification cards were confiscated and more arrests were likely.

One student was treated for minor injuries at the student infirmary and at least one was reported treated for facial injuries at Oxford - Lafayette Hospital. There were no serious injuries reported.

Violence broke out on the campus several hours after an organized bonfire rally for the Ole Miss-LSU football game. Male students milled near Kincannon dormitory about 11:30 Thursday night and by midnightt he crowd numbered several hundred.

There had been rumors of the panty raid for several days. The crowd went to Deaton and Somerville, girls dorms, but the group dwindled to about 200 students when violence erupted. Both dormitories were reported damaged, windows smashed and some students broke into the dormitories but no rooms were entered.

The car belonging to Campus Police Chief Burns Tatum was rolled down a hill and crashed into a fire plug. Windows of the car were broken and the upholstery torn.

As Sheriff B o y c e Bratton drove into the mob his car windows were smashed by flying rocks. One campus policeman was injured when hit on the head by a rock.

Dean Frank Moak, dean of students, said he heard rumors of a panty raid earlier Thursday evening and went to the campus.

At about 11:30 all girls dormitorles began usual panty raid safety preparations — all lights were t u r n e d out, doors to rooms were locked, elevators were taken to the top floors, and residents were told to stay away from windows.

Throughout the raid Ole Miss Chancellor J. D. Williams stood guard near LeBauve Dormitory which houses the two Ole Miss Negro students. A university spokesman said the two were not involved in the demonstration in anyway.

At one time during the raid a student shouted, "Lets get the Negroes."

"No, we want panties," the crowd shouted back.

An anonymous letter appearing Thursday in the student newspaper, The Mississippian, called for a spontaneous pep rally "minus the cheer leaders and the Associated Student Body."

"Here it is the week of the LSU game; while the LSU campus is rocked by demonstrations, the students at Ole Miss are sitting quietly on their hands. Whatever happened to the famous Ole Miss spirit?" the letter asked.

The writer said he was not advocating mob violence "but how about a little enthusiasm."

Last night Ole Miss students got off their hands, on to their feet, and for a few, no doubt, out of school.

The letter w a s answered affirmatively.

The *Jackson* (Miss.) *Daily News*, Friday, October 30, 1964.

The compulsion which projected these students into the midst of Mississippi is not strange or foreign to the South or America; it is woven into the fabric of our history. It is no different from the experience of the South when large numbers of able-bodied men from the northern hills of Alabama risked their lives to go through the Confederate lines to join the Union Army when the South tried to overthrow our government with force and violence. And there were countless examples even before that—at the founding of our country, for example. What student of American history is not familiar with the name of the French general, Marquis de Lafayette, who aided so nobly in the winning of the first American Revolution as a soldier in the Continental Army? And Lafayette was rewarded by American support of the French Revolution which occurred a few years afterward.

IV

The Courts: Federal Law in Mississippi

> Uncle tarnished the image respected
> of a man always fair,
> though sometimes right—
> and other times wrong.
>
> He gutted the strings of my harp,
> On which I played Compassion
> And Freedom Songs.
>
> My eyes no longer look to the Hill:
> From which no strength comes.
> Now I only feel the sinew
> Of the Freedom Fighter's arms.
>   —The Wisdom of Dawley

IT'S POETIC TRUTH that a lot of things in this life aren't what they seem to be.

Bloodhounds are an example.

Most people consider them to be merely soulful-looking hounds, low-slung, with long ears, friendly, and possessed of an acute sense of smell that makes them excellent for finding things—people. Prisoners at the Mississippi penitentiary view this supposedly kind old dog differently. The Mississippi prison system is a vast complex of force and dehumanization designed to make the most out of a huge supply of prison labor. There are roads to be built, ditches to be drained and cotton to be hoed and picked. (The largest cotton subsidy in the United States is paid to the Mississippi prison system, which owns and operates the nation's largest cotton-acreage allotment.)

Much of the work of the prisoners during the day requires that they be outside of the walls and barbed-wire fences of their night-time confinement. The authorities know that one of the compulsive thoughts of every "forced guest" is to leave—by escaping or other-wise.

To discourage escape, new prisoners are "entertained" with a demonstration that causes a "second look": the yapping, yowling dogs straining at the leashes are released within a confine where there is a dummy dressed in prison attire. The prisoners watch in horror, while the powerful dogs rip away with their teeth at the area on the dummy where the sexual organs would be if the dummy were human. The dogs are trained to find and castrate.

Just as the prisoners re-evaluate and take a second look at the bloodhounds, the Mississippi Summer Project suggests that the federal government should be looked at a second time and re-evaluated.

A prevalent concept is to consider our nation to be a country with 50 state governments and one large federal government with its own separate and distinct character.

This premise and oversimplification—of necessity—is not as true as it once *may* have been. At many points the federal government and the state governments, though not one and the same, become an alloy, so fused with each other as to deny *meaningful* distinction.

In other words, there is the Mississippi federal government, the New York federal government, the California federal government, and so on, for each of the several states of the United States. When the question *"What are you going to do to enable us to see the fall?"* was asked of John Doar of the Justice Department in Oxford, Ohio, at the orientation program for the summer volunteers, it was a re-quest for the employment of federal protection. If the request had been granted, it would have meant the employment of federal judges, federal juries and federal policemen.*

How does *federal* law enforcement differ from Mississippi law enforcement—in Mississippi?

Federal Judges

A person engaged in the Mississippi Summer Project in 1964 didn't have to take a plane to Washington, D.C., to see the federal government. To see it, he had only to go to the nearest federal court and look into the face of the federal judge. In Jackson, Mississippi, this would have involved going to the Post Office Building on Capital Street and catching an elevator to the upper floors. Not knowing where the courtroom was located, he might have stopped in the clerk's office for the United States District Court for the Southern District of Mississippi. Or he could have gone into the office of the United States Marshal or the United States District Attorney.

The clerk's office, marshal's office and United States District Attorney's office would have presented a "sea of white faces" which would have given directions to the courtroom with varying degrees of hostility. The counterparts of these offices in the local state courts of Hinds County would have appeared no different—all white.

Upon entering the courtroom presided over by the Hon. W. Harold Cox (a schoolmate of Senator James O. Eastland), the visitor's eyes would have been sullied by a large (15-by-30-foot) mural above the judge's bench. Gazing from left to right, the visitor would have seen the slaves picking cotton and getting their bags weighed by a white overseer. Next he would have seen in the mural a tall white man with a broad-brimmed hat with his right arm in front of a white woman holding a baby while a girl with blond hair, appearing to be about 10 years of age, stands nearby. With his left hand the tall white planter helps an aged white woman—

---

* In spite of repeated begging and demands for the United States Civil Rights Commission to come with its subpoena powers and conduct hearings, for five years the Commission was kept out of the state.

in black with shoulders stooped—maintain her delicate stance. And then there is an equally tall white minister looking learned and holding the "holy book." To the minister's left is a collection of young white men reading blueprints and constructing a building which contrasts sharply with the shabbiness of the slave shack at the opposite side of the painting.

Underneath the mural would sit Judge Cox.

Judge Cox and the two other judges who comprise the federal judiciary of Mississippi interpret the Constitution and laws of the United States. Unless and until their decisions are appealed to a higher court, their decisions *are* the "Constitution." Unless and until their acts are appealed, they *are* the federal government.

Their decisions are as predictable and consistent as the decisions of their counterparts in the state courts of Mississippi. Their decisions are so predictable that it is an accident or miracle when a person who files a case in the court pertaining to civil rights doesn't have to appeal. The results would be no different in a Mississippi state court. In other words, the federal courts of Mississippi are just as *good* as the state courts of Mississippi.

One can understand why things are so similar if he considers an ancient definition of a judge: "A judge is a lawyer with political friends." To become either a state judge or a federal judge in Mississippi (or any other state), one must have friends in politics.

To become a judge in Mississippi, one must be a friend of persons like Senator James O. Eastland, the White Citizens Council and ex-Governor Ross Barnett.

Civil rights cases in the federal courts are characterized by delay and frustration—and sometimes *honest* statements of their opinions by the federal judges. In one voting suit, on March 8, 1964, the Hon. W. Harold Cox was quoted as saying: "I am not interested in whether the registrar is going to give a registration test to a bunch of niggers on a voter drive."

Attorney General Robert F. Kennedy, who had concurred in the appointment of Judge Cox (the first Kennedy appointee) to the federal bench by his brother, President Kennedy, was asked by a reporter why persons known to have such strong segregationist views had been selected. The Attorney General replied: "I'm very proud of the judges that have been appointed."

During the successful campaign of Robert Kennedy for the election to the United States Senate from New York, his opponent, Senator Kenneth Keating, made much of the matter. This was unfair. Whether the administration of the federal government had been in the hands of the Democrats or the Republicans, in Mississippi the results would have been the same—as the appointment of the late Judge Ben Cameron of Mississippi to the United States Court of Appeals for the Fifth Circuit proved. When a federal judge who does not properly reflect the mores of the local political structure gets appointed by some accident or clever concealment, his life becomes miserable. Judges Waite Warring of South Carolina and Skelly Wright of Louisiana are examples of why the federal courts are a reflection of the political attitude of the states in which they preside—or else. These judges were hounded out of the South because of decisions favoring integration.

The State of Mississippi, the church-burning capital of the world, did not like its citizens to testify about the denial of civil rights and passed a state law making it a Mississippi offense for a person to give false information to any federal officer or agency, the definition of false being anything that Mississippi didn't like. Using his judicial power, Judge Cox embarked on a similar venture in the federal courts. In October, 1964, Judge Cox cited in contempt Robert Hauberg, the United States District Attorney for the Southern District of Mississippi, for refusing to sign an indictment for perjury against persons who had testified that there was racial discrimination against Negroes in a suit regarding the denial of the right to vote.

The U.S. District Attorney, himself in complete agreement with Judge Cox, tearfully declined because the Acting Attorney General of the United States, Nicholas Katzenbach, had ordered no signing. (Under the rules governing the federal courts, an indictment handed down by a grand jury is not effective until signed by the United States Attorney for the federal district in which the grand jury is convened.) On appeal of the contempt to the U.S. Court of Ap-

peals for the Fifth Circuit, Judge Cox was represented by Mississippi's Attorney General, Joe Patterson.

Mississippi doesn't want its Negro citizens—or any other citizens—bringing suits to stop, change, alter or correct illegal practices
that are a denial of Constitutional rights. This control is maintained
in part by the fact that there are only four lawyers (including R. Jess
Brown, Carsie Hall and Jack Young) in the entire state who will
handle racially controversial cases. The federal judges in Mississippi
voiced approval of the Mississippi desire by issuing rulings to bar
the many out-of-state attorneys servicing the Mississippi Freedom
Summer from the federal courts unless and until they could get
local Mississippi lawyers involved in each case.

This was a critical matter because of the physical impossibility
of the willing Mississippi lawyers' being all over the state. There
were more than 1,000 arrests by Mississippi policemen during the
Summer Project, and practically all of these arrests were removed
by filing a petition to the federal courts. Judge Cox insisted at once
that each petition for removal be for only one person and that
each petition be accompanied by a $500 cost bond.

Through an appeal of the case of *Michael Lefton v. City of
Hattiesburg* in mid-April, 1964, to the U.S. Court of Appeals for
the Fifth Circuit, these Judge Cox requirements were flushed away.

In summation, with regard to the federal judiciary one finds that
if the state has racial segregation as a policy, the federal judges—
who are judges solely because they have racist political friends—
reflect, endorse and implement that policy, just as the state courts
do. Because the things that exist in Mississippi exist in a raw and
ugly form, they are easily detected and analyzed. But the same
guidelines and results are true of the other 49 states. Yes, there will
be distinctions between the federal and state courts; but those distinctions are without meaningful differences.

Judges are but one part of the federal government and federal
law enforcement. Another important part of the federal law enforcement is the juries—that collection of persons which decides whether
to indict or not to indict, which decides on innocence or guilt, which

decides the property rights or lack of them for the citizens in a state where a federal court is sitting.

This problem of juries in Mississippi and the South could and should be avoided by the following statute:

U.S. Code, Section 332, Title 10
Use of militia and armed forces to enforce federal authority.

Whenever the President considers that unlawful obstructions, combinations, or assemblages, or rebellion against the authority of the United States, *make it impracticable to enforce the laws* of the United States in any State or Territory *by the ordinary* course of judicial proceedings, he may call into Federal service such as the militia of any State, and use such of the armed forces, as he considers necessary to enforce those laws or to suppress the rebellion. (Aug. 10, 1956, ch. 1041, 70A Stat. 15.) (Emphasis added.)

Federal Juries

The federal juries in each of the 50 states are expressions of the federal government—and replicas of the juries found in each of the state's court systems.

Mississippi is no exception.

SNCC made many efforts to secure "federal protection" for those who were going to be engaged in the Mississippi Summer Project of 1964. One such effort was a hearing before a special panel held on June 8, 1964, at the National Theater in Washington, D.C. Persons from Mississippi testified about violence in the state—including, among others, Mrs. Fannie Lou Hamer (philosopher from the cotton fields of Ruleville), George Greene (SNCC field secretary and racing driver) and Hartman Turnbow (Tchula farmer whose Remington automatic rifle was called upon to speak a truth). In addition to the oral testimony, there was also the introduction of pertinent documents, all of which appeared in the Congressional Records of June 15, 1964, and June 16, 1964.

William Higgs, white ex-Mississippi lawyer, provided the hearing with a legal memorandum setting forth the various acts of Congress under which the federal government could act to protect the lives of citizens before a lynching. (See last section of this chapter.)

Larry Speiser of the American Civil Liberties Union (ACLU) spoke with regard to an exchange of letters between his office and that of Burke Marshall, Assistant Attorney General of the United States and head of the Civil Rights Division. Speiser had asked for more federal prosecutions of those officials of a state who deprive a citizen of his Constitutional rights. Such prosecutions are permissible under Title 18, United States Code, Section 242:

Deprivation of rights under color of law.

Whoever, under color of any law, statute, ordinance, regulation, or custom, willfully subjects any inhabitant of any State, Territory, or District to the deprivation of any rights, privileges, or immunities secured or protected by the Constitution or laws of the United States, or to different punishments, pains, or penalties, on account of such inhabitant being an alien, or by reason of his color, or race, than are prescribed for the punishment of citizens, shall be fined not more than $1,000 or imprisoned not more than one year, or both. (June 25, 1948, ch. 645, 62 Stat. 696.)

Quoting in part from Burke Marshall's letter of reply, Speiser said this:

He [Burke Marshall] said, "It is not true, as you suggest, that there have been few if any prosecutions under section 242 in recent years. For the same period as mentioned above, *eight* cases involving police or prison brutality were presented to Federal grand juries sitting in the State of Mississippi."

The period he [Burke Marshall] is referring to was between January, 1962, to February 28, 1963—14 months—in which there had been a total of 102 complaints filed alleging deprivation of civil rights in the State of Mississippi and they were received and investigated.

Now, of those 102 complaints, they presented *eight* cases to the Federal grand jury sitting in the State of Mississippi. On *six* of them the grand juries refused to return indictments. Of the two cases in which indictments were returned, one went to trial, defendant was acquitted by the verdict of the jury.

"The trial of the remaining case was expected to take place in the near future." This was back in March of 1963.

"I think you will agree this reflects a vigorous enforcement policy on the part of this department."

In his letter, Mr. Marshall indicated one reason for not filing more charges against State and local officials, he said. "But I will not permit the filing of a criminal information where I am not convinced *evidence will support a conviction* and sustain the judgment on appeal . . ." (Emphasis supplied.)

The remarks of the Assistant Attorney General, as reported by Speiser, were most revealing.

"Evidence that will support a conviction" is evidence that proves to the satisfaction of a jury beyond a reasonable doubt that a crime has been committed and that the particular defendant before the jury committed that crime.

This is remarkable for two reasons.

First, this level of proof is *not* required in any other federal prosecutions, tax frauds, narcotics, thefts of government property and what have you. It is a uniquely high level of proof. In all other areas, the Justice Department prosecutes if it has a *prima facie* case, a case in which there are the bare facts of the commission of a crime. "Reasonable doubt" suggests an almost absolute certainty that the person charged with the crime is guilty.

The second reason goes to the nature of the jury before which these matters are brought. White, southern juries can't quite believe that a civil rights worker—a Negro—can have a crime committed against him. The FBI report for the fiscal year of 1964 substantiates this conclusion. The report states that the FBI handled 3,340 civil rights cases during the year with only 5 convictions.

The circle of logic used by the federal government to neglect its duty to protect citizens shows that the federal government is either dumb or dishonest. If the federal juries were constitutionally proper, there would be a big difference in the statistics. To prove either this dumbness or dishonesty, one has but to look at Neshoba County, Mississippi, the county where the city of Philadelphia is located and where James Chaney, Mickey Schwerner and Andrew Goodman were killed.

Under the Constitution and laws of the United States, almost without exception, one is entitled to be tried for the commission of a crime in the locality in which the crime is supposed to have occurred.

All of the facts known about the lynching of the three civil rights workers show that the act of lynching occurred in Neshoba County. Neshoba County is located in the federal judicial area of Mississippi known as the Eastern Division of the Southern District of Mississippi. In addition to Neshoba, there are seven other Mississippi counties which comprise this judicial area: Clarke, Jasper, Lauderdale, Noxubee, Kemper, Newton, and Wayne.

The jury for one charged with committing a federal crime in this area should come from these counties. By clearly established law of long enunciation, juries have to be representative of the general population in the areas where the juries are drawn. In other words, if there is a certain area from which a jury is drawn that has a general adult population composed of 33 per cent Negroes, 22 per cent Mexican-Americans, 15 per cent Chinese-Americans, and 30 per cent whites, the jury roll of 1,000 names should come close to reflecting the same percentages. Any gross discrepancy in the proportional representation on that over-all jury panel, if not properly explained—and this is very hard to do—renders any and all indictments of the grand jury (the jury that decides whether to indict persons for alleged crimes) selected from the panel void, illegal and invalid. It also renders any and all verdicts of guilty by a petit jury (a jury that sits on the trial of a case and decides guilt or liability) void, illegal and invalid.

In the 8-county area in which Neshoba is located, the census shows that there are 103,472 persons 21 years of age or over. Racially this number is divided into 68,353 whites and 35,119 Negroes (33.9 per cent).

Yet the federal grand jury summoned in Mississippi in September, 1964, to hear the evidence in which indictments were gotten against Sheriff Lawrence Rainey, Deputy Sheriff Cecil Price and several others on the alleged charges of beating and intimidating and coercing Negroes and depriving them of their rights had only one Negro member out of the 33 persons called (23 regulars and 10 alternates).

Unofficial reports indicate that the failure of this grand jury to hand down indictments in September, 1964, against certain persons for the lynching of the three civil rights workers was by a margin of one vote; 12 of 23 votes are needed for an indictment.

This one Negro in 33 jurors is not an oddity. A check of the records in the office of the U.S. Clerk in Meridian, Mississippi (the place where the federal district court of the area is located), revealed that in September, 1964, a panel of 50 persons was called to try cases and only 2 Negroes were on that panel. And this is from counties where the adult Negro population comprises 33.9 per cent of the total adult population.

Needless to say, the federal juries in Mississippi are exactly alike and just as *good* as the state court juries. They are so *good* that a New York lawyer, Arthur Kinoy, asserts the obvious: "There isn't a criminal conviction in Mississippi that could stand up if the jury question of representation is raised."*

By no means is the invalid jury system described peculiar to Mississippi. Albany, Georgia, where the political forces of the community successfully threatened noncooperation with the Kennedy Administration unless it brought criminal actions against the integration leaders of the community, provides another example. On flimsy evidence, which in no way dulled the stench of persecution, the Justice Department (our guardian of civil rights) indicted and convicted nine persons in the community who had been active in pushing the once-world-famous Movement for civil rights.

One of the victims of the upside-down "justice" was Miss Joni Rabinowitz, a SNCC volunteer in Albany during 1963.† In the brief before the United States Court of Appeals for the Fifth Circuit is found the Mississippi-like information:

Rabinowitz v. U.S., No. 21256: The master jury box from which both the grand and petit juries were chosen contained 1,985 names. Of these, 117, or 5.8%, were Negroes. By contrast the Macon Division of the Middle District of Georgia has a population of 211,306 persons over the age of 21, of whom 73,014, 34.55%, were Negroes.

* Mel Wulf of the American Civil Liberties Union recently filed a suit in the Mississippi Federal Court to force the federal court to stop excluding Negroes from juries.

† An excellent pamphlet discussing the Albany cases is *Upside Down Justice* by the Southern Conference Education Fund, 4403 Virginia Avenue, Louisville, Kentucky.

Luckily for the Southern judicial system, the federal government has not seen fit to take note of the following statute in any active manner in Mississippi or elsewhere.

Section 243, Title 18, U.S. Code. *Exclusion of jurors on account of race or color.*

No citizen possessing all other qualifications which are or may be prescribed by law shall be disqualified for service as grand or petit juror in any court of the United States, or of any State on account of race, color, or previous condition of servitude; and whoever, being an officer or other person charged with any duty in the selection or summoning of jurors, excludes or fails to summon any citizen for such cause shall be fined not more than $5,000. (June 25, 1948, ch. 645, 62 Stat. 696.)

It is impossible to locate the federal government which passed this statute in the courthouses of Mississippi.

The Federal Police Force

Unhappily, the federal police force is just as good as the federal judges and juries.

The federal police force consists of the Secret Service, U.S. marshals, Treasury Department agents and the FBI. With its 6,140 agents, the FBI constitutes the overwhelming majority of this federal police force and is the branch of the federal police force most often involved in the efforts to protect the rights of those engaged in the civil rights movements—or the lack of such efforts.

Because the FBI is a thoroughly segregated agency, one has no difficulty explaining the conduct of the agents in the South. (The little city of Norfolk, Virginia, with only 300 policemen, has more Negro policemen on its 300-man force than the FBI has on its 6,000-man force.) The FBI in the South is just as good as the city and state policemen of the south, and the Civil Rights Movement knows it.

To secure protection from the federal government during the Summer Project, SNCC issued a series of news releases throughout the spring and summer explaining the plight of those who work in the civil rights movement in Mississippi. One such news release described the FBI: ". . . in Mississippi they are always white, generally southern, *and usually from Mississippi. Like the state law enforcement officers,* these FBI Agents often serve to obstruct rather than aid the administration of justice in civil rights cases." (Emphasis supplied.)

During the Summer Project, this basic position of the FBI didn't change. Chief Ben Collins of Clarksdale, Mississippi, has been repeatedly accused by the white and Negro civil rights workers of being involved in acts of intimidation and brutality—all of which Collins denies. During July, Ben Collins was asked about this matter by a northern reporter and he boasted that the FBI had not bothered him about these charges, so "evidently there's not anything to it." He added, "The FBI comes in here every day and we have coffee every day. We're good friends."

This *friendly* federal police force posture continued on beyond the summer even as the civil rights program continued beyond the summer. On October 28, 1964, in McComb, Mississippi, another vivid example of the FBI friendship was given in a SNCC report after 18 persons had been arrested in that city while attempting to register:

All 18 people—voter registration workers and prospective applicants—were released today—CHARGES DROPPED.
No reason for the release was given by Pike County officials. . . .
Five of those jailed reported some kind of physical abuse while in jail. Mrs. Aylene Quinn reported being bruised when an electrical jail door was slammed on her. Mrs. Spinks had her arm twisted very badly. Rev. Malcolm Campbell, Douglas Jenkins and Marshall Ganz [Campbell from Canada, Jenkins from McComb and Ganz from California and SNCC staff] reported having been kicked, knocked around or arms twisted in some painful way.
Mendy Samstein, white SNCC worker from New York, actually saw Mrs. Spinks being pushed around and having her arm twisted by a man who later turned out to be a *state investigator.* Then after Mendy talked with the other four who had been physically hurt, it turned out that the same man had done the work in each case. This is the same man who told Ursula Junk when she was arrested in September that she "ain't got no rights in Mississippi."
As they were released from jail and taken outside of the jail, Mendy noticed the man standing around. He went over to him and asked his name but the man would not give it out. Mendy then walked over to the

FBI agents standing there, explained to him that this state investigator had been harassing people in jail, and asked them to come with him so that he could identify the man to them. Then the FBI men and Mendy started walking toward the door into which the state investigator had disappeared and just at the entrance a large group of state troopers surrounded them and blocked the doorway.

At that point the FBI men began to move away as if to indicate that they were not with Mendy. Mendy went after them and said that he wanted to identify the man to them and they said something to the effect of "don't tell us how to run our investigations." Mendy then said that he had a right to tell them how to run investigations since he had seen the man twist Mrs. Spinks' arm. They then mumbled something about come down to the office. Then the state investigator walked out of the building. Mendy then pointed him out to the agents. They walked away with no comment.

Later, John Beecher, a SNCC volunteer in McComb, reported that the same state investigator had come a few days earlier to the McComb Freedom House with the same FBI agents and that they seemed to be quite friendly.

Even J. Edgar Hoover, FBI director, admits to the nature of the Mississippi law enforcement officials:

> Around Philadelphia, Miss., law enforcement is practically nil and many times sheriffs and deputies participate in crime.
> —November 19, 1904, Washington *Post*

Yet the conduct of the FBI agents described in the SNCC report is not uncommon and is to be expected. Many FBI agents resign from the FBI to assume "investigation jobs" for the southern states, as did Hugh Clegg, the former FBI official who, as special assistant to the Chancellor of Ole Miss, did such an outstanding job of helping the state defy the admission of James Meredith to the university.

The *friendliness* by the FBI agents is but an extension of the attitude of the director of the bureau, J. Edgar Hoover. On Hoover's visit to Jackson, Mississippi, on June 10, 1964, to open up a branch office of the FBI in Mississippi, a great deal of time was spent by Hoover visiting with Governor Paul B. Johnson. One reporter called it a "love feast." Quite lavishly Hoover praised Governor Johnson as a "man I greatly admire."

The hundreds in Mississippi engaged in the Summer Project—as well as the nation itself—were stunned.

It was difficult to understand how Hoover could be so crude.

This Paul Johnson whom Hoover was praising was the same Paul Johnson who, after being called a "moderate by Mississippi standards" by a column of Drew Pearson, hurriedly convened a press conference to deny that he was "moderate" and buttressed his self-praise by making extended remarks extolling the virtues of the White Citizens Council. This was the same Paul Johnson who, as Lieutenant Governor of Mississippi, had taken advantage of Governor Ross Barnett's transportation difficulties in getting from Jackson to Oxford by grabbing some of the "glory" of defying the federal marshals as they sought to enroll James Meredith. This was the same Paul B. Johnson who had defeated a Republican opponent, Rubell Phillips, in the fall of 1963 by convincing the white voters of Mississippi that he hated "niggers" more than Phillips did. And this is the same Paul B. Johnson who is awaiting trial for criminal contempt of the orders of the United States Court of Appeals for the Fifth Circuit ordering Ole Miss integration—a step forced on the Justice Department by an incensed Court of Appeals even though the Justice Department wanted to drop the whole matter for fear of embarrassing the Kennedy Administration, which had a not-too-well-known degree of complicity in the acts of defiance of Barnett and Johnson.*

The earlier visit of Allen Dulles, former director of the Central Intelligence Agency (CIA), to Mississippi had been of the same order as the Hoover visit.

There is little need to belabor the truth that there is not one mystical federal government in Washington and that the federal government is a somewhat imperfect chameleon with a character in each state similar to the character of the state. The most cursory examination proves the obvious, especially in Mississippi:

---

* Frank E. Smith, *Congressman from Mississippi*, p. 305, discusses private arrangements with the Kennedy Administration to allow integration of Ole Miss while publicly feigning defiance. Similar arrangements were made for a charade at the University of Alabama in 1963, when Governor George Wallace "stood in the schoolhouse door," and by Eisenhower in Little Rock, Arkansas, in 1957.

• The federally subsidized national guard is racially segregated in Mississippi and elsewhere in the South.

• The federal postal system mirrors the patterns of segregation locally. Patronage is handled in Mississippi and elsewhere in the South by racist officials of states and reflects their racial views.

• The federal school lunch program is racially administered with Negro schools getting the worst of it.

• Farm subsidies are racially administered to the detriment of southern Negroes in Mississippi and elsewhere.

• Federal installations (both military and civilian) show patterns of racial limitations on employment, assignment and promotion.

• State unemployment services (federally subsidized) are racially segregated.

• Hospitals built with federal funds deny service because of race or segregate in dispensing available service.

You name it. It's all totally segregated or only tokenly integrated. The chameleon nature of the federal government either permits or requires the similarity between the federal and state governments.

Mississippi and the Mississippi Summer Project provide a relatively uncluttered view of our nation. For nowhere else is the relationship between the state government and the federal government so deep and substantial.

For every $3 in federal taxes collected from the state of Mississippi, the state received approximately $6.50 in return, plus other moneys that aren't divisible as to what exact share of the benefit went to the state: $270,793,000 federal tax collected and $644,617,217 federal moneys spent. The excess of moneys spent by the federal government over what is collected, or approximately $373,824,217, constitutes more than 30 per cent of the annual income of the state.

In spite of this involvement, the federal administration—both Democratic and Republican—feigned helplessness to protect the lives of persons involved in the Mississippi Summer Project. (This lie was refuted by public assertions of the National Lawyers Guild in a legal memorandum presented to President Lyndon B. Johnson and also by the statement of 29 of the nation's outstanding law professors. No credible source has agreed with the federal government's assertions of helplessness.)

READERS' VIEWPOINT

Can Mississippi Afford Goldwater?

Editor — I would like to comment on what I think is the most important and the most ignored feature of the current political campaign.

Mississippi just cannot afford Goldwater—or any other brand of economic conservatism! A rich state (i. e., one which pays more to the Federal treasury than it receives in Federal funds) can afford to advocate conservatism. A poor state (Mississippi receives more than $3 for every $1 paid in Federal taxes) cannot.

What part of the federal expenditures in Mississippi should be deleted from the budget? Shall we give up the $186 million which came into the state for prime military contracts in the fiscal year 1963, or the $78 million for prime NASA contracts? Shall we do without social security payments ($127 million) or maybe the school milk and lunch porgrams ($7 million)?

Who needs the Federal fund for college construction, research, and fellowships which totaled $10 million for the period 1961-63, or the college student loan program of $3.8 million and the college housing loan program of $15 million over the same period? Maybe the $3.7 million in Federal vocational education funds is expendable?

The Federal highway construction program brought $116.-8 million into the state during 1961-1963 and created 17.7 million man-hours of employment.

The 60,136 veterans and their dependents receive $4.4 million in monthly payments in the State of Mississippi. Mississippi farmers received $18.2 million in Government payments in the year 1963.

Do you really feel that Mississippi, with the lowest per capita income in the United States, con afford to give up the assistance that it gets from the other states — because that is what this inbalance (Between payments to and receipts from the Federal Government) actually reflects?

Lynn Johnson
707 Lakeland Dr.
Jackson, Miss.

Letter to the editor which appeared on the editorial page of the *Jackson* (Miss.) *Daily News,* Friday, October 30, 1964, p. 9.

In spite of the involvement of the federal government in Mississippi and the fact that the efforts of SNCC, CORE and the other civil rights groups working in the state are actually performing a function that is really not their affair, but is the prime business of government (insuring the enjoyment of Constitutional rights by citizens long denied those rights), these civil rights workers were less protected than Peace Corpsmen working in faraway continents. Even to this date, the FBI asserts that "it can only investigate, not protect."

This statement was only true when the persons seeking the protection were not important enough to risk impinging upon the "state-federal" relationship. While Hoover of the FBI was in Jackson, Mississippi, mouthing this statement in July, the same night some 50 FBI agents, with guns bared, surrounded a church in McComb, Mississippi, to *investigate* because there was a Congressman inside the church speaking to the Movement. When Congressman Don Edwards (Dem., Calif.) left, the *investigation* ended.

The summer that wouldn't end—the Mississippi Freedom Summer of 1964—if it does nothing more, should teach some and remind others that with regard to ending the racism of America the federal government is not so much helpless as it is unwilling.

All of the "great" social legislation passed in recent times to end the pressing problems of our nation (poverty program, surplus food program, urban renewal, manpower development and training, farmers home administration, crop support program, area redevelopment administration, welfare program, etc.) is drafted to maintain local direction and control of the federal money and power. This enables the "things-as-they-are people"—be they in Mississippi or in Montana—to maintain the status quo.

What the federal government doesn't do directly to perpetuate and reinforce local power blocks, it does indirectly.

Pontius Pilate-like, at the orientation of the summer volunteers in Oxford, Ohio, the federal government, through John Doar of the Justice Department, washed its hands. The federal government in effect said that the Constitutional rights to both life and liberty are placed "in the hands of local law enforcement agencies," i.e.,

Sheriff Lawrence Rainey of Philadelphia and Chief Ben Collins of Clarksdale.

The results of the hand-washing were both inevitable and deadly.

There's need for a second look at the federal government, the government with the nickname "Uncle Sam."

Though world pressure had mounted to such an extent that the federal police force by November 18, 1964, had arrested or assisted in the arrest of approximately 25 persons out of the thousands guilty of civil rights deprivations in Mississippi, on the same day the widely reported utterances of the Hon. J. Edgar Hoover, director of the FBI, indicated that the arrests were merely a temporary phenomenon:

> Over and over the FBI Director emphasized that it is not his agency's business to guard anyone. This, he said, includes protecting the President and "wet nursing" those "who go down to reform the South."
>
> November 19, 1964, Washington Post

Hoover's other comments of November 18, 1964, were the beginning of a bizarre episode in the prosecution of the accused killers of the three civil rights workers in Neshoba County.

On November 18, Hoover criticized the Warren Commission (the group which had investigated the murder of President John F. Kennedy), berated the judiciary of the nation for "coddling the convicted," and called the noted civil rights leader, Dr. Martin Luther King, a "notorious liar."

These charges, which were repeated several times, have never been retracted.

National reaction was swift.

Civil rights organizations, liberal groups and the northern press (including *The New York Times,* the Washington *Post* and the New York *Herald Tribune*) either joined in demanding the ouster of Hoover or criticized the incompetence or inaction of the FBI. Other forces equally as influential demanded that nothing be done to Hoover. On both sides the pressure mounted. The potential destructive effect on President Lyndon B. Johnson's plans for the "Great Society" was obvious.

For reasons not yet clear, on Wednesday, December 2, 1964,

Martin Luther King suddenly decided to make a pilgrimage to the office of Hoover in Washington. The two of them, plus some aides, spent more than an hour in private consultation. It is not known what Hoover said to King or what Hoover might have shown him. As an intimidated King left the conference he made few comments, but he did state that Hoover had not apologized.

King's going to Hoover dissipated some of the pressure. This was the first step. The second step occurred on Friday, December 4, 1964.

Sheriff Lawrence Rainey of Neshoba County and his deputy, Cecil Price, along with 19 others, were arrested by the FBI on charges of violating the civil rights of Chaney, Goodman and Schwerner by killing them. The news was treated sensationally, with some papers putting out special editions to hail the event. The critics of the inaction of the FBI and the Justice Department became flatterers of the two organizations.

The pressure was off—completely. Gone were the demands for Hoover's retirement. Praise was effusive.

Six days later, Thursday, December 10, 1964, at a preliminary hearing before the United States Commissioner in Meridian, Mississippi, Esther Carter, the charges against the sheriff and others were dropped. The function of a preliminary hearing is to determine if there is enough evidence to justify holding an arrested person until a federal grand jury can be convened to decide if the accused person should be indicted.

At the preliminary hearing the government gave evidence—raising doubts as to whether it had any.

An FBI agent merely *said* that he had a written confession from one of the 21 men implicating all of them in the murders. The defense lawyers objected, and the FBI agent's statement about what he had in written form was not considered—and correctly so.

Casual television viewers of *The Defenders* and *Perry Mason* recognized the FBI agent's statement as being hearsay of the rankest kind. But a spokesman for the Justice Department pretended to be startled. He said:

"In the experience of the department, the refusal by a U.S. Commissioner to accept a law enforcement officer's report of a signed confession at a preliminary hearing is totally without precedent."

Lawyers who regularly practice in the criminal courts hope that the spokesman for the Justice Department was "misquoted." For if the spokesman wasn't misquoted, the Justice Department is admitting that it has wrongfully caused a lot of persons to be held for grand juries illegally. Hearsay is incompetent evidence, and persons should not be deprived of their liberty by the use of incompetent evidence—the kind of evidence that is not permitted in court.

Conveniently, the civil rights organizations abandoned their lawyers and began to repeat the utterance of the Justice Department spokesman as if it were gospel. The liberal press of the nation did the same. If any newspaper had made a simple inquiry to a competent lawyer, it would have found the answer: Esther Carter, United States Commissioner for the Eastern Division of the Southern District of Mississippi, was correct in dismissing the charges when the only evidence was the word of an FBI agent that he had some evidence. And the onus wouldn't have shifted from the FBI.

The pattern seems to be set.

Each step and episode of the attempted prosecution of those accused of the murders of the three civil rights workers in Neshoba will be a farce, with the federal agency and the public-relations outlets coming out the victor and the concept of justice being the loser. No matter what the outcome of any number of arrests, charges and releases, the nature of the federal government and the function of the FBI might well be studied and questioned.

There's a need to remember that the work of SNCC, CORE and the others in the South—getting people registered as voters, trying to feed and clothe them during the winter months, and trying to secure protection for people from the violence—is not the real function of any private organization; it is the function of the federal government because of the nature of state governments. We must also remember that there ought not to be occasions when supporting organizations—private in nature—are needed to assist these civil rights organizations as they go about trying to do the federal government's job.

V

Supporting Organizations

I've seen daylight breaking high above the bough,
I've found my destination and I've made my vow:
So whether you abhor me or deride me or ignore me,
Mighty mountains loom before me,
And I won't stop now.

—*Naomi Long Nadgett*
Greenwood, Mississippi, Freedom School

PARTIALLY because of the indifference of the northern press during
the early stages of the planning of the Mississippi Summer Project,
and partially because SNCC had no money to supply COFO with
postage, during the spring of 1964 the Mississippi spokesmen gained
the initiative in the field of public relations.

Jimmy Ward, editor of the Jackson *Daily News,* and others began
calling the Summer Project an "invasion."

Incestuously, this propaganda was sucked back into the minds
of its propagators. . . . Vast expenditures for additional policemen
(the Highway Patrol forces and the Jackson police were doubled)
and armament (including a $13,000 tank for Jackson) were made;
vacations were canceled. Mississippi prepared for what its propaganda had created: a state of war.

This armament became a million-dollar monument to the power
of two lies, one announced and the other "concealed." The announced purpose was that the military might would be used to repel

the "invaders." The unspoken one was that the might was intended
for the preservation of school segregation in the fall of 1964, when
the federal courts had ordered token integration to begin. Be that as
it may, the Summer Project was an "invasion" and the summer
volunteers were "troops" who were part of a vast northern "army."

This army had its medical corps, chaplains, signal corps, "U.S.O."
and "judge advocate general department" (lawyers).

The Medical Committee for Human Rights

Every army needs a medical corps.

The troops involved in the Mississippi Summer Project of 1964
were no exception; they needed a medical corps, and they had one.
It was the Medical Committee For Human Rights, which was
founded on June 27, 1964.

The idea for the utilization of the professional skills of those
in the medical science had many sources, and no one person should
be given the credit. If any persons should be singled out of the many,
they should be Dr. Tom Levin and Dr. Marvin Belsky, who have
pushed this program so hard.

Understandably, parents have a lot of concern for their kids, and
this concern was translated into positive results, because many of
the more than 800 volunteers in the Summer Project had mothers,
fathers, aunts, uncles and brothers who were in the medical field.
The Medical Committee for Human Rights provided these relatives
with a legitimate excuse to be on the scene and to render service
while at the same time not seeming to protect or guard those whom
they loved.

There were others in the medical profession who thought that
the work of this committee would provide them with a chance to
participate in a meaningful way in supporting a Movement that
the totality of their hearts and beings wanted to see succeed. Whatever the *prime* motivation for the involvement, the results were
commendable.

The Medical Committee was but one genius of the Movement in
Mississippi; it provided more and more opportunities for people to

feel that they were worth something, that they were not just machines consumed by their own selfishness. For years the civil rights efforts indicated, by implication, that the only things those persons living in northern communities could do for the civil rights effort were to donate money, send telegrams and walk picket lines when some matter deserved a show of bodies.

Few concerned people find it completely satisfactory to be involved in pursuing their ideals by merely giving money—although it's greatly needed. Concerned people are more than money machines. Fortunately for SNCC, as it was organizing the Summer Project, it stumbled on to this. A place for those with medical skills was found.

This medical group established what it called a "medical presence" for the civil rights movement in Mississippi. This presence was achieved by contacting all 57 Negro doctors in the state and setting up liaison. In addition to the Negro physicians, some six white doctors practicing in Mississippi gave help, as did one or two medical institutions.

This contact was made easy by the character of the northern doctors involved, whose national reputations extended to Mississippi. Colleagues who knew the northern doctors only by reputation eagerly sought out contact with the specialists.

With this entree the Medical Committee was able to establish a rudimentary system of care for the urgent medical needs of the civil rights workers in many parts of the state, although not in all. It set up nine major stations and many more substations for emergencies, along with a referral system in to Jackson (where the best medical facilities of Mississippi are located) and beyond when necessary.

During the months of June, July and August, 1964, the Medical Committee sent 100 representatives into the state, including doctors, nurses, counselors and other medical workers, who performed medical tasks short of the actual practice of medicine. Among those who went were such specialists as psychiatrists, pediatricians, dermatologists, orthopedic surgeons, cardiologists, and registered nurses.

As these persons served, they learned. They saw and felt the interlocking chain of exploitation, poverty, discrimination, disease and human neglect that damns the South in the eyes of the world. From interviews they learned that the health problems of Negroes in Mississippi not only shocked the outsider but also were considered vital political issues that older Negroes, especially, were willing to fight about.

Wherever the members of the medical teams stopped—freedom schools, community centers, homes, and crossroad gatherings—they heard complaints about the high costs of medical care, the inadequate and callous treatment in segregated offices and facilities, the utter lack of state programs in such important medical areas as chronic diseases. To the surprise of some, they found local people who could place the medical problems in an historical-political perspective and liken the medical situation to the school situation of 100 years ago.

(The first public schools in Mississippi and the South were created by the Reconstruction legislatures. There were no schools for either the slaves or the poor white persons. The planters, who controlled the states, were wealthy enough not to need schools; they could employ tutors for their children.)

Added to the medical problems of the state, which stemmed from the lack of medical aid programs, were the problems involved in programs that were supposed to exist. The Medical Committee for Human Rights, in its report prepared and published on August 16, 1964, described the malfunctioning of the "existing" medical programs:

We have found there to be many programs, inadequate though they may be, that Mississippi provides on paper to maintain the health of its people. These range from the prenatal clinic, to the checking of school children's eyesight and hearing, to the pittance in medical assistance for the aged on welfare. But even these programs barely reach out to the rural Negro.

One can only say that there is a conspiracy of silence when one seeks to discover what programs are available. Too often in too many parts of the state and in Jackson itself, our medical teams—as well as the COFO workers—have been refused information on these programs. And so often as to be all but universal, these programs are unknown to the rural poor, who spend their medical moneys on doctoring for ultimate emergencies—many of which might have been avoided with preventive medical care that is even now currently available.

It would be a great service to make known to the people in each county just what services are available now, at what cost, at what time, and where. Our teams and some of the COFO projects have made a beginning at this. It should be expanded and systematized. And this information will in most cases *not* be available for the asking, but must be dug out painstakingly and tactfully from the [white] patients themselves who use the facilities.

This information, by the way, can provide part of the factual underpinning for a health program for the future.

Equally in danger of malfunctioning, the medical teams found, was the veteran staff of COFO, especially the SNCC workers, who constitute 80 per cent of the staff. (The Congress of Racial Equality (CORE), being more affluent, can, and often does, pay its staff members in excess of $100 weekly. The SNCC field secretaries get $9.64 weekly—when it's available.)

In a world where life is valuable, the COFO staff members are slightly more than precious because they are the *true believers,* the ones who, more than any group in America today, show promise of bringing the nation up to the status of the "beloved community," where, suddenly, it may be more important to send the children of white and black laborers to college than to send astronauts to the moon. These young men and women are the ones threatening to alter the nation's values so drastically, so that, without notice, the value of new hospitals may someday exceed the esteem of new launching pads for Saturn rockets.

The starting place is Mississippi, a jungle that extracts its toll even as it is transformed. Far too long has the COFO staff lived the life of a chicken in a den of jackals. Far too long have these people worked in communities where their existence has depended upon the inaccuracy of a sheriff's aim or the faultiness of a bomber's fuse. The COFO staff is tired—continuously; malnourished—continuously; tense—continuously; and frustrated—continuously. And the medical teams knew it. The doctors found everything from infected mosquito bites and badly decaying teeth to broken glasses.

The Medical Committee reminded the staff members repeatedly of the fact known to all: that eventually the physical condition of the staff would lead to suffering in both efficiency and morale. Physical examinations were given to the staff and individual recommendations were made based on the medical findings. Local physicians prescribed treatment and medicines where indicated.

As the medical team members served in Mississippi they became addicts.

The "mystique" of the Movement infected them.

Regardless of whether the motivation for the individual member of the Medical Committee coming to Mississippi had been shallow or profound, the heat, horror and commonplace heroics impelled him toward several conclusions: that this is a serious struggle for serious stakes; that we all have to be more than summer soldiers; that, just as the Movement goes on from the summer, we must go on too; that, to the extent possible, we must not let this summer end.

In August, as it was learned that the Summer Project wouldn't stop, the Medical Committee for Human Rights said that it wouldn't conclude and announced its plans for the future:

1. *A group health plan*—to secure, if possible, the enrollment of the staff continuing in Mississippi in a group health plan of medical and hospital insurance.

2. *Health education.* "We think that we have a role to play with regard to the freedom schools and the community centers. It's not to provide doctors or nurses to go to them, at least in any significant numbers. It's to work with the COFO staff to prepare materials and an actual training course for COFO workers and local people in various fields of health: first aid, personal hygiene, sex education, nutrition, and mother and child care."

3. *Health research.* "COFO began, before we did, in analyzing the health problem of the Mississippi Negro. There is much more to be done: to learn more about the distribution of federal and Public Health Service funds; to find out what moneys might be available; to develop programs for involving the federal government in more direct and meaningful ways in the Mississippi health picture; to develop strategies to desegregate hospitals. Beyond money, we must

develop pilot studies and field programs, often with foundation support, in areas that Mississippi has failed to touch such as mental health for children, dental services for the rural areas, and the like."

4. *Professional training.* "It is a disgrace and a scandal in America that Mississippi Negroes have no access to medical school; that in the last four years there has no longer been a colored nursing school; that the midwives, so important to the Negro mothers in the rural areas, are so little trained and supervised. We think that we have a role to play in this area that is important for the dignity of the Negro and for the assurances of his health."

5. *Rest and recreation.* The Medical Committee is developing facilities for a rest and recreation program to accommodate physically overworked and mentally strained COFO workers who have been in the field for long periods without adequate food, hygiene and rest.

The Medical Committee is committed to continue. "As long as there is a COFO, there will be doctors," Dr. Robert Axelrod has stated. Many doctors throughout the nation have learned of the committee's work, and hundreds of applications have poured into the office of the committee at 211 West 56th Street, New York, New York, to be assigned to work in Mississippi.

As the summer volunteers remained in part in Mississippi, so did the Medical Committee for Human Rights remain—in part.

Photographic Corps

In addition to the photographers of the national news media, COFO had its own photographic staff.

SNCC field secretary Willie Blue, after extensive training in New York by a "motion-picture committee" headed by Pete Smollet and Hortense Beveridge (working out of the Calpenny Studios), was equipped with 16-millimeter and 8-millimeter cameras and covered the state on assignments.

"Still-picture" coverage was provided by the Southern Documentary Project, headed by Matt Herron, who directed three other professional photographers. The activities of these project members were in addition to the efforts of Cliff Vaughs, SNCC field secretary, who for over a year has been COFO's "photographer in residence."

The "U.S.O."*

The cultural corps of the Summer Project had two units: the Mississippi Caravan of Music and the Free Southern Theater.

Consisting of an integrated troupe of eight persons headed by its founders, John O'Neal and Gil Moses, and Jackie Washington, the gifted singer, the Free Southern Theater toured the freedom schools and community centers, presenting the documentary historical play of Martin Duberman, *In White America.*

Although some were critical because there were no Mississippians in the cast and in some of the communities parts of the play were "over the heads" of a few, the production got mostly rave reviews from culturally parched audiences, which drank in the drama as the roots of the cotton plant gulp water after a drought.

One native Mississippian who had never seen a play before described his reaction to the production of the Free Southern Theater: "I sat there on the edge of the seat, with one hand holding me to it, to keep from jumping up and screaming through the veil of heaven, 'Yes! Tell it!' With the other hand, I was wiping tears from my eyes that were laden with love, sorrow, joy, pity—and hate. I was born in Mississippi. And by the act of God or a cracker sheriff I'll probably die here. They were telling my story on that stage. Oh, they were telling it . . . and telling it like it *really* is."

Amen.

From its base in New Orleans, where new plays are being prepared, the Free Southern Theater is coming into Mississippi and other parts of the Deep South again and again, feeding the souls through the senses and stopping the changes of seasons by not letting the work begun during the summer of 1964 end—and not letting the summer end.

* During the years of World War II and after, the entertainment of the American soldier was carried out by the United Service Organization (U.S.O.).

Ordinarily one would think that sending folk singers to Mississippi (the home of Mississippi John Hurt, Big Bill Bronzy and other giants of soul music) would be like taking salt water to San Francisco or coal to Kentucky.

Not so.

For the most part, the Mississippi Negroes—and the whites, too—are not organized within their own communities for cultural and recreational activities. Thousands of rural churches—those that haven't been burned down—meet only once and sometimes twice a month, "when the preacher makes his circuit." In the hundreds of joints where the sheriff's liquor is sold, the people are either without music or dependent upon a tired jukebox with music from another world.

Because of the Mississippi Caravan of Music, coordinated by Bob and Susan Cohen during the Summer Project, the 30 project centers throughout the state had plenty of what one bard called "soul" music.

The singers and musicians traveled around the state in groups. After completing a program at one freedom school or community center, the caravan traveled to another, usually a trip of no more than one or two hours. Once there, say in the afternoon, the members held an informal workshop with the students. These "workshops"—a better name would have been "playshops"—generally wound up with whatever the singers or children were most interested in: anything from folk dancing and African rounds to English ballads and learning the banjo chords for "Skip to My Lou." After time out for supper, there was a mass meeting with singing or perhaps a "hootenanny," where the adult population of the community attended with the younger people, who were at the freedom school during the day. It was not uncommon for these evening sessions to go on for more than three hours.

The Mississippi Caravan of Music was a success for a lot of reasons. It worked at giving renewed status to the music of Huddie Leadbetter and Big Bill Bronzy and the others whom Mississippians had been taught to hate because they were both black and Mississippian. The caravan was a success also because of the kind of people who gave their time to it during the Summer Project: Len Chandler, Bob Cohen, Judy Collins, Jim Crockett, Barbara Dane, Dick Davey, Alix Dobkin, the Eastgate Singers (Adam and Paul Cochran, James Mason and Jim Christy), Jim and Jean Golver, Carolyn Hester, Greg Hildebrand, Roger Johnson, Peter La Farge, Julius Lester, Phil Ochs, Cordell Reagan, Pete Seeger, David Segál, Ricky Sherover, Gil Turner, Jackie Washington and Don Winkleman.

And the caravan didn't end. Guitar whammers, banjo pluckers, harmonica squealers, and singers of all kinds are still *stealing away* a week from the bright lights of the concert stages and the dim lights of funk-filled cafés to tour the Mississippi freedom schools and community centers, where they experience the realities of singing the verse of "We Shall Overcome" that says "we are not afraid" within a circle of locked arms—while knowing that the building has been promised to be bombed.

"Chaplain Corps"

Not only did the National Council of Churches (NCC) provide the place for the orientation of the "troops" (Western College for Women in Oxford, Ohio) and convene a gathering of educators in New York City in the late spring to help construct the curriculum of the freedom school, but it also saturated the State of Mississippi with a heavenly host of ministers, priests and rabbis during the summer months—400 of them on a rotating basis.

Given the title of "resident director" and set up in a Jackson office at 507½ North Farish Street, the Rev. Warren McKenna would have been more aptly called "resident conductor": his ministers flowed in and out of the state in a constant stream.

Supposedly the prime function of the clergy was to act as "minister-counselors to volunteers in projects." Translated into Movement language, this meant that the clergymen licked stamps, ran mimeograph machines, drafted leaflets, drove cars, mopped floors, outran sheriffs, inhabited jails, got heads split, canvassed for voters, taught at freedom schools, led singing, taught crafts and occasionally preached at a local Negro church. In other words, the

clergymen did what everybody else in the Summer Project did—
any job that needed doing at the particular moment.

So "regular" were the clergymen that some of the atheists began
to wonder what corrupting influence was cleansing religion of so
much of its stodginess: it was enough to shake one's profoundly
religious views that churches have no place in an earthly hell.

Because of their church credentials, the clergymen were able to
establish considerable contact with the Mississippi clergy, both
white and black. For what it was worth, there were thousands
of covert meetings during the summer in the offices and homes of
white ministers with drawn shades.

Even the lawyers were impressed. A guild-sponsored attorney,
Eugene Crane of Chicago, who was stationed in Hattiesburg (in the
southeastern area of Mississippi where Rabbi Arthur Lelyveld of
Cleveland, Ohio, was beaten with a metal pipe), described the
Hattiesburg operation of the National Council of Churches clergy-
men:

> They set up a house in Hattiesburg and one of the rooms had 14
> mattresses spread on the floor. There was a 30-gallon hot water heater
> which supplied constant hot water to provide for 20 people to take two
> showers a day. This they felt could only have been done through
> "Divine intervention."
>
> The ministers were extremely active and extremely militant. They
> seemed to be a cohesive element. They helped us in many instances in
> approaching the police structure and arranging bail in some cases. They
> have developed some contact with the police department. They seemed
> to have developed a great deal of contact in the community. On one oc-
> casion they were able to raise bond money from unknown sources within
> two hours to release one defendant.
>
> The ministers also seemed to be very interested in active militant
> action by the local community people and were active out in the com-
> munities themselves constantly. After canvassing with the voter registra-
> tion and Freedom Registration in Negro neighborhoods, they finally
> switched to the canvassing in the white neighborhood.

These were not summer chaplains to summer soldiers.

Just as the Mississippi power structure thought—hoped—the National Council of Churches would flee the state at the end of August,
the NCC Commission on Race and Religion shifted itself into the

Delta Ministry, a project to deal with the problems of automation in the cotton fields of Mississippi, where thousands are nearly starving because the chopping of cotton is now done by "poisoning" the fields (spraying with chemicals) and the picking is done by a host of machines that don't need to eat.

The Delta Ministry will seek to get as many of the dispossessed persons on relief as are eligible, and in some cases there may be direct aid to those ineligible for relief by the National Council of Churches through the months long beyond that part of year mortals call summer.

Legal Corps

The last census of Mississippi shows the state to have a population of 2,178,141 persons, with 42.3 per cent of that population, or 920,595 persons, composed of black would-be citizens.

The best available figures show that there are 2,100 lawyers in the state, or close to one lawyer per 1,000 persons—if, and only if, you don't want to challenge the systematic exclusion of Negroes from juries; if you don't object to racial signs and racial segregation in the court and the community; if you are not litigating against a white person and insisting that your black skin not be sacrificed to perpetuate the "white fictions" of those who run Mississippi.

If you fall in the category of one of these "if's," then there are only four lawyers in Mississippi: three black barristers and one white one. It would appear that this grouping should include the 300 young white people working throughout the state today with SNCC (they're not *white* in the Mississippi definition) and the 920,595 Negroes who at any fortuitous moment may find part of their lives (or all) and part of their property (or all) taken away "legal-like" by some Mississippi court, either state or federal.

How drastic the ratio changes for the "if's."

Instead of one lawyer per 1,000 persons, it becomes one lawyer per every 230,250 persons. The Student Nonviolent Coordinating Committee decided that additional legal help would be needed for the Summer Project of 1964 . . . and three legal groups responded.

One group was composed of law students solely, operating under the banner: Law Students Civil Rights Research Council. It was the duty of Hunter Morey, SNCC field secretary and legal coordinator for COFO, to assign these law students to areas of responsibility throughout the state. The students prepared arrest data, collected affidavits, contacted the FBI, collected evidence of voting discrimination, and "clerked" for whatever lawyers happened to be in the same part of the state where the law students were assigned—lawyers from either the Lawyers Guild Committee for Legal Aid to the South (CLAS) or the Lawyers Constitutional Defense Committee (LCDC).

During the summer of 1964, there were 15 such students who served for two months or more: William Robinson, Sherwin Kaplan, Alan M. Lerner, Lowell Johnston, Dan Perlman, Miss Cornelia McDougal, George Johnson, Mike Starr, Mike Smith, Bob Watkins, Richard Wheelock, Larry Hansen, Bennett Gershman, Leonard Edwards and Clinton Hopson.

The LCDC was composed of the Lawyers Committee for Civil Rights Under Law (called the "President's Committee" because it was formed out of a conference of lawyers called to the White House by President Kennedy during the hot summer of 1963), the NAACP Legal Defense and Educational Fund, Inc. (the Ink Fund), the American Jewish Committee, CORE, the American Jewish Congress, and the American Civil Liberties Union (ACLU). This group placed 40 lawyers in the state on a rotating basis and stationed another 20 at two places outside of the state—Memphis, Tennessee, and New Orleans, Louisiana.

The credit of the sizable entourage of lawyers operating in the state for the Summer Project under the sponsorship of the LCDC must be given to the Guild, the third part of the legal triumvirate.

The Guild (a national bar association of more than 25 years' existence) became involved in the civil rights movement of the 1960's shortly before the annual conference of the SNCC staff held in Atlanta in the late summer of 1962.

As fate would have it, this SNCC conference came on the heels of a series of confrontations between SNCC and Jack Greenberg's

NAACP Legal Defense and Educational Fund, Inc. (the Ink Fund).

Never having had money, SNCC has always depended upon those with resources to do what they could. Greenberg's Ink Fund publicly billed itself as "the legal arm of the entire civil rights movement" and had handled several cases involving arrests of SNCC field secretaries throughout the South. Initially the Ink Fund had indicated that it would probably handle any case that SNCC asked it to handle. But that was before the Ink Fund really understood the aggressive nature of SNCC. SNCC was pushy and pushing. It had protests going hard, fast and furious in Alabama, Mississippi and Georgia. Moments after each arrest, Greenberg would get a collect call for legal help. The pushiness of SNCC was extending and distending the carefully allocated Ink Fund budget and staff. Greenberg's response was to indicate to SNCC that it should cease being so aggressive, because the Ink Fund thought that a "point had been proven" and that there was no need for new cases before the number of old cases of arrests had tapered down considerably.

The Ink Fund's suggestion was based on consideration of sound Ink Fund fiscal policies. SNCC's opposition was based on its ingrained dedication to attacking and attacking—again, again, again—the citadels of Southern segregation.

Wisely, the Ink Fund pressured for a slowdown by indicating that it didn't intend to take care of the defense of persons arrested because of the far-flung SNCC efforts. This *promise* had far-reaching implications for the young student organization, which was then entirely dependent upon the Ink Fund for legal aid. There were thought to be no alternatives.

In this setting three lawyers from the National Lawyers Guild's newly formed committee dealing with civil rights were invited to address the SNCC staff conference for an hour—and they whaled!

Irving Rosenfeld of Los Angeles flung answers back as fast as the questions were hurled at him by the SNCC staffers about the role of the lawyer as it should be. Vic Rabinowitz of New York kept opening eyes with regard to the creative use of the law in supplementing boycotts, sit-ins and other integration efforts by use of the federal regulatory agencies, such as the Federal Communications Commission, and by employing some of the old labor cases to enjoin Chief Laurie Pritchette of Albany from preventing all public expression of free speech by the Movement in that city.

The third Guild lawyer of the conference—who was referred to by the odd name of "Snake Doctor"—kept encouraging the filing of some sort of legal monstrosity called an "Omnibus Integration Suit."

SNCC wasn't *important* then, in 1962. The United States Justice Department declined to send a representative, so the three Guild lawyers were allowed to spill over into the period allocated in the conference schedule for remarks by the Justice Department.

The staff loved it.

They bored into the three lawyers again and again with any question that came to their minds. "What about citizen arrests?" "What sorry lawyer can I get to come to Arkansas and file one of those suits y'all talking about?" "What do you do when there ain't no lawyer and they are proceeding with your trial?" "What should you do when your lawyer tells you to sit on the segregated side of the courtroom and you don't wanna?" "Why aren't the NAACP lawyers like you guys?" "What can be done to get us on the aggressive legally instead of waiting around for another arrest?" "How can we force the FBI to act?"

A thousand questions were asked and a thousand questions were answered. (The answer to many was, "I don't know. But I'll research it.") Over the meals, into the night, the questions and answers flowed as the SNCC staff gulped in the presence of the three Guild lawyers, who were responsive, unaloof and "regular" and seemed to know *where it was at.*

Two days after this conference ended, Jack Greenberg, accompanied by Wiley Branton, was back in Atlanta at the SNCC national office. The Ink Fund pulled out a "blank check" and gave it to SNCC. Greenberg assured the SNCC leadership that he had been misunderstood. "All cases will be handled. Just call."

In the fall of 1963, during the mock Freedom Election balloting for Governor of Mississippi, COFO brought 100 northern students into the state to help; they came from Yale and Stanford universities. These volunteers supplemented the regular COFO staff of 100.

Sole reliance at that time for legal aid was on Greenberg's Ink Fund. It sent no additional legal personnel into the state for the stepped-up project. Good business and fiscal policies would not permit it.

Bad were the results. Jess Brown, Jack Young, and Carsie Hall (three-fourths of the civil rights lawyers in the state), who were inundated by the impossible case loads from the ordinary constant arrests of the Mississippi civil rights workers in ordinary Mississippi times, were drowned by the influx of new cases from the Freedom Election.

SNCC was appalled.

Somebody remembered the Guild and the 1962 conference in Atlanta that had gone so well everyone had tried to find out *where it was at*. SNCC invited the Guild to extend its limited operations in the civil rights field (in Virginia, North Carolina and Louisiana) into Mississippi.

It did.

Then it became fiscally possible for the Ink Fund to send more lawyers into the state and to spend more money during the Mississippi Summer Project of 1964—but not before the Ink Fund had begged, cajoled and threatened in an effort to regain its former monopoly with SNCC in Mississippi.

SNCC didn't budge.

Greenberg did.

The operation of the Guild in the Mississippi Summer Project of 1964, in which it brought into the state 69 lawyers on a rotating basis, was typical of the way that both lawyer groups (LCDC and the Guild) functioned.

A plan was drafted for complete legal coverage of what was called "60 lawyer weeks." Broken down, this meant that a given lawyer might volunteer to come to Mississippi and stay for one week, in which event the Guild would have "one lawyer week." If that same lawyer had volunteered for two weeks, there would be "two lawyer weeks."

The figure of 60 lawyer weeks was selected because of anticipation that there would be need for coverage in five different areas of the state, representing the five Congressional districts of the state. One lawyer for each of the five areas for the 12 weeks of the Summer Project came to 60 lawyer weeks.

In addition to the lawyers in the state, a reserve system was set up whereby 90 other lawyers volunteered to spend at least 40 hours during the summer preparing briefs, legal memoranda, and the other work that didn't require on-the-scene presence.

The customary day for the changing of "shifts" was Sunday, and the most popular form of transportation was flying. Usually George Crockett of Detroit got involved in a shuttling service to the airport —taking 6 to 10 lawyers out to the airport and bringing 6 to 10 back from the airport. As the Guild's Mississippi Project director, based in Jackson for the summer, he began his orientation of the incoming lawyers at the Jackson airport and on the 20-minute ride back. Crockett described the beginning of that orientation for life— or death—in Mississippi this way: "It would be interesting if you could hear some of our conversations coming from the airport driving to the city of Jackson because nine times out of ten they have a completely false impression of what they will encounter when they get off the plane. They were surprised that they were not even arrested or that nobody insulted them, or that type of thing.

"They would be frightened—and who isn't frightened in Mississippi?—and the job would be to get *some* of the fear out without at the same time making them too complacent.

"We'd tell them the ropes as we understood them: that it's their primary responsibility to get people out of jail and not to get themselves into jail."

Similarities between the Guild legal operation and that of the LCDC existed in the matters of bail and federal removal actions. Both groups had a bail fund, even though each summer volunteer was supposed to have $500 bail money as part of his equipment for coming into the state. One reason for the bail fund was that a lot of the people in the Summer Project were local Mississippians who hadn't seen $500 in their lives. (Work in the cotton fields from sunrise to sunset was paid for at the rate of $2.50 to $3 per day.)

The second reason was that the bail money arrangement of the volunteer often consisted of phoning or sending a telegram to someone in the North. Getting the bail money to Mississippi could take a day or so, because the Western Union office in Mississippi's largest city, Jackson, is not open all night and the situation is worse in other communities. Once a summer volunteer is in jail—especially if he is white—deadly consequences can follow. All the guard has to do is tell the other prisoners: "Here's one of those nigger lovers from the North!"

With the more than 1,000 arrests during the months of June, July and August, both legal groups filed petitions which took the cases out of the hands of the state judges and put them in the hands of the federal judges. Paradoxically, the reason that the petitions gave for transferring the case from the state courts to the federal courts was that the civil rights worker could not get a fair trial in the state court. As proof of this assertion, the removal petitions filed by the lawyers pointed out that the juries of the state courts either totally excluded Negroes or only tokenly included them. Secondly, the removal petition asserted that no fair trial could be gotten in the state courts because Negroes were denied the right to vote and therefore didn't help elect the state court judges, who, as a result, could be responsive to rights only in so far as prejudiced white voters viewed those rights.

The paradox is provided by the fact that the very reasons given for no fair trial in the state courts—*from* which the cases were being removed—were true of the federal courts—*to* which the cases were being removed.

During the summer months the law enforcement agencies accused those engaged in the Movement of a wide range of charges: picketing without a permit, disorderly conduct, traffic violations, carrying a concealed weapon (fingernail file), interfering with an officer in the performance of his duty, failing to move on, et cetera. Only once was charged with a felony. (Felonies are crimes for which one may spend more than a year in jail—serious criminal offenses.)

The charges were minor ones: misdemeanors.

This was deliberate.

Mississippi law was certain that the summer would end, that all of the high-powered lawyers would go home, and that all of the summer volunteers would go home. Charging someone with a felony might mean his staying, if for no other reason than to defend himself from the serious charge.

The word "summer" became irrelevant as the Ink Fund and the Guild both set up their Jackson offices on a permanent basis to follow through on the cases begun during the summer . . . and to follow through on future calls from COFO for massive legal assistance, should it be needed . . . and to work with the general counsel employed by COFO at the end of August, 1964.

More often than not, when the individual lawyers working with the two committees of lawyers reached the ends of the periods for which they had initially volunteered, the long-distance phones back to their offices in the North would get "hot." The volunteer lawyers would work at changing schedules in their offices in the North to be able to stay a little longer. Mississippi had "hooked them."

From the response of the lawyer organizations remaining, it is apparent that the individual lawyers were not the only ones so addicted—much to the glory and benefit of COFO.

The change of seasons seems to have ended in the land of the Pearl and Mississippi rivers. For the lawyers who volunteered for a season, the summer hasn't ended.*

* In addition to the legal organizations, there were several unattached lawyers who rendered specific service such as the firm of Kunstler, Kunstler and Kinoy (KKK), which filed several sweeping federal suits seeking to force the intervention of the federal judiciary on the side of the Movement. Morton Stavis of New Jersey joined "KKK" in these actions.

One notation of the legal coordinator of COFO, Hunter Morey, showed a case involving the death sentence (armed robbery) against John P. Henry in Ruleville, which was dismissed after the intervention of a lawyer referred to as the "Snake Doctor." This type of result certainly wasn't typical; the local power structure must have forgotten momentarily that Ruleville is in Mississippi.

PART TWO

VI

Freedom Schools

Of course he forbade her to give me any further instruction, telling her in the first place that to do so was unlawful, as it was also unsafe, "for," said he, "if you give a nigger an inch he will take an ell. Learning will spoil the best nigger in the world.

"If he learns to read the Bible it will forever unfit him to be a slave. He should know nothing but the will of the master, and learn to obey it.

"As to himself, learning will do him no good, but a great deal of harm, making him disconsolate and unhappy.

"If you teach him how to read, he'll want to know how to write, and this accomplished, he'll be running away with himself." Such was the tenor of Master Hugh's oracular exposition.

"Very well," thought I. "Knowledge unfits a child to be a slave" . . . and from that moment I understood the direct pathway from slavery to freedom.

—Frederick Douglass

IF FOR ONE MOMENT we think that the Negroes of the South, of Mississippi, are fools, simpletons, childlike creatures with the bodies of men and the minds of infants because they don't leave the South, it is we who are the idiots. Though perhaps unlettered, unsung and even unwashed, the Negro with his "Dumb Darkie" routine is responding, on his level, to the basic problem of this day—survival.

His critics in the North who cannot understand can find that understanding in the answer to two questions: what will he find in the Harlems? What are we doing when we laugh at the joke of a boss that isn't funny and accept any lie that appears in enough papers or magazines?

More than it has ever been for years, the problem of today and tomorrow is that of survival—staving off the ultimate rendezvous.

For all there is the threat of nuclear destruction. For many there is the threat of a slower death from starvation with its parched lips and blue sleep before passing through eternity. And for Mississippians the odds are unfavorably increased by the legion of the brave sharpshooters, bomb tossers and decapitators.

Though the facts are to the contrary, the Mississippi Negro sees his problem as the problem of color. He knows with unshakable certainty that his poverty, starvation and brutalizing are based on color; the signs—though he may not be able to read them—tell him this, and the "oppressor" keeps saying "nigger" as his black body is robbed of its manhood. Thus the Negro has a convenient one-word explanation for his ills: race.

Eyes in black bodies look at, but don't see, their counterparts in white skins who are bereft of the Negro's convenient explanation: white people are forced to seek their philosophical escape from their hells in a caricature, which mawkishly causes their whiteishness to shout louder and louder, so that sheer volume will convince itself, "All is well. All is well! ALL IS VERY WELL!!"

How piteous are both and all, but yet not at all. Are men to be blamed for getting wet when pushed into a river? Is there guilt in having a reality made of fictions when the manipulators (power structure) deny access to other than make-believe?

Unhappily, but understandably, the public schools are the arch tools of the fictions and the conformity to "Alice in Mississippi-land," which answer the Negroes' question of "Who am I?" with the word "nigger." To the white person's question of "Who am I?" the answer is "your skin."

This is especially disappointing because education is valued so highly by the oppressed as an instrument of partial or total escape from whatever the oppression happens to be—sex, race, age, religion. Jews denied the right to own land, ghettoized, and slaughtered whenever it served a political gain of a power structure learned that an educated man is a useful man and a useful man is a less persecuted man among the persecuted—for a time. Skills in the arts, sciences and professions made a person a little less "Jewish" at a moment of convenience of the persecutor, and acquiring these skills was less offensive to the persecuted than deliberate uncircumcising, shunning the synagogues or assuming a "goy" name.

And so in Mississippi the feeling is that education makes one a little less "black."

Why am I persecuted?

"Black" is $2.50 for a 14-hour day in the Mississippi cotton fields. "Black" is stepping off the sidewalk for a white person 20 years younger than you, and being cheated at the store (be it white- or black-owned) where you cash your welfare checks, and being robbed of land, labor, health and self-esteem while seeing yourself in the image perpetuated by the First National Bank, the Mississippi Power and Light Company and U.S. Senator James Eastland.

"Black" is sharing the *man's* opinion and hatred of poor white people, many of whom live, suffer and die as badly as Negroes without the *comforting* prison of pigmentation as an explanation.

What does the majority culture have that I want?

Because mechanization has become a reality for you in Mississippi (85 per cent of the cotton picked in the Delta last year was picked by machines), you find yourself somehow crowding your *vast* personal belongings into a $3.75, black, tin-covered suitcase, wrapping a lunch of chicken and baked sweet potatoes and taking the savings, from the little that you didn't have, to buy a ticket north on the Illinois Central Railroad, the Freedom Train.

What does the majority culture have that I don't want?

If perchance you had decided on that trip north to freedom and had gone to begin it on June 28, 1964, you might have been confused. It seems that the Freedom Train was running both ways as groups of whites and a sprinkling of young Negroes—freedom-school teachers—were coming to the place you were leaving: Mississippi.

Not a brighter, more beautiful day in the world has ever come to pass than Sunday, June 28, 1964, in Mississippi. It was the sort of day on which you'd praise all the good gods in the heavens for being alive to see it—except that there was a part of you that was dead, brutally dead, deadly dead, somewhere in Neshoba County near Philadelphia, where god is named Sheriff Lawrence Rainey and the archangel is Deputy Cecil Price.

On this day 275 more persons arrived in Mississippi from Oxford, Ohio, after having attended the second orientation session for the summer volunteers coming into Mississippi. Most of these arrivals were freedom-school teachers.

There were several reasons why these teachers were an encouraging sight for the desperateness of those summer volunteers who had preceded them. When the first group of volunteers had left Oxford on June 20, 1964, death for them in Mississippi had been merely an often-discussed probability. When these teachers arrived on June 28, death in Mississippi during the summer had become an actuality —even though in the far corners of the most pessimistic minds was retained hope that the three were still alive.

The presence of these teachers for the freedom schools was also encouraging because the freedom schools had been singled out for special attention by the Mississippi power structure. The legislators had dredged up from fetid pits a bill to make it illegal to have freedom schools. Copies of this bill had been given to many, if not all, of those in the teacher-training session of the Oxford, Ohio, orientation period—Senate Bill No. 1969:

BE IT ENACTED BY THE LEGISLATURE OF THE STATE OF MISSISSIPPI: *Section 1.* Any person, groups of persons, associations and corporations conducting a school in any county within this state shall first apply to the county superintendent of education thereof for a license to conduct such school.

If, after due examination, said county superintendent of education shall determine the said school is in fact for bona fide educational purposes, that said school does not intend to counsel and encourage disobedience to the laws of the State of Mississippi, and that the conduct of said school is in the public interest, he shall forthwith issue a license to the persons, groups of persons, associations or corporations applying for same.

Section 2. Should any person, group of persons, associations or corporations conduct any type school without obtaining a license as herein before provided, they shall together with any individual acting as professor, teachers, or instructors in said school be guilty of a misdemeanor which shall be punished by a fine of not less than One Hundred Dollars ($100.00) nor more than Five Hundred Dollars ($500.00) and/or confinement in the county jail for a period of not less than thirty (30) days nor more than six (6) months.

In the face of this actual intimidation of deaths and laws, the arrival of the teachers was the rainbow sign that the Mississippi Summer Project would at least begin, that the deaths couldn't stop it.

> We have walked through the shadow of death—
> We've had to walk it all by ourself.
> But we'll never turn back . . .
> No, we'll never turn back.

My God, they looked good getting off the train in Jackson; and they must have been just as imposing a sight in the other communities along the way as the Freedom Train brought them in.

Nine persons came into Jackson that day from the Oxford, Ohio, orientation session. Several of us went down to the dull, dirty, Illinois Central Station. As usual, the train was late—15 minutes late. The cops were on time—seven in uniforms and an equal number in plain clothes. We too were on time. So were the local hoodlums. Everybody with an interest in the arrival was there.

Why was the Jackson police force out in such representative numbers to meet the train? To intimidate or to protect? And to protect whom? Doubts were soon removed. One of the nine incoming persons, Stephen Smith, 19, of Marion, Iowa, went to retrieve his bag, which had been placed in the street by persons unknown. Unsuspectingly, he bent over to pick up the bag. A foot slammed into him. His assailant, not satisfied yet, pursued his course. Smith was subjected to smashing blows to the face with fists. Gleefully watching the beating were three, baby-blue-uniform-shirt-wearing members of the Jackson 400-man police force. Taking notes was an FBI agent.

What do I have that I want to keep?

For seven 28-hour-days in Oxford the teachers had been subjected to a well-organized inundation of facts—beyond that of their physical survival—about Mississippi schools, the probable conditions under which they would teach, the nature of their probable students, and the purposes of the freedom schools. The information flowed into their minds from stacks of mimeographed materials about the condition of the Negro in Mississippi, from lectures from members of the COFO staff, and from interpretations of conditions by Staughton Lynd.

Staughton was the state coordinator of the freedom schools during the first two months of their existence, July and August. The Mississippi power structure might have noted, ominously, that he had an excellent background for the job: he is youngish, frugal, a Quaker, a history professor whose field is the American Revolution. Immediately prior to his assumption of the duties of coordinating the freedom schools, he had spent three years in northern Georgia in a rural cooperative community, followed by three years more at Spelman College, a Negro woman's college in Atlanta. During the spring of 1964 he announced his resignation from Spelman in protest against restrictions on academic freedom of both students and faculty and was immediately recruited to join the faculty of Yale University, a white Ivy League School. During the planning stages, Staughton had been one of the two coordinators. His colleague, a Negro, found himself unable to fulfill his commitment to serve as summer coordinator and fear arrived.

Quickly the future teachers had learned that the best description in one word of Mississippi schools—for both black and white—is "lousy." They had learned that in Mississippi the counties appropriate funds for education to supplement minimum funds coming from the state government and had looked aghast at such figures as the following for appropriation per pupil:

North Pike County (McComb) (44% non-white)		*South Pike County* (Magnolia)	
white	$30.89	white	$59.55
Negro	00.76	Negro	1.35
Forrest County (28% non-white)		*City of Hattiesburg*	
white	$67.76	white	$115.96
Negro	34.19	Negro	61.69

The freedom-school teachers had been shown information that indicated open hostility to education with such facts as these: 9 counties of the state's 82 counties had no public high schools for either race; to stave off the integration of Ole Miss, the state was willing to close down all colleges—or, if they remained open, to discard their accreditation because the one thing that the state schools existed for in the minds of so many (to provide an athletic program for football and basketball) could go on without any accreditation; in Mississippi a law to require the superintendent of prisons to have a high-school education was not acceptable; and often in the rural schools the students could study astronomy through the holes in the roofs and archaeology through the cracks in the floors.

In Oxford the word had been passed along that many Mississippi teachers had to sign oaths not to participate in civil rights activities, should not attempt to vote (if Negro), could not openly endorse the Republican party (if either white or Negro) and had to teach that slavery was a happy period for Negroes (and superior to their present life) and that the Ku Klux Klan had saved the South from the ravishing hordes of Northerners who had raped white women and stolen the resources of the South.

In other words, they had learned that the closed society that often exists in other parts of the country had become a "locked" society in Mississippi and that, to make sure that it's locked forever, Negro teachers, to maintain jobs, could not permit the classes—many with 50 students in each—to ask questions. Proof of this had been given by the example of the expulsion of Negro students who had raised the question inadvertently of "What about the Freedom Rides?"

Why are we (teacher-student) in a freedom school?

From Staughton Lynd, mimeographed material and the COFO staff, the teachers had been informed that the purpose of the freedom schools *". . . is to provide an educational experience for students which will make it possible for them to challenge the myths of our society, to perceive more clearly its realities, and to find alternatives, and, ultimately, new direction for action.*

"The kind of activities you will be developing will fall into three general areas: 1·) academic work, 2) recreation and cultural activities, 3) leadership development . . . These three will be integrated into one learning experience, rather than . . . the kind of fragmented learning and living that characterizes much of contemporary education."

In short, the freedom schools were to develop leaders . . . in a land where such a title can reward one with an early grave . . . as was proven by the *purge* following the 1954 school integration decision of the United States Supreme Court. In response to the decision, school desegregation petitions were filed in 1954 by Negro Mississippians in Jackson, Vicksburg, Yazoo City, Biloxi and other larger Mississippi communities. Where a petition was filed, two things occurred as surely as night followed day: an organizer of the White Citizens Council slithered into town, and a wave of threats, harassment and violence erupted against Negro leaders.

In Brookhaven a Negro was shot on the courthouse steps for attempting to register. In Belzoni economic reprisals caused all but three of the Negro voters to withdraw their names from the voting list. Of the three holdouts, the Rev. George Lee was killed, Gus Courts was shot and left the state, and the third person, Mrs. George Lee, kept her name on the list—but wouldn't take that long march through the valley of death to the polling place.

Finding disfavor in target practice when he was the target, Dr. T. M. Howard of Mount Bayou joined Gus Courts in Chicago, and the screaming silence on the integration front in Mississippi gave mute proclamation that the Citizens Council had used well the time given by a slow, if not indifferent, federal government. On the finger of nubbed hands one could tally the Negro leaders: "Doc" Aaron Henry in Clarksdale, Merryl Lindsey of Holly Springs, the indomitable Amzie Moore of Cleveland, Mississippi, and one or two others. There was little change until 1962, when SNCC blossomed in the state.

Bluntly the teachers had been told that they had about eight weeks to develop those leaders needed and that there'd be no need to search for them; every morning when they said "hello" the leadership potential would be standing there before them. The need was for revolutionary leaders, and attending the freedom schools was an act of defiance of Mississippi, a state where defiance, by definition, is revolutionary.

The teachers-to-be had been told that most of their students would be from the "block," the "outs" who were not part of the Negro middle class of Mississippi (which is composed primarily of teachers) and who were dissatisfied; and that knowledge abounds in the Negro communities about the subtle forms of ignorance and subservience to the State of Mississippi inflicted in the regular public schools.

From a single-spaced, eight-page, legal-size document headed "Notes on Teaching in Mississippi," the same theme had been pushed over and over again: "The purpose of the freedom schools is to help them begin to question." This was the guideline asserted by Jane Stembridge (SNCC's executive secretary in 1961), who also sought to answer for the teachers this question: What will the students demand of you?

The answer was this: "They will demand that you be honest. Honesty is an attitude toward life which is communicated by everything you do. Since you, too, will be in the learning situation— honesty means that you will *ask* questions as well as answer them. It means that if you don't know something, you will say so. It means that you will not "act" a part in the attempt to compensate for all they've endured in Mississippi. You can't compensate for that, and they don't want you to try. It would not be *real,* and the greatest contribution that you can make to them is to be real."

Questions constantly asserted themselves as the keys to opening the doors of the closed society in which black and white were not to probe, inquire or challenge. ("It's so because it is so. Your cotton bales came to just $3.16 less than what you owe for the furnishings I gave you for the year. Nice going.")

This was one question: *What's to be done . . . and who will do it?*

Charles Cobb, SNCC field secretary, hinted at some of the answers when he wrote the following in those same "Notes on Teaching in Mississippi":

Repression is the law; oppression, a way of life—regimented by the judicial and executive branches of the state government, rigidly enforced by state police machinery, with veering from the path of "our way of life" not tolerated at all. Here, an idea of your own is a subversion that must be squelched; for each bit of intellectual initiative represents the threat of a probe into the way of denial. Learning here means only learning to stay in your place. Your place is to be satisfied—a "good nigger."

They have learned the learning necessary for immediate survival: that silence is safest, so volunteer nothing; that the teacher is the state, and tell them only what they want to hear; that the law and learning are white man's law and learning.

There is hope and there is dissatisfaction—feebly articulated—both born out of the desperation of needed alternatives not given. This is the generation that has silently made the vow of no more raped mothers—no more castrated fathers; that looks for an alternative to a lifetime of bent, burnt, and broken backs, minds and souls. Where creativity must be molded from the rhythm of a muttered "white son-of-a-bitch"; from the roar of a hunger-bloated belly . . .

There is the waiting, not to be taught, but to reach out and meet and join together, and to change. The tiredness of being told it must be, 'cause that's white folks' business, must be met with the insistence that it's their business. They know that anyway. It's because their parents didn't make it their business that they're being so systematically destroyed. What they must see is the link between a rotting shack and a rotting America.

The freedom-school teachers had occasion to consider well these interpretive statements of Charley Cobb, for it was Charley who was the mother-father of the idea of having freedom schools as part of the Mississippi Summer Project. Charley is an SNCC field secretary who has postponed for another year the pursuit of his own college career at Howard University, where his talents as a gifted creative writer were being polished, to remain in Mississippi. He presented the idea of freedom schools to one of the early planning conferences of the Freedom Summer. With the characteristic calm, quiet persistence of those like him who have found internal security in their personal lives by giving them meaning and direction, Charley pushed the idea. It wasn't necessary for him to push too long before Bob Moses and the other staff members were pushing along with him.

Mendy Julius Samstein, another SNCC field secretary, had contributed to the freedom-school notes by detailing some of the problems of freedom-school teaching. His suggestion had focused on the facts of facilities for the schools: they'll all be *scrounged,* "and if you are white, you will almost certainly be the first white civil rights workers to come to the town to stay. You will need to deal with the problem of your novelty as well as with the educational challenge."

The *words* had been given.

Frightened of life, death, the students, themselves, and every other matter that they could crowd into their concern in the short space allotted between their arrival and the beginning of the schools' tensions, the teachers began their tasks.

It was a hot morning in early July when the freedom schools, the *temple of questions,* opened.

One day that date, July 7, 1964, will be cursed by the power structure of Mississippi and celebrated by the lovers of human dignity as the point of the beginning of the end—the end and the downfall of the empire of Mississippi, the political subdivision, the state that exhibits best the worst found anywhere in America.

As the overly scrubbed, intensely alert and eager students poured into the churches, lodge halls, storefronts, sheds and open fields that served as school facilities, both teachers and students trembled with the excitement of one taking his first trip to the moon. From the beginning, the schools were a challenge to the insistent principle that everyone had talked about so much: flexibility.

Where the initial plans had been for only the tenth, eleventh and twelfth grades, one found sitting in the informal circles youngsters with the smooth black faces and wondering eyes of the impish ages of nine and ten who were mere fifth-graders. Flexibility. And there just behind teen-age boys—with slender, cotton-picking muscles— were sets of gnarled hands and the care-chiseled faces of grandmothers, some of whom said they thought they were in the seventies (birth records for the old are almost nonexistent). Flexibility.

Where Tom Wahman and Staughton Lynd had thought that there would be only 20 or so schools to be planned for, 50 of them had sprouted before the end of the summer. Where a mere 1,000 students had been hoped for, 3,000 eventually came.

To meet all these changes and challenges, flexibility became the rigid rule.

While those in charge of coordination and administration worked to resolve the logistical problems of swollen enrollments, the tasks of education proceeded in the first 23 schools to be opened, which were scattered throughout the state in 19 communities: Columbus, West Point, Holly Springs, Greenwood, Holmes County, Ruleville, Bolivar County, Greenville, Clarksdale, Vicksburg, Canton, Madison County, Carthage, Meridian, Hattiesburg, Pascagoula, Moss Point, Gulfport and Laurel.

Happily, the concern about the ability of the rural Negro communities to accept the white teachers readily was a wasted concern. After a day or so and a few touches of the white skin and blond tresses, the white teachers ceased to be "white" in a Mississippi sense. The first-name basis between students and teachers, the obvious sincerity, and the informality of the classroom situation all contributed to the breaking of any barriers that existed and enhanced the learning situation: if there were chairs, they were arranged in circles rather than rows; no one was required to participate in any classroom activity while in class; to go to the toilet or outhouse, one did not need to raise a hand to get permission; not disturbing others was the only consideration requested of the students.

And, most important of all, the teachers asked the students questions and the students talked: the students could and did say what they thought to be important, and no idea was ridiculed or forbidden—an immeasurably traumatic joy for the souls of young black folk.

Almost always there was the push of the students into fields where they could be creative. Where there was a mimeograph machine, weekly newspapers were written, typed and published by the students. Where there was a record player or some musical instrument to be played, assignments were given to describe the sounds in words and even to compose songs and words. Rorschach-like colors were splashed on large sheets of paper to be described from the students' experiences. Class organization was encouraged, with presidents and subofficers to carry out functions within the class and to teach the fundamentals of parliamentary procedures.

Role playing was used extensively. To learn Negro history, the students would portray three generations of Negro families. Often the teachers of history in the freedom schools would begin each day at a point on which it appeared that the students' recognition might fasten long enough to guide them onward rather than to follow a prescribed text. Flexibility was based on the needs of the students.

Contemporary events were utilized to the fullest. For example, newspaper stories, such as the one in the Jackson *Clarion Ledger* asserting that the freedom schools were teaching violation of the law, were used as the basis for civic lessons. Classes, when held out of doors, would sometimes take advantage of the presence of passers-by. One day three Negro ladies trudged by, looking angry and forlorn, on their way back from the courthouse, where they had just learned that their applications for voter registration had been rejected. The teacher called them over to tell what had happened. Thus the students learned of the registration procedures and how to help their parents pass the exams. Flexibility again.

Poems were read, such as Langston Hughes' "Blues":

> When the shoestring break
> On *both* of your shoes
> And you're in a hurry—
> That's the blues.

To these poems and others by Frost, Gertrude Stein and e. e. cummings, the students were asked to respond by writing their own poems, which on some occasions created anguishing but vital opportunities for self-exploration. The class situation in Harmony, Mississippi, where Allen Gould, 20, of Detroit, Michigan, a student of Wayne University, used this device, provides an example.

The Negroes of Harmony are a closely knit, fiercely proud group with an above-average number of persons in their midst who own small tracts of land, from which they eke out a living growing cotton and beef cattle. Some 12 miles away is Neshoba County.

Classes were held out of doors. (The community center had not been built at that time.)

Several students read their poems—one was about household chores; another told about the first time the poet had heard the word "freedom"—and for their originality and ideas the poems received the reward of applause from the class.

Then Ida Ruth Griffin, 13, unlike those before her, decided that she would stand and read her poem. The sun shone on her soft brown face, causing it to glisten. Her eyes sparkled with a deep fire as her voice came forth melodiously and with just a slight dramatic tinge; she read in a slow cadence:

> I am Mississippi-fed,
> I am Mississippi-bred,
> Nothing but a poor, black boy.
>
> I am a Mississippi slave,
> I shall be buried in a Mississippi grave,
> Nothing but a poor, dead boy.

The rustle of the leaves seemed hushed and the blades of grass appeared to be straining to hear.

She finished.

There was silence, a silence that lingered. The eager young faces grew sullen and flushed with anger as if somehow a scab had been ripped from an old sore or Ida Ruth's poetry had betrayed all that they were learning of denying the myths of Negro inferiority.

On the silence lingered until the floodgates of scorn poured forth from others in the class. In an angry chorus they responded with fierce refutations: "We're not black slaves!"

The teacher, Gould, felt the compelling urge to speak in an effort to save this brown, beautiful and unknown young bard from more verbal attacks, but his tongue was stilled. All along the desire had been to encourage the students to think and to express those thoughts, and expressing opinions often includes speaking opinions other than what a teacher might think.

"She's right," spoke another student, a tall reedy girl with a sharp mind. "We certainly are. Can your poppa vote? Can mine? Can our folks eat anywhere they want to?"

Silence engulfed the class again momentarily, and then everyone began a cacophony of talking and thinking aloud, scattering ideas.

Gould's chest filled with the joy of seeing the sun rising in alert minds that were heretofore damned by the oppression of conformity.

The black giant was stirring.

And there was more to push the capacity of the students to the outer limits, to make them reach beyond any preguessed borders. The original plans had called for the teaching of only reading, writing, basic mathematics, *revolution* and Negro history. After the first few days of contact, there was expansion to include typing (many of the freedom-school teachers had brought portables), algebra, physics and French.

Imagine students coming to the Mt. Nebo Church in Jackson and being greeted at the door of the classroom by a willowy blonde (5 feet 8 inches, 113 pounds)—Wendy Heil, from a home in Westchester, New York—with the strange words, "Bon jour" . . . and then seeing on the board other strange words: "Nous serons vanqueurs—nous l'affirmons."

For the whole hour there was an intensely exciting challenge between students and teacher as the teacher pointed to herself and said, "Je m'appelle Wendy Heil," and then walked over to a student and asked, "Comment vous appellez-vous?" The joy was electrifying as the first student guessed and replied, "Ida Bell Johnson"! And then from that small beginning, without a word of English during the whole class, Wendy picked up objects, pronounced the French names in exaggerated fashion, and had the students repeat them. Pantomime was used extensively.

The first hour closed with a test: objects were held up and the students recalled the names given earlier and pronounced them in a French laden with a Mississippi drawl.

Then Wendy began giving the pronunciation of the words on the board, "Nous serons vanqueurs," slowly and with repetition until all could give the same pronunciation. Following this, Wendy began humming the tune of "We Shall Overcome," and then she sang the words she had just taught. With unbounded exhilaration of discovery, the students sang, causing the theme song of the Movement, "We Shall Overcome," to reverberate to the sky in a way that it had never done before—in Mississippi French.

The black giant had stirred some more.

The French course (like the arts, crafts and science classes) was symbolic of what the students don't get in all but a few Mississippi high schools and was an adjunct of the basic remedial courses that were such a vital part of the freedom schools: reading, writing and mathematics. More often than not, the students knew no algebra for the reason that they had never been exposed to it. It wasn't taught in their schools. More often than not, the high-school seniors could read on only a fourth- or fifth-grade level. Reading, too, was not *taught* by the teachers in the regular Mississippi schools—who were themselves victims of the state's indifference, which guarantees promotions through grammar school, high school and college merely if the student has another birthday.

Word games, letter games, oral reading, story writing, free access to the odd collection of books which constituted the library possessed by each Freedom School—any device, tactic or trick that would push the students into the use of language was used. And the same was done with numbers. Moreover, to all of this was added individual tutoring. Knowledge-starved minds ravenously gulped in the information—in many instances causing the teachers to spend extra-long hours of preparation in the evenings to insure that the challenge of the students was fully satisfied each day.

As good as the purely academic efforts were, and as desperately needed as they were, the freedom schools were not mere educational feasting tables to supplement the skimpy diet of knowledge of regular schools.

The freedom schools were—and are—a collection of institutions to train leaders, and for that reason approximately half of the average of nine hours spent daily in school was utilized in a *direct* approach to develop Mississippi leaders.

Serving as the basic teaching material for leadership was the *Curriculum Guide for Freedom Schools,* by Noel Day. Out of the need for training material for students attending classes in Boston churches and lodge halls during the boycotts against Boston's token integration, Day had prepared a curriculum; with appropriate adaptations and revisions, this Boston curriculum became the bible for leadership training in Mississippi. This curriculum, in mimeographed form, was divided into seven units:

1. Comparison of the student's reality with that of others (the way the students live and the way others live).
2. North to Freedom? (The Negro in the North.)
3. Examining the apparent reality (the "better lives" that whites live).
4. Introducing the *Power Structure*.
5. The poor Negro and the poor white.
6. Material things versus soul things.
7. The Movement.

Interwoven into Noel Day's freedom-school curriculum were extensive reading and discussion of Negro history and hundreds of questions along the margins for the teachers to ask. Truly the training was a training of questions, because in addition to the questions suggested in each unit of the curriculum there were two additional sets of questions that were to be reintroduced periodically: a "basic set of questions" and a "secondary set of questions."

The basic set was this:

1. Why are we (teachers and students) in freedom school?
2. What is the Freedom Movement?
3. What alternatives does the Freedom Movement offer us?

Undergirding the basic set was this secondary set:

1. What does the majority culture have that we want?
2. What does the majority culture have that we don't want?
3. What do we have that we want to keep?

Relied upon heavily in the first unit, as a comparison with the students' reality, was a mimeographed pamphlet which described analytically the development of Hitler's Germany and the oppression of the Jews as they sought to accommodate themselves to terror. Throughout the unit were questions designed to provoke questions, answers and discussions of similarities in the attitude of the Negro toward the power structure of Mississippi and the attitude and adjustment of the Jews to the power structure of Hitler's Germany. Frightening were the parallels discovered as the teachers and students probed ever deeper with questions, questions, questions, questions.

The "North to Freedom" unit was frankly designed to raise questions and evaluations of whether freedom was north in order that the students might place the "advantages" of the North in more realistic terms: a place that isn't heaven while not fully like hell (Mississippi). The hope was that the evaluation would cause more of the students to consider remaining in Mississippi instead of dedicating the totality of their beings to flight. (SNCC's statistics show that 54 per cent of the college graduates of Mississippi in 1963 left the state.)

Teachers strove to present the questions and to elicit the answers without denying the basic fact that one means of surviving sometimes is to run away—and that flight does not always show a lack of courage.

Aiding the discussion of this unit during the summer was the eruption of black rebellions in Harlem, Rochester, Jersey City, Philadelphia (Pennsylvania) and other northern communities. Again and again the teachers stressed that part of the basic problem of getting things in the North was that there the Negroes were a minority . . . while in Mississippi, in scores of counties, the Negroes were a majority, constituting nearly half of the state's population.

But there were problems. The freedom-school teachers—mostly Northerners themselves—on one hand were well equipepd to describe the ghetto life of northern Negroes; on the other hand these same teachers had stirred the alert and eager minds in the black bodies to challenge, to think and to question. These students knew well that this was a *Summer* Project, that come the fall the teachers would hop on the Illinois Central (Freedom Train) and ride in style across the Ohio River (the Red Sea) to the Promised Land.

In the learning situation the teachers did not coddle or protect the students from facts. For their own comfort, the teachers taught too well or the students learned too much. One student bore into the heart of his teacher: "I believe what you have been trying to say. This is our land. It's worth staying and fighting for. I'm gonna be here when those leaves over yonder are gold. If you believe what you're teaching, where should you be?"

The prison walls crumbled a little more.

The black giant was stirring.

The third unit of the curriculum, through a series of questions, brought forth how white persons and Negroes lived. One of its primary values was the destruction of the myth that all white people live better than all Negroes. And then the unit took the students further. Most of the teachers were white and from northern suburbia. Analyzing their own lives in the North in the same fashion that life was being analyzed in Mississippi, many of the teachers pointed out the drastic shortcomings of the tension-ridden, insecure life of those "middle class" people (like the teachers' parents) who would have heart attacks if a Jew, Negro or Chinese-American moved into their neighborhoods; who haven't expressed an honest idea in public since the first payment on one of their several mortgages; whose ulcerated, psychotherapied, martini-drenched lives are composed totally of the deadest, sickest fictions that the most successful Madison Avenue huckster can sell in a world tottering on the brink of ultimate destruction.

Then followed the unit on the "Power Structure." Through questions, this unit sought to reformulate the thinking of the students to see who the people are who are the real bosses of the state and the particular county in which the students lived—who are the men who *really* determine whether the Negroes and whites starve, live or die; who manipulate the laws, the courts, the schools. As the discussion progressed, more and more the students changed their language. Instead of the old "the white folks don't want," there was "the power structure has decided." Through this unit the students began to see that friends and foes cannot be determined by skin, that a John Brown is more a friend than a Booker T. Washington.

From their own experiences they discovered what they already knew: that not all white people had a voice in running either the state or the county—that, in fact, there were just a few: the sheriff, the banker, the large-plantation owner, the northern-based corporation owning a local factory.

"The poor Negro and the poor white" unit and the other two were developed by the same method: probing questions that always enlightened—and sometimes hurt.

The "schools of question"—the freedom schools—had as adjuncts 13 community centers throughout the state where there were classes for the very old, for mothers with children, and for preschoolers in such areas as literacy, art, music, dance, recreation, day care and health. Miss Annell Ponder, Southern Christian Leadership Conference (SCLC), field secretary, was the director of the community centers.

Serving in the same adjunct role was the Mississippi Student Union (MSU), which is a state-wide organization of Negro high-school students in the state. It was the convention of the MSU in early August, 1964, which provided an unwanted but crucial test of the effectiveness of the freedom schools in developing leaders with minds that would reach beyond the mental prisons designed by the power structure.

Happily, the freedom schools came out of the testing situation "A-O.K." The MSU-Freedom School Convention in Meridian, Mississippi, on August 6, 7, 8, after a lot of heated wrangling over wording and the blessed chaos of exuberance of souls that have but moments ago broken their chains, the backward, dull, imbecilic, slothful Mississippi students—according to the myths of the society—issued the following proclamations to Mississippi, the nation and the world:

PUBLIC ACCOMMODATIONS

1. We resolve that the Public Accommodations and Public Facilities sections of the Civil Rights Act of 1964 be enforced.
2. We demand new and better recreation facilities for all.
3. We support the right of the Negro people and their white supporters to test the Civil Rights Act via demonstrations such as sit-ins. We are not urging a bloodbath through this means; we are simply demanding our Constitutional right to public assembly and seeking to test the Federal government's position.
4. Conversion of public accommodations into private clubs should be treated as a violation of the Civil Rights Act of 1964.

HOUSING

The home, being the center of a child's life as well as the center of a family's, must have certain facilities in order for it to be a home and not just a building in which one eats, sleeps, and prepares to leave for the rest of the day.
Therefore, be it resolved:
   1. That there be an equal-opportunity-to-buy law which permits all

persons to purchase a home in any section of town in which he can afford to live.

2. That a rent control law be passed and that one should pay according to the condition of the house.
3. That a building code for home construction be established which includes the following minimum housing requirements:
   a. a complete bathroom unit
   b. a kitchen sink
   c. a central heating system
   d. insulated walls and ceiling
   e. a laundry room and pantry space
   f. an adequate wiring system providing for at least three electrical outlets in the living room and kitchen and at least two such outlets in the bedroom and bathroom
   g. at least a quarter of an acre of land per building lot
   h. a basement and attic
4. That zoning regulations be enacted and enforced to keep undesirable and unsightly industries and commercial operations away from residential neighborhoods.
5. That slums be cleared, and a low-cost federal housing project be established to house these people.
6. That federal aid be given for the improvement of houses, with long-term, low-interest loans.
7. That the federal government provide money for new housing developments in the state. Anyone could buy these houses with a down payment and low monthly rate. There must be absolutely no discrimination. The federal government should take action if this law is not complied with.
8. That a federal law make sure that the projects are integrated and that they are run fairly.
9. That there be lower taxes on improvements in the houses so that more people will fix up their homes.
10. That the federal government buy and sell land at low rates to people who want to build homes.

EDUCATION

In an age where machines are rapidly replacing manual labor, job opportunities and economic security increasingly require higher levels of education. We therefore demand:

1. Better facilities in all schools. These would include textbooks, laboratories, air conditioning, heating, recreation, and lunch rooms.
2. A broader curriculum including vocational subjects and foreign languages.
3. Low-fee adult classes for better jobs.

4. That the school year consist of nine (9) consecutive months.
5. Exchange programs and public kindergartens.
6. Better-qualified teachers with salaries according to qualification.
7. Forced retirement (women at 62, men at 65).
8. Special schools for mentally retarded and treatment and care of cerebral palsy victims.
9. That taxpayers' money not be used to provide private schools.
10. That all schools be integrated and equal throughout the country.
11. Academic freedom for teachers and students.
12. That teachers be able to join any political organization to fight for Civil Rights without fear of being fired.
13. That teacher brutality be eliminated.

HEALTH

1. Each school should have fully-developed health, first aid, and physical education programs. These programs should be assisted by at least one registered nurse.
2. Mobile units, chest X rays semiannually and a check-up at least once a year by licensed doctors, the local health department or a clinic should be provided by the local or state government.
3. All medical facilities should have both integrated staff and integrated facilities for all patients.
4. Mental health facilities should be integrated and better staffed.
5. Homes for the aged should be created.
6. Free medical care should be provided for all those who are not able to pay the cost of hospital bills.
7. We demand state and local government inspection of all health facilities.
8. All doctors should be paid by skill, not by race.
9. Titles should be given to the staff.
10. The federal government should help the organization pay the salaries of workers.
11. All patients should be addressed properly.
12. We actively seek the abolition of any sterilization act which serves punishment, voluntary or involuntary, for any offense.
13. In a reasonable time we seek the establishment of a center for the treatment and care of cerebral palsy victims.

FOREIGN AFFAIRS

1. The United States should stop supporting dictatorships in other countries and should support that government which the majority of the people want.
2. Whereas the policy of apartheid in the Republic of South Africa is detrimental to all the people of that country and against the concepts of

equality and justice, we ask that the United States impose economic sanctions in order to end this policy.

3. We ask that there be an equitable balance between the domestic and foreign economic and social support provided by our country.

FEDERAL AID

1. We demand that a public works program be set up by the federal government to create jobs for the unemployed.

2. Because of discrimination in the past, we demand preferential treatment for the Negro in the granting of federal aid in education and training programs until integration is accomplished.

3. To help fight unemployment, we demand that federal funds be lent communities to set up industries and whole towns which shall be publicly owned by the communities. For example: textile and paper mills, stores, schools, job relocation programs for those put out of work by automation, job retraining centers, recreational facilities, banks, hospitals.

4. We demand that Social Security benefits should be given according to need and not according to how much one earned previously. In addition, we demand guaranteed income of at least $3,000 annually for every citizen.

5. The federal government should give aid to students who wish to study for the professions and who do not have the necessary funds.

6. We feel that federal aid in Mississippi is not being distributed equally among the people. Therefore we adopt Title VI of the Civil Rights Law which deals with federal aid. We demand federal agents appointed to Mississippi expressly for this purpose. We demand that action be taken against the State of Mississippi so that this aid may be distributed fairly.

7. We demand that the federal government divert part of the funds now used for defense into additional federal aid appropriations.

8. We demand that the federal government refuse to contract with corporations that employ nonunion labor, engage in unfair labor practices, or practice racial discrimination.

JOB DISCRIMINATION

1. We demand: That the federal government immediately open to Negroes all employment opportunities and recruitment programs under its auspices, such as in post offices, Veterans Hospitals and defense bases.

2. That the fair employment section (Title VII) of the 1964 Civil Rights Law be immediately and fully enforced.

3. The guarantee of fair employment be extended fully to all aspects of labor, particularly job training programs.

4. We encourage the establishment of more unions in Mississippi, to attract more industry to the state.

5. We will encourage and support more strikes for better jobs and

adequate pay. During the strikes the employers should be enjoined from having others replace the striking workers.

6. Vocational institutions must be established for high-school graduates and dropouts.

7. The federal minimum wage law be extended to include *all* workers, especially agricultural and domestic workers.

8. Cotton planting allotments to be made on the basis of family size.

9. We want an extension of the Manpower Retraining program.

10. Whenever a factory is automated, management must find new jobs for the workers.

11. Workers should be paid in accordance with their qualifications and the type of work done.

THE PLANTATION SYSTEM

1. The federal government should force plantation owners to build and maintain fair tenant housing.

2. In cases where the plantation farmers are not being adequately paid according to the Minimum Wage Law, the government should intervene on behalf of the farmers in a suit against the plantation owner.

CIVIL LIBERTIES

1. Citizens of Mississippi should be entitled to employ out-of-state lawyers.

2. Section Two of the Fourteenth Amendment should be enforced, specifically in Mississippi and other Southern States, until the voter registration practices are changed.

3. The citizens should have the privilege of exercising their Constitutional rights
   a. to assemble,
   b. to petition,
   c. to freedom of the press,
   d. to freedom of speech

in such ways as picketing, passing out leaflets and demonstrations. We oppose all laws that deprive citizens of the above rights.

4. We want the abolition of the House Un-American Activities Committee because it deprives citizens of their Constitutional rights.

5. We resolve that the Freedom Movement should accept people regardless of religion, race, political views or national origin if they comply with the rules of the movement.

LAW ENFORCEMENT

1. We want qualified Negroes appointed to the police force in large numbers. We want them to be able to arrest anyone breaking the law, regardless of race, creed or color.

2. All police must possess warrants when they demand to enter a house and search the premises. In the absence of a search warrant, the police must give a reasonable explanation of what they are looking for. In any case, with or without a warrant, no damage should be done unnecessarily to property, and if damage is done, it should be paid for.

3. A national committee should be set up to check police procedures, to insure the safety of people in jail: their food, sleeping and health facilities; to protect them from mobs and see that no violence is done to them.

4. All cases against law enforcement agencies or involving civil rights should be tried in federal courts.

5. Law enforcement officials should provide protection against such hate groups as the KKK. Police and public officials should not belong to any group that encourages or practices violence.

CITY MAINTENANCE

1. The city should finance paving and widening of the streets and installing of drain systems in them.

2. Sidewalks must be placed along all paved streets.

3. A better system of garbage disposal, including more frequent pickups, must be devised.

4. Streets should be adequately lighted.

5. We oppose nuclear testing in residential areas.

VOTING

1. The poll tax must be eliminated.

2. Writing and interpreting of the Constitution is to be eliminated.

3. We demand further that registration procedures be administered without discrimination, and that all intimidation of prospective voters be ended through federal supervision and investigation by the FBI and Justice Department.

4. We want guards posted at ballot boxes during counting of votes.

5. The minimum age for voting should be lowered to 18 years.

6. We seek for legislation to require the county registrar or one of his deputies to keep the voter registration books open five days a week except during holidays, and open noon hours and early evening so that they would be accessible to day workers. Registrars should be required by law to treat all people seeking to register equally.

DIRECT ACTION

1. To support Ruleville, we call for a state-wide school demonstration, urging teachers to vote and asking for better, integrated schools.

2. We support nonviolence, picketing and demonstrations.

With all of its rawness and ugliness, there is something about Mississippi and the South that "hooks" you.

After a lifetime—be it short or long—of being convinced by your surroundings that you aren't anything more than an insignificant, selfish, parasitic bug among millions of other similar bugs called humans, the experience of being in the South and being creative— and seeing your little efforts aid in the qualitative changes in the lives of warm, lovable humans willing to tackle the massive problems that you and your kind have avoided facing—makes you feel traumatically and suddenly as if your life has real meaning so long as it is in this sort of setting and you are doing this sort of work: saving yourself and your society (the good part of it) by helping others save themselves.

"Am I a 'summer soldier'?" the summer volunteer had to ask himself as the days in August spent themselves toward an end. "What about all the threats I've heard from the power structure which have sullied my ears, such as, 'We'll take care of the niggers when y'all gone.'?"

What's the answer to the challenge of the students who have said, "I'm gonna be here when those leaves over yonder are gold. If you believe what you're teaching, where should you be?"

Those who came to teach were taught.

Nearly 300 of the 800 *summer* volunteers dropped the adjective; they became *volunteers* and remained in Mississippi and saw the beautiful foliage of the vast virgin forest land turn brown and gold.

Staughton Lynd and Tom Wahman moved on to their obligations at Yale and New York universities, respectively. Into the vacated position of freedom-school coordinator moved Mrs. Liz Fusco, who had been in charge of the Indianola freedom schools during the summer.

Mrs. Fusco is a "mite" of a woman, about five feet tall and nearly 100 pounds, whose beautiful face and soft, long, dark-brunette hair enhance the impression she gives of being a hummingbird as she flits about doing four things at once. To the amazement of less artistic souls in the Movement, she has every office in the state decorated with art from the freedom schools and eagerly displays the poetry and writing of one of her 2,000 students around the state, which she has picked up during one of the incessant trips she has been taking—everywhere—since September. There's a bit of incongruity about it all for the unprepared stranger. Though co-ordinator of the year-round freedom schools that wouldn't let the summer end, she looks not a bit of her 20-odd years and easily would be mistaken for a high-school senior in her teens who was a bit precocious.

Even the most casual look at a report prepared for the end of September shows that all the activity on her part is provoked by busy circumstances:

FREEDOM CENTERS—WHAT'S HAPPENING
Sept., 1964

1. *Marks:* Regular schools are on split session for cotton picking. The freedom school is teaching the regular curriculum of Mississippi 1964 and Negro history, etc., and some algebra, in the evenings. They are trying to get a place for a community center. Four high school kids from the Mississippi Student Union went to register in the white school.

2. *Mound Bayou:* Project director John Bradford is conducting classes in local government. Classes meet every evening:

Monday—voter registration education
Tuesday—welfare and community improvement
Wednesday—an executive committee of 10 or 12 adults
Thursday—local government
Friday—songs

Every Wednesday there is an MSU [Mississippi Student Union] meeting, at which there is both planning for direct action and discussion of Negro history.

3. *Ruleville:* Kindergarten in the daytime, high school and adults in the evenings. Extensive use of library.

The little kids have mornings of free play, singing, games, stories, acting of nursery rhymes, nature walks, simple dances, basic carpentry.

The adults meet two nights a week for reading and discussion. The MSU kids hold Sunday-afternoon meetings instead of Saturday-night dances, then refreshments.

4. *Holly Springs:* There are two freedom schools in Benton County, even though the kids are picking cotton. Classes in voter registration and Negro history are going on. Next door to the one school is a community center, which the teen-age girls are staffing for library and TV in the evenings. *There is a nurse in Holly Springs.*

5. *Itta Bena:* Just getting started. On Tuesday evenings people come over from Greenwood to teach voter registration to the adults.

6. *Meridian:* Good integration of freedom school and community center activities: a theater group, citizenship seminars, book discussion, individual tutorial, etc. There is a sculptor there who will be traveling around the state, spending about two or three weeks in each project; under his direction the kids are doing "*wild* sculpturing."

7. *Greenwood:* Tutorial every afternoon 3:30-6, 10 students. On Monday, Wednesday, and Thursday nights a college prep course: reading comprehension, vocabulary drill, novels (this week, *Go Tell It on the Mountain*). Six kids, perhaps more soon. There is a local lady who has been running a kindergarten for years. Study hall. The staff has had communication teachers at the high school.

Greenwood has tapes: from KPFA in California: lectures by Baldwin, Lomax, and speeches by King and by professors of history and political science. *708 Ave. N.*

8. *Indianola:* Day program for little kids: reading and writing, African dancing, geography, Negro history and science. Library. Evening program for adults and teen-agers.

9. *Cleveland:* The MSU is active in school, refusing by letter to raise money by the campus queen drive. Talking about eating in public places and boycotting stores.

10. *Tupelo:* No place to have classes, but there is some teaching going on in private homes.

11. *Natchez:* Strong MSU, tutoring, discussion, newspaper.

12. *Moss Point:* MSU working on school integration and the petition part of the groundwork for the state-wide Freedom Study Day (alias boycott). (*sic*)

13. *Biloxi:* All of the staff is working on building a new community center and the library and new office. The adult Nonviolent Action Association (12 members) is working to raise funds and to feed the workers.

14. *McComb:* Afterschool tutoring, 4-6. Weekend classes Saturday and Sunday, 4-6, combination of American politics, problems of civil rights movement (FDP as solution?), world history, current events (focusing on the election). Adult evening classes in citizenship. Library.

15. *Canton:* The community center is open with a full recreation program every night and games on the weekend. Library and reading program, study hall planned, perhaps tutorial.

16. *Belzoni:* Just getting started, has no place. The MSU is meeting.

17. *Columbus:* The Young Democrat Club (alias MSU) is writing letters to Congressmen in addition to working out grievances against the schools. Most of the summer's FS kids are on the football team or in the band.

18. *Greenville:* Tutorials, literacy work in homes. Action against the

city's new school regulations: entrance fee raised to $3.50, special fee for kids not living with natural parents, refusal of admission to girls who are pregnant or who have children.

19. *Hattiesburg:* Community centers are open or about to open, with plans for one in each area: local people working, day care and recreation center at Palmer's Crossing.

20. *Tchula:* In process of building new community center. Freedom-school staff mostly in jail.

21. *Philadelphia:* Library functioning well; voter registration classes and expectation of beginning regular classes as soon as cotton picking is over.

22. *Clarksdale:* Study hall every day 4-9 P.M., individual tutorials.

23. *Aberdeen:* The basis for a freedom school in 10-15 kids hanging around.

24. *Shaw:* Citizenship classes for adults. ADULTS and kids very active in MSU-type action with regard to the schools—kids have decided to go back to school October 1 even though their demands weren't met, in anticipation of the state-wide action.

25. *Holmes County:* Adopted by Iowa communities, working on literacy. Local participation in new community center is county-wide!

Figures released by the United States Civil Rights Commission in 1964 showed that 98.5 per cent of the Negro students in the South were in segregated schools. This figure screams that something fundamental is wrong. In 1964, ten years had passed since the United States Supreme Court had mandated the end of school segregation.

Figures for the North for the same year provide no comfort. Something more than 70 per cent of all the Negro students in the North were in racially segregated schools.

In the South and in Mississippi the segregated school means that the worst of what the community has to offer will be typified by the Negro schools. There is no difference in the North.

In the South and Mississippi the Negro student is oppressed and stifled. For similar and slightly different reasons, the Negro student in a Chicago school is treated the same.

Freedom schools were, and are, needed in Philadelphia, Mississippi . . . and its northern namesake. And wasn't the basic curriculum that worked so well in Mississippi born of the school boycott led by Noel Day against token integration of the Boston schools? There is no need to pile on the evidence by citing Harlem, Detroit, Los Angeles, St. Louis and other cities.

The fact that the schools of northern communities differ only in a matter of degree from those in southern communities is neither a secret fact nor a newly discovered fact. Mississippi didn't create an awareness of the problem; what the Mississippi Summer Project of 1964 gave America was an awareness of a solution.

Optimism about the freedom schools is well supported: 1,000 students were hoped for in Mississippi and 3,000 came; the schools were conceived of as a six-to-eight-week effort; they are in fact as permanent as the Movement and a desire for a better life.

Comparison with the growth of the Catholic Church in America reveals part of the potential of the system of freedom schools in Mississippi.

In 200 years the Roman Catholic Church increased from the smallest to the largest church in the nation, claiming some 40,000,-000 adherents, or one-fifth of the total population of America. Although as late as 1908 the Catholic Church of America was still of only missionary status, it is now the most powerful branch of the faith. And the single most important factor in this amazing pace of growth has been the system of parochial schools.

Both the freedom schools and the parochial schools teach the four "R's." Parochial schools teach reading, 'riting, 'rithmetic and religion. Freedom schools teach reading, 'riting, 'rithmetic and *revolution*. The growth of the parochial schools was enhanced by the dedication of those taking the vows of the religious orders for poverty. Vows are not taken in the Movement, but ends up impoverished.

The Mississippi freedom schools are demonstrating what can be done; and if the problems of oppressive, inferior education—to insure the disinheritment of the disinherited—can be wrestled with in Mississippi and headed in the right direction, who is there to say that it can't be done in Cleveland, Ohio, and elsewhere?

The freedom schools crassly call liars those who say that nothing can be done until the government acts. Had you been a student at one of those freedom schools, you would have learned why the gov-

RIGHTS WORKERS PLANNING FOR '65

Student Movement to Stress Poverty in the North

By FRED POWLEDGE

A group of young civil rights activists are making plans for a comprehensive program in two Northern states next summer. The program would be modeled in many ways on last summer's Mississippi civil rights campaign.

William Strickland, the executive director of the Northern Student Movement, said yesterday that the summer program would not involve Negroes alone, but would seek to "organize people around poverty."

Mr. Strickland, a 27-year-old Negro who majored in psychology at Harvard, is representative of a large number of young persons in the civil rights movement who feel that, in his words, "Integration is no longer the issue. The issue is poverty."

An estimated 300 young persons from the North, most of them college students, started on Friday a weekend conference sponsored by the Northern Student Movement at Columbia University. The conference was expected to produce some details of the projected Northern summer campaign.

Mr. Strickland said two states had been selected for intensive organizing, one in the Midwest and one in the Northeast, but that they probably would not be identified until the end of the year.

He said the projects would include attempts to set up community centers, operated by and for "the inhabitants of the ghetto; "tutorial projects for the inhabitants who need them, and possibly rent strikes.

"Ultimately," he said in an interview, "the problem of poverty is a political problem, and it can only be dealt with by the political organization of the poor. We hope that the program will result in some political organization, too."

Would Combine Efforts

Mr. Strickland said the Mississippi experience showed that small, city-wide efforts to bring change were not very effective against ingrown traditions and discrimination. It is the thinking of the student movement now, he said, that seven or eight cities in each of the two states should put their efforts together.

In the Mississippi Freedom Summer project, which was led by a coalition of young civil rights workers, "Freedom schools" were established, voter registration was attempted, and a challenge to the state's all-white Democratic party was carried before the eyes of the nation at the Democratic National Convention in Atlantic City.

The Northern Student Movement was begun in 1961 as a Northern fund-raising arm of the Southern-based Student Nonviolent Coordinating Committee. The group maintains 73 affiliates on Northern campuses. Mr. Strickland estimated that 3.000 to 4,000 persons were involved in its work.

ernment hasn't acted: the power structure of our community wants things as they are.

To those who have listened—and there have been many—the freedom schools have said that those in the leadership of our communities are there because those with power in the community have placed them there. Any organization of the millions in the slums of the North would realign power, and power would have to be shared with people who aren't *fit*. So it's best that the sleeping and unorganized giants in the North remain just that way—sleeping and unorganized—with escape for only the lucky or the exceptional.

Howard Zinn (SNCC adviser, Boston University professor and eminent author) poses a question for America as penetrating as any asked in the Mississippi freedom schools as a result of his observations of their operation in Mississippi:

> Is there, in the floating, prosperous, nervous, American social order of the sixties, a national equivalent to the excitement of the civil rights Movement, one strong enough in its pull to create a motivation for learning that even the enticements of monetary success cannot match?
>
> *Would it be possible to declare boldly that the aim of the schools is to find solutions for poverty, for injustice and for race and national hatred, and to turn all educational efforts into a national striving for these solutions?*

To answer these questions "YES" by many is considered too dangerous. We must also ask ourselves this: Is there any state where the disinherited, realizing that it is they, more than anyone else, who must force the changes in the conditions of their disinheritment—as has been started in Mississippi—would not alter the status of things as they are within the political machinery of those states?

No.

Not yet.

Nevertheless, the fact of the freedom schools started people thinking—white as well as black—and it occurred to some, quite logically, that the next step up might well be organizational work among the white people of the state as well.

VII

"White Folks" Project

> I'm tempted to thank God for being white.
> But I hesitate.
> I'm neither proud of myself
> Or our society which forces such a temptation on me
> —and gives so little in return.
>
> —*The Wisdom of Dawley*

NOTE: *To protect people and places from reprisals, some names and locations have been disguised. The events described are true.*

ONE AUGUST MORNING IN 1964 two casually dressed fellows in their twenties, each with leaflets and Freedom Registration forms rolled into a baton in one hand, crossed a street in the Point Cadet section of Biloxi, Mississippi.

Stepping sprightly and forcing themselves to appear nonchalant in spite of the feeling that hundreds of hostile eyes were piercing their backs, they walked up on the porch of the first house. It was a wooden frame building whose ancient coat of paint had long since surrendered to the salty air blowing from the Gulf waters a few blocks away.

Like the other homes in this all-white, low-income neighborhood, this first building seemed tired and brooding from the tropical heat as its drabness contrasted with the brightness of the wild red and orange flowers growing untended in the yard. In this area lived mostly seasonal workers from the shrimp and oyster boats as well as those who eked out a living working as guides, laborers, maintenance men and taxi drivers serving the tourist business.

The taller of the two young men, Kirk Morris, knocked at the door, fidgeted uncomfortably, rubbed his right forearm where his white skin had reddened from a painful sunburn, and pushed from his face a lock of wild blond hair which had resisted the intimidation of the combing given shortly before he'd left the Biloxi SNCC headquarters.

His co-worker, Paul Dumas, smiled at their nervousness. Both sweated. The leaves of the palm trees across the street were motionless; no breeze stirred in the 90-degree heat.

Heavy footsteps approached the door from the inside. The door opened. The two saw standing in front of them a barefoot man in his forties, with thinning black hair, a pockmark-grated face, and slender arms that told of his outdoor work by their crimson color, which ended where a shirt had protected him from the poaching rays of the sun.

There was silence.

The occupant of the house stared, and his blue eyes grew wider in disbelief. It was as if one answered his door one morning to find a nude woman standing there selling *Liberator* magazines.

Paul Dumas was the cause.

His smooth black skin, tapered muscular limbs and unconsciously perfect posture as he stood at the doorway to the house was not an acceptable event in this neighborhood, where even the garbage collectors were white.

The tenant of the house gulped, almost swallowing the golf-ball-size wad of chewing tobacco which distended his jaw. "Well, come in," he said.

The canvassing team entered the house, introduced themselves, but made no offer to shake hands because their befuddled host's hand had not been held out.

The dialogue began. Both fellows, though from states farther north, spoke in a rural cadence with deliberation; they didn't want to use any "big word" that might not be understood or might alienate this man whose education appeared to be "Mississippi-bad" (poor even by Mississippi standards).

Their host spoke in a drawl as thick as the good oyster stew so common in this area of oyster fishermen.

"How come you Freedom Riders are coming in here?" the man asked, full of curiosity.

"We aren't Freedom Riders. We're seeing folks like you to get them on the side of the Mississippi Freedom Democratic Party," Kirk Morris said.

"Well, we ain't had no trouble with niggers around here. Everything is fine. We're not worried about them."

Calmly, Paul Dumas replied to this, saying, "We're not talking about Negro problems. We're trying to organize a new political party which will do something about getting some better streets, stronger labor unions, and some federal programs to help people who need jobs."

"Well, you're going to have niggers in this, aren't you?"

"Yes, there'll be Negroes," Kirk said. "We want everybody having the same problems to work together. And if they need jobs, we want everybody who needs a job to get one. If the problem is schools, we want everybody who needs an education to have a chance to go to schools. We feel that the Mississippi schools are bad because the state is poor and got two sets of schools going."

"I don't see nothing wrong with our schools."

"Let me ask you something," Dumas said as he came back into the dialogue. "You know that oil refinery that Standard Oil opened over in Pascagoula. They're bringing in a bunch of people from California to work in that plant. Here you got jobs paying three and four dollars an hour and the company can't find people from local schools able to do the work. So they bring folks from other places who went to good schools to get those jobs. You and I know that folks around here should have the learning for those jobs. Don't we need them more than the people in California?"

The host nodded in agreement. Sensing that his Negro co-worker had developed a rapport, Kirk Morris let the two of them do the rest of the talking. The subject shifted to getting a signature on the Freedom Registration.

"What help are you getting now from the regular Democrats?" Paul asked rhetorically.

The host became defensive. "Well, all politicians are no good. None of them do anything. One set is as bad as another," the host said.

"Wait a minute. There's a 5-cent sales tax. When we buy two dollars' worth of groceries, we've gotta pay ten cents in taxes. What kinda jobs, schools and highways are we getting for this?"

The conversation went on for nearly an hour. The civil rights workers pressed for a signature without seeming "pushy." They explained in detail that the Freedom Democratic Party was not the "nigger party" but the party for people like their host, who weren't really represented by the regular Democrats; that things were bad for all people in Mississippi because of the indifference of the politicians; and that Negroes and "thinking white people like yourself" have to change things.

The civil rights workers left the house exchanging smiles and well-wishes with the host, who hadn't signed but had said, "I'll think it over 'bout a week. If'n you around here then, stop and I'll let you know."

A point had been proved. Integrated teams could canvass in white neighborhoods in Mississippi.

Systematically other houses in the same block were approached, but not all people welcomed the teams that were integrated. Nor were the strictly white pairs of canvassers welcomed at every door in Biloxi. For three weeks, a dozen or so persons, in integrated and nonintegrated teams, canvassed in the poor white neighborhoods of the city. At worst they were told to leave. At best they were offered some beverage—soft or hard—and talked with for as long as two hours in some homes. There was no kicking down the steps or threats of violence anywhere. Almost everywhere there was curiosity . . . even when there were situations of "racial baiting."

For example, a team of canvassers consisting of a fellow and a girl was invited into a home where the first statement the man said was this: "I've been a member of the Ku Klux Klan for years. What do you have to say about that?" Since the man and his wife showed an undertone of curiosity, the two summer volunteers "played it cool" and kept talking without accepting his challenges to argue. After 15 minutes the team announced that it was leaving. The white man closed the conversation on the same tone that it had begun.

"You people are a bunch of damned fools. You don't understand Mississippi." The team had walked out of the house and was beyond the picket fence of the well-kept lawn when the supposed Klan member called out: "Hey! Wait a minute!" They stopped. The Klan member picked a bouquet of red and yellow roses from the flower garden and gave them to the girl summer volunteer. "Good luck. But I still think you're crazy," he told them as the girl thanked him for the unsolicited kindness.

This grass-roots political action of going to homes was new to Mississippi, so new that many of the people contacted in the white neighborhoods didn't know what the word "canvassing" meant—causing the summer volunteers to abandon its use. From three weeks of this kind of effort (from the first week of August, 1964, until time to leave for the National Democratic Convention in Atlantic City, which began on August 22), the White Community Project could show several achievements:

1. Twenty members of the white community of Biloxi had signed the Freedom Registration forms. These forms merely contained basic information about name, age, residence and how long the person has lived in the state. Persons all over the state, both black and white, were signing these forms, in part to show that they felt that their interests were not being represented by the controlling Democratic Party.

By non-Mississippi standards, the figure 20 does not sound impressive. But in Mississippi it's phenomenal. It increased the number of white persons in the state *openly* supporting the Mississippi Freedom Democratic Party from approximately 2 persons (the Rev. and Mrs. Edwin King of Tougaloo College) to 22.

2. The "White Folks" Project recruited in those three weeks two

additional Mississippi white persons, who got involved in full, *open* commitment to the Mississippi Freedom Movement: Robert Williams and his wife Lois from Biloxi. Williams was a thing of beauty to see in his blunt, lovable rawness when representatives of the Biloxi power structure tried to frighten him. A policeman awesomely and belligerently asked him, "What do you think you are?" And Williams replied, "A goddamned Freedom Fighter!" A high city official asked him, "How'd you feel if somebody blew your head off?" And Williams stormed out, slamming the office door, after promising, "About the same way you'll feel when my buddies get the bastard who did it."

Robert Williams was among the 68 delegates of the Mississippi Freedom Democratic Party who challenged the seating of the regular Democrats at the Democratic National Convention in Atlantic City in August, 1964.

Liz Khrone, a summer volunteer working in the Biloxi White Community Pilot Project, is immodest in her praise of Williams: "Six more like him in Mississippi and the state would move into the category of magnificent."

3. Theory was proven. The integrated teams of canvassers in the white community proved what few believed and most doubted: that a Negro could work among white persons in Mississippi as hundreds of white persons had worked among Negroes for the Freedom Movement. In many ways the reports from the pilot project showed that canvassing was more effective when integrated teams did it. There was less of the charges of "communist" by those being canvassed, and the dialogue was refreshingly healthier as many of the white persons talked *with* a Negro for the first time in their lives rather than *at* him. The importance of this arises from the fact that SNCC insists that the organization of white persons in Mississippi take place in a setting which emphasizes the problems of the disinherited of both races.

4. Myths were disproven. The poor white Mississippian is mostly conceived of in demonic terms: "The red-necked cracker with snuff spittle streaming down his jaw, a gun in his pocket and a lynch rope on his shoulder." But they are warm humans whose stomachs

ache when they aren't fed, who bleed when they are cut, whose souls thirst for a better life for themselves and those they love. The meaningfulness of this "discovery" can be appreciated only in the context of the moving force of the stereotype which makes the poor white cracker the enemy, the person whose proximity to you causes the adrenal glands to flow and your reaction to be like that of cattle when their nostrils gulp in the whiff of a hungry jackal pack.

Intellectually, few persons in the Movement accept the stereotype of the poor white man of the South feverishly boiling in a caldron of his own hate. Psychologically, the results are somewhat different. The experiences of the "White Folks" Project in Biloxi provided experiences which helped the *intellectual* to become also the *emotional* attitude.

In other words, the experiences provided an opportunity to know on a deeper level that the stereotype of the poor white man was as "accurate" as the stereotype of the Negro.

5. Insight was gained as to the desires and needs of poor white persons. The canvassing and its resulting discussions revealed that there was dissatisfaction. Better schools, more jobs, health facilities, stronger unions, and cooperatives were among the things for which the white disinherited of Biloxi longed.

The summer volunteers talked with them about how to fulfill the desire to reorganize the fishermen's union, which had been disbanded for illegal price-fixing and whose treasurer had run off with the money. The fishermen with whom they talked wanted an oyster cooperative. The fishermen get about $2 per gallon of unopened oysters, and restaurants sell them opened for $6 and $7 per gallon. Large factories in the area have machines that do the opening and get a large portion of the profit from the oyster fishing by serving as the middlemen. The fishermen want the cooperative in order to employ their wives and to become their own "middlemen." And such a project could work, because the hand-opened oysters command a better price than the machine-opened ones.

Community centers, freedom schools and voter education were all found to be things that the poor whites of the community desired. In short, the efforts in Biloxi removed any thoughts in the Mississippi Freedom Movement that there were a large number of persons in the state—with white skins—who were something less than human.

There's a familiar sociological idea that groups are more immoral than individuals, and the experiences of those organizing in Biloxi supported this sociological idea. The absence of open hostility except from officials of the city and the lack of blind submission to the "Southern Line" about civil rights by most of the individuals contacted—who were some of the same people who attacked Negroes with chains at a beach wade-in during the summer of 1960 and spent several days shooting up Negro homes as an aftermath—were shocking.

Comparison of the three-week experiences and gains of the White Community Project which went into Biloxi "cold" (without a local person to open doors and arrange contacts) with similar efforts in all Negro situations in Mississippi places the pilot project in the category of exceptional. In some "Negro" situations it has taken four and five months to achieve similar results.

The exploration of the possibilities of organizing white people during the Mississippi Summer Project of 1964 was consistent with the history of SNCC. It was almost inevitable.

When SNCC was formed in 1960, it was a campus-based civil rights organization with primary emphasis on organizing southern Negro college students for racial protests. At the suggestion of Jane Stembridge (a southern white coed, who was SNCC's executive secretary in 1961) and Anne Braden (editor of the *Southern Patriot* and one of the South's leading white integrationists) and with a grant from the Southern Conference Educational Fund (SCEF), SNCC employed a southern white college student, Robert Zellner, to travel around the South, organizing white students for the integration drive.

In the fall of 1963, Zellner enrolled in Brandeis University's graduate school and was succeeded by Sam Shirah. At this point SNCC's efforts had changed from organizing students on campuses to organizing Negro field hands in cotton fields; it had gone from the schools to the community.

Sam Shirah pushed the idea that just as SNCC had shifted its main thrust from organizing Negro schools to organizing Negro communities, he ought to shift from organizing southern white students to southern white communities. His idea was readily accepted.

With encouragement from Bayard Rustin and Anne Braden and more encouragement and some personnel from the newly organized Southern Students Organizing Conference (SSOC), the idea was implemented as part of the Mississippi Summer Project.

Except for Sam Shirah, none of the 25 white summer volunteers and staff—most of whom were Southerners—had had any previous experience in organizing. Seven of the volunteers were assigned to four communities—Jackson, Greenville, Meridian and Vicksburg—where they helped the local human-relations councils and committees to save public education. School integration was imminent for Mississippi in the fall of 1964, and there was assiduous talk of closing the schools rather than allowing them to be integrated.

In these four communities the work of the volunteers consisted, for the most part, of mailing literature that explained to the business and professional groups of the communities the role and function of the Mississippi Summer Project, which had been widely misinterpreted by the news media of Mississippi in scare stories. Considerable literature was also mailed to encourage keeping the schools open and avoiding violence in connection with those integrated school openings. Some personal visitations were made to ministers and persons suspected of having "liberal" thinking.

The bulk of the volunteers, 18 persons (5 girls and 13 boys), were concentrated in Biloxi. Not knowing what to expect and having no contacts, the group arrived in the city on July 1, 1964, unencumbered by any rigid plans or programs. They were feeling their way. Ed Hamlett, who was the ostensible leader of the group, was strongly persuaded that efforts ought to be concentrated on building contacts with the white ministers, businessmen and professional persons. With some misgivings on the part of two-thirds of the group, the efforts were begun. Over 30 ministers in Biloxi were reached by visiting teams. Others in the professional class were also contacted. The results were devoid of encouragement.

"Seems that the scaredest white men in the state are the business and professional people. They've just enough of nothing to think that they have something," Charles Smith, one of the Biloxi volunteers, commented.

At the end of the first month, a retreat was held at the Highlander Folk Center in Knoxville, Tennessee, by those working in the White Community Project. With the experience of more than a quarter of a century of organizing in the South as a guide, Myles Horton—who is the director of the Highlander Folk Center—posed the right questions. The volunteers in the White Community Project gave the right answers: those 10 who thought that the effort could best be spent contacting the poor white people of the community returned to Biloxi and worked with the poor white persons; the others took assignments bolstering the staffs mailing literature and sipping clandestine cups of tea in the homes of white ministers and professionals.

At the end of August the Biloxi volunteers left for the Democratic National Convention in Atlantic City, New Jersey.

Happily, this was not the end of a beginning, but the spread of a start. This aspect of the Mississippi Summer Project didn't end.

The idea had taken roots.

A summer's flirtation had become a marriage, "in sickness and in health, for better or worse, until . . ." Four of the Biloxi project members made a synthesis of the good and bad techniques used. During the early days of September the staff and volunteers received a mimeographed recruiting leaflet for the mighty *Army of Gideon:*

WE MUST BE ALLIES . . .
RACE HAS LED US BOTH TO POVERTY

COFO's experimental white community project in Biloxi has forced an inescapable conclusion: our existing experience organizing the white poor of Mississippi must be developed into a major portion of the COFO program in the coming year. No matter how difficult the task, every effort must be made, by those of us who share the dream of an interracial movement of the poor, to establish programs in white communities in twenty counties by the end of next year.

This means that we need people, i.e., personnel and leadership, to undertake a most difficult, dangerous, and fascinating task of community organization. There are a few requirements for these people. They must have an understanding of the poverty of the Southern white poor. They must be able to communicate a concern for that poverty without precipitating or reinforcing fear and hostility toward the Negro and the freedom movement. They must have training in the field under COFO's sophisticated programs. The leadership must be willing to stay in the field for several years, the personnel for several months. White skin is required only of those who have the initial task of sounding out the potential community leadership as unobtrusively as possible. If enough of those leaders respond favorably to the idea of COFO programs with which to fight their own poverty, then they will invite COFO staff in to help them run their program.

PLEASE SEEK OUT people who are interested in working with this program and get them in touch with White Folks Program, 1017 Lynch St., Jackson, Mississippi. There is a great freedom of choice over jobs in this movement. Its bureaucracy does not bite, does not stick people into convenient cogs. People are encouraged to do the job they think they can do best. No one should have the fear that his humanness will be sacrificed to the cause.

The important work to be done is with poor folks and not with moderates and liberals. The white poor have the political need of decent jobs, housing, education, and health. The movement must go to them and help them develop their own leadership rather than demand that the moderates and the liberals fight their political battles for them. The greatest thing about the freedom movement in Mississippi (and what the rest of the country should consider very seriously) is that the people themselves are voicing their own political needs.

Both politically and in human terms, the freedom movement has no other choice but to develop the white folks program. The resistance in the past within the movement to the white poor program has not been to the idea or to the necessity, but has reflected a frank recognition that people who know how to do the job are not available and that the hostility of the white poor to the movement makes it a near-impossible task. The populist movement and the labor movement both failed to resolve the issue of race. It is the responsibility of the freedom movement, before the threat of the movement to the white poor further increases, to include them in our efforts.

Politically, the freedom movement cannot succeed as a Negro movement for two reasons: First, a solid black vote can never be a political majority of the state or the South. Neither can a solid voting block of the white poor. Only 42.3% of Mississippi and roughly 20% of the

South is Negro. In only 27 of 82 counties in Mississippi are Negroes a majority, and in eleven of those, they are bare majorities of less than 60%. Negro political control of these counties would eventually lead to partition (Pakistan was created out of Muslim sections of India). Separate black societies is an impossible solution in as interdependent a society as ours.

Secondly, a racial political order can never be a stable one. Not only would that order create a chaotic standstill in legislative chambers, it would also create nothing less than a racial war among the people. For the freedom movement to follow the insane path toward that order would create a revengeful Samson who destroys himself in order to destroy the nation which oppressed his people. Hopes for human rights would suffer a destructive blow if race were to block the possibility of the South solving its problems of poverty. It is important to note that the creation of a political voice of poor folks stands to improve the economy for all. There is no reason for the middle and upper classes to be threatened by the development of decent jobs, education, housing, and health for all.

In human terms, the freedom movement has the clear imperative to include the white poor chained to the Negro at the bottom of the economic ladder. It is clear from the U.S. Census of Mississippi (p. 132) that this is true:

Negro family income of less than $1,000/yr.—65,711 households
      "   "   " from $1,000 to $2,000/yr.—51,640   "
      Total—28% of population 117,351   "
White family income of less than $1,000/yr.—32,751 households
      "   "   " from $1,000 to $2,000/yr.—38,622   "
      Total—12.7% of population 71,373   "

Almost one-third of the really poor folks in the state are white.

Personnel for the program will come from interested staff and volunteers with a couple of months' experience in the movement. Hopefully, white SNCC and CORE field secretaries will undertake the leadership of this program in Mississippi and the rest of the South. Disgusted labor organizers who want a fresh approach provide a second resource. The experimental projects now under way of the Students for a Democratic Society (SDS) may develop some good community organizers they could spare for work in the South, as could the Hazard movement. Highlander Folk School, in all probability, would continue to provide orientation and workshops for the white folks program. Effort will not be spared to recruit personnel from Southern colleges (even in

Mississippi) as well as from Northern and Western schools. Hopefully, this recruiting effort will mean that one-third of COFO's work in Mississippi by the end of three years will be with white poor folks.

Northerner and Southerner, black and white, should be encouraged to join this effort. The white task force which moves into the community first will spend a couple of months finding the potential leadership of the program by talking to people individuallly, and disassociated from COFO, in the bars and restaurants, churches and ball games. The task force should interest the people in decent jobs, etc., for poor folks; overcome their hostility to the movement; and encourage them to organize and run their own program. COFO would provide the financial and personnel resources to make the program work. COFO would draw on both white and black sources of people to establish interracial programs to fight the battle for decent jobs, etc. That fight will eventually draw the two groups together.

By the middle of September, 1964, a small group of SNCC field secretaries had scattered themselves around 5 counties, a figure that hopefully will increase to 20 counties with the influx of several thousand northern students in Mississippi in the summer of 1965.

Mostly, now, these volunteers just talk and ask questions while responding to help in whatever emergencies arise in the communities, such as the birth of a baby or a calf, securing enrollment of blind children in the crowded state school, filling out Social Security application forms for illiterates, reading mail, and catching hogs that have broken out of pens and threaten to ruin a crop.

But always there are the questions: "What do you think of having a community center where we can have classes in reading for the older people, show movies or help the kids who are falling behind in school?" "Do you want me to write a letter and send off some of this dirt so we can know how it should be *poisoned* and fertilized?" "If we could get some agricultural students down from the North, could they help us much around here?" "Will you be able to put up a student when summertime comes?" "Since our problem is better crops, roads and hospitals, how does the Klan help these things?"

Then there is always the letter writing to northern organizations for help. It's evident that the poverty program of the federal government will never be even a trickle of help in Mississippi. Letters to the National Farmers Union are sent: "Help." Letters are sent to national cooperative organizations: "Help!" The poor white farmers are overcharged by the merchants in town and short-counted by the operators of the cotton gins. (Five bales come out only four, top-grade cotton is second-grade, and a challenge gets a threat—"Take your cotton elsewhere" . . . when "elsewhere" either doesn't exist or is 40 miles away.) Generally the letters are ignored by indifferent secretaries away up north or get unconcerned formal replies: "At this time our organization does not extend itself any further than Ohio. We suggest that you make inquiry with the appropriate agency of the State of Mississippi."

But still a volunteer walks down from an $8-a-month cabin, climbs into a donated 1950 Plymouth, drives down the road farther, asks more questions, lends a hand with a chore if need be, and writes more letters.

Somehow those working in the "White Folks" Project go on in spite of little immediate tangible gains, probably because they know they will succeed. Or perhaps it's because they know that they can't afford to fail, lest Hitler's mother spawns another and he comes into these same predominantly white communities screeching loudly the lies that were only suggested during the 1964 Presidential campaign: "Your wives are unsafe because the niggers aren't contained. Your stomach is bloated because the niggers are taking white men's jobs. America has only a few jobs left; why should the coons have them?"

There *are* a few signs of encouragement, though. Those with whom the volunteers talk are told of the connection with SNCC and COFO and that before long Negro field secretaries will be in to help with getting the things done for folks in this community. There are smiles as the white field secretaries are called "nigger lovers," and there is no venom in the voices as they say, "I wouldn't care if a bear came in here if'n we can just get something done."

Then, too, there are negative signs of success. Three State Highway patrolmen beat a merchant in the Whitfork County seat when he told them: "Nigger lover or not, I think they are helping our people. Nobody else had tried to do what they were doing. I'm not going to stop selling them food."

And even though the SNCC field secretaries miss a meal or at least postpone it for a long time—because there is no money for the $9.64 salaries during a particular week—things don't get too bad. There is hope. Come the summer of 1965, with the influx of more troops, enough hell will be raised so that an indifferent nation and state will suddenly discover that there are ways of distributing some of the millions of tons of surplus food rotting in caves and storage bins to the people in a county or over the state without first getting permission from the Mississippi power structure.

There is hope because land has been tentatively selected for the construction of a community center—because there are people who wonder why there wasn't a freedom school here for white people last summer.

Mrs. Fannie Lou Hamer was once asked if her goal was equality with the white man. She answered: "No. What would I look like fighting for equality with the white man? I don't want to go down that low. I want the *true democracy* that'll raise me and that white man up." Those who know her best will tell you that she isn't talking about just the Mississippi white man . . . but America.

Credence for Mrs. Hamer's philosophical truth is provided when we view the country as it *is*, in perhaps a painful ugliness, rather than the way we would have it be. This nation is *not* composed of 49 states and a foreign island named Mississippi; damned or blessed, America is composed of 50 Mississippis which vary from each other in degrees—and at a given moment when a New York cop shoots a Negro youth in the back 20 yards away for refusing to halt for a traffic ticket there may be no degree of difference . . . and if there be, who among us can make the distinction?

Mississippi schools are bad—the worst in the nation. Other schools are good only when compared with places like Mississippi. And where is there a place in this nation where the fecal odors of racism can't be sniffed, even though we spray self-righteously with "pine mist" and "room freshener"?

The old who are poor languish in a damnable neglect in Mississippi, and those of limited means grow up unnecessarily scarred for their short lives, solely because money denies them access to proper medical care. Tell us now when you view the same conditions in Michigan and say that they are better . . . tell us what they are better than. Mississippi? How strange it must seem *not* to be able to say the same thing about a soldier, sailor or marine stationed in this nation or in a far-flung outpost of the world.

The fact of the matter is that Negroes and whites in Mississippi suffer as do the poor, aged and infirm all over the nation because of an immoral kind of indifference that is the direct by-product of the slavery—both in and out of chains—that is part of our nation from its very birth; that slavery was sanctified by both the Bible and the "founding fathers," who wrote into their Constitution that black men were to be counted as only three-fifths human.

After the Constitution a tortuous process began: the development of a system of ignoring the shrieks, cries and moans of the raped, dehumanized, castrated black millions whose labor created wealth for this nation. As a country, America succeeded immeasurably well in this fiendish mental pursuit of being callous. But, alas, our nation succeeded too well. We could be indifferent to the degradation of the *blacks* because we weren't black and nobody was chaining our souls. We learned to be indifferent to everything and everyone except those things which *immediately* threatened our little bungalows in Shaker Heights or Westchester County or Beverly Hills. How else can we justify—nay, explain—starving people in our nation and the world, with millions of tons of food rotting in our storage bins? How, when one President, John F. Kennedy, can say, on April 10, 1963, that ". . . one-sixth of our people [Americans] live below minimal levels of health, housing, food and education," do we rationalize $50,000,000,000 for military expenditures and a mere $1,000,000,000, at best, for an antipoverty program?

A lot of comfortable persons won't let themselves know that for millions the American dream comes closer to being a nightmare in a world where rain means that everyone must get up to move beds from leaks, where babies' lips are reddened and sore from constant washing so as not to attract the bite of a cat-size rat, and where entire families live for weeks on nothing but flour, grits and grease gravy.

There are at least 20,000,000 such people in the world's richest nation, and Mississippi, with its average personal income of $1,379 (or 56.4 per cent of the national average) for 1963, has more than its proportional share.

Depending on how hungry or how unhealthy people have to be before you call them "poor," there are perhaps 54,000,000 such persons—"one-third of a nation," some say. Every state, every region has them; in a few unfortunate places like Appalachia and Mississippi there is scarcely anyone else. Nowhere are these poor persons considered tourist attractions; few local chambers of commerce advertise them; our cities and communities are designed to hide them; they are largely "invisible."

And all of this indifference and planned unawareness stems from three centuries of a national conspiracy to encourage black men to remain in a place designed for them at the inception of the nation— at the bottom of everything—where they were to remain quietly "invisible" and quietly ignored, mute census figures, and *good niggers.*

Even today most of the "comfortables" in our nation don't really believe that the price has been too high in spite of their own insecurity in suburbia after arising out of the poverty of the ghettos. How does one comfortably eat a sirloin steak in front of a starving urchin? And isn't it more uncomfortable if by some miracle that urchin grows up and you feel his ominous presence as you leave the opera with your mink coat on, or pass through the ghettos on the elevated train, or read of burglaries, or learn that his cup overflowed one night and he ran through the streets of Harlem unafraid even of the death-laden men in blue uniforms who were put there to guard his *cage?*

Those same dispossessed and disinherited people—to a more intense degree—are in Mississippi. The power structure (Senators, bankers, utility owners, planters and sheriffs) of Mississippi is disturbed too. Their power, both within the state and in the national governing bodies, where they control the military expenditures and the federal judiciary, is being threatened by the efforts of SNCC. The Mississippi Summer Project of 1964, with its freedom schools, northern white "troops," community centers and other forms for organizing the Negroes of the state, has threatened.

And more threatening is the organization of the poor white Mississippians. Mississippi, like the other states of the nation, still makes pretenses that the government is directed by the dictates of a democratically selected set of officials and democratically passed laws, i.e., a majority rule.

Mississippi, like other states, is in fact controlled by a power element which derives its power from the abstension of vast numbers from the democratic processes. (The alternative form in some northern states has been to control narrowly the possible choices of the electorate by having a well-run "in-group" (sometimes called a "machine").

There is a realization in Mississippi—by even the most naïve— that if the poor whites of the state (at least one-third of the abjectly poor in the state are white) and the poor Negroes of the state, who have far more in common than it is safe to enunciate, join hands around, through, and in spite of the veil of color, the present power arrangement will be changed. This is precisely what must be done to resolve the pressing matters of poverty, health and education in Mississippi—indeed, in the nation.

Nowhere in history can there be found an example to the contrary, unless it be an exception which proves the rule. No meaningful steps were taken to insure the vote for women until the women organized and raised hell to the extent of making the rest of the nation concerned (i.e., inconvenienced) about the problem that sorely pressed upon women's souls. Meaningful labor legislation in our nation didn't come until there were millions who had banded themselves together to assert their felt needs for collective bargaining. For reasons not quite clear as of this moment, the factory employees engaged in such uncouth things as "sit-down" strikes and, instead of employing the good offices of the National Association of Manufacturers to serve labor's interests, formed their own groups.

And, for what it's worth, the recent civil rights legislation came as a token effort to calm a mighty rumbling of black discontent that had been expressed both in and out of the Negro organizational structure.

It would not be amiss at this point to state that what Mrs. Hamer referred to as the *true democracy*—which she wanted herself and the white man to raise up—is the one that can be created only by the uncomfortable black man and the uncomfortable white man wresting some of the power from the *comfortables*. As the suffragettes, labor unions and others have done, so must the impoverished.

The problem of the uncomfortable or impoverished is accelerated by recent technological advances, which are described in such terms as "automation" and "cybernation." The problems will hit the South in a frightening degree even before disturbing so deeply other areas of the nation, primarily because there are no unions to impede the speed of the inevitable.

Technology is an even greater threat to the South, because one of the basic reasons for many of the plants' having opened in these states in the past has been the cheap labor and the protection of that cheap labor for the manufacturer by the use of "right-to-work laws." A machine is just as cheap in Milwaukee as it is in Meridian—and probably cheaper because there isn't the added shipping cost of bringing it South.

With fewer jobs in the South and Negroes demanding a redistribution of the scarcity of them by the employment of more Negroes in areas heretofore excluded, a setting of urgency is created in order to avoid the *Fire Next Time,* where the morality of survival will be operative in Mississippi and elsewhere: that morality which justifies what you feel you must do as you take a 12-gauge shotgun, kill a man, let him drop to the ground, take his package of meat, and carry it home to your starving family, knowing full well that it is better that you and your family live than your unasked benefactor.

Happily, SNCC is not the only organization acting on its knowledge that the solution to the problem of the *uncomfortables* can come only out of effective organization by the *uncomfortables* to satisfy their pressing needs. Another is the Southern Conference Educational Fund (SCEF), which has begun a similar project in

Eastern Tennessee and Kentucky. The Students for a Democratic Society (SDS) have begun a project in Baltimore, Maryland—called the Union for Jobs and Income Now (U-JOIN)—which is organizing black and white unemployed persons to pressure for consideration from the comfortable persons of the power structure of Maryland and the federal government.

Because Mississippi is Mississippi, failure of SNCC to effectuate an integrated organization of the poor white persons of that state will probably result in the greatest national disaster, because of the fertile breeding ground for undisguised "super-Americanism" provided by the strength of the Klan and the Citizens Councils of the state.

On the other hand, the success of the "White Folks" Project in Mississippi would wildly encourage and provoke similar organizations nationwide. . . .

It is a truth: "If it can be done in Mississippi, who is there who can say that it can't be done everywhere?"

During the summer of 1964, the "White Folks" Project began; neither it nor the summer has ended.

VIII

Mississippi Freedom Democratic Party

Midway

I've come this far to freedom
And I won't turn back.
I'm changing to the highway
From my old dirt track.
I'm coming and I'm going
And I'm stretching and I'm growing
And I'll reap what I've been sowing
Or my skin's not black;
I've prayed and slaved and waited
And I've sung my song.
You've slashed me and you've treed me
And you've everything but freed me,
But in time you'll know you need me
And it won't be long.

*—Unknown Student of the
Mississippi Freedom Schools*

In 1876 Rutherford B. Hayes was the Republican candidate for President of the United States. Neither Hayes nor his Democratic opponent, Samuel Tilden, received sufficient electoral votes to win the election. There were disputed vote counts in several of the southern states which would be used by Congress to determine the victor. Hayes met with some distinguished white Southern gentlemen to discuss what arrangements could be made with regard to the South, where millions of ex-slaves lived. It was the period of Reconstruction.

The Negro vote was large enough to elect hundreds of black men to public office, including the House of Representatives and the Senate of the United States. A working coalition between the ex-slaves and poor whites had infused the South with progressive legislation, such as laws creating public schools, which would have been impossible to enact if the ex-slaveowners dominated.

A "compromise" was worked out.

Hayes was given the Presidency and the federal troops were withdrawn from the South, enabling the former slaveowners to massacre their way back to power. In return, the former slaveowners supported the tariff policies, industrial-expansion practices and railroad grants so earnestly desired by northern businesses.

When the troops were withdrawn and Reconstruction gasped for breath, the white population of Mississippi joined its brethren across the South in *redemption*. Redemption meant restoration of absolute white rule. Redemption meant nullification of the Fourteenth and Fifteenth Amendments to the Constitution . . . and the power that black citizens had exercised under them.

The method used was "genocide."

The method was effective. In less than 20 years the blood of millions of black lambs had washed away all the guilty stains of a South that had *lost* a war.

Negro voters became almost extinct. (In 1890 in Mississippi there were 189,884 Negro voters and 118,870 white voters. Today there are 23,801 Negro voters and more than 500,000 white voters.) As it was in Mississippi, so it was throughout the South.

With the destruction of Negro political power by use of "nigger barbecues," the way was clear for Mississippi to build, through its state government, a society in which black "arrogance and aspiration" would be as treasonable as it was impossible.

Jim Crow was born.

A violent cram course was conducted in black docility. The South was successful; in survival techniques the Negro was an apt student. The lesson was taught that "privileges" and facilities were for *whites only* . . . including the voting booth. Within 19 years after the last southern Negro Congressman left the House of Representatives in 1901, the black Mississippian had learned that everything he did was a privilege, everything he had was a gift. Negroes who objected either died or left for Chicago. By 1920 it could be said that there were only two kinds of Negroes in Mississippi: happy ones and dead ones.

Thus, in 1954 the laws of racial segregation first enacted in the 1890's and early 1900's had become "ancient traditions and customs," which garnered another concession in line with the *compromise* of President Hayes of 1876; that victory was the phrase "deliberate speed" in the school desegregation decision of the United States Supreme Court.

But even "deliberate speed" was too fast to a Mississippi power clique which shouted, "Never!"

Mississippi in 1954 defeated a series of White Citizens Council chapters, which eventually flushed their influence, by way of cooperating chapters, over half of the United States. It was not until 1961 that there was any challenge to the absoluteness of the "Mississippi way of life," and this challenge was the Freedom Rides.

Though the Freedom Rides (consisting of teams of bus passengers riding throughout the South and integrating the facilities of the larger terminals) were shocking and spectacular to Mississippi, which was the prime focal point of this national demonstration, they didn't constitute a threat to the Mississippi status quo. The results were not lasting. Even today, in 1965, it is a courageous Negro who will sit on the white side of the Jackson, Mississippi, bus terminal only to have the cop on duty take a walk down a long block . . . as other brave white males question the Negro's sanity and desire to live.

The lack of lasting effect of the Freedom Rides is understandable. ALL of Mississippi is hard-core. ALL of the local and state governments are committed to total segregation. Elected officials can personally lead physical attacks on those in integrated facilities and be succored by the knowledge that the more vicious the attack, the more likely re-election.

It was difficult not to reach the conclusion that in Mississippi the racial composition of the electorate had to be changed in order for there to be a basis for *moderation* or a forum for negotiation.

Voter registration became the prime focus of the Movement in Mississippi. It began on an "organized" scale with the arrival of Bob Moses in McComb, Mississippi, in 1961. In 1962 the voter registration work spread northward to the Mississippi Delta.

For three years the Movement tried to get people registered in a long and not too dull grind that produced droplets of Negro voters in a situation that requires a mighty river of voter registration to be effective. The movement plodded along. Canvassing, persuading, and counseling possible suicide (going to register) took up most of the workers' time—when they were not in dilapidated jails. Beatings were always a certainty. Lynch mobs and shootings, though infrequent, were never unlikely. But the trickle of new voters was so slow that it would take a score of centuries to get results.

It was a very tired and discouraged Bob Moses who talked with Dr. L. Ben Wyckoff and his wife, Jersey, in Atlanta during the spring of 1963. The contact was initiated because SNCC had just begun its plans for a programed learning course for teaching literacy in Mississippi. Ben Wyckoff is one of the leading world authorities on the subject. One of the topics covered in the conversation was the theory of the teaching machines and "reinforcement." Reinforcement is a psychological term for reward or punishment. According to Ben Wyckoff, it is a well-established principle of learning that one learns better and faster if the reward or punishment for answering a question (reinforcement) is closely associated in time with the giving of an answer.

Consciously and unconsciously, the idea must have fermented within Bob Moses. It was related to the whole problem of registration and political organizing in Mississippi. The most discouraging aspect of the work was the feeling that it would be so long before even the trickle of voters registered could participate and feel that the risks undertaken were worth it. Reinforcement. Because of the poll-tax law of Mississippi, it was not unusual for there to be a two-year delay between registration and the first date of being eligible to vote. To vote in state elections, one has to have paid a poll tax for two consecutive years. Poll-tax payments are received for only one year at a time and only during a special time of the year; no double payments are permitted. Hence, the reinforcement is poor.

By the close of the summer of 1963, an idea had jelled which would improve the reinforcement: the Freedom Vote Campaign. In the fall of 1963, Aaron Henry (a Negro pharmacist from Clarksdale, Mississippi) and the Rev. Edwin King (a white chaplain at the predominantly Negro Tougaloo College, just outside of Jackson, Mississippi) ran as candidates for Governor and Lieutenant Governor, respectively, from the Freedom Party. Also listed on the Freedom Ballot were the candidates of the Mississippi Republican and Democratic parties for Governor and Lieutenant Governor.

The purpose of the Freedom Vote was to provide political education for the Negroes of the state, who had so little to do with the elective processes, and to compile evidence to disprove the constant assertion that the voting among Negroes was slight because of apathy—a concept that hardly seems to need disproving. Every adult in the state who was a resident was eligible to participate in the Freedom Election. Some 93,000 Negroes—voting at polling places set up in Negro barbershops, stores and beauty shops and on fenders of convenient cars—participated in the election. If proof was needed that Negroes were eager to vote, eager for political activity, eager to register, the Freedom Vote Campaign of November, 1963, provided that proof.

The Freedom Vote Campaign of 1963 provided positive and quick reinforcement. Needless to say, Henry and King won by an overwhelming margin. Aiding in the project for the first time were large numbers of northern white college volunteers who had taken two weeks off from school.

The months between November, 1963, and February, 1964, were relatively quiet in Mississippi. The biggest event during this period was Freedom Day in Hattiesburg, which began on January 22 and resulted in several weeks of continuous picketing of the courthouse as hundreds of local Negroes tried to register. A federal court order against the registrar there—handed down after three years of legal hassling—asking that he stop the discriminatory registration practices, had precipitated Freedom Day. On hand to participate was George Ballis, editor of a labor paper in Fresno, California.

At the urging of Bob Moses, Jack Minnis of the SNCC research department convened a meeting in Atlanta, Georgia, on February 1, 1964, to consider plans on how to make a national project of Mississippi during the summer of 1964. Hardly had the idea been approved of challenging the traditional Democrats at the National Convention in August before George Ballis gave the political party of the Freedom Movement a name.

Mississippi Freedom Democratic Party (MFDP) was the name Ballis used.

Along with two others (Mrs. Beverly Axelrod, San Francisco civil rights lawyer par excellence, and Claude Hurst of Fresno), Ballis introduced a resolution at the California Democratic Council held in Long Beach, California, February 21-23, 1964, which called for the seating of the MFDP delegates in Atlantic City.

With a burst of enthusiasm, there was unanimous adoption of the Ballis resolution on February 23, 1964.

But still the program of challenge was not off the launching pad.

The hope was that the major civil rights organizations—the National Association for the Advancement of Colored People, Martin Luther King's Southern Christian Leadership Conference, and the Congress of Racial Equality—would join with the Mississippi Freedom Democratic Party in pressing the challenge.

Unity was almost imperative. SNCC was nearly broke—as usual —and couldn't subsidize the challenge. State conventions had to be contacted to secure resolutions in support of the seating of the Mississippi Freedom Democrats. A massive collection of disciplined demonstrators had to be mobilized in Atlantic City in order to make it difficult for President Lyndon B. Johnson to follow his proclivity to capitulate to a southern coalition which wouldn't want the Freedom Democrats seated.

Some signs were encouraging. While attending a meeting of liberals in Washington, D.C., Bob Moses outlined the programs for the Mississippi Freedom Summer, coming in a few months. Present was Joseph Rauh, vice-president of the Americans for Democratic Action (ADA), dictator of the Democratic party of the District of Columbia, general counsel for Walter Reuther's United Automobile Workers (UAW), and confidant of Hubert H. Humphrey.

"If there's a challenge," he said, "if there's anybody at the Democratic Convention challenging the seating of the outlaw Mississippi Democrats [the traditional Mississippi Democrats], I'll help make sure that the challengers are seated."

Jack Pratt, employee of the Commission on Religion and Race of the National Council of Churches, nudged Bob. "Did you hear what Rauh said?" he asked. "Did you hear it?"

Bob had heard it.

They approached Rauh after the close of the meeting. Again Rauh gave assurances of help if there was a challenge to the traditional Mississippi Democrats. The offer seemed a godsend. For a challenge to be successful, there had to be money to pay expenses. Rauh's contact with Reuther and the UAW might provide a source for defraying part of the costs. For a Freedom Party challenge to be successful, support from Democratic delegations from northern states was essential. The UAW and the ADA had the reputations of being the most powerful liberal forces within the Democratic Party which could help. Feelers were made for a later appointment when Bob Moses could involve Miss Ella J. Baker (one-half of the SNCC advisory staff) and some others in a conference concerning the help that Rauh would be willing to offer.

Some signs were discouraging.

After securing assurances from CORE of full support—along with the CORE assignment of Norman Hill to work with Ella Baker and others on the Mississippi challenge—the Moses-Baker-

Hill trio journeyed to Atlantic City to the National Convention of the UAW (which was held March 20-26) to see Walter Reuther, president of the union.

Because the challenge had started in typical SNCC fashion—moneyless—it was hoped that a confrontation with Reuther would result in both moral and *financial* support. Mrs. Mildred Jefferies, a Democratic State Committeewoman of Michigan and a member of the UAW, arranged a luncheon between Reuther and representatives of student organizations at the convention. Moses of SNCC, representatives of the Students for a Democratic Society (SDS), and persons from the Northern Student Movement (NSM) spoke at the luncheon and presented ideas.

When Reuther responded, it was as if he had heard nothing that had been said. His remarks were confined to the projection of plans he had about the utilization of appropriations from the poverty program.

From the convention the next major conference was in Washington, D.C., at the offices of Joseph Rauh. Rauh was asked to be counsel for the Mississippi challenge. It was made clear that there wasn't money to pay legal fees.

Rauh accepted.

Calling upon his experiences in challenges at prior Democratic conventions, Rauh offered helpful suggestions: as much as possible, the procedures followed by the Freedom Democrats had to be these: first, to participate in the precinct, county and state conventions of the traditional Mississippi Democrats and, second, when frustrated in this attempt, to follow procedures approximating the procedures of the traditional Democrats as closely as possible.

It was pointed out that a brief should be submitted to the Credentials Committee of the Party and that research personnel would be needed in the preparation of the brief. Because Miss Eleanor Holmes, graduating student at Yale Law School, would not be available until May or later, when graduation and some sort of legal examinations took place, the services of H. Miles Jaffe were secured. Jaffe was from the Washington Human Rights Project directed by William Higgs. Shortly after the research work began, the full-time volunteer services of a sociologist, Dr. Danny Foss, were used.

But the hour was late. The end of April was approaching and the broad coalition for support, finance and demonstration forces wasn't materializing. Already a lot of conventions of northern Democrats had been held, and they could not now be approached for resolutions in support of the Mississippi Freedom Democratic Party. CORE was having internal problems: Norman Hill had resigned in a huff in a policy dispute with James Farmer and others within CORE.

And Bayard Rustin was fiddling. While *committed* to recruiting and organizing tens of thousands for the Democratic Convention, he was yet uncommitted. None of the grand plans had been executed. Rustin seemed unwilling to do anything until he had built a broad coalition of the UAW, CORE, SNCC and SCLC for personnel and for finance, including a salary for Rustin equal to his abilities.

Ella Baker acted. The proposal was made and accepted that the work of organizing the demonstration be separated from the work of gaining support for the challenge within the Democratic parties throughout the North. On borrowed money, and with SNCC's $10-a-week staff personnel, an office was opened in Washington, D.C., on April 24 for the Mississippi Freedom Democratic Party.

With a little over three months left until the Convention, the scurrying began. Ella Baker acted as coordinator of the office. Walt Tillow, Bernard Conn, Reginald Robinson, Alex Stein, Charles Sherrod, Leslie McLemore, Miss Barbara Jones and Frank Smith manned the office, wrote letters and made speeches before the state conventions in key states when money permitted travel. Senators and Congressmen in Washington, D.C., were badgered for support.

But things did not seem encouraging. Success of the challenge would depend on the ability to get national attention: a few hundred demonstrators outside of Convention Hall could be ignored; tens of thousands could not. Much was in the hands of Rustin.

In this mixed setting of successes and procrastinations, the MFDP held its kickoff rally at the Masonic Temple on Lynch Street in Jackson, Mississippi, on Sunday, April 26.

I was there.

For several days Mississippi had been shrouded in gloomy rain. Saturday, the day before, at the state-wide meeting of high-school students, a bare 85 showed up; hundreds had been expected. At the gigantic kickoff rally the vastness of the auditorium, which could seat thousands, engulfed the feeble attendance of 200. There was a sense of impertinence and irrelevance: these few dare to dream of challenging the traditional Mississippi Democrats, who could command the powers of all of the southern politicians and the allegiance of President Johnson (who, in turn, would get the support of the civil rights leaders, such as Roy Wilkins, Martin Luther King and James Farmer, and such powerful figures as Walter Reuther, Congressman William Dawson of Chicago and Congressman Charles Diggs of Detroit—all of whom could contrive reasons to show that support of President Johnson was not support of the South even as the President supported Mississippi).

The scene bordered on the ridiculous. It was ridiculous by any standard other than that of SNCC. But one could not help but wonder if even SNCC had gone beyond the pale of rationality in this case. (Months later, on August 6, the Masonic Temple was packed to capacity with 2,500 at the MFDP state convention.)

As the rally was drawing to a close, Bob Moses came in fresh off a plane from the North but stale from the despairs of his missions. Some form of support that he had sought and had been promised had been denied. His appearance at the rally was perfunctory. As soon as circumstances permitted, Bob left, trudged to his room a few blocks away, and withdrew in its relative quietness for three days.

Laurence Guyot, robust SNCC field secretary, native Mississippian and newly elected chairman of the Mississippi Freedom Democratic Party at the state-wide rally, collapsed in exhaustion from weeks of overwork. John O'Neal took Guyot to an apartment and summoned a doctor. Tony Gray, husband of the Freedom Democratic candidate in the coming June 2 Democratic primary, Mrs.

Victoria Gray, was mad. "All the colored folks in the state should be here. They are all dressed up. Church is over. They don't have anywhere else to go. I know," he said in condemnation of the attendance.

But the indomitable Lois Chaffee, CORE field secretary, seemed to take the matter in stride. Lois, as dutiful as she will be until death summons her to turn in her COFO button, sang the closing "We Shall Overcome" with the others and scampered across the street and down half a block to where COFO headquarters was and bowed her head in rapt attention over a pile of material on her cubicle desk that she was determined to read in order to prepare some sort of summary report.

A huge Labrador dog spotted Lois running across the street and followed her into the office. Lois often fed him. Shaking his rich burned-brown-colored hair of the moisture as he stood near Lois in the office to get her attention, the dog's odor reminded those nearby of another task left undone: his bath.

MFDP's kickoff was not overly impressive.

In May, 1964, in Mississippi four candidates from the Mississippi Freedom Democratic Party had qualified to run in the Democratic primary of June 2. Mrs. Victoria Gray of Hattiesburg was opposing Senator John Stennis. The Rev. John Cameron was the sole competition for the incumbent Congressman, William M. Comers of the Fifth Congressional District, who was second-in-command of the House Rules Committee. James Monroe Houston, a 74-year-old retired machinist from Vicksburg with a civil rights record dating back to 1934, was the Freedom Party candidate in the Third Congressional District of Mississippi. Up in the Second Congressional District, Mrs. Fannie Lou Hamer was the Congressional candidate.

The political posture of Mrs. Hamer was representative of the attitude of the three other Freedom Party candidates.

"My candidacy is directed to whites as well as Negroes," she said. "All Mississippians, white and Negro alike, are the victims of this all-white, one-party power structure. I'm running against Jamie Whitten, and we mustn't forget that Jamie used his position on the

House Appropriations Subcommittee of Agriculture to kill a bill that would have trained 2,400 tractor drivers in Greenwood. Six hundred of those to be trained were white!" That was her exhortation anywhere a church, lodge hall or corner store could be found where folks would listen.

Wherever a speech was made, solicitations for Freedom Registrations on the Freedom books were sought by Freedom registrars.

This Freedom Registration served as a method of organizing Negroes throughout the state, gave some focus to the attempts of Negroes to register in the official books of the county, and formed the basis of participation in Freedom Elections. Irritating the Mississippi power structure now is the knowledge that every time any official election is held, a Freedom Election is held. Each Freedom Election stirs the black giant more as it develops a greater yearning to substitute the real ballot for the symbolic one.

"Games" have a way of becoming real.

Read or write or not, one can register for the Freedom Ballot. An "X" mark is considered sufficient if there is a witness. Philosophically the practical position is taken that it is both illegal and immoral to deny, discourage, demean and prevent Negroes from getting educations—as is done by the power of Mississippi—and then penalize the poorly educated—the group in which the system of oppression has been most successful—as being unfit.

Only two requirements were promulgated for the Freedom Registration: to be 21 or over and to be a resident of the state.

While Cameron, Gray, Houston and Hamer were campaigning in Mississippi, support was developing elsewhere. On May 21 the Young Democratic Club of the University of Virginia passed a resolution calling for the seating of the Freedom Democrats.

On June 2 the four candidates of the MFDP were defeated in the primary election. Or were they? Thousands of names were added to the Freedom Registration books and carefully filed away with the names of the 93,000 others who had registered in November, 1963. Careful documentation of the intimidation and harassment of each of the candidates was filed with the Freedom Registrations, to be hurried to the protective setting of Atlanta. In Atlanta copies were made on microfilm.

Encouragement was found in the announcement made during the early part of June by the subcommittee on the allocation of delegates to the Democratic National Convention: party loyalty was a prerequisite for delegations to be seated, a requirement that the traditional Mississippi delegation could never satisfy.

On June 13 the Americans for Democratic Action (ADA) passed a resolution calling for "rejection of the racist Mississippi Democratic Delegation" and the seating of the "integrated Freedom Democratic Party." The resolution was significant. Its significance is found in the ADA's status as the most powerful "liberal" wing of the Democratic Party. Much of the credit for Adlai Stevenson's getting the Democratic Presidential nomination in 1952 and 1956 goes to the ADA. Past presidents of the ADA include such persons as Vice-President Hubert H. Humphrey. Joseph Rauh, national counsel for the UAW, was a high official in the organization, as was Walter Reuther of the UAW. To those who believe in "signs," this was a good one.

The language of the ADA resolution sounded exactly like what the Freedom Democrats wanted to hear most: "It would make a mockery of everything that the Democratic Party stands for," the promulgators of the resolution had said. A copy was sent to the national chairman of the Democratic National Committee.

More state delegations were meeting. More letters, personal contacts and phone calls were being made, asking for help. There was furious scrambling by the Washington office of the Freedom Democratic Party to do the *difficult* in the few days left.

On June 14 in Lansing, Michigan, the state Democratic convention unanimously adopted a resolution calling for the seating of the Freedom Democrats.

On June 15, on a motion of Sylvia Hunter of Manhattan, seconded by Ray Guenter and John English, the New York delegation to the National Convention went on record favoring the seating of the MFDP.

June 16, 1964, was like no day had been since Mississippi came into existence.

To the north some 500 miles, there were hundreds of youthful college people ready to turn back the evils of the century of oppression since the Civil War: Oxford, Ohio, was the place. To the east in Atlanta, Georgia, SNCC was moving its national office to Greenwood, Mississippi, in the Delta. Within Mississippi a scab was being pulled off a sore, revealing a carefully concealed lie: the lie that the delegates to the Democratic National Convention are selected in accordance with the laws.

In Mississippi there are 1,884 voting precincts. Each of these precincts was supposed to have a meeting on June 16 at 10 A.M. at the regular place where the ballots are cast. At the precinct meetings delegates to the 82 county conventions were supposed to be elected. From the 82 county conventions, delegates were supposed to be elected to attend the caucus of the five Congressional districts; the district caucuses were to select the delegates to the state convention and name the delegates to the National Convention of the Democratic Party, subject to the approval of the state convention. But this just doesn't happen.

The sampling derived from the experiences of Negroes in trying to find these precinct meetings indicates that three-fourths, or 1,413, of the precincts don't bother to have a meeting. Canvasses by phone couldn't produce persons listed as white voters in towns who had ever heard of a precinct meeting.

Not every precinct in the state was covered by the integration workers, but the sampling was sufficiently broad to reveal the pattern of Mississippi politics. The refusals of the traditional Democrats to allow Negroes to participate in the selection of the delegates to the National Convention were documented in affidavits. The report on Ruleville, Mississippi, was typical:

"June 16, 1964, Ruleville, located in Sunflower County where Senator Eastland's plantation is. Eight Negro voters went to the place where the precinct meeting should have been held, the regular polling place. They tried to open the door of the Community House. It was locked. They called out. No one answered. Then at 10:05 A.M. the Negro voters convened the precinct meeting on the lawn of the Community House. A resolution was passed pledging support of the National Democratic Party. Delegates were elected for the county convention. After a short prayer and singing 'We Shall

Overcome,' the precinct meeting adjourned. The entire operation was filmed by CBS News, TV."

Affidavits of similar frustrated attempts throughout the state were presented to the Credentials Committee in Atlantic City to deal with the question of which delegates were legal—the Freedom Democrats or the traditional Democrats.

On June 19 in Oxford, Ohio, at the orientation session, William Kunstler (New York lawyer and father of one of the 300 volunteers present, Karen) announced the filing of a federal suit attacking, among other things, section 3107 of the Mississippi Code, which provided for the selection of the Democratic Presidential electors after the holding of the National Convention. This statute made it impossible for a traditional Democrat to give assurances that the candidates of the National Party would appear on a Mississippi ballot because the decision was in the hands of the Mississippi state convention, held after the National Convention.

Who was legal?

June 30, 1964, the platform of the Mississippi State Democratic Party was released. It was against everything: civil rights, poll-tax amendments, the United Nations, et cetera. It further made the determination of the legal delegation at Atlantic City easier by asserting, "We reject and oppose the platforms of both national parties and their candidates."

On July 2, Ella J. Baker sent a telegram to the Oregon state convention of Democrats asking for support in the seating fight. In the telegram was a quote of Governor Brown of California expressing approval of the support given to the Freedom Democrats by California: "I could not be more pleased. The traditional Democratic Party [of Mississippi] was so far out of tune with the National Democratic Party that it should not be allowed near the Convention Hall." (Governor Brown recanted from this position at the National Convention.) On July 5 word came back from Oregon pledging support for the Freedom Democrats. On July 6 the District of Columbia came out for support of the Freedom Democrats.

Then came the bogey man: Goldwater. The 1964 National Convention of the Republican Party selected Barry Goldwater as Presidential nominee. The Presidential election was characterized then as a contest between "good and evil, Johnson and Goldwater, sanity and a madman." Goldwater's election to the Presidency of the United States was likened unto destroying the world. Northerners who were supporting the Freedom Democrats began a re-evaluation.

To beef up support within Mississippi for the challenge and to increase the freedom registration, Dr. Martin Luther King was brought into Mississippi for a five-day speaking tour. James Farmer (national director of CORE), Bayard Rustin (who calls himself the "Lone Wolf of Civil Rights"), Ella J. Baker, James Forman and Bob Moses of SNCC, and others gathered in Jackson while the Rev. King was there to have a "high-level" conference on the Atlantic City challenge.

The two most important items to be resolved were money to carry on the challenge and the organizing of the demonstrators. Pledges of some financial support were secured from all the civil rights groups represented at the meeting. When discussion began, Bayard Rustin was still insisting that he would marshal and organize the tens of thousands of demonstrators for the Convention. It is believed that later in the day there was a long-distance phone call to Rustin from a friend in Detroit. At the evening session he reversed his position. He began making impossible requests, such as putting both the securing of support for the challenge and the organization of the demonstrations under his control and placing the need tor large sums of money under his exclusive direction. Though Bayard insisted that he hadn't fully rejected the idea of organizing the demonstrations and wanted to think it over for a few days, it was apparent that he was lost. The hour had grown late.

It was too late to marshal and organize large numbers of demonstrators. Bayard's decision—because so much reliance had been placed on him and because the time had run out—was a bitter revelation.

On Saturday, July 24, on the "Senate Cloakroom" television program, Senator Paul Douglas of Illinois projected the idea of seating both delegations from Mississippi and splitting the vote, as had been done in ten of twenty-seven challenges in the history of the Democratic National Convention. The Martin Luther King tour of the state was completed on the same date.

The days raced by until the eve of the Democratic Convention. President Lyndon B. Johnson and his advisers wrote a script to be followed at the "Johnson Convention." He would pretend to be undecided on a running mate, and this would give the unspectacular Convention some drama which might hold TV audiences.

The leading actors of the drama would be Hubert H. Humphrey (to make sure that the Alabama and Mississippi seating challenges were handled expeditiously) and the former Governor of Pennsylvania, David Lawrence, as the head of the Credentials Committee (which makes the decision as to who gets seated).

Making sure that the rules of the Convention could be bent, twisted, broken and discarded and that convenient new ones could be enacted to serve the purposes of the "Great Society" was the trusted Governor Carl Sanders of Georgia.

The end of the script had a climax that called for the Freedom Democrats to march into the Convention to the roll of drums and blare of trumpets to take seats as "honored guests" or "fraternal members" or anything except the "Mississippi delegation." After all, there was a fiery dragon named Goldwater that had to be slain.

The traditional Democratic Party of Mississippi came to the Convention with *certainty* in its favor:

1. The group knew that 3 of its delegates would be seated as the other 65 stalked out in feigned indignation at being asked to take an oath of loyalty to the Party.
2. The group knew that the Freedom Democratic Party would not be allowed as part of the Mississippi delegation.

This certainty had come from two sources. Governor Paul B. Johnson, in a private session, had informed the delegation of the phone call received from President Lyndon B. Johnson and then had proceeded to brag about the call to the press (Jackson *Daily News,* August 13, 1964).

The other source was Douglass Wynn of Mississippi, who was one of the delegates. Wynn's seven-year-old daughter has President Lyndon B. Johnson for a godfather. Wynn's father-in-law is Ed

Clark of Austin, Texas. Clark, an ardent friend of President Johnson and one of the most influential lobbyists in America, is reputed to be the puppeteer of six United States Senators.

In addition, it was known that Johnson was running scared: five delegations from the South had promised to walk out of the Convention if the Freedom Democrats were seated. Things were certain. Yet there was still a role that the traditional Mississippi Democrats had to play: they had to come to the Convention.

If no traditional Democrats had shown up, it would have been immeasurably more difficult for President Johnson to have justified *not* seating the Freedom Democrats. Millions of Negro voters and other liberals in key northern states would not have understood and might have made Election Day a "fishing day" by staying away from the polls.

In spite of the awesome power of President Johnson and the southern block of Democrats, the Freedom Democrats were not without some power. Firstly, they had an ironclad legal posture for being seated as the delegates for Mississippi, inasmuch as they had irrefutable legal evidence that

1. Negro voters in Mississippi (and most of the white) had been illegally denied access to the delegate-selection machinery of the Democratic party in Mississippi and all other political processes of the state. Freely and repeatedly the delegation of Freedom Democrats reminded everyone that for the National Convention to say that the traditional Democrats were "legal" was for the National Democratic Convention to endorse the fraud, violence and trickery used to keep Negroes out of the few precinct meetings held on June 16.
2. The traditional Democrats had systematically and consistently prevented Negro voter registration by every statute, custom and lynch rope available.
3. Under no circumstances would the traditional Mississippi Democrats support the National Party or the national candidates.

Secondly—for what it may have been worth—Freedom Democrats had the guilt of a nation on their side, arising out of centuries of slavery, exploitation and segregation. The discovery of the bodies of Chaney, Goodman and Schwerner on August 4 was still fresh enough, when the Democratic National Convention opened, to be remembered.

Thirdly, the Freedom Democratic Party had the support of resolutions from 9 important Democratic Party delegations (including Michigan, California, New York and Oregon), 25 Democratic Congressmen (including Mrs. Edith Green, William F. Ryan, Philip Burton, James Roosevelt, Gus Hawkins and Robert W. Kastenmeier) and more than a score of vigorous supporters scattered about the Convention.

Fourthly, there was public focus. The news media hadn't bought the bit about President Johnson's not knowing who his Vice-Presidential candidate would be. For the news media the only issue seemed to be Mississippi, so they zeroed in on the Freedom Democrats.

Finally, there was determination. The Freedom Democrats were determined to get something meaningful out of the Convention, such as being seated as *representatives for Mississippi* in exchange for the position of peril that they had assumed by the mere act of coming to the Convention. (On August 13 the Attorney General of Mississippi had secured an injunction against the MFDP in the state courts. In addition, the promise had been made to jail the delegates if they went to Atlantic City.)

During the afternoon of Saturday, August 2, the curtain was raised. The grand drama began with the hearing of the Credentials Committee of the Convention in the Grand Ballroom of Convention Hall.

IX

Democratic National Convention

"Seek ye first the political kingdom
and all other things shall be added."
—President Kwame Nkrumah
of Ghana

BEING A NEWSLESS DAY, relatively speaking, every major television network, every major newspaper and all of the important columnists of America were present. Every actor knew his part, save a few: the delegates of the Freedom Democratic Party of Mississippi, who were not about to play "make-believe."

The testimony began. America stood still as a Mississippi truth unfolded from the eloquent tongues of its immediate victims. Aaron Henry spoke. The Rev. Edwin King spoke. And then came Mrs. Fannie Lou Hamer, and she shared with the world, the best she could with words, some of the indescribable horrors inflicted by traditional Mississippi Democrats when a Negro tries to vote.

Breaths grew short; each throat had that sort of choked feeling, as if one's heart was going to come out through it. Faces of men and women, blacks and whites, Credential Committee members and just plain spectators were washed in their own tears. Even the whispers of Mrs. Hamer's voice damned a nation, for in them you could hear and see Herbert Lee, Medgar Evers, James Chaney, Andy Goodman, Mickey Schwerner and a million bodies gulped by Mississippi rivers during three centuries. She told her story . . .

". . . They beat me and they beat me with the long flat blackjack.

I screamed to God in pain. My dress worked itself up. I tried to pull it down. They beat my arms until I had no feeling in them. After a while the first man beating my arm grew numb from tiredness. The other man, who was holding me, was given the blackjack. Then he began beating me. I can't . . ." Mrs. Hamer was sobbing.

In the White House there was panic.

Hurriedly President Johnson ordered his own television press conference. But the notice had been too short. By the time the cameramen had set up, Mrs. Hamer had almost finished. President Johnson went on national television and made some comments about some matter about poverty or something. Few can recall what he said; there was nothing that impressed one as being either important or urgent. But it was long. It did cut off Mrs. Rita Schwerner, widow of Mickey, and the others. But if the President had intended to keep the world from hearing the 45 minutes of testimony of the Freedom Democrats, he surely failed. Later in the evening the radio and television networks played the recorded and filmed testimony blocked by President Johnson's inane news conference. And the papers the following day told the story in print.

Thousands of telegrams, letters and calls poured like a torrential rain in to the members of the Credentials Committee.

The seven Negro members of the Credentials Committee (which included such persons as Mrs. Todd Duncan of Washington, D.C.) became "uncontrollable." They, too, were indignant and angry, as were the magnificent lady from Oregon, Congresswoman Edith Green, and Congressman Kastenmeier.

"The best-laid plans of Presidents and Men often go astray." That was the way that Joe Jordan characterized the hearing of Saturday, August 22, in a paraphrase of Robert Burns.

The script had to be rewritten because of that *awful* session the Freedom Democrats had conducted before the Credentials Committee. Something had to be done to create the impression of concession to the MFDP.

The Master Political Dramatist did rewrite the ending. The new script called for giving "delegate status" to two persons selected by Hubert H. Humphrey: they were Aaron Henry and the Rev. Edwin

King. While other delegates at the Convention would be the delegates of Maryland, California and so forth, these two hand-picked
delegates of Humphrey from the 68 in the Freedom Democratic
Party would be the delegates of a mystical land like Valhalla; they
would be the delegates-at-large. To sweeten the pie, there would be
an unenforceable resolution calling on southern Democratic parties
to integrate their slates of Convention delegates, as is done in the
northern states.

The marching into the Convention to the roll of drums and blare
of the band was rewritten into the new ending. It was a *must* that
the Freedom Democratic delegates make a public show of being
grateful.

On Monday, August 24, in spite of a lot of hard selling by Joseph
Rauh, Congressman Charles Diggs, the Rev. Martin Luther King,
Jack Pratt of the National Council of Churches, Congressman
William Dawson, and a half a dozen others of similar mind, it be-
came obvious that the Freedom Democratic delegation had come to
be seated to represent Mississippi and not a place named "at-large."

The adamant position of the Freedom delegates was frightening.
President Johnson demanded that people *follow leadership*—especially since he was the leader. The position that Senator Humphrey sought as Vice-Presidential candidate was being endangered.
If the Freedom Democrats pushed successfully to the point of a floor
fight on seating, or otherwise displeased the southern delegations,
President Johnson appeared to have made it clear that he would
select a man for Vice-President who had no liberal image or one
who was a southerner like himself.

The early votes in the Credentials Committee made it certain
that the Freedom Democrats would never be allowed to represent
Mississippi by a decision of that committee. The thing feared was
that the Freedom Democrats could muster enough support for a
floor vote on seating them. To get the floor vote in the Convention,
the Freedom Democrats needed 11 members of the Credentials
Committee to sign a minority report calling for the seating of the
MFDP. Then there were needed 8 delegations to call for a roll-call
vote on the seating. The magic figures were 11 and 8.

The 8 was quickly taken care of. Walter Reuther, who was flown into Atlantic City on an emergency mission which tore him away from crucial UAW contract negotiations with the automobile industry, and Senator Humphrey quickly ascertained that the 8 delegations which the Freedom Democrats were counting on for a roll-call vote included Puerto Rico, the Virgin Islands, the District of Columbia and Guam. A call was made. Governor Carl Sanders hurriedly had the Rules Committee of the Convention make a regulation that only delegations from states could ask for a roll-call vote.

By Tuesday, August 25, the matter of the 11 signatures of members of the Credentials Committee needed for a minority report calling for the seating of the Freedom Democrats was handled.

Joseph Rauh, lawyer for the Freedom Democrats, was also general counsel for the United Automobile Workers of America, whose president was Walter Reuther. The position as general counsel pays several tens of thousands of dollars per year. For reasons not known, when time came for signing a minority report, Rauh did not sign, although he had promised to do so repeatedly.

Congressman Charles Diggs, who, like Rauh, was a member of the Credentials Committee, wouldn't sign a minority report. The Michigan delegation to the Convention was furious and made strong accusations as to the reasons why Diggs didn't sign and otherwise sided with the wishes of President Johnson rather than those of the Freedom Democrats.

Martin Luther King changed. On Saturday, August 22, and on Sunday and Monday he had repeatedly called for the seating of the Freedom Democratic Party to represent Mississippi. With the aid of Bayard Rustin, the Messrs. Reuther, Humphrey and Johnson had caused the Rev. King, whose organization (SCLC) receives substantial contributions from organized labor, *to see the light.*

Other members of the Credentials Committee who supported the Freedom Democrats were promised no judgeships for their husbands; one was promised no poverty program in his Congressional district; another had his employer call him and remind him that continued support of the Freedom Democrats might be the loss of a government contract that the firm was seeking; another was told that her job with a high official of the city of New York was not helped by her support of the Freedom Democrats.

The various messages from the master politicians got across. The support of the Freedom Democrats dwindled from 18 to 4 on the Credentials Committee.

Tuesday, August 25, was a sad day.

The nearly 100,000 miles of travel by members of the Washington office of the Freedom Democrats, the hundreds of telephone calls, the countless hours spent talking with Congressmen and delegations —both at home and in Atlantic City—were all for nought. The people on the Credentials Committee and in the delegations of the various states all had personal hopes, desires and ambitions. The Master Politician knew this. He reminded as many as were weak that to oppose his wishes would mean an end to those hopes, desires and ambitions.

With all of the actors back in place and following both the script and the leadership, the issue of who would be seated for Mississippi, which had been postponed until things had been arranged (a shrewd leader never allows a matter to come to a vote unless he is certain that the outcome is "desirable"), was placed back on the agenda of the Convention for Tuesday night, August 25. On a doubtful voice vote the recommendation of the Credentials Committee was "adopted" by the Convention.

But there was another scene to be played.

It involved a role to be enacted by the Freedom Party delegation. The delegates were supposed to be pleased, to be happy. They weren't. They wanted to represent Mississippi. If they couldn't be seated as the sole delegation from Mississippi, they wanted the plan proposed by Congresswoman Edith Green: to give the loyalty oath to both delegations and divide the vote equally among those who took it—which would have meant only three of the traditional Democrats in the Mississippi section until the first Negro delegate took his seat . . . and then there would have been no traditional Democrats, because not even for President Johnson could a Mississippi politician sit near a Negro.

Credentials Committee Report on Mississippi

ATLANTIC CITY, Aug. 25 (UPI)—Text of the Credentials Committee report on the Mississippi delegation case:

1. We recommend the seating as the delegates and alternates from Mississippi those members of the regular Democratic Party of Mississippi who subscribe to the following assurance:

We, the undersigned members of the Mississippi delegation to the 1964 Democratic National Convention hereby each formally assure the convention of our intention to support the convention's nominees in the forthcoming general election.

2. We recommend that the convention instruct the Democratic National Committee that it shall include in the call for the 1968 Democratic National Convention the following amended first paragraph:

It is the understanding that a State Democratic Party, in selecting and certifying delegates to the Democratic National Convention, thereby undertakes to assure that voters in the state, regardless of race, color, creed or national origin, will have the opportunity to participate fully in Party affairs, and to cast their election ballots for the presidential and vice presidential nominees selected by said convention, and for electors pledged formally and in good conscience to the election of these presidential and vice presidential nominees, under the Democratic Party label and designation.

3. We recommend that the convention adopt the following resolution:

Resolved: That the chairman of the Democratic National Committee shall establish a special committee to aid the state Democratic parties in fully meeting the responsibilities and assurances required for inclusion in the call for the 1968 Democratic National Convention, said committee to report to the Democratic National Committee concerning its efforts and findings and said report to be available to the 1968 convention and the committees thereof.

4. We recommend that the members of the delegation of the Freedom Democratic Party, like the Democrats proposed, but not seated, as members of the Oregon, Puerto Rico and Virgin Islands delegations, be welcomed as honored guests of this convention.

5. Wholly apart from the question of the contest as to the delegates from Mississippi and in recognition of the unusual circumstances presented at the hearing, and without setting any precedent for the future, it is recommended that Dr. Aaron Henry, chairman, and the Reverend Edwin King, national committeeman-designate, of the Freedom Democratic Party, be accorded full delegate status, in a special category of delegates-at-large of this convention, to be seated as the chairman of the convention may direct.

From a United Press International release, Atlantic City, August 25, 1964; the text of the Credentials Committee report on the Mississippi delegation case.

The Freedom Democrats didn't want the "at-large" or "fraternal" status that was being offered.

"It's a token of rights on the back row that we get in Mississippi. We didn't come all this way for that mess again," said Mrs. Hamer.

Thus, on Tuesday night, August 25, when the Convention session began, when all was supposed to be happy and pretty, President Johnson and millions of other television viewers found a scene in which the three traditional Democrats were under the platform in the custody of a Presidential aide. Outside in the Mississippi section were sitting members of the Freedom Democratic Party. With their bodies they were telling the world that they didn't like the farce that had been planned for them. In the news media that night this MFDP assumption of the seats upstaged everything else that the Convention did. Rough members of a sergeant-at-arms force were summoned away from the delegation by a call reputed to have come directly from President Johnson. The effect on Negro voters of seeing Negroes bodily hauled out of the Convention—a Convention that the Negroes were risking death to attend—would have been disastrous.

Leadership wasn't being followed.

A troubled and angry MFDP delegation gathered at the Union Temple Baptist Church on Wednesday, August 26, at 10:00 A.M.

It was known that Aaron Henry, Martin Luther King, and Edwin King had agreed to the proposed "at-large" delegation plan and with Senator Humphrey's naming of the two delegates.

Again the total MFDP delegation's vote showed overwhelming rejection of the "at-large" status and then condemned the insulting spectacle of Hubert H. Humphrey purporting to pick representatives for the MFDP. And while this discussion and voting was going on, unknown to the delegation, seats in Convention Hall a few blocks away were being removed from the Mississippi section—save for three—in order to block another sit-in, which had the potential of explosively alienating Negro voters.

After much effort, Aaron Henry, who was personally anxious to take the at-large seat designated for him by the then Senator

Humphrey, got the other 63 Negro members and 4 white members of the delegation to hear speakers after lunch who favored acceptance of the plan adopted by the Democratic National Convention and rejected a dozen times by the MFDP.

It was a time for extreme action and heroic effort to get stubborn Mississippians to accept what had been decreed for them from Washington. Senator Humphrey was informed of the MFDP's further rejection and condemnation. President Johnson was alerted. Another upstaging could not be tolerated.

On the afternoon of Wednesday, August 26, the "Big Guns" poured the message on the MFDP delegates: "Follow leadership!" Bayard Rustin, after announcing that he had been sent to the Convention by Walter Reuther to give the Mississippi people the *message,* insisted that the Freedom Movement needed white allies. Therefore, he said, the MFDP should accept the "at-large" offer: "Be at large, but be." Senator Wayne Morse categorically said that the MFDP had won a "victory" and that the victory should be "accepted." Jack Pratt of the National Council of Churches did the same.

James Farmer (national director of CORE), embittered by the inner conflict between his conscience and what pressure was forcing him to do, spoke both for and against acting the role desired.

The Rev. Martin Luther King summoned all of his eloquence and attempted to convince the delegates that the world was in their hands: "This is the greatest decision you'll ever have to make in your lifetime. And the weight of this decision will affect not only what takes place in America, but throughout the world."

Speakers told the delegates that acceptance meant a grand ceremony of the MFDP delegates marching into the Convention with the eyes of the world upon them; that the chairman of the Convention would call out to the two delegates-at-large; that Aaron Henry would get a chance to say, "I, Aaron Henry of Clarksdale, Mississippi, and delegate-at-large, cast two votes for President Lyndon B. Johnson."

The speechmaking for acceptance ended. The 68 MFDP delegates excluded everyone (visitors, friends, reporters and SNCC and CORE staff) and held a long, private caucus.

Again they rejected the script and the role written for them by President Johnson.

A phone call relaying the decision to the White House was made.

Contrary to his announced plans, contrary to all precedent, President Lyndon B. Johnson immediately decided to come into the Convention prior to his being nominated. The Freedom Democratic Party could not be permitted an evening of prime time of nationally televised interviews, during which they might tell all why the "at-large" status was unworthy of acceptance—even while there were people in Mississippi writing epitaphs for the delegates.

Again the MFDP delegates got into the Convention on Wednesday night with borrowed credentials. At the Mississippi section they found three traditional Mississippi Democrats surrounded by a score of suit-wearing men with shielded guns (*Newsweek* magazine said that they were FBI agents and Secret Service men). To the consternation of the "establishment," the delegates stood there for the rest of the proceedings. And they looked beautiful.

Even the tired, aging, 53-year-old boy wonder, Bayard Rustin, was moved to commend the Freedom delegates for not accepting the "back-of-the-bus" surrender that he had worked so hard to force upon them.

"I want to apologize to you people. I opposed a lot that went on here that you wanted. But when I think of those big, black, ugly and beautiful asses in the seats of those nice, lily-white, dainty, traditional Mississippi delegates, I'm happy!

"Yes. Go out into the streets of the nation and demonstrate. Not to keep Lyndon Johnson honest. But to make him less crooked."

The hundreds gathered on the boardwalk in front of Convention Hall for the final demonstration cheered Bayard's belated candor. Smiling and tired, Bayard bobbed his bushy head of gray hair a few times. And then he walked off beyond the view of the crowd into the dark of the night to pursue matters of politics, leaving behind a once-vibrant conscience that he couldn't use in his practical endeavors.

It was reported that the southerners accepted the "at-large" status readily and laughed. The northern newspapers, almost without exception, praised the "at-large" plan. But the fear was that the stench might have been detected by Negro voters in key northern states, who might accept the position urged by the great comedian, Dick Gregory, who had said that if the Freedom Democratic Party were not seated, Negroes should go fishing on Election Day.

It was for this reason that so much effort was spent to get the Freedom Democrats to endorse what was done. Being denied this, the Democratic National Committee engaged the services of the Rev. Martin Luther King and Bayard Rustin to tour the larger urban communities of the North. Their mission was to encourage Negroes not to go fishing.

With regard to the Mississippi Convention challenge, there appeared to be three operative philosophical levels. One was the attitude of the southern delegates. Crudely stated, the position of the South was this: "Damn Johnson if the Freedom Democrats are seated representing Mississippi; our votes will go to the Republican Presidential nominee, Barry Goldwater." With this position they had power. No arrangement was made at the Convention that met their disapproval. Their strength came from their willingness to renounce. As usual, their outlook was practical. The type of challenge emerging from Mississippi could not be encouraged. There is no southern state (and few northern states) which doesn't exclude vast numbers from really participating in the machinery of party organization. Also, do not forget that most whites in Mississippi didn't get a chance to help select the delegates to the convention either.

Another operative philosophy was the one of the Humphrey-Bayard Rustin-Reuther-type group. Theirs seemed to be one of getting their objective accomplished, and "too bad that we'll have to run over everybody and every concept that gets in our way." This, too, is a powerful operating guide.

The third philosophical approach was that affecting the decisions of the Freedom Democrats, who seemed to be saying in everything that they did at the Convention, "We are the legal and moral owners of the prestige and seats allocated at the Convention to the Democrats of Mississippi. We want those seats. But if we are refused them we will still go back to Mississippi and elsewhere and work to see that the national candidates and National Party are triumphant."

Had the Freedom Democrats possessed more power they would have been seated. They could be characterized as *not* having legal as well as moral force on their side only by a tortuous mind that could also assert that the government of Nazi Germany which destroyed millions of lives (in a shorter period than was done in Mississippi) was "legal."

The chairman of the traditional Democrats of Mississippi, Bidwell Adams, in so many words admitted this: "They could seat them *if they wanted to*. They could seat a dozen dead dodos brought there [the National Democratic Convention] in a silver casket and nobody could do anything about it."

With only slight variations, the year 1964 suggests that there will be a similar challenge from the Freedom Democrats of the seating of the traditional Democrats at the National Convention in 1968. The signs point to an expansion. There will be, it appears, challenges by Freedom Democrats from Georgia, Alabama and Arkansas in addition to Mississippi.

So be it.

True to their promise, the Mississippi Freedom Democrats worked for the national candidates when they returned home. True to the MFDP's predictions and proofs, the traditional Democrats carried their state for the Republican Presidential candidate, Goldwater. True to the pattern of the Freedom Democratic Party, a mock election was conducted simultaneously with the holding of the Presidential elections.

Several hundred northern students volunteered for the period of October 20 through November 4, 1964, to assist in that election. The political program of the summer had not ended. A telegram from Laurence Guyot on October 30, 1964, to the national chairman of the Democratic Party gave evidence that the Mississippi reaction had not ended either.

MISSISSIPPI FREEDOM DEMOCRATIC PARTY
52½ SHORT STREET
JACKSON, MISSISSIPPI

Chairman, Laurence Guyot
State Executive Committee
Mr. Lee Dilworth, Holly Springs
Mrs. Victoria Jackson Gray, Hattiesburg
Mrs. Fannie Lou Hamer, Ruleville
Mrs. Annie Devine, Canton
Miss Peggy Conner, Hattiesburg

October 30, 1964

John Bailey
Democratic National Committee Chairman
Washington, D.C.

The Mississippi Freedom Democratic Party has been actively campaigning for President Lyndon B. Johnson and Hubert Humphrey, seeking votes both in the regular election and in our own Freedom Vote—an election designed to give disfranchised Negroes in the state an opportunity to make their choice for political office known. This telegram is in protest of the often brutal actions of private citizens and law enforcement officials that occur in a closed society. In the following cases we witness not only the oppression of a minority group, but the oppression of a minority opinion. We request that the Democratic Party conduct an investigation of the following incidents and/or refer us to the appropriate body for actions against persons committing the following unfair campaign practices and illegal acts suppressing political organizing in Mississippi.

Laurence Guyot

BELZONI
Oct. 1: Six campaign workers arrested on charges of "criminal syndicalism" while distributing registration leaflets.
Oct. 15: Four more campaign workers arrested on "criminal syndicalism." Bond for eight of them totaled $16,000.

INDIANOLA
Oct. 20: FDP volunteer worker kicked and hit in face by local white man.

Photographer for SNCC, in the city to photograph FDP activity, beaten outside city by whites.

Oct. 21: Insurance canceled on church after it was used for campaign meeting.

Oct. 22: Small plane passed several times over FDP rally of 250 people, dropping flare and explosives.

Oct. 26: FDP volunteer worker hit with fists in face at courthouse while escorting 4 local Negroes to apply for voter registration test.

Oct. 28: Tear-gas bomb thrown through window of home of FDP supporter lodging volunteer workers. Arson attempt at SNCC freedom-school building which has been used for FDP meetings.

Oct. 29: Police used night sticks to break up FDP rally on lawn of freedom school, beating 2 Negro women, one of whom is an amputee. 13 arrested for "resisting an officer."

TCHULA
Oct. 24: Home of Hartman Turnbow, FDP delegate to the Democratic National Convention in August, 1964, and active state-wide campaigner, shot into. 4 bullets lodged in wall.

JACKSON
Oct. 24: 7 persons arrested while passing out LBJ-Humphrey leaflets in downtown area. Charged with "distributing leaflets without a permit." Bond for $100 each.

LAMBERT
Oct. 20: 5 campaign workers run out of town by 2 whites as they were canvassing for the Johnson-Humphrey ticket.

MARKS
Oct. 21: Campaign worker forced off highway, beaten by 4 whites and urinated upon: suffered concussion.

PASCAGOULA
Oct. 26: Two campaign workers arrested on false traffic charges.

COLUMBUS
Oct. 26: Campaign worker arrested for "disorderly conduct" and "distributing leaflets without a permit" while passing out Johnson leaflets.

COLUMBUS
Oct. 28: Campaign worker arrested on 2 false traffic charges.

McCOMB
Oct. 23: Campaigning clergymen arrested for "distributing leaflets without a permit" while passing out Voting literature. 13 campaign workers

arrested for "operating a food-handling establishment without a permit" at private home used to lodge workers.

MAGNOLIA
Oct. 26: 29 persons arrested for trespassing in parking lot of Pike County Courthouse as they debarked from cars to make applications to register to vote. $100 bond for each.

Oct. 27: 14 persons again arrested on same charges at same place while attempting to apply to register to vote. Campaign worker arrested while attempting to communicate with jailed person. 6 people physically abused while in jail.

RULEVILLE
Oct. 24: Rocks thrown through window of only Negro merchant in town who dared to post Democratic posters.

Oct. 29: Shots fired through same window riddling pictures of Johnson, Humphrey, and local candidate.

HOLLY SPRINGS
Oct. 16: Cross burned before home of newly registered voter.

CANTON
Oct. 27: Campaign worker arrested on false traffic charges.

QUITMAN
Oct. 28: 3 campaign workers arrested on false charge of car theft.

BATESVILLE
Oct. 26: Firecrackers set off at campaign headquarters.

TALLAHATCHIE
Oct. 26: 2 campaign workers threatened by policemen, had gun pulled on them as they were talking in café.

There is a saying that "there's no rest for the wicked."

On November 28, 1964, in Washington, D.C., the Freedom Democratic Party embarked on another project to disturb what tranquillity Mississippi may have left: a challenge of the seating of five Mississippi Congressmen elected, by reason of systematic exclusion of Negroes from the electorate.

As various representatives of northern groups, gathered to support this challenge, stood up at the November 28 meeting to give their names (such persons as Jesse Gray of the Harlem rent-strike group, Al Raby of the Freedom Democrat clubs of Chicago,

Cleveland Students for a Democratic Society, and Noel Day of Boston), a tone of increased militancy emerged. Missing were groups with strong ties to the Johnson Administration, such as the NAACP, Martin Luther King's SCLC, the Urban League, and CORE.

The challenge idea, as described to the group by lawyers Ben Smith of New Orleans and Arthur Kinoy of New York, seemed so obvious that it's a wonder that civil rights groups had not employed the challenge before. Under the provisions of Title 2, United States Code, Sections 201 through 226, governing the procedure, any person who has run for office and been defeated can invoke the challenge:

Section 201. Whenever any person intends to contest an election of any Member of the House of Representatives of the United States, he shall, within thirty days after the result of such election shall have been determined by the officer or board of canvassers authorized by law to determine the same, give notice, in writing, to the Member whose seat he designs to contest, of his intention to contest the same, and, in such notice, shall specify particularly the grounds upon which he relies in the contest. (R.S. 105.)

As projected on November 28, 1964, the petitions of challenge were formally filed on December 4, 1964 (the same day that Sheriff Lawrence Rainey, Deputy Cecil Price and 19 other white Mississippians were arrested and charged with killing the 3 civil rights workers, only to have the charges dismissed a few days later by United States Commissioners at preliminary hearings).

The next steps consisted of Congressmen friendly to the MFDP (among them William F. Ryan of New York, Phillip Burton of California, John Conyers of Michigan, and Adam C. Powell of New York) challenging (on the opening day of Congress, January 4, 1965) the right of the five Mississippi representatives to be sworn in and to occupy seats pending the determination of the challenge by the Subcommittee on Elections and Privileges of the House of Representatives. One third of the House, 149 Congressmen voted with the MFDP to unseat the Mississippi Congressmen-elect.

After that, the teams of lawyers went to Mississippi armed with federal subpoena power and gathered evidence of terror and other devices to exclude Negroes from voting in the state. And then both sides submitted such evidence as they had gathered along with a brief to the Subcommittee on Elections and Privileges for a determination of who shall sit.

Thus the summer of 1964 rolls onward.

For selfish reasons, many northern Congressmen, as prejudiced as those from Mississippi, are giving the Congressional challenge of the MFDP valuable support. These Congressmen seek through the MFDP challenge to effectuate reforms in the seniority system, which gives awesome power to the Southerners over the government of the United States. The northern Congressmen aided because they want some of that same power.

So be it.

Thus the Freedom Democratic Party of Mississippi, which arose out of a mock political action, is now making a *mockery* of the fraudulent nature of the Democratic Party of Mississippi, which has the key to what is known to be a "closed society." Regardless of the outcome of the continuing programs of the MFDP, it is certain that the Mississippi Freedom Democratic Party is insisting itself into a position of prominence in the realms of conscious modern American History.

LIST OF APPENDICES

APPENDIX I

THE PHILADELPHIA, MISSISSIPPI, CASE

CHRONOLOGY OF CONTACTS WITH AGENTS OF THE FEDERAL GOVERNMENT

Sunday, June 21

10:00 PM:* H. F. Helgesen, Jackson FBI agent, was contacted by law student Sherwin Kaplan. Helgesen was informed that the party was missing and was given the three names. An investigation was asked for; Helgesen said something like, "Keep me informed of what happens."

10:30 PM: A Mr. Schwelb, a Justice Department lawyer, was called from the Meridian COFO office. Schwelb was in Meridian at the time. He was informed of the disapearance of the party.

11:00 PM: Jackson COFO called Schwelb at approximately 11:00, but he gave no indication of having taken any action.

12:00 PM: Robert Weil from Jackson COFO called Schwelb and gave him the license number of the missing car and further information on the addresses of the missing people. Weil requested an investigation. Schwelb stated that the FBI was not a police force and that he was not yet sure whether any federal offense had occurred; so he could not act. He was informed of the provision in the US code providing for FBI arrests; he still insisted that he did not have authority.

12:00 PM: Weil also called Helgesen at this time. Helgesen took in the information curtly and did not allow a chance for further conversation. Weil also called the Mississippi Highway Patrol, with similar results.

---

* All times are Central Standard Time (CST), except where otherwise indicated.

Monday, June 22

1:00 AM:
(EDT, 2 hrs. ahead of Mississippi

Ron Carver of the Atlanta SNCC office called John Doar of the Justice Department in Washington, D.C., and informed him of the case. He said he was concerned, and asked to be kept informed. He said he would look into the case. He suggested that the Mississippi State Highway Patrol be alerted.

3-4:00 AM:
(CST)

John Doar was called again by Atlanta SNCC. He repeated that he would attempt to see what the Justice Department could do.

6:00 AM:

On being called again, Doar replied that "I have invested the FBI with the power to look into this matter."

7:30 AM:

Information concerning the arrest on traffic charges of the three which had been gathered from the Philadelphia jailer's wife was phoned in to the Jackson FBI office. The agent said he would give the information to FBI agent Helgesen, whom we had contacted the night before.

8:30 AM:

New information from the jailer's wife, Mrs. Herring, to the effect that the three had been released at 6:00 PM plus the results of phone calls to various neighboring jails were called in to Agent Helgesen. Helgesen said he could do nothing until called by the New Orleans FBI office.

9:00 AM:

Robert Weil in Jackson called the Highway Patrol. Though they had been called at least four times during the night, they did not seem to know about the case.

9:15 AM:

Attorney Doar was called again at 9:15 from Atlanta and apprised of new developments.

11:00 AM:

Helgesen was called and given new information reported by some white contacts in Philadelphia to the effect that the three were still in jail at 9:00 PM and, appeared to have been beaten, though not seriously. Helgesen said he would "take the necessary action." He said that the alleged beating threw new light on the FBI's role in the case. He said he would call our source.

12:00 PM:

Helgesen was called again. He said that he had only called New Orleans and had not received instructions to investigate.

12:15 PM: Atlanta SNCC called Jackson and said they had spoken to Agent Mayner in New Orleans, who had said he had received no orders from Washington.

1:00 PM: Meridian informed the Jackson office that Marvin Rich, public relations director of CORE, and James Farmer, executive director of CORE, had contacted FBI Agent Delloch, second-in-command of the FBI, as well as Lee White, Presidential Assistant, and Burke Marshall, head of the Civil Rights Division of the Justice Department. Rich and Farmer said that if they got no action from the FBI, they would call the President. Meridian also informed us that Farmer in Washington had called the FBI in New Orleans. Henry Wolf, attorney for the Goodman family, called to say that Robert Kennedy had been contacted.

1:40 PM: Meridian reported that attempts had been made to call local air force bases to institute an air search, but were unsuccessful. Atlanta SNCC called John Doar; he was speaking on another line. They left word for him to call back.

2:10 PM: Our source with the white contacts in Philadelphia reported that as of that hour the FBI had not yet called him, as Helgesen had promised he would two hours earlier. Meridian reported that Marvin Rich was calling the Defense Department to try to institute an air search. Stormy weather developed later in the afternoon in the Meridian Philadelphia area, however.

2:45 PM: Atlanta informed us that calls were made to Burke Marshall and John Doar at 2:30 and 2:45 PM respectively. Word was left, as the two men could not be reached by phone.

2:55 PM: It was reported that reporters had been permitted to go through the Philadelphia jail and were satisfied that the three were not there.

3:30 PM: As of this time neither the Atlanta nor the Jackson offices had received any return phone calls from Doar or Marshall, nor did the FBI office in Jackson have any word from them.

5:20 PM: Doar called Atlanta. He informed them that the Mississippi Highway Patrol had put out an ALL POINTS ALERT bulletin and that both the sheriff of Neshoba County and the FBI were searching. The sheriff claimed that the trio were last seen heading South on Route 19 toward Meridian.

8:00 PM: Bill Light in Jackson called Agent Helgesen. He was asked five times if the FBI was investigating the case. Five times Helgesen answered, "All inquiries are to be directed to the Justice Department in Washington."

8:45 PM: Meridian reported that they called Doar in Washington. Doar was busy. A collect call was placed to John Doar at his home in Washington, from Meridian. He would not accept the call.

9:30 PM: Reporters called from Philadelphia that four FBI agents from the New Orleans office were in Philadelphia. No men from the Justice Department were reported. The FBI agents reportedly were talking to people and were planning to launch a road search and investigation in the morning.

10:00 PM: UPI reported that Edwin Guthman of the Justice Department in Washington had announced that the FBI was ordered into the case to determine whether the trio were being held against their will or whether there was a violation of civil rights involved.

Tuesday, June 23

8:40 AM: Meridian called to say that Marvin Rich had informed them that the Air Force might come by. As of this time, nothing had been heard from them.

10:10 AM: Meridian informed us that John Proctor and Harry Saizan, FBI agents, were in the Meridian office. They were investigating, asking questions, and getting photographs of Schwerner. We were told that Nathan Schwerner (Mickey's father) has an appointment with Lee White, Presidential Ass't.

1:00 PM: Meridian called to tell us that Marvin Rich had made contact with the White House (with Lee White). He was told that the Naval Air Station near Meridian was available to the FBI for an air search. Rich asked for an FBI head agent out in the field. Rich said he was going to call New Orleans. Meridian informed us that some Meridian citizens with private planes were thinking of conducting their own air search, in case of further defaulting by the Defense Department. One of these people was Negro Charles Young.

Newsman Burn Rotman said helicopters are flying around the Philadelphia area. Marvin Rich said that the President was to call back to CORE in New York.

2:10 PM: The Naval Air Station near Meridian was called. They said that as far as they knew, no search was being conducted. There were only student flights taking place in the area.

2:50 PM: Mr. Henry Wolf, attorney for the Goodmans, called. He said that the Goodmans and Mr. Schwerner, accompanied by Representative William Fitz Ryan of New York and others, had spent over an hour talking to Attorney General Robert Kennedy. Kennedy assured them that all authorities were working on the case and that Navy helicopters were searching the area. He told us that they had an appointment to see Lee White soon afterward.

He also informed us that there was hope that President Johnson would make a statement to the nation.

3:55 PM: Meridian heard that local radio station WMOX broadcasted that the FBI had found the car, charred and burned and cold. There was no trace of the missing persons.

5:15 PM: Attorney Wolf informed us that Mr. and Mrs. Goodman, Mr. Schwerner, and two Congressmen saw President Johnson for about 21 minutes this afternoon. While they were there, they received the news that the car had been found. Johnson assured them that the Federal Government was doing everything it could.

5:25 PM: Attorney Larry Warren heard a confirming report on local radio that a Navy Helicopter was being used in the search. The sexton of the Methodist Church which had been burned June 16 in Philadelphia informed us that the FBI had been working on the burning case since Friday, June 19.

6:00 PM: WRBC news report on Gov. Johnson's afternoon press conference; Johnson had sent two plain-clothesmen into the area to assist the FBI in the search. Gov. Johnson had not called President Johnson or the Justice Department, but he was working with the FBI.

7:30 PM: Martin Popper, who is Att'y. Wolf's partner for the Goodmans, called to describe the trip to Washington. On the trip were Mr. and Mrs. Goodman, Mr. Schwerner, Congressmen Ryan and Reed, and Popper.

They first went to see Kennedy. Katzenbach, Marshall and others were with him. This visit was apparently the first thing on Mr. Kennedy's agenda after his arrival from Massachusetts. Mr. Kennedy told the group that the Department of Justice was doing everything possible, and that he was using the maximum resources available to him, including personal resources. He told them the President also expressed concern. The FBI, according to Mr. Kennedy, was acting on the assumption that this was a kidnaping; it was on this assumption that they are assuming jurisdiction on the case.

The parents' group made it clear that the Federal Government must make every effort to: (1) find the boys, and (2) protect the rest of the workers in the state. They made a special point that what was needed was not just investigation, but protection.

Kennedy said that the government was making a statement to Mississippians, urging them to come forward if they had any information. He assured them that they would be protected by the Federal Government. Kennedy said he personally would report to the President on new developments.

The group then went to the White House. They met the Presidential assistants Lee White and Myer Feldman. The parents were told there was a possibility that military personnel might be used in the search; that Navy helicopters were already being used; that the President had told McNamara to advise J. Edgar Hoover that military personnel were available to Hoover.

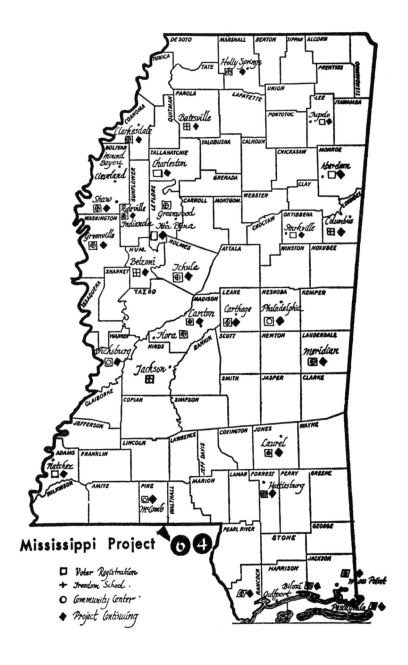

DE SOTO · MARSHALL · BENTON · TIPPAH · ALCORN

TUNICA · TATE · *Holly Springs* ◼◆ · PRENTISS · TISHOMINGO

PANOLA · LAFAYETTE · UNION · LEE ◼◆ · ITAWAMBA

COAHOMA · QUITMAN · *Batesville* ◼◆ · PONTOTOC · *Tupelo* ◼◆ · MONROE

Clarksdale ◼◆ · TALLAHATCHIE · *Charleston* ◻◆ · YALOBUSHA · CALHOUN · CHICKASAW · *Aberdeen* ⊕◼◆

BOLIVAR · *Mound Bayou* · *Cleveland* ⊕ · GRENADA · WEBSTER · CLAY

Shaw ⊕ · SUNFLOWER · *Ruleville* ◻◆ · *Greenwood* · CARROLL · MONTGOM. · OKTIBBEHA · *Columbus* ⊕◆

WASHINGTON · *Indianola* ◼ · LEFLORE · *Itta Bena* ◼◆ · CHOCTAW · *Starkville* •◻

Greenville ⊕◆ · HOLMES · ATTALA · WINSTON · NOXUBEE

HUM. · *Belzoni* ⊕ · *Tchula* ◆⊕ · LEAKE · NESHOBA · KEMPER

SHARKEY · YAZOO · MADISON · *Carthage* ◻◆ · *Philadelphia* ◻◆

ISSAQUENA · *Canton* ◻◆ · SCOTT · NEWTON · LAUDERDALE · *Meridian* ⊕◼◆

WARREN · *Flora* ◻ · HINDS · RANKIN

Vicksburg ◻ · *Jackson* ⊞ · SMITH · JASPER · CLARKE

CLAIBORNE · COPIAH · SIMPSON

JEFFERSON · LINCOLN · LAWRENCE · COVINGTON · JONES · WAYNE

ADAMS · *Natchez* ◻ · FRANKLIN · JEFF DAVIS · *Laurel* ◻◆

WILKINSON · AMITE · PIKE · *McComb* ◻◆ · WALTHALL · MARION · LAMAR · FORREST · PERRY · GREENE

Hattiesburg ◻◆

PEARL RIVER · STONE · GEORGE

JACKSON

HARRISON · ◼◆ *Moss Point*

RANCOCK · ⊗ · *Biloxi* ◼◻ · *Pascagoula* ◼◆

Gulfport

Mississippi Project ⑥④

◻ *Voter Registration*
✛ *Freedom School*
○ *Community Center*
◆ *Project Continuing*

APPENDIX II

COFO AND THE SUMMER PROJECT

MISSISSIPPI PROJECT, 1964-1965

PROJECT	DIRECTOR	MAILING ADDRESS	PHONE
Aberdeen	Joe Maurer	Box 133	369-9076
Batesville		Route 2, Box 20	563-9731
Belzoni	Willie Shaw	268 Wallington	1445
Biloxi	Dick Flowers	732 Main Street	436-9654
Canton	George Raymond	838 Lutz	859-9944
Carthage		% Williams Store Route 2, Carthage	6081
Clarksdale	Lafayette Surney	429 Yazoo Ave.	624-9167
Cleveland	Lois Rogers	614 Church St.	843-5458
Columbus	Don White	1212 17 St. N.	328-9719
Greenville	Muriel Tillinghaust	901½ Nelson	335-2173
Greenwood	Mary Lane	708 Ave. N.	453-1282
Gulfport	Henry Bailey	2905 Harrison St.	863-9550
Hattiesburg	Sandy Leigh	507 Mobile St.	584-9993
Holly Springs	Cleveland Sellers	100 Rust Ave.	1257
Indianola	John Harris	Box 30	1112
Itta Bena	Willie McGhee	153 Love Street	254-7811
Jackson		853½ Short Street	352-9605
Laurel	Jeff Smith	518 E. First St.	428-7057
McComb	Jesse Harris	702 Wall Street	684-9414
Meridian	Preston Ponder	2505½ Fifth St.	482-6013
Moss Point	Charles Mansor	609 Bowen	475-9069
Mound Bayou	John Bradford	P.O. Box 443	57-M
Natchez	Chico Neblett	611 S. Wall St.	442-1298
Philadelphia	James Collier	% Meridian COFO	656-2451
Pascagoula		% Biloxi	
Ruleville	John Harris	Box 275	756-9980
Shaw	Mary Sue Gellatly	Box 547	
Starkville	Ronald Bridgeforth	10 Henderson St.	
Tchula	Hollis Watkins	Route 2, Box 56A	5989
Tupelo	Isaac Coleman	1132 Hilda Drive	842-9963
Valley View	Andrew Green	Route 1	859-4361
Vicksburg	Dennis Brown	1016 Hossley	636-5967

PROSPECTUS FOR THE MISSISSIPPI FREEDOM SUMMER

"It can be argued that in the history of the United States democracy has produced great leaders in great crises. Sad as it may be, the opposite has been true in Mississippi. As yet there is little evidence that the society of the closed mind will ever possess the moral resources to reform itself, or the capacity for self-examination, or even the tolerance of self-examination."

from *Mississippi: The Closed Society*
by James W. Silver

It has become evident to the civil rights groups involved in the struggle for freedom in Mississippi that political and social justice cannot be won without the massive aid of the country as a whole, backed by the power and authority of the federal government. Little hope exists that the political leaders of Mississippi will steer even a moderate course in the near future (Governor Johnson's inaugural speech notwithstanding); in fact, the contrary seems true: as the winds of change grow stronger, the threatened political elite of Mississippi becomes more intransigent and fanatical in its support of the status quo. The closed society of Mississippi is, as Professor Silver asserts, without the moral resources to reform itself. And Negro efforts to win the right to vote cannot succeed against the extensive legal weapons and police powers of local and state officials without a nationwide mobilization of support.

A program is planned for this summer which will involve the massive participation of Americans dedicated to the elimination of racial oppression. Scores of college students, law students, medical students, teachers, professors, ministers, technicians, folk artists and lawyers from all over the country have already volunteered to work in Mississippi this summer—and hundreds more are being recruited.

Why a project of this size?

1. Projects of the size of those of the last three summers (100 to 150 workers) are rendered ineffective quickly by police threats and detention of members.

2. Previous projects have gotten no national publicity on the crucial issue of voting rights and, hence, have little national support either from public opinion or from the federal government. A large number of students from the North making the necessary sacrifices to go South would make abundanty clear to the government and the public that

this is not a situation which can be ignored any longer, and would project an image of cooperation between Northern and white people and Southern Negro people to the nation which will reduce fears of an impending race war.

3. Because of the lack of numbers in the past, all workers in Mississippi have had to devote themselves to voter registration, leaving no manpower for stopgap community education projects which can reduce illiteracy as well as raise the level of education of Negroes. Both of these activities are, naturally, essential to the project's emphasis on voting.

4. Bail money cannot be provided for jailed workers; hence, a large number of people going South would prevent the project from being halted in its initial stages by immediate arrests. Indeed, what will probably happen in some communities is the filling of jails with civil rights workers to overflowing, forcing the community to realize that it cannot dispense with the problem of Negroes' attempting to register simply by jailing "outsiders."

Why this summer?

Mississippi at this juncture in the movement has received too little attention—that is, attention to what the state's attitude really is—and has presented COFO with a major policy decision. Either the civil rights struggle has to continue, as it has for the past few years, with small projects in selected communities with no real progress on any fronts, or there must be a task force of such a size as to force either the state and the municipal governments to change their social and legal structures, or the federal government to intervene on behalf of the constitutional rights of its citizens.

Since 1964 is an election year, the clear-cut issue of voting rights should be brought out in the open. Many SNCC and CORE workers in Mississippi hold the view that Negroes will never vote in large numbers until federal marshals intervene. At any rate, many Americans must be made to realize that the voting rights they so often take for granted involve considerable risk for Negroes in the South. In the larger context of the national civil rights movement, enough progress has been made during the last year that there can be no turning back. Major victories in Mississippi, recognized as the stronghold of racial intolerance in the South, would speed immeasurably the breaking down of legal and social discrimination in both North and South.

The project is seen as a response to the Washington March and an attempt to assure that in the Presidential election year of 1964 all American citizens are given the franchise. The people at work on the project are neither working at odds with the federal government nor at war with the State of Mississippi. The impetus is *not against* Mississippi but for the right to vote, the ability to read, the aspirations and the training to work.

Direction of the Project:

This summer's work in Mississippi is sponsored by COFO, the Council of Federated Organizations, which includes the Student Nonviolent Coordinating Committee (SNCC), the Southern Christian Leadership Conference (SCLC), the Congress of Racial Equality (CORE) and the NAACP, as well as Mississippi community groups. Within the state COFO has made extensive preparations since mid-January to develop structured programs which will put to creative use the talents and energies of the hundreds of expected summer volunteers.

Voter Registration: This will be the most concentrated level of activity. Voter registration workers will be involved in an intensive summer drive to encourage as many Negroes as possible to register. They will participate in COFO's Freedom Registration, launched in early February, to register over 400,000 Negroes on Freedom Registration books. These books will be set up in local Negro establishments and will have simplified standards of registration (the literacy test and the requirement demanding an interpretation of a section of the Mississippi Constitution will be eliminated). Freedom Registration books will serve as the basis of a challenge of the official books of the state and the validity of "official" elections this fall. Finally, registration workers will assist in the campaigns of Freedom candidates, who are expected to run for seats in all five of the State's Congressional districts and for the seat of Senator John Stennis, who is up for re-election.

Freedom Schools:

1. *General Description.* About 25 Freedom Schools are planned, of two varieties: day schools in about 20–25 towns (commitments still pending in some communities) and one or two boarding, or residential, schools on college campuses. Although the local communities can provide school buildings, some furnishings, and staff housing (and, for residential schools, student housing), all equipment, supplies and staff will have to come from outside. A nationwide recruitment program is underway to find and train the people and solicit the equipment needed. In the schools, the typical day will be hard study in the morning, an afternoon break (because it's too hot for an academic program) and less formal evening activities. Because the afternoons are free, students will have an opportunity to work with the COFO staff in other areas of the Mississippi Freedom Summer program, and the additional experience will enrich their contribution to the Freedom School sessions.

a. *Day Schools.* The day schools will accommodate about 50

students, with a staff of 15. There are 20 communities, located in all five Congressional districts of the state, where the people in the community have indicated that they want a Freedom School and are cooperating in finding facilities and housing. These are the towns of some size, where the local Negro communities can provide housing for the staff, and where a suitable building can be located and safely leased. The day schools will attract high-school students from the immediate area only, since there are no provisions planned for living in, but there will be organized contacts—exchanges, sports events, etc.— between day Freedom Schools across the State. The sessions will present similar but not identical material, so the students can profitably attend one or both sessions. This will allow some adjustment for students who must work during the cotton-picking season, and faculty people who are unable to stay six weeks.

b. *Boarding Schools.* The one or two boarding schools will accommodate 150 to 200 students apiece, in a college-campus atmosphere. There will be one six-week session of the boarding schools. The curriculum will be similar to that of the day schools, but on a more intensive level, and with an additional goal of bringing together and training high-quality student leadership. The boarding schools will recruit students who have displayed some leadership potential and can profit from the more intensive approach.

c. *Curriculum.* The aim of the Freedom Schools' curriculum will be to challenge the student's curiosity about the world, introduce him to his particularly "Negro" cultural background, and teach him basic literacy skills in one integrated problem. That is, the students will study problem areas in the world, such as the administration of justice, or the relation between state and federal authority. Each problem area will be built around a specific episode which is close to the experience of Mississippi students. The whole question of the court system, and the place of law in our lives, with many relevant ramifications, can be dealt with in connection with the study of how one civil rights case went through the courts and was ultimately decided in favor of the defendant. The episode of Congressman Jamie Whitten's tractor deal, where Whitten quashed a federal program to train over 2,000 tractor drivers in the Mississippi Delta (because it would have been integrated), can lead one into the whole area of state and federal relations. The campaign of Mrs. Fannie Lou Hamer for Congress (running against Jamie Whitten) provides a basis for studying all the forces which are against her, and which have worked against a Negro's even attempting to run for Congress in Mississippi. Planning the COFO project to challenge the regular Mississippi delegation at the Democratic National Convention provides the starting-point for a study of the whole Presidential nomination and election procedures. These and other "case studies" which are used to explore larger problem areas in society will be offered to the students. The Negro history outline, as presently planned, will be divided into sections to be coordinated with the problem-area presentation. In this context, students will be given practice activities to improve their skill with reading and writing. Writing press releases, leaflets, etc., for the political campaigns is one example. Writing affidavits and reports of arrests, demonstrations, trials, etc., which occur during the summer in their towns, will be another. Using the telephone as a campaign tool will both help the political candidates and help students to improve their techniques in speaking effectively in a somewhat formal situation. By using a multidimensional, integrated program, the curriculum can be more easily absorbed into the direct experience of the students.

d. *Students.* Students for the Freedom Schools will be recruited through established contacts with ministers, educators, and other organizational contacts in the state. Around a hundred applications have already been returned, and we do not anticipate that written applications will form the bulk of the students selected. A state-wide student organization, the Mississippi Student Union, has recently been formed, and will be important to the recruitment of students. Students who have shown evidence of leadership potential will be encouraged to attend the state-wide boarding schools, to meet students from other parts of the state, and lay the foundation for a much broader student movement.

e. *Staff.* Both professional and nonprofessional teachers will participate in the staffing of the schools. Professional teachers will be sponsored by the professional teachers' associations, the National Council of Churches, the Presbyterian Church and other institutions with educational resources. The nonprofessional teachers will be selected from among the applicants for the summer project. A special delegation of Chicago high-school students, who have taught Negro history to other students their own age under the auspices of Chicago's Amistad Society, will work as student teachers in the Negro history program.

f. *Schedule.* The boarding-school staff and staff for the first session of the day schools will go through a general orientation program with the community center staff, probably held at Mt. Beaulah. This orientation will run July 8-12. On July 13, the boarding schools and the first session of the day schools will receive students. Orientation for the teaching staff of the second session of the day schools will be held August 5-9. On August 10, the second session of the day schools will start classes. The sessions will end on August 22 for the boarding school and August 30 for the second-session day schools.

Community Centers: The community centers program projects a network of community centers across the state. Conceived as a long-range institution, these centers will provide a structure for a sweeping range of recreational and educational programs. In doing this, they will not only serve basic needs of Negro communities now ignored by the social service provisions of the State, but will form a dynamic focus for the development of community organization. The educational features of the centers will include job-training programs for the unskilled and unemployed, literacy and remedial programs for adults as well as young people, public health programs such as prenatal and infant care, basic nutrition, etc., to alleviate some of the serious health problems of Negro Mississipians, adult education workshops which would deal with family relations, federal service programs, home improvement and other information vital to the needs of Negro communities, and also extracurricular programs for grade-school and high-school students to supplement educational deficiencies and provide opportunity for critical thought and creative expression. Each center would have a well-rounded library because Negroes in many communities now have no access to an adequate library.

Though the community centers program is primarily educational, some of each center's resources would be used to provide much-needed recreational facilities for the Negro community. In most communities in Mississippi the only recreation outside of taverns is the movies, and for Negroes this means segregated movies. If there is a movie theater in the Negro community, it is old, run-down, and shows mostly out-of-date, third-rate Hollywood films. The film program of the centers will not only provide a more agreeable atmosphere for movies; it will bring films of serious content which are almost never shown in Mississippi, where ideas are rigidly controlled. Other recreational offerings will be: music appreciation classes, arts and crafts workshops, drama groups, discussion clubs on current events, literature and Negro achievement, etc., pen-pal clubs, organized sports (where equipment allows), and occasional special performances by outside entertainers, such as folk festivals, jazz concerts, etc.; organized storytelling for young children will be entertaining, and will introduce them to the resources of the center's library and to reading for pleasure in general.

Special Projects:

a. Research Project—A number of summer workers will devote themselves to research on the economic and political life of Mississippi. Some of this work can be done outside the state, but much will need resources which can be found only in Mississippi. In addition, a number of people will be asked to live in white communities to survey attitudes and record reactions to summer happenings.

b. Legal Projects—A team of lawyers and at least 100 law students are expected to come to Mississippi to launch a massive legal offensive against the official tyranny of the State of Mississippi. Law students will be dispersed to projects around the State to serve as legal advisers to voter registration workers and to local people. Others will be concentrated in key areas where they will engage in legal research and begin to prepare suits against the State and local officials and to challenge every law that deprives Negroes of their freedom.

c. White Communities—Until now there has been no systematic attempt by people interested in the elimination of hate and bigotry to work within the white communities of the Deep South. It is the intention of the Mississippi Summer Project to do just that. In the past year, a significant number of Southern white students have been drawn into the movement. Using students from upper Southern states, such as Tennessee, and occasionally native Mississippians, SNCC hopes to develop programs within Mississippi's white community. These programs will deal directly with the problems of the white people. While almost all Negroes in Mississippi are denied the right to vote, statistics clearly indicate that a majority of whites are excluded as well. In addition, poverty and illiteracy can be found in abundance among Mississippi whites. There is in fact a clear area for Southern white students to work in, for in many ways Mississippi has imprisoned her white people along with her blacks. This project will be pilot and experimental and the results are unpredictable. But the effort to organize and educate whites in the direction of democracy and decency can no longer be delayed.

d. The Theater Project—Sponsored by the Tougaloo Drama Department, this summer will also mark the beginning of a repertory theater in Jackson, Mississippi. The actors will be Negro Mississippians; the plays will dramatize the experience of the Negro in Mississippi and in America; the stage will be the churches, community centers and fields of rural Mississippi.

Using the theater as an instrument of education as well as a source of entertainment, a new area of protest will be opened.

MEMORANDUM ON MISSISSIPPI SUMMER PROJECT

TO: MEMBERS OF THE UNITED STATES CONGRESS
FROM: COUNCIL OF FEDERATED ORGANIZATIONS
DATE: JUNE 3, 1964

MISSISSIPPI RIGHTS DRIVE PLANNED; STATE OFFICIALS MOBILIZE FOR SUMMER

A massive education, community improvement, and voter registration drive is being launched in the State of Mississippi this summer by the Council of Federated Organizations (COFO), a civil rights coalition comprised of the Congress of Racial Equality, the National Association for the Advancement of Colored People, the Southern Christian Leadership Conference, and the Student Nonviolent Coordinating Committee. The National Council of Churches has joined the civil rights groups in this extensive drive. Hundreds of clergymen, students, teachers, lawyers and others will be going to Mississippi to volunteer for this project. (See attached article: *New York Times,* Sunday, May 17, 1964.)

COFO is concerned about the physical safety of summer volunteers because of Mississippi's long record of violence against civil rights workers. (See attached documented chronology of violence: From April 4, 1963, *Congressional Record.*)

The State has passed five bills designed to halt demonstrations and has other proposals before it which would legalize the blatant harassment of our education and voter registration workers. (See attached: "Mississippi Readies Laws for 'Freedom Summer.'")

A powerful police force is being mobilized both locally and state-wide by Mississippi law enforcement officials in a response to the summer project. (See attached article: *Newsweek,* February 24, 1964.)

PROPOSED ACTION TO PREVENT VIOLENCE AND MAINTAIN ORDER

In order to prevent possible violence and chaos—and to save lives— COFO is attempting to secure a federal presence in Mississippi *before* any tragic incidents occur. Public hearings before a panel of ten distinguished Americans are scheduled for June 8th at the National Theatre. Local Mississippians and Constitutional lawyers will testify as to the need for and legality of Federal action. Leaders of the COFO project are attempting to secure an appointment with President Johnson to confer on steps which should be taken. (See attached article: *New York Post,* May 27, 1964.)

ACTIONS REQUESTED OF MEMBERS OF CONGRESS
This briefing is an attempt to enlist your help. We are asking you to
take the following steps:

1. Attend the June 8th hearings and plan to make a public statement on the basis of the testimony you hear that day.
2. In a few weeks, COFO will be sending you a list of the names
of your constituents who will be working with us in Mississippi. We
urge that you bring their presence in Mississippi to the attention of
your colleagues and that you seek the aid of your colleagues in obtaining Federal protection for your constituents.
3. Contact the Justice Department, in writing, individually, or as a
group, and urge that the Department take the following specific steps
in order to insure that the Constitution is upheld in Mississippi this
summer and that summer project volunteers are protected.

a. Assign several U.S. Marshals in every county or locality where
there will be COFO projects designed to secure the constitutional
rights for the Negro citizens of Mississippi. (The power of the
Attorney General to do this is found under Section 549, Title 28,
U.S. Code; and Section 3053, Title 18, U.S. Code.)
b. Set up a full-time branch office on a temporary basis in several
key Mississippi cities, i.e., Greenwood, Hattiesburg, Jackson, and
Batesville. (There are currently U.S. Attorney's offices in the first
three cities. It is quite within reason to request that the Justice Department establish fully staffed operations in these cities, as well as
Batesville, for the summer.)
c. Inform, by mail or otherwise, various Mississippi law enforcement officials both on the state and local level of Federal laws regarding intimidation and harm of citizens of the United States who
are exercising their Constitutional rights and that the Attorney
General make it clear to these officials that prosecution as well as
the active use of Federal preventative force will be swift and sure.
d. Notify Governor Paul Johnson that the Justice Department
intends to take whatever means are necessary to guarantee the
Constitutional rights of U.S. citizens who are in the State of
Mississippi this summer.
e. Recommend to President Johnson the immediate use of Section
332 of Title 10 of the U.S. Code since it is absolutely apparent that
Constitutional rights cannot be currently enforced in any courts
within the State of Mississippi and that such deprivations are going
on in spite of any actions by the Federal courts. (Refer to Section
332 of Title 10 in the Appendix of the Legal Memo attached which

refers, in part, to situations in which it is "impracticable to enforce the laws of the United States in any state or territory by the ordinary course of Judicial proceedings." The 1963 report of the Civil Rights Commission states: "The conclusion is inevitable that present legal remedies for voter discrimination are inadequate." One might cite, for example, *U.S.* v. *Lynd,* Forest County, Mississippi, instituted in 1960, which has yet to have a final effective decree allowing Negroes to freely register to vote.)

f. Meet with the leaders of the Mississippi civil rights project and recommend that President Johnson meet with them also.

4. Assign one person in your office to act as a liaison with COFO in the event that incidents similar to those which took place in Canton, Mississippi, this past week occur this summer. We would request that your office cooperate with the following procedure if and when incidents occur this summer.

a. The COFO office in Mississippi will phone the details of any incidents directly and immediately to the COFO office in Washington, D.C. COFO's legal advisers will determine under which statutes the Federal Government has the power to act in any given situation and will relate this information to your office.

b. With the attached legal memo to refer to, we would request your office to phone the Justice Department and urge that they take immediate action to bring relief to our volunteers and to resolve the situation.

c. The Justice Department will furnish you with a complete report. It has been the history of the Justice Department, in the majority of instances, to reply that they have insufficient information and/or power to act in a given situation. The COFO line to Mississippi should provide fast and accurate details on events in that State. We hope to point out to you, in the attached memo, that the Federal government has the power to act in Mississippi *before* any incidents occur; there is little doubt that the legal power exists under which the Justice Department may act in the event that Constitutional rights are violated.

d. If the Justice Department does not take swift and incisive action in the event of an incident in the State of Mississippi, COFO will request that your office make an additional inquiry upon receipt of the Justice Department report if it appears to be inadequate.

The Council of Federated Organizations sincerely hopes that it will not be necessary to use the above procedure. However, because of our serious concern for the safety of summer project volunteers and because of our apprehension at the visible mobilization of the State of Mississippi in response to the project, we strongly urge you to develop the mechanisms within your own office to respond to our appeal if it is necessary.

It cannot be stated too many times that our basic goal is to obtain Federal preventative action *before* any more names are added to the list of civil rights martyrs. It is to this that we hope you will direct your efforts at this time by urging the Justice Department to take the steps we have outlined.

MISSISSIPPI SUMMER PROJECT: RUNNING SUMMARY OF INCIDENTS

JUNE 16: *Philadelphia:* Mt. Zion Baptist Church burns to ground. Fire starts soon after Negro mass meeting adjourns. Three Negroes beaten by whites. Church was freedom-school site. *State-wide:* Negroes attempt to attend Democratic Party precinct conventions for the first time in this century. Results vary. Two Negroes, two whites elected in Jackson.

JUNE 17: *Vicksburg:* Summer volunteer arrested for driving while intoxicated. Not allowed phone call. Held overnight. Acquitted at trial next day.

JUNE 20: *Fayette:* Police, citizens order SNCC worker out of his house. He flees, but when car recovered two days later his camera, food, and personal documents are missing.

JUNE 21: *Brandon* (Rankin Co.) Molotov cocktail explodes in basement of Sweet Rest Church of Christ Holiness. Fire; minor damage.
McComb: Homes of two civil rights workers planning to house summer volunteers bombed. One damaged extensively. Seven dynamite sticks left on lawn of third home with no civil rights ties.
Meridian: Three civil rights workers missing after short trip to Philadelphia.

JUNE 22: *Clarksdale:* Four volunteers arrested on vagrancy charges while engaged in voter registration work. Held 3½ hours, released.
Brandon: Negro youth killed in hit-and-run accident.

JUNE 23: *Philadelphia:* Missing car found burned; no sign of three workers. Car was on list circulated state-wide by Canton White Citizens Council.
Jackson: Shots fired at home of Rev. R. L. T. Smith. White

man escapes on foot, reportedly picked up by a city truck. (Smith's home is under 24-hour guard.)

Moss Point: Knights of Pythias Hall fire-bombed. Arson attempt on side of building. Damage slight. Used for voter rallies.

Moss Point: Two summer volunteers picked up as they leave cafe, relax on private lawn. Taken by police at 85 m.p.h. without lights at night to Pascagoula jail. Held in "protective custody" overnight, then released.

Jackson: Civil rights worker held eight hours after receiving $5 change for a $20 bill.

Jackson: White car fires shot at Henderson's cafe. Negroes pursue. Three shots fired, hitting one Negro in head twice.

Clarksdale: Local pastor, a civil rights leader, arrested for reckless and drunk driving. He is a total abstainer.

State-wide: Negroes try to attend Democratic Party county conventions. Participation systematically discouraged.

Ruleville: Look, Time reporters covering voter rally at Williams chapel, chased out of town by car at speeds up to 85 m.p.h. Early next morning, nine Negro homes, cars hit by bottles thrown from similar car.

JUNE 24: *Meridan:* Threat: "You G. D. people are going to get bombed."

Hollandale: Police, mayor tell summer volunteer he can't live in Negro section of town and register voters.

Drew: Thirty volunteers, staff workers engaged in voter registration meet open hostility from whites. Weapons shown.

Canton: Civil rights car hit by bullet.

Collins: 40 M-1 rifles, 1,000 rounds of ammunition stolen from National Guard armory.

JUNE 25: *Ruleville:* Williams Chapel fire-bombed. Damage slight. Eight plastic bags with gasoline found later outside building.

Jackson: Two separate arrests of volunteers on minor traffic charges. Seven questioned in one case; charges dropped in other. (Law student presented his own case.)

Philadelphia: Southern newsman's car deliberately rammed by local citizen. Newsman gets two tickets.

Itta Bena: Two volunteers working with local Negro, handing out literature for voter registration rally, taken to gas station-bus stop by four white men who tell them: "If you speak in town tonight, you'll never leave here."

Greenville: Federal building demonstration. No harassment.

Durant: Civil rights worker's car stopped on highway for repairs. Driver charged with illegal parking. $60 bond paid.

JUNE 26: *Hattiesburg:* Hate literature from whites: "Beware, good Negro citizens. When we come to get the agitators, stay away."

Columbus: Seven voter registration workers arrested for distributing literature without a city permit. Bond: $400 each.

Itta Bena: FBI arrests three local residents for June 25 incident. Two are released on $2,000 bail, one on $1,000.

Clinton: Church of Holy Ghost arson. Kerosene spilled on floor, lit after local white pastor speaks to Negro Bible class. (Fifth fire-bombing in 10 days.)

Holmes County: Two staffers detained for illegal parking, no Mississippi permit. One arrested. Bond $60.

Holly Springs: Harassment: beer cans tossed at volunteers, car tires slashed.

Greenwood: Freedom House call: "You'd better not go to sleep or you won't get up."

Greenwood: Voter registration worker picked up by police, released after questioning.

Jackson: CORE field secretary beaten at Hinds County jail while a federal prisoner. Third beating of a civil rights worker at same jail in two months, second of federal prisoner.

Canton: Two volunteers picked up by police, told all out-of-town visitors must register with them. Registered, released.

Belzoni: Three arrested for disturbing the peace. Two released without charges, third held on $100 bond.

JUNE 27: *Batesville:* Local person helping voter registration gets obvious harassment ticket for illegal parking outside courthouse.

Vicksburg: Threatening call: "We're going to get you."

Philadelphia: Local Negro contact has bottle thrown through window of home. Threatening note attached.

Greenwood: Several phone harassments; bomb threat.

Doddsville: Highway Patrol kills 34-year-old Negro with history of mental illness. Local deputy who knew Negro with patrolman. Mother asks to see body. Police reply: "Get that hollering woman away." Ruled "justifiable homicide" in 17 hours.

Jackson: Two phone threats: "We're going to kill you white SOBs."

JUNE 28:   *Jackson:* Civil rights worker held 8½ hours without charges; stopped for no reason while driving near COFO office. (Mississippi law permits holding for 72 hours "for investigation.")

Vicksburg: High-school girl tells friends COFO "going to get it."

Canton: Threatening calls throughout the night.

Ruleville: Mayor tells visiting white Methodist chaplain he cannot attend white Methodist services: "You came here to live with Negroes, so you can go to church with them, too." He does, with three volunteers.

Batesville: Report local Negro man beaten, missing.

Jackson: "Hospitality Month" in Mississippi: white volunteer kicked over from behind, slugged on arrival from Oxford at local train station.

JUNE 29:   *Hattiesburg:* Two cars owned by volunteers shot by four whites in pickup truck at 1:00 A.M. No injuries, $100 damage to each car. Three witnesses. (Owners were sleeping two blocks away.)

Columbus: Six carloads of whites drive up on lawn of Freedom House. Five flee before police arrive. Police question, release two men in sixth car.

Hattiesburg: Civil rights worker charged with reckless driving, failure to give proper signal. Held overnight, paid fine.

Biloxi: Volunteers in White Community Program turned away from hotel.

Hattiesburg: Phone rings. Volunteer hears tape recording of last 20 seconds of his previous conversation. Someone goofed!

Columbus: Restaurants serving volunteers threatened.

JUNE 30:   *Vicksburg:* Negro woman threatened for registering to vote.

Ruleville: Man loses job for housing white volunteers.

Jackson: Car circles office with gun, threatens teen-ager: "Want to shoot some pool, nigger?"

Jackson: Volunteer charged with reckless driving. Fine $34. (He moved from one traffic lane to another in integrated car.)

Holly Springs: White teen-agers scream profanities, throw rocks at office from passing car.

Hattiesburg: Whites in pickup truck with guns visible drive past office several times. FBI checks June 29 car shooting.

Holly Springs: SNCC staff worker jumped by local white who threatens to shoot both him and his office with 12-gauge shotgun.

Harmony: Freedom-school teachers arrive. School superintendent announces first Negro summer school in memory of local residents.

Tchula: Two carloads of highway patrolmen start excessively close watch on volunteer. Ended 48 hours later.

Oakland: Police find body of white man, badly mangled by hit-run driver, no identification at all. (Later found no civil rights tie.)

Greenville: Report that on June 19 a Negro porter at Greenville General Hospital was beaten by policeman with billy club there. Porter charged with resisting arrest and disturbing the peace.

JULY 1: *Holly Springs:* Justice of Peace (and Mayor) has local farmer arrested on assault and battery charges in June 30 incident. Bail set at $1,000.

Clarksdale: Pickup truck tries to run down SNCC worker and volunteer. License plates hidden.

Gulfport: Police threaten to hurt children of lady housing civil rights workers. Workers plan to move elsewhere.

JULY 2: *Harmony:* Sheriff, school superintendent tell community abandoned buildings may not be used for freedom school. Cross burned, tacks strewn in Negro community.

Vicksburg: Whites chase, shoot at Negro on motorcycle.

Hattiesburg: Two voter registration canvassers followed and questioned by men describing themselves as state officials.

Hattiesburg: School superintendent threatens all janitors who participate in civil rights activity. Ditto at Holiday Inn.

Hattiesburg: Local police stop Negro girl, five white boys en route home. Policeman curses, threatens arrest, slaps one boy.

Batesville: Panola County Sheriff Carl Hubbard detains several persons housing civil rights workers, spends most of night in courtyard where many workers are living.

Meridian: White teen-age girl throws bottle at civil rights group outside church, cuts leg of local Negro girl.

Canton: Local police turn on sirens, play music on loudspeaker near COFO office, fail to answer phone calls.

Gulfport: Two voter registration workers threatened: "Things are fine around here; we don't want them to change." Man grabs volunteer's shirt: "I'm going to whip your ass." Workers run.

JULY 3: *Meridian:* Volunteer's car goes through *green* light, hits local station wagon. Volunteer charged with running light, reckless driving. Bond $122.

So So: The "Greasy Spoon," a Negro grocery and teen spot, is bombed. Damage minor. Sheriff's deputy says there is no civil rights motive for the bombing, calls it "senseless."

Greenwood: Three visiting Congressmen witness voter registration, call it discriminatory.

Toogaloo: En route to Canton, four civil rights girls are chased by two cars driven by whites. They decide to stop here (in Jackson) for safety.

Jackson: Lots of phone harassment. WATS line goes dead, then rings—a technical impossibility.

Columbus: Police impound volunteer's car—claim it's stolen because transfer papers are not notarized.

Itta Bena: Police question two volunteers about robbery, say they were only ones in vicinity. No charges filed.

Greenwood: Two tagless cars drive continually past office.

Moss Point: Police, white citizens pressure Negro cafe owners not to serve civil rights workers. Policeman says white racist in town has gun on his person, grenade in a satchel.

Harmony: Sheriff, superintendent post "no trespassing" sign at abandoned school. Local citizens move books, other materials to Negro church. Police flash lights on homes.

JULY 4: *Laurel:* Police barely prevent large racial clash after two Negroes, two whites injured in attempt to integrate drive-in. Police fail to respond to calls for help from injured Negroes.

Clarksdale: Local manager says Negroes going to courthouse will be discharged: "I have a large contract with the head of the White Citizens Council, and I'm not going to lose thousands of dollars for one of you."

Batesville: Volunteer, local worker chased 30 miles by car.

JULY 5: *Greenville:* Local citizens test several restaurants. The eating places are closed either before or after testing.

Ruleville: Local segregationist visits COFO office, has a very friendly argument with civil rights workers. Police ask him to leave. He refuses. Charged with disorderly conduct. Fined.

Laurel: Civil rights worker who witnessed and reported the

July 4 incident is arrested. Police say he has 4-6 months left to serve on previous sentence.

Columbus: St. Louis (Mo.) Negro beaten by whites who mistake him for a "Freedom Rider." En route to a funeral, he's fined $75.

Laurel: Two volunteers questioned by police who stop their integrated car as it leaves Sunday school. Charges dropped against driver, but passenger arrested on vagrancy charge. She left pocketbook in car at police station, gets 10 days suspended sentence.

Jackson: NAACP integrates local hotels without major incident. Individuals integrate many other places on their own.

Jackson: Local woman's leg cut by bottle thrown at COFO office.

JULY 6: *Jackson:* Voter registration group harassed by police who say "One man, one vote" sticker has been found on city car. They threaten arrest for trespassing if anyone will sign charge.

Jackson: McCraven-Hill Missionary Baptist Church damaged by kerosene fire. Church has no ties to civil rights movement.

Clarksdale: Station wagon plays "chicken" with civil rights workers going home.

Jackson: Negro youth slugged by white who flees in truck.

Moss Point: Negro woman shot twice at voter rally, singing "We Shall Overcome." Three Negroes arrested when they pursue car from which they believe shots were fired. White car not checked.

Greenwood: Harassment call: "I just shot one of your workers . . ."

Itta Bena: Local police, sheriff hold civil rights worker incommunicado, trigger wide search by federal authorities, SNCC.

Hattiesburg: Owner's wife pulls pistol as 15-25 youngsters try to integrate drive-in. Youngsters run, are arrested and put in drunk tank by police. Three are roughed up.

Raleigh: Methodist and Baptist churches burned to ground.

JULY 7: *Shaw:* Stores refuse to cash volunteer's traveler's check.

Shaw: Police ask all volunteers to register. Only four do not.

Clarksdale: Sheriff asks white minister driving integrated car: "Are you married to them niggers? You ain't no minister; you're a SOB troublemaker . . . I'm gonna stay on your back until I get you."

Vicksburg: White boys throw bottle, break windshield of car waiting to pick up freedom-school student.

Greenwood: Six young students picketing jailhouse ("Stop Police Brutality," "One Man, One Vote") arrested. So are three others with them.

JULY 8: *McComb:* SNCC Freedom House bombed; two injured. Despite numerous requests by Congressmen, attorneys, pastors (and a personal visit with the mayor—who also heads the White Citizens Council), no local police were seen in the area prior to the bombing. 15 FBI agents, several packing pistols, show up during day. 150 local citizens attend rally same night.

Hattiesburg: Rev. Robert Beech of National Council of Churches arrested on false pretense charge after allegedly overdrawing his bank account $70. Bail set at $2,000.

Ruleville: Volunteer bodily ejected from county circuit clerk's office for accompanying local woman to voter registration.

Columbus: Three volunteers arrested on trespass charges after stopping at a gas station for a soft drink. Friendly conversation there until attendant says, "You boys should be on the road." They leave immediately. He files charges. Bail $500 to $1,000 each.

Clarksdale: Bomb threat.

Hattiesburg: Bottle thrown at picnic by passing car. No plates.

Holly Springs: Civil rights worker arrested. Reckless driving. $250.

Clarksdale: Police chief in Lafayette tells Negro cafes not to serve volunteers.

Vicksburg: Bomb threat.

JULY 9: *Greenwood:* Local insurance salesman slugs volunteer during voter canvas. Follows in car and rebeats.

Yazoo City: Folk singer arrested for reckless driving. Quick fine.

Clarksdale: Volunteer arrested for taking pictures in courtroom. Photos taken in hall after police chief sprayed room deodorant on two girls.

Gulfport: Four arrested for refusing to leave local people and cross street on police orders as they near courthouse. Held on $500 bond for violating anti-picketing law.

Vicksburg: Freedom-school students stoned en route to class.

Moss Point: Five Negroes fired from jobs for attending mass rally. Woman fired from work for housing two volunteers.

Clarksdale: Police chief visits office when another white man comes to turn off electricity.

Gulfport: Police urge volunteer to leave for his own protection or face charges of inciting to riot.

JULY 10: *Clarksdale:* Chairs removed from libraries. NAACP youths refused service at two restaurants.

Hattiesburg: Rabbi, two volunteers, two local teen-agers attacked by two men as they walked in uninhabited area. Assailants escape after attacking three men. On emerging from hospital, rabbi says Jews in Mississippi should "stand up for decency and freedom with all risks involved" or leave the state.

Vicksburg: Four civil rights workers chased by two cars, one of which has a man with revolver.

Jackson: J. Edgar Hoover opens Jackson FBI office, first state-wide center since 1946. Cites efficiency as reason. Says 153 agents now in state. Says FBI can give civil rights workers "no protection" (beyond reports based on complaints and directions for investigation from civil rights division of Justice Department).

Greenwood: SNCC staff member arrested on public profanity charge. Policeman overheard him say, "We've got to get some damn organization in our office." Bail: $15.

Moss Point: Howard Kirschenbaum, only volunteer to leave the MSP because of arrests and harassment, returns with $2,000 in gifts from New York.

JULY 11: *Shaw:* Local Negro offered $400 by five whites to bomb SNCC Freedom House, $40 for list of residents' home addresses.

Laurel: Four young Negroes injured during and after attempts to integrate Kress' lunch counter, where Negroes had eaten earlier.

Canton: Small fire bomb thrown at Freedom House lawn.

Vicksburg: Amateur bomb thrown through window of Negro cafe.

Canton: Volunteer arrested on traffic charges while delivering freedom-school books.

Browning: Pleasant Plan Missionary Baptist Church burns to ground. Whites sought to buy it, Negroes would not sell.

Laurel: Local NAACP president received two death threats both for July 19.

Holly Springs: Integrated staff picnic broken up by police.

Clarksdale: NAACP member testing barbershop driven out at gunpoint.

Harmony: Police visit local Negroes who have had contact with COFO volunteers, staff, forcing them to sign peace bonds. Police come armed with a warrant to search for liquor.

Greenwood: Local Negro woman hit in chest by white man, while accompanied by two volunteers. No police cooperation in getting assailants.

JULY 12: *Canton:* Two summer volunteers, visitor refused admission to First Methodist Church. Volunteers had been welcomed a week earlier.

Greenwood: Bomb threat.

Jackson: Half-body found in Mississippi identified as Charles Moore, former Alcorn A&M student. Second half-body found in river. (In mid-April, more than 700 students, all Negroes, were summarily dismissed from Alcorn after a nonviolent general grievance demonstration.)

Jackson: White teen-agers slash Negro woman's tires, spit in face of volunteer coed after integrated group eats at drive-in.

Jackson: Elderly man attacks Negro woman at Greyhound coffee shop. She is treated for cut head, hand, then charged with disturbing the peace. Out on $50 bond. Assailant escapes.

Biloxi: Volunteer picked up while canvassing, informed of complaints by local residents, released.

Itta Bena: Local woman attacked by two white boys while baby-sitting. Both her arms cut.

Natchez: Jerusalem Baptist and Bethel Methodist Churches burned to ground. Home of Negro contractor in Natchez fire-bombed.

JULY 13: *Clarksdale:* Negro volunteer chased out of white laundromat, picked up by police for failure to signal turn, taken to jail and beaten. Sheriff says: "You're a nigger and you're going to stay a nigger." Charged with resisting arrest, out on $64 bond.

Clarksdale: Chief voter registrar closes courthouse for next few days. Stated reason: court in session, no time for registration.

Clarksdale: Owner of electric company has project leader pointed out to him, then fingers knife in his presence.

JULY 14: *Canton:* Man threatened with job loss if youngster continues in freedom school. Youngster stays.

Drew: Police chief, local citizens protest Albuquerque *Journal* article based on volunteer's letter home. Volunteer says letter was edited.

Hattiesburg: State Sovereignty Commission visits office.

Vicksburg: Milkman's assistant loses job because he attends the freedom school.

Vicksburg: SNCC team confirms burning of Bovina Community Center July 7.

Drew: Police pick up James Dann for distributing literature without permit. Later, seven people arrested for distributing literature without a permit and blocking the sidewalk. $100-$200 bond.

Holly Springs: Oxford police chief told civil rights worker he should not come back to town. Chief threatened to hit Negro over head, especially if he did not speak to others with proper respect. (No major changes.)

Laurel: Gas bomb thrown at local Negro's home.

Batesville: Movie which had upstairs for Negroes now offers admission only to whites.

Canton: Three white men pursue five civil rights workers in car en route home.

JULY 15: *Biloxi:* Two arrested in traffic harassment case.

Clarksdale: Another traffic arrest: improper turn.

McComb: Freedom school enrolls 35 here.

Drew: 25 arrested for willfully and unlawfully using the sidewalks and the streets during voter registration rally. Citizens Council met at 9 A.M.

Gulfport: Civil rights worker arrested for putting posters on a telephone pole. City ordinance. Bond $50.

JULY 16: *Canton:* Volunteers report they were beaten by police last night following arrest with truck carrying freedom registration supplies, books, miscellany. Bond set at $150 each.

Greenwood: Freedom Day—111 arrests, including 13 juveniles. Group includes 98 adults, of whom 9 were SNCC staff and 13 volunteers.

Vicksburg: White man comes to door of home where volunteer staying. Has pistol showing in holster. Asks to see owner of house. At another home housing workers, car circles block 10-15 minutes.

Greenwood: Silas McGhee, local resident, picked up by three whites, forced to enter cab of their pickup truck at gunpoint, then beaten with pipe and plank. Incident occurs just after he leaves FBI office. He returns there; agents take him to hospital. He has been active in attempts to integrate theater.

Greenville: Freedom Day: 101 people took test, 100 more came too late. No arrests.

Hattiesburg: Two voter canvassers stopped by police.

Hattiesburg: Police question those who complain about inadequate protection for those going to freedom school, may charge them with threatening mayor.

Indianola: Of those arrested in Drew July 15, 10 women are being held at county jail and 15 men at county farm near here. Superintendent of farm tells lawyer he can't guarantee safety of those at the farm. FBI advised.

Laurel: Volunteer canvassing accosted by two white boys who accuse him of not being from Mississippi, knock materials from hand and run.

Cleveland: Freedom Day: 25 to 30 picket without incident. About 20 of 25 from Shaw group register. More than 50 from other communities came, of whom 30 registered. Process slow but polite. Ten regular and 45 auxiliary police allow only those registering or picketing on courthouse grounds.

JULY 17: *McComb:* Mount Zion Hill Baptist Church in Pike County bombed or burned to ground. Pastor of this church had let project use his McComb Church, St. Mary's.

Philadelphia: Columbia law student and a writer beaten with chain by two middle-aged white men in early afternoon.

Greenwood: 15 staff and volunteers on hunger strike until let out of jail after being brought in during massive freedom-day arrests.

Greenwood: Greenwood and Drew mass arrest cases have been removed to federal court and bonds reduced to $200 out of state, $100 for residents.

Yazoo: Three Negro men, late teens or early twenties, arrested for looking at a white girl.

Greenwood: White summer volunteer harassed by three white men while putting up voter registration poster.

JULY 18: *Lauderdale:* Two summer volunteers arrested for willful trespass while discussing voter registration on front porch of two Negro women; no complaint made by women.

Hattiesburg: Kilmer Estus Keyes, white, of Collins, Mississippi, turned self in to local police in connection with beating of rabbi and two workers last week. Charged with assault; out on $2,500 property bond. (Eventually fined $500 and given 90-day suspended sentence.)

Batesville: 8 people detained one and one-half hours by sheriff who was "trying to see if there is a state ordinance against the passing out of leaflets." Statute not found; released into crowd of whites standing about. Local volunteer hit hard in jaw by white man.

Starkville: Police chief followed two volunteers to various stops in Negro cafes, delivered lengthy "anti-agitator" speech directed at local Negroes talking to volunteers. Lengthy verbal abuse by police chief, directed to the voter registration workers.

JULY 19:   *Columbus:* Two voter registration workers detained in jail in Aberdeen for four hours after being picked up as suspicious strangers and refusing to be driven out of town and left on highway by police.

Greenwood: Mass arrest victims still at city jail and county farm. No visiting privileges at farm—among those there is a 78-year-old man who is in need of medicine which no one has been able to bring to him.

Oxford: An Ole Miss student who has contacts at Rust College (Negro) had his seat covers slashed while car parked outside faculty home, threatening note left. He has had much harassment before, but cannot get administration to act.

Biloxi: Voter registration worker chased, threatened by two men in pickup truck.

Biloxi: White Community Project worker arrested for trespass in white restaurant where he had worked for one day until owner discovered he was a civil rights worker. Owner turned him into police when he went back to restaurant.

Batesville: Town marshals threatened volunteers at mass meeting in Crowder (13–15 miles away). Said "Lucky I have no gun in here . . . wish I didn't have my badge on . . ."

JULY 20:   *Greenville:* Nine shots fired at car workers went to mass meeting in. Two workers threatened that white mob would form at place where they were staying.

Hattiesburg: White volunteer beaten downtown as left bank with two other freedom-school teachers. Assailant hit from behind. No words exchanged. Volunteers and attacker charged with assault.

Ruleville: Two workers ordered out of cafe. Doors locked with people inside.

Greenwood: Both barrels of shotgun fired at worker's car.

Greenwood: Trial of mass arrest victims held despite filing of petition to remove case to federal courts. Defendants remained mute on basis of violation of Constitutional rights. Convicted of violation of picket law—30 days, $100 fine.

Clarksdale: Three workers (girls) of newly formed Clarksdale Youth Action Group arrested for trespass outside local cafe in Negro section.

McComb: SNCC field secretary hit on side of head by white man as both stopped their cars for red light at intersection of two state roads and federal highway.

JULY 21: *Lexington:* Volunteer hit in face and body with fists by white man while waiting outside courthouse to take part in voter registration campaign.

Laurel: Rights workers believe the second ouster of summer project workers from a rented office here this summer is due to "intimidation" of local Negro realtors by white persons opposed to the project.

Clarksdale: Volunteer arrested for running red light, paid fine.

Holly Springs: $200 bond levied on volunteer for failure to have a car inspection sticker.

McComb: Freedom-school enrollment reaches 75 in this "hard-core" area.

Greenwood: Windows of three Negro cafes broken. Windows of volunteer's car also broken.

Natchez: Within 45 minutes after 3 SNCC workers arrived in this area to set up a summer project office, one is arrested for failure to stop at stop sign. Police chief tells him police knew of their movements "every minute of the day." Continual following by police.

Doodleville: Three Negro youths in company of white volunteer picked up and held for "investigation" at Club 400 by police. Volunteer later arrested for "improper tags." Negro youths released on bond; amount not known.

Clarksdale: Two precinct meetings of the Mississippi Freedom Democratic Party attracted 160 persons here.

JULY 22: *Jackson:* Volunteer beaten with billy clubs by two whites at a major downtown intersection. Police officer who returned the beaten volunteer and two colleagues to the COFO office indicated that a complaint had been filled out and a pickup call had been issued for any cars matching the assailants'!

McComb: Mt. Vernon Missionary Baptist Church, organized more than 80 years ago, found burned. FBI, sheriff, and police uncovered no clues. Fire officially listed as "of undetermined origin." Neither the pastor nor his church is in any way affiliated with the civil rights movement.

Tchula: Driver of car carrying man who attacked volunteer here yesterday reportedly arrested.

Natchez: Local Negro taken into police custody today while walking along street with two SNCC field secretaries.

Greenville: Local Negro arrested for forgery while passing out voter registration leaflets with several other local citizens. After being questioned about civil rights activity here, released for lack of evidence on forgery charge.

Natchez: Mayor tells SNCC field secretary that most of the nationally publicized shipment of arms to white terrorist groups in this area has been done in Adams Co., as opposed to the city. Police continue to follow the SNCC workers "every minute."

JULY 23: *Tchula:* SNCC staff member followed out of Jackson, arrested by police on speeding charge.

Canton: White volunteer and Negro CORE staff member harassed by a group of white men while canvassing for voter registration. CORE staffer struck five times with wooden cane by one of the whites. The workers were on porch of some potential Negro registrants when white drove up.

Moss Pt.: Volunteer arrested today for improper turning, released on $40 bond.

Durant: Volunteer assailed today while canvassing for voter registration. Two white men approached him and asked what it would take to get him out of town; volunteer replied he was not quite ready to leave. After approximately 10 minutes of talk, one man began to punch him, then left after several minutes of blows.

Granada: SNCC staff member arrested for speeding.

Moss Pt.: At mass meeting last night, $33 was collected for a woman who lost her job two weeks ago for housing COFO volunteers. Several people pledge to give 50¢ a week indefinitely to help pay hospital expenses of local resident who received back and side wounds when shots were fired into voter registration mass meeting July 6.

Shaw: Local white woman tells local Negro woman that she

plans to watch mail and those Negroes who get letters from "freedom riders" (presumably summer project volunteers) would "get hell after they leave." Mail is picked up at a post-office box.

Jackson: Surprise—police court acquits three local youths on public drunk charges. Trio were arrested July 21 in Club 400 at Doodleville.

Harmony: Local residents plan to start construction of a wooden frame building for use as a permanent community center to be staffed by project volunteers.

Meridian: Hearing continued to July 30 for omnibus suit filed against Ku Klux Klan, Sheriff Rainey, Deputy Sheriff Price, the White Citizens Council, and others in attempt to enjoin acts of violence on the part of defendants and the classes of officials and citizens they represent. This hearing is the first of its kind in Mississippi.

JULY 24:   *Holly Springs:* Voter registration worker arrested for "disturbing the public peace" at a Holly Springs Freedom Day is being held on $500 bond. Volunteer charged with "using profanity in front of more than two people" after using two-way radio to inform office of profanities local policeman told potential Negro registrants on courthouse steps. Police insisted that the 40–50 potential registrants walk to the courthouse steps one by one, eight feet apart, and have a police escort from steps to registrar's office. Approximately 55 helmeted highway patrolmen and 35 helmeted local police were stationed at the courthouse for Freedom Day. Their presence in such numbers prompted cancellation of planned integrated picketing of the courthouse.

McComb: Amite County's Rose Hill Church reported burned last night. Owner of a local Negro club near Freedom House arrested and beaten. Officer tells owner, "Now that you've got white folks in here, you're getting uppity."

Ruleville: A Negro woman ordered off the bus and handled roughly by driver when she sat down next to white man. All but two passengers got off.

Ruleville: Rabbi and summer volunteer are "forcibly ejected" from office of Drew City attorney, where they had gone to attend a meeting of the parents of children detained and then released July 15.

Jackson, Meridian: FDP holds precinct meetings.

JULY 25:   *Greenwood:* Ten to 15 workers handing out freedom Registration forms prompt at least three incidents: 1) SNCC worker Eli Zeretsky approached by three whites who took his clipboard from him and tore up forms. Police stood by, refused to act unless Zeretsky knew assailants' names and filed complaint with a judge. 2) White volunteer Adam Kline was jumped from behind and hit on head; police refused aid. 3) Volunteer William Hodes, white, threatened by local whites in presence of police, who refused to make arrest and refused to give name of citizen involved so that complaint could be filed.

Greenwood: Shot fired at home of Silas McGhee, the young man whose beating in local movie theater prompted first arrests under the 1964 Civil Rights Act.

Canton: First FDP county convention adopted resolution of loyalty to principles of National Democratic Party for strong and enforceable civil rights plank in platform. Approximately 300 people attend, of whom 102 were voting delegates elected by precincts.

Hattiesburg: Home of two local FDP leaders bombed between 1 and 4 A.M. Broken whisky bottle found indicated "molotov cocktail" type of device. Used on home of Mr. and Mrs. Boyd, FDP temporary chairman and secretary.

Ruleville: Rock smashed windshield of local Negro housing civil rights workers; car parked in his yard.

Drew: Affidavit received from parent of one of Negro children arrested after July 15 rally: mayor and city attorney called meeting of parents, told them defense would not be provided unless children signed statement disavowing association with "the Communists coming into town." According to affidavit, city attorney called Congressman Don Edwards (D.-Cal.) a Communist and said Edwards has been "Castro's secretary." Summer volunteer and rabbi were forcibly ejected from room when they tried to attend the meeting yesterday.

Clarksdale: Bottle thrown through office window last night.

JULY 26: *McComb:* Two bombs were thrown at the home of a local civil rights leader. As the first bomb was thrown, leader's wife fired at car with shotgun. When car's lights were seen approaching again, her husband ran outside but was knocked to ground by second explosion before he had time to fire. About 50 people attended a voter registration meeting at this home today.

Batesville: Tear-gas bomb explodes behind home in which five civil rights workers are living, forcing occupants to leave. Sheriff and deputy arrived approximately 30 minutes later, found grenade still hot, handled it a good deal so that FBI found it covered with police fingerprints.

Mileston: SNCC car burned outside home housing volunteers.

Mileston: Volunteer approached in store by two whites who ask where he lived. He pointed to community center. They go to their car, take a pistol each from trunk, put them in their belts, come back and tell volunteer they would "find out what was going on" when they "came back."

Canton: Church Council of Canton voted in June to keep all summer civil rights workers from attending services. One Presbyterian church took exception and admitted volunteers until today, when two white volunteers were turned away by three white men who told them they had "caused too much dissension in church." At a Methodist Church, four white volunteers were refused attendance for third week in row. As they left church, a group assembled around their car, shoved them into the car, and slammed the door with such force the window cracked. Their car was followed to its destination by pickup truck.

Greenwood: Silas McGhee, the young man whose July 16 beating led to first arrests under civil rights act, and his brother Jake are mobbed by 150–200 whites as they leave theater after they walked from theater to car. Jake hit repeatedly by whites. Both receive cuts and abrasions of face and shoulders and glass in eyes when a Coke bottle is thrown through car window. Both treated at LeFlore Co. Hospital, then trapped there with SNCC staff members until 1 A.M. as cars of armed whites blocked all roads leading out of hospital. FBI, local police, highway patrol, and sheriff refuse protection out of hospital until 1 A.M. After more than three hours of waiting behind locked doors, the sheriff followed SNCC staff and McGhee car to their destinations.

JULY 27: *Jackson:* Aaron Henry, Ed King, Mrs. Victoria Gray replied publicly to Sen. Douglas' (D.–Ill.) "conciliatory suggestion" that no Mississippians be seated at convention or the delegation be half Dixiecrat, half Democratic: "We are dubious of value of delegation that is half slave, half free."

Canton: On arrival at bus station, five NCC ministers are threatened by seven local whites. When ministers try to leave station in car with two local Negro housewives, their car is trapped in narrow, one-way alley for two hours. One local white stops his car in front of them, the other stops in rear. Separate crowds of 100 whites, 50 Negroes gather. Local Negro alerts CORE staff, who send pickup truck to scene and persuade local sheriff to let ministers drive out of alley. *Greenwood:* Brick thrown through window of Negro barbershop in neighborhood where freedom registration was held.

McComb: White volunteer arrested for "failure to yield the right of way" as he drives a group of local Negro children for voter registration canvassing and leaflet distribution for an FDP precinct meeting. Fined $16.50.

Mayersville: Precinct meeting held in Moon Lake Baptist Church. Owner of plantation across street threatened to burn the church if any more civil rights meetings were held there. (2,399 Negroes here out of total population of 3,576.)

Batesville and Holly Springs: Precinct and county meetings. *Gulfport:* Precinct meetings.

JULY 28: *Itta Bena:* Voter registration house broken into during night. Front porch supports broken, leaving badly sagging roof. Door half torn off, all windows broken. Posters urging citizens to vote for Fannie Lou Hamer in Democratic primary ripped off. Volunteers have received several threatening phone calls about the house and voter registration activities there.

Holly Springs: Police cars surrounding school where FDP precinct meeting was being held are themselves surrounded by approximately 200 Negro FDP participants singing freedom songs. Participants gathered around cars as they left school late at night. Police record license of every car at school, stop about 70 drivers to check licenses, arrest five on various traffic charges. School superintendent said he would burn or tear down school if meeting were held there.

Vicksburg: Precinct meetings—FDP.

Clarksdale: FDP county meeting.

JULY 29: *Hollandale:* A Negro SNCC staff member chased from a traditionally white barbershop by a razor-wielding barber: "If you don't get out of here, I'll kill you."

Ruleville: A plantation worker fired for being a freedom registrant and attending two voter registration rallies. Plantation renter tells Negro: "Get off the place and don't come back. You're messed up in the voter registration and I don't want to have anything to do with you." (This type of incident occurs often; it is seldom reported in detail.)

Greenville: FDP precinct meetings.

Gulfport: County meeting—FDP.

JULY 30:   *Meridian:* The Mount Moriah Baptist Church, a Negro church located in a completely white neighborhood, burned to ground last night. Although many homes are located close to the site, the fire department was not notified until too late to halt the fire.

Gulfport: Local Negro volunteer forced into car at gunpoint last night, blindfolded, and taken into a room at a location he guessed to be Biloxi. Five men question him at length about COFO activities. They offer to pay him well for information about people and organizations who contact COFO. He was not injured or molested, except for one man repeatedly poking him with a gun. FBI investigating.

Drew: Negro SNCC volunteer and Ruleville Negro volunteer arrested in Drew for distributing leaflets for FDP on public property without permit. Total bond for two: $600.

Meridian: County meeting.

Laurel: Precinct and county meetings.

JULY 31:   *Brandon:* Pleasant Grove Missionary Baptist Church burned to ground last night. Fire department came to scene, left before fire put out, stating they had "been called too late." A butane tank was burned next to church. FBI investigating.

Carthage: Rev. Edward K. Heininger, NCC volunteer, and John Polacheck, summer volunteer, brutally beaten in office of Dr. Thaggard, Sr., in Madden today. Polacheck had gone to clinic yesterday for medical treatment, but left when he was told to go to Negro waiting room (he is white). He came back today with minister, and both were met in waiting room by doctor who began berating Heininger for his civil rights work. While they were talking, Heininger was hit from behind. Polacheck estimates that between 5 and 10 men beat them for approximately 5 minutes. Heininger reported that the doctor pushed him from the front into the punches of his assailants. Heininger was knocked unconscious, suffered severe injury to the left eye with possible internal injury to the eye, severe lacerations of scalp and face, contusions on back of neck, bad cut on left ear, and swelling of mouth and lips with possible injury to gums. Polacheck got to their car parked outside clinic and pulled in the minister, who was on his back outside the car. One of several whites standing around car grabbed keys. A deputy sheriff arrived, handcuffed Heininger and Polacheck and jailed them for disturbing peace: the doctor had reported they had used profanity. They were released on cash bond of $100 each after being brought to station in a non-officially marked pickup truck and car. Trial set for Aug. 27.

Meridian: White summer volunteer arrested for reckless driving and speeding. He was not informed of charges until after being held at police station under arrest. At station, he was asked whether he was "sure" what his race is, and was hit on hand when reached for ticket to see what charges were being placed against him.

Greenwood: Silas McGhee and a summer volunteer arrested for driving with improper vehicle license. Both cars had temporary 7-day Tennessee license tags. Negro SNCC worker reported the arrests to Greenwood office over car radio, then was arrested for resisting arrest. Total bond: $200.

Batesville: Three shots fired late last night past Negro home where five volunteers stay. July 26 the same home was tear-gas-bombed. A local white reportedly has threatened to kill the homeowner if he does not oust the volunteers.

Shaw: Three white volunteers made to leave Negro high-school cafeteria where they had been invited to a fund-raising supper. They were warmly received by students and supervising teacher, but were told by principal they must first secure permission of superintendent to enter school. One volunteer called this an "excellent demonstration of the fact that not only Negroes but whites also are not free in Mississippi."

Ruleville: Precinct meetings.

AUG. 1: *Holly Springs:* Wayne Yancy, 21-year-old volunteer from Chicago, killed in head-on collision here today. He was passenger in car driven by SNCC worker Charles Scales. Both are Negro. Highway patrol claimed Scales passed another car near hill crest, crossed yellow line, hit oncoming car. He was charged with manslaughter, hospitalized with injuries. SNCC staffer and summer volunteer nurse who tried to visit him were bodily thrown out of hospital in Memphis, Tenn.

Greenwood: Two local Negro volunteers arrested for disorderly conduct in front of store belonging to police officer Henderson, who dragged a pregnant Negro woman on pavement during Freedom Day demonstration. At police station, officers twisted one volunteer's arms behind him, kicked him, shoved his head three times against a concrete wall, hit him in mouth with stick, shoved and kicked him into cell, kicked him 7 more times after he fell to floor—and then refused him a doctor. Bail originally set at $50 each. White volunteer arrested same night on Negro business street. He was treated roughly by police during arrest. Officers pushed, kicked and stamped on his feet at station. FBI visited him within minutes of his confinement to ask if he had been beaten. Bond originally set at $100. When SNCC workers arrived to bail out all three, they discovered bond had been raised to $200 each. All three were bailed out.

Canton: Six civil rights workers—five white, one Negro—handing out freedom registration forms in downtown Canton jailed.

Vicksburg: FDP county meeting held at courthouse, first FDP meeting to be held in gov't. building.

Ruleville, Moss Pt., Jackson: County meetings.

McComb: In White America production at freedom school.

AUG. 2: *Greenwood:* Summer volunteer arrested on Justice of Peace warrant for assault with deadly weapon. Arrest apparently connected with breaking of window in store owned by police officer Henderson. Volunteer not near store, but had been calling jail all night to obtain information on other arrests. She was held for four hours and released on $1,000 bond.

Greewood: Annie Lee Turner, the pregnant 15-year-old Greenwood Negro whom officer Henderson reportedly dragged across the pavement during Freedom Day, arrested today while among group of local youth gathered in front of Henderson's store. Henderson came, ordered them to disperse, then reportedly dragged Mrs. Turner to waiting police car. She was held on $50 bond for disturbing the peace. A police blockade, with tear-gas equipment, was maintained at Henderson's store for 2 hours

Greenwood: Local resident arrested today while in his front yard. He reported that police car drove by, an officer made obscene gestures, the Negro laughed, the car backed up, and the Negro was arrested for profanity. Bond: $50.

Greenwood: Shortly after midnight four shots were fired at SNCC office from passing car.

Jackson: Report of local Negro man beaten very badly after being arrested for an accident.

Natchez: Passing car fires shots at Archie Curtis Funeral Home. Curtis was beaten last Feb. by hooded men on desolate road outside city. He was lured to spot by unidentified caller who told him a woman was dying of heart attack. Earlier, Curtis had participated in vote drive.

Canton: Shot fired from car passing approximately 50 feet from Freedom House.

Greenville: County meeting, FDP.

Hattiesburg: In White America tours freedom schools.

AUG.   3:   *Columbus:* Police arrest Negro volunteer for driving without a license and charge SNCC project director with allowing him to do so. Bail set at $300 and $100, respectively.

Batesville: SNCC project director Charles Weaver and summer volunteer Benjamin Graham arrested while trying to get names of 25 potential Negro voter registrants lined up outside courthourse. Weaver arrested while talking with another volunteer, who had been ordered out of courthouse by registrar. Graham arrested when he inquired what police were doing to Weaver. Both charged with interfering with officer. (The registrar is under federal injunction to facilitate registration.)

Greenwood: White volunteer arrested on John Doe warrant for assault and battery. Arrest stems from his participation in freedom registration drive. Elderly white man with limp came up while volunteer was distributing FDP registration forms Aug. 1 and stepped on his foot. He asked if volunteer wanted to "punch me in the face." Volunteer did not reply. Today he was picked up from across the street from Greenwood SNCC office. Two police, one with club, served warrant and grabbed him. He is held on $100 bond. (This is 8th arrest in Greenwood this weekend. At least three of previous arrests involved extensive police brutality at jail.)

Jackson: Local Negro volunteer arrested for vagrancy in front of drugstore near his home. He had an SNCC button on his shirt, reportedly did not have his draft card with him. He is held on $225 property bond.

Clarksdale: White Church of Christ minister and white summer volunteer refused admission to white Church of Christ. Church members felt they were "exploiting the church."

AUG.   4:   *Washington, D.C.:* FBI announces that two of three bodies found near Philadelphia last night have been identified as Andrew Goodman and Michael Schwerner. (Third subsequently identified as James Chaney.)

Shaw: Negro schools closed indefinitely following student boycott. This was triggered by Negro principal's request that three white volunteers leave cafeteria where they'd been invited for school fund-raising dinner last Friday. Students declared boycott of cafeteria, asked Student Union to assemble their grievances, then called a general boycott of the schools which was supported by 75 per cent of students. The Union called the boycott "because of the inadequate education we're getting." Its demands included up-to-date texts, a well-stocked library with Negro history materials, workshops and laboratories, foreign languages and other courses needed for college entrance. Principal relayed these requests to white school superintendent, then notified students schools would be closed. Heavily armed sheriff's deputies in helmets soon arrived on scene.

Moss Pt.: Approximately 62 persons arrested during voter registration meeting held on front lawn of SNCC office. Five were civil rights workers, rest local Negro citizens. The orderly meeting had been in process for 15 minutes when as assistant deputy sheriff gave the group 5 minutes to disperse. Group stayed. Within minutes 18 helmeted policemen with guns, bayonets, and clubs surrounded them; 15 minutes later a prison bus drove up. Ten police cars and two motorcycles—total of 40 officers—accumulated. All at meeting were put in bus and taken to jail. They were held for breach of the peace on $300 cash or $600 property bond each.

Cleveland: Fifty potential Negro registrants lined up at courthouse this morning, accompanied by 13 civil rights workers. Negroes were admitted one by one at 45-minute intervals. Leaflets were given them without incident. But when civil rights workers moved across street, all 13 arrested for distributing pamphlets among pedestrians. Charges based on anti-litter ordinance. Bond: $300 each.

Marks: LCDC attorney received head injuries, including large gash over one eye, when he was thrown against police car by city marshal. Attorney arrested for "obstructing officer in performance of duties" and held on $200 bail. He had gone to Marks to check detention of voter registration worker, when he saw marshal had stopped car filled with civil rights workers. He went over to investigate and the incident followed.

Jackson: After being refused service at small cafe, local volunteer chased by white man in pickup truck who fired two shots at him.

McComb: Pete Seeger held folk music workshops at Mc-Comb freedom school this morning following evening concert last night.

Hattiesburg: Seeger conducted folk music workshops in two freedom schools this afternoon. *In White America* at the freedom schools here.

Meridian: Community concert by Seeger in support of summer project. Four people refused service at supposedly integrated "Dairy Queen." Bus driver refused to pick up person wearing CORE shirt.

Cleveland: Car with 3 or 4 armed whites circled house of local volunteer between midnight and 1 A.M., parked briefly about 100 yards from her home.

AUG. 5: *McComb:* Two teen-age Negro boys, students at McComb freedom school, have received harassing phone calls from two white girls. Boys were arrested few days ago, and yesterday were sentenced to year in jail each under Mississippi's recent phone harassment law.

Natchez: Mt. Pilgrim Baptist church in Finwick reported burned last night.

Shaw: Thirty-five parents are organizing association to meet with school board and high-school faculty. In addition to students' demands which led to boycott and closing of schools, parents will take action against inadequate school lunch program, problems of split session and mechanics of desegregation in school system there.

Jackson: Community concert by Pete Seeger.

Gulfport: Free Southern Theater production of *In White America.*

AUG. 6: *Jackson:* Approximately 300 delegates from precinct meetings and county conventions attended first State Convention of the Mississippi Freedom Democratic Party. Alternates and observers bring total attendance to 1,000. Slate of 68 delegates and alternates was elected to represent Mississippi at National Democratic Convention. Hattiesburg housewife Mrs. Victoria Gray elected National Committeewoman, and Rev. Ed King, white chaplain of Mississippi's private, interracial Tougaloo College, elected National Committeeman, Dr. Aaron Henry, Clarksdale pharmacist and president of state NAACP, named permanent chairman of Convention and chairman of National Convention delegation. After Convention, newly elected State Executive Committee named Pass Christian resident Laurence Guyot chairman and Hattiesburg resident Mrs. Peggy J. Connor secretary of Party. Mrs. Fannie Lou Hamer, candidate for Congress in Mississippi's 2nd District, named vice-chairman of delegation and Mrs. Annie Devine of Canton, secretary. Address of keynoter Miss Ella J. Baker, currently coordinator of Washington office of FDP, received standing ovation and sparked spontaneous marching and freedom song in hall. Among resolutions adopted were statement of loyalty to National Democratic Party platform and candidates.

Gulfport: In White America, Free Southern Theater production, at freedom schools.

AUG. 7: *Meridian:* Over 200 persons gathered at four churches to take part in memorial procession for slain civil rights worker James Chaney. Walking in silence, two abreast, in somber dress, the mourners joined approximately 400 others for memorial service at First Union Church. Procession and service followed private burial of Chaney in Meridian. Immediately following service, Free Southern Theater production of *In White America* was presented at church in conjunction with freedom-school convention which began here tonight.

Jackson: A. Phillip Randolf, president of American Negro Labor Council and long-time head of Brotherhood of Sleeping Car Porters, addressed mass meeting of students and parents of Jackson freedom schools which opened this week.

Aberdeen: Integrated group refused service at Tom Restaurant and Elkin Theater.

Jackson: SNCC staffer Ivanhoe Donaldson arrested for improper driver's license. He was not in car at time of arrest. There were four integrated cars in front of house at which he was picked up. Bond: $50.

Jackson: White coed volunteer Mary Zeno and local Negro volunteer Rommie Drain chased by white man with pistol in belt as they canvassed for voter registration.

Jackson: Freedom-school coordinator Tom Wahman arrested and fined $17 for failing to yield proper lane.

AUG. 8: *Jackson:* N.Y. pathologist David M. Spain, M.D., reported today after post-mortem examination of body of James

Chaney, "In lay terminology—the jaw was shattered, the left shoulder and upper arm were reduced to a pulp, the right forearm was broken completely across at several points, and the skull bones were broken and pushed in toward the brain. Under the circumstances, these injuries could only be the result of an extremely severe beating with either a blunt instrument or chain. The other fractures of the skull and ribs were the result of bullet wounds. It is impossible to determine whether the deceased died from the beating before the bullet wounds were inflicted. In my extensive experience of 25 years as a pathologist and as a medical examiner, I have never witnessed bones so severely shattered, except in tremendously high-speed accidents, such as airplane crashes."

Hattiesburg: Two men, Clifton Archie Keys, 51, and his nephew Estus Keys, 31, were tried today for the July 10 beating of Rabbi Arthur Lelyveld, 51, of Cleveland, Ohio. Pair pleaded *nolo contendere*, waived arraignment, and paid fines of $500 each. They also received 90-day suspended sentences on condition of good behavior. The charge was changed by District Attorney James Finch from assault and battery with intent to maim to simple assault and battery.

Meridian: Approximately 150 outstanding students from throughout state gathered for freedom-school convention here today. Resolutions brought by student delegates from their community freedom schools were divided into four groups: Foreign Relations, Medical Care, Education, and Public Accommodations, and workshops held in each area. *Seeds of Freedom*, a Holly Springs freedom-school production based on life and death of Medgar Evers, was performed during evening, as well as Free Southern production of *In White America*.

Tallahatchie: Four members of a local family—the first Negro family to attempt to register to vote from this county in several decades—have been steadily harassed since they attempted to register last Tuesday. On Tuesday night two truckloads of whites with guns came by at 6 P.M., 10 P.M., and 3 A.M. shouting obscenities and threats. They have been back several times, and the family is now afraid to go to work in the fields. The County Registrar is currently under a court injunction to determine the qualification of Negro registrants by the same standards as whites, not to limit

Negro registrants to coming in one at a time, and not to use the Constitutional interpretation section of the registration form. Approximately 70 per cent of the county's population is Negro. SNCC voter registration activity began here two weeks ago.

Shaw: Two cross burnings here were reported night of Aug 6–7. Both were apparently intended to frighten local families involved in civil rights work.

AUG. 9: *Mileston:* Shortly after midnight a bomb was thrown in road approximately 40 yards from new freedom center. Thrown by whites from passing car, the bomb left a hole approximately one foot deep and 5 or 6 feet wide in road. There were no injuries.

Aberdeen: Two or three canisters of tear gas were found on lawn of Freedom House here. Local police arrived and removed canisters before FBI could take fingerprints.

Canton: In White America produced here tonight.

AUG. 10: *Marigold:* An elderly Negro man was shot to death in a gas station here this morning. Although reports vary, it seems confirmed that the man ordered gas and either had forgotten his billfold and could not pay, or received more gas than he had ordered and refused to pay for the extra. The gas station attendant began to beat him. A local policeman shot and killed the Negro, who was unarmed.

Aberdeen: Two local Negro voter registration workers were stopped and given speeding tickets here after they and approximately 20 other Negroes attempted to integrate the downstairs section of the Elkins movie theater. CDC lawyer Abe Weitzman and law student Richard Wheelock were harassed as they observed the integration attempt. Their car was kicked by local white citizen, and they were stopped and questioned by police. They were followed back to Columbus by police car and carload of whites. The two given speeding tickets were driving 25 mph in a 30 mph zone. A third local Negro who participated in integration attempt was ticketed for improper lights. His lights were in order.

Canton: In White America presented here tonight.

AUG. 11: *Gluckstadt:* Mt. Pleasant Church in Gluckstadt burned to ground last night. It had been used daily as freedom school site. Within minutes after leaving site, white volunteer Jim Ohls arrested for reckless driving.

Aberdeen: White volunteer Joel Bernard attacked by local

white man today while engaged in voter registration canvassing. Volunteer was with local Negro filling out freedom
registration form when white man drove up in pickup
truck, questioned him about what he was doing, struck
him to ground, and punched him several times. Bernard
managed to break away, and was searching for telephone
when police passed by. While he was explaining incident
to police, his attacker—who had been following in his
truck—came out and began threatening once again. Bernard
taken to station for questioning, was refused use of telephone, and was refused protection back to office. He sustained bruises and grazed arm.

Ruleville: Mrs. Fannie Lou Hamer, candidate for Congress,
suffered brutal beating in county jail in Winona for her
voter registration activities, is again being threatened. One
of men involved in her earlier beating has been passing
by her home today in pickup truck, pointing her out to a
series of companions. Mrs. Hamer, who suffered a permanent back injury from her earlier beating, states she feels
the man "is up to something drastic."

Cleveland: Preliminary hearing held this morning on fatal
shooting yesterday of 60-year-old Negro Neimiah Montgomery by police officer Leonard Yarborrow of Marigold
force. Witnesses testified that Montgomery went berserk
soon after he drove into station, when attendant asked to be
paid. Montgomery reportedly ran across highway to trailer
and got hammer, then threatened to kill woman. Service
station attendant got an ax handle and he and Montgomery
struggled for it. Officer Yarborrow arrived and reportedly
tried to subdue Montgomery. Officer shot him twice, both
bullets going into heart. This was viewed at hearing as
justifiable homicide while acting in line of duty.

Anguilla: Two local Negro civil rights workers, Louis
Grant and Bob Wright, arrested this evening while handing out leaflets advertising Freedom Day in Rolling Fork.
Leaflets urged voter registration. (Bond set later at $200
on anti-littering charge.)

AUG. 12:   *Aberdeen:* Potential Negro registrants taken to courthouse
today found it closed. Officials there said registrar was sick.
There is no deputy registrar.

Greenwood: Six local Negro youths arrested today while
standing in front of Doris' store in Baptist Town, singing.

At least one beaten. Doctor and nurse dispatched to jail. Charges unknown.

Charleston: 24 Negro citizens attempted to register at Tallahatchie Co. courthouse here yesterday. Approximately 93 armed whites gathered. Cars and trucks with guns prominently displayed were double- and triple-parked in front of courthouse. Potential registrants were able to take test quickly as registrar is under federal injunction to cease discrimination. Sheriff also under federal injunction restraining him for intimidating Negro applicants.

Ruleville: Students at local Negro school organizing to force teachers to register to vote. Only one is registered. They are also pressing to improve school conditions, and to stop practice of students' financing school's operations. Classes reportedly have class field days when students go out in field and pick cotton to raise money for school.

Ruleville: Mrs. Hamer threatened with murder in telephone call to her home tonight.

Oak Ridge (near Vicksburg): Three people who have supported FDP beaten and shot at last night by men with hoods over their heads and in robes. Henry Ollins, his wife Lucy, and their next-door neighbor Thomas Hick attacked by three carloads of men. Attackers broke doors of both houses and fired high-powered rifle at Hick's house. Both Mr. and Mrs. Ollins beaten; she sustained damaged hip, while he suffered rather severe beating, according to Vicksburg hospital. Hick managed to wrest hood off one of men, and has delivered it to sheriff. According to MSP spokesman, "Warren Co. prides itself on not having a White Citizens Council, let alone a KKK."

Ocean Springs (near Gulfport): In two separate incidents, two local Negro men shot at here today. 19-year-old city employee Calvin Galloway cutting grass near beach when three white men drove by and fired pistol shots. Second incident involved man about 50, Barney Brooks. His attackers may have been same at those of Galloway. Neither was hit by shots.

Biloxi: Rental of local store for precinct meeting canceled by owner today when SNCC poster put up. Local people reportedly told him they feared he was going to "move the nigras in."

Brandon: St. Matthew's Baptist Church here burned to

ground last night. Fire department spokesman told AP that department was unable to stop the fire.

Hattiesburg: Mrs. Dorethea Jackson, local Negro woman, arrested yesterday when she would not give her seat to white woman on bus. Mrs. Jackson reportedly was pulled off bus by policeman. She asserted that knife was planted in her purse. Charges as yet unknown.

Lexington: In White America produced here.

AUG. 13:   *Canton:* 18-year-old Gluckstadt freedom-school student, whose school site was burned to ground two days ago, arrested today for alleged reckless driving and attempting to run Constable Bruno Holly off road.

Ocean Springs: Report here of third shooting in 24 hours at local Negro citizens, none hit. Also here last night, three white women in pickup truck attempted to run over local Negro woman.

Cleveland: Local Negro reported that Willie Carter, another Negro Cleveland resident, offered $200 by Shaw chief of police W. H. Griffin "to get rid of" three local Negroes —Elijah Smith, Aaron German, and Charles Bond—who are active in voter registration activity. Carter reportedly accepted offer, but second man reported it to COFO.

Columbus: Summer volunteer Ron Bridgeforth jailed at Starkville today on charges of refusing to be fingerprinted and photographed. He had gone to courthouse to pay parking fine. Bond: $500.

Ruleville: 19-year-old white volunteer Joseph Smith arrested this evening in Drew on charges of "conduct tending to incite a breach of peace" while passing high-school campus. He is in Drew City jail; bond not set.

Greenwood: Production of *In White America.*

AUG. 14:   *McComb:* Supermarket across street from church site of McComb freedom school bombed before 1 A.M. today. All windows shattered and walls and roofing damaged. Blast, which left large hole in ground, almost knocked down voter registration worker in Freedom House two blocks away. Immediately after explosion, white SNCC staffer Mendy Samstein ran outside, jumped into car, passed by car with two white men in it, followed car until he could record license; he had seen car before and found it listed on McComb SNCC's "suspicious car" list. Law student Clint Hopson arrested for interfering with officer as he worked his way through crowd at bomb site and spoke with one of officers there. He was released on $52.50 bail. Local voter registration worker Roy Lee arrested when he returned to scene of bombing and charged with inciting to riot, threatening life of policeman, cursing, and disorderly conduct. Being held on $900 bond. McComb SNCC spokesmen stated he was arrested for no apparent reason.

Natchez: Tavern next door to Freedom House here bombed tonight. Owners of tavern, an integrated couple, live in home attached to it. Tavern owned by Jake Fisherman and Evangeline Thronton. He is white, she, Negro. Natchez SNCC spokesmen report that police were circulating through crowd of several hundred spectators, stating that "the wrong place" had been bombed. Firemen told one of voter registration workers there (whom they did not recognize), "Those outside agitators are in that house. The bomb was set for that house. They're here to stir up trouble. George Greene rents that place." Greene is 20-year-old SNCC staff member working in Natchez.

Aberdeen: Elkins Theater closed down today rather than integrate. There have been two integration attempts at theater Aug. 6 and 11.

Aberdeen: 24 voter registration workers had to wait outside courthouse here last night as local Negro volunteer Leon Smith tried for traffic violation. When Smith's lawyer inquired why workers were not permitted in courtroom, judge said, "I don't hold trials for monkeys." As workers waited outside, large group of whites gathered, many with baseball bats. This morning local volunteer Sammy Bets, who tried to attend trial, fired without being given any reason by his white employer, one of white crowd outside courthouse last night.

Aberdeen: Three local voter registration workers given traffic tickets as they drove home from registration meeting last night. This is third time this week that this form of harassment used by police.

Hattiesburg: Local Negro citizen Willie Mae Martin re-arrested last night in connection with charge of resisting arrest and interferring with police officer last March. Billy McDonald, another Hattiesburg Negro resident, and FDP chairman Laurence Guyot arrested at same time, McDonald on same charge as Miss Martin and Guyot solely for interfering. Because of legal misunderstandings, three did not know they were scheduled to appear for hearing to be held six months after their charge. Miss Martin and McDonald assigned $200 bond and 30 days imprisonment, and Guyot $100 and 30 days. It is doubtful that Guyot will be released before the Democratic National Convention.

Ruleville: Local attorney has informed voter registration workers here that any white volunteer staying overnight in Negro section of Drew, a small town near here, would be arrested.

Columbus: Local voter registration volunteer John Luther Bell jailed at nearby West Point today on charges of larceny and disturbing peace. He was arrested while canvassing for potential Negro registrants. Bell was one of three outstanding students selected as delegate to freedom-school convention in Meridian Aug. 8-10.

Hattiesburg: Freedom-school teacher Sandra Adickes, UFT volunteer, arrested today when she attempted to have six of her students check out books from public library deemed for whites only. After they were refused applications for cards, they sat down at tables to read magazines. Short time later police chief Hugh Herrin walked in and announced library was being closed. Everyone made to leave library, which Mayor Claude F. Pittman now states was closed for inventory. This is second time this year it has closed for inventory. Miss Adickes and students were followed by police from time they left library. They went to integrated lunch counter, where waitress said she would serve only Negroes. UFT volunteer arrested outside lunch counter and released under $100 bond on a vagrancy charge.

Greenwood: White women owners of grocery store here fired with shotguns on crowd of 75–100 Negro pickets today. Their "Happy Day" store has been object of civil rights boycott for past several days. There were no injuries reported. Police arrived shortly after shooting and dispersed pickets.

Columbus: LCDC Attorney Tom Connelly arrested on charges of reckless driving today after pickup truck rammed into his parked car. Local white citizen Travis Hamilton ran his truck into Connelly's car, smashing door, shattering window, and injuring passenger and law student Richard Wheeler (cut on arm by flying glass). Connelly released after several hours on $110 bond. As Connelly was being driven home from District Attorney's office by summer volunteer Steve Fraser, their car was met by highway patrol roadblock. Fraser was given ticket for improper license. Roadblock then ended.

Canton: Bullet fired at Freedom House at approximately 10 P.M. from passing car. No injuries or apparent damage. Police came immediately upon being informed and were cooperative.

Indianola: Local white resident Joe Hopkins today drove to freedom school while classes in session, questioned volunteer about presence of N.Y. reporter and Attorney Andrew Goldman, fumbled with rifle, drove off. Earlier, Hopkins told Negro family living next door to freedom-school site that civil rights workers "better get out of there." He said, "I'm going to blow up that place." Two Negro citizens also told summer volunteer that several white men planned to "shoot up the place" tonight. Local police stated they would patrol area all night.

AUG. 15: *Jackson:* Between 10:30 P.M. and 12:30 A.M., voter registration worker beaten over head with baseball bat outside COFO office, carload of one white and four local Negro voter registration workers was shot at 8 to 10 times, four crosses were burned simultaneously, and local student shot by white man: white volunteer Philip Hocker working on pickup truck across street from COFO office as three other workers—two Negro, one white—sat in car behind him lighting his work with headlights. Another car double-parked beside car and truck. Young white man wearing Bermuda shorts went up to Hocker, hit him on back of head with bat, and continued to hit him after he fell to street. At 10:45 Hocker taken from office to Baptist hospital, still bleeding about the head. At 11, crosses burning at Lynch St. and Terry Rd. approximately three blocks from COFO office; at Sun-n-Sands Hotel, where many project lawyers, doctors, ministers, and national press correspondents stay; at Millsaps College; and at Valley Rd. and Hwy. 80, site of soon-to-be-integrated public school. White summer volunteer and four local Negro voter registration workers shot at 8 to 10 times by two white men in car as they drove through Jackson. Civil rights workers stopped when they saw parked police car. Officer, after hearing Smith's statement, sent out report over radio that "we got some colored people who say some niggers were shooting at them." As soon as Oldsmobile containing attackers came close, police drove off. Investigating plain-clothes man found 5 bullets in the car. Willie Gynes was shot in leg by white man in car passing a teen dance here. Gynes is in the emergency ward of University Hospital.

Meridian: Two local Negro voter registration volunteers, Sam Brown and David McClinton, and SNCC staffer Preston Ponder fired upon today while driving Hwy. 11 in Jasper Co. Shot hit and cracked front window of trio's car as they returned from investigating beating several weeks ago of schoolteacher and her mother.

Greenwood: SNCC staffer Jesse Harris arrested today for disturbing peace. Arrest made under warrant, presumably in connection with boycott currently in operation against several stores here.

Greenwood: Silas McGhee, young man whose brutal beating led to first arrests under 1964 Civil Rights Act, shot in face tonight as he sat in car outside Lulu's restaurant. McGhee alone in car when shot fired by white man in passing car. He was rushed to University Hospital in Jackson in critical condition. McGhee initially brought to Leflore Hospital here. Staff reportedly unable to remove bullet, which entered through left side of face near temple and lodged near left side throat. Two SNCC staffers refused admittance to hospital because they were not wearing shirts; they had taken off their shirts to help stop McGhee's bleeding.

Laurel: Volunteer and three local Negro voter registration workers beaten today after sitting down for service at theoretically integrated Kress' department store lunch counter. Ten whites approached as Levelle Keys, James House, Larry McGill and Ben Hartfield being served. Two of whites beat group with baseball bats. Hartfield knocked unconscious. Woman pulled pistol on McGill. His mother yelled, "Don't kill my son," to woman who pulled pistol. For this remark, McGill's assailant reportedly filed assault charge against his mother. SNCC staffer Fred Richardson entered store earlier, was asked to leave because he had a camera. Richardson outside Kress' when incident occurred and was himself beaten by whites who gathered at scene when he called police. His camera taken by one of his attackers. Police arrived and warrants were sworn out against several of the attackers.

AUG. 16: *McComb:* McComb office raided at 1:30 A.M. by 24 policemen in five cars, representing city police, sheriffs and deputies, and highway patrol. Warrants were for illegal liquor. None was found, but officers spent good deal of time reading letters and literature found in office. The workers had just returned from an evening of convassing bars and restaurants in McComb area, announcing rallies and Freedom Days. These were planned in response to a period of increased violence and harassment by local white community.

Greenwood: Several hundred local Negro citizens gathered at Friendship Baptist Church here to protest shooting of McGhee. Approximately 100 of those who had gathered in church came to SNCC office after meeting. Police in full riot garb, with tear-gas equipment, blocked off both ends of street on which office is located until angry crowd dispersed.

Philadelphia: Memorial service held today for civil rights workers James Chaney, Michael Schwerner, and Andrew Goodman, who were slain here June 21 after inspecting burned-out church site of a freedom school.

Laurel: White volunteer David Goodyear beaten unconscious at gas station here today, and his companion, white volunteer Linnelle Barrett, was kicked and stepped upon. They were outside their car when two white men approached and asked if they were civil rights workers. When they replied "yes," several whites milling around closed in and began beating them. Police came in three cars immediately after being notified. Within an hour after incident, police—on basis of license number—picked up assailants' car. Gas station attendant closed station and left before police arrived. Two of Goodyear's teeth were loosened.

AUG. 17: *Hattiesburg:* Four voter registration workers, 3 white and 1 Negro, arrested on vagrancy charges here as they left public library which had refused them service. Susan Patterson, Ben Achtenburg, Tom Edwards, and Bill Jones held on $100 cash bond or $250 property bond.

Ruleville: Three local Negro youths picked up by police here and held for half an hour for distributing announcements of tonight's production of *In White America.*

Laurel: Anthony Lynn hit twice by passing white citizen as he stood on street corner here today. Lynn was with local Negro citizen whom he had just accompanied to courthouse to take voter registration test. Lynn called police and pointed out his assailant to them. Assailant denied everything; police had both file affidavits.

Gulfport: Volunteer Steve Miller badly beaten today by passing white man as he left Carnegie Library. Miller sustained severe bruises on jaw, right temple, and head, and is suffering from amnesia. County police officer arrived at scene, but left without providing any aid. Taxi then refused to take him to hospital. Civil rights workers arrived at hospital with Miller about one hour after beating. They were made to wait another two hours for doctor. Assailant walked by police officer and commented, "I got me one." Workers went to city police, who refused to take action for lack of complaint. Warrant filed by one of witnesses at whom assailant had swung but not hit. Miller not capable of filing warrant. Sheriff is investigating.

Indianola: Approximately 25 white citizens, some of whom were reportedly White Citizen's Council members, attended this evening's performance of *In White America.* Eight to 10 helmeted police arrived in two cars, said there would be no trouble. Play features integrated cast of 8; it describes suppressions and victories of American Negro in his own country.

Winona Co.: White volunteer Tim Morrison arrested here for faulty driver's license and fined $18.

Clarksdale: Franklin Delano Roosevelt III arrested and fined for speeding while going 25 mph in 35 mph zone. Roosevelt has been doing research on project to bring aid to civil rights workers.

AUG. 18: *McComb:* After series of bombings and intimidation, first Southwest Mississippi Freedom Day was peacefully conducted here today. 25 potential Negro registrants went to courthouse, 23 of whom permitted to take test. Registrar processed one applicant every 45 minutes. Police and FBI agents were at Pike Co. courthouse in Magnolia throughout day. (Of Pike Co.'s 35,063 Negro voting-age citizens, 207 (3%) registered, as contrasted to 9,989 registered whites representing 82.1%.) Over 200 local Negro citizens attended mass meeting here last night to protest terrorist activities brought against Negro citizens and voter registration workers in this hard-core area.

McComb: Attempted house-burning reported by SNCC spokesmen today. At 1:30 A.M. local Negro resident Vera Brown, whose daughter is active in civil rights movement here, woke up to smell of smoke. Gasoline-filled jar found smoking under house. Conflagration was smothered with little damage. Mrs. Brown plans to attempt to register as part of Freedom Day.

Philadelphia: Shortly before 11 P.M., Aug. 15, car stopped across street from freedom-school headquarters here and driver kept single-barreled shotgun pointed at office for about 5 minutes, left, and returned second time. When two freedom-school teachers filed warrant about incident with district attorney, official put on it that party was COFO worker who made $9.64 a week, "lives off people in community, and has no other visible means of support." Freedom-school coordinator Ralph Featherstone refused to sign affidavit with this addition. His companion, volunteer Walter Kaufman, did sign complaint. Name of man with gun is known; action on case is awaited. Aug. 16 a rumor began spreading that office and motel across street from it, where workers eat, would be bombed. By Aug. 17 rumor was widespread—woman at motel was threatened and told workers she could not feed them any more. FBI watched office all night; local police took no action. This morning Deputy Sheriff Price, officer who arrested James Chaney, Michael Schwerner, and Andrew Goodman, came to office and took films of all workers. He came by three times. He reportedly has been questioning local Negro citizens as to the workers' activities. Today local Negro citizen beaten by white man when he went into store with Negro girl. Philadelphia staff reports man could be taken for white and was probably thought to be project worker. He came to office after leaving doctor's office. He was frightened and refused to contact local police. FBI contacted, and man questioned for about ½ hour. One agent reportedly was "very hostile."

Greenwood: Jake McGhee, younger brother of Silas, arrested here this morning for traffic violation. His mother, Mrs. Laura McGhee, hit in chest by desk sergeant when she went to pay fine. Mrs. McGhee hit officer in nose; officer went for gun. Greenwood staff members George Greene and Ed Rudd held policeman's hand till another officer came in and calmed him down. Jake fined $100 for improper license and impersonation. Warrant issued for Mrs. McGhee's arrest for assaulting officer.

Jackson: 17-year-old Negro from Columbus formally announced plans today to seek state charter for Mississippi Young Democrat Club. Melvin L. Whitfield assumed presidency of new Young Democratic group at their Aug. 10 convention in Meridian, which included representatives from about 25 Mississippi communities. He will represent body, along with 9 other Mississippi officers, at meeting of National Committee of Young Democratic Clubs of America Aug. 21–23 in Atlantic City. Group, thus far all-Negro, learned few weeks ago that existing Young Democratic organization in Mississippi has never been granted charter by national body. Spokesman noted, "Our organization, in keeping with principles stated in constitution of Young Democratic Clubs of America, is open to anyone who is between ages of 16 and 40 who 'professes, and demonstrates allegiance to principles of National Democratic Party,' regardless of race or creed."

Gulfport: Man who yesterday beat volunteer Steve Miller today was arrested and charged with assault. Gulfport resident James Robert Thomas released on $200 bond. Thomas has only been charged with assault as warrant against him was filed by Miller's companion Charles Wheeler, who was not hit. Miller will swear out warrant when able.

Vicksburg: Early this morning, bottle hurled through window of barbershop owned by Mr. Eddie Thomas, Warren Co. FDP delegate.

McComb: As white volunteer Marshall Ganz drove back from Pike Co. courthouse in Magnolia to transport potential Negro registrants, he was followed by four men in unmarked pickup truck. When he stopped at red light, one man quickly got out of truck and began running at him. Ganz quickly drove off and was followed by truck back to McComb. Passenger in truck threw bottle which narrowly missed going through window of Ganz' car.

Natchez: Five-gallon can of gasoline, a bomblike apparatus, found under Blue Moon bar here. Bar belongs to Jake Fisher, whose brother's bar was found bombed in Louisiana over the weekend.

Yazoo City: Two local Negro citizens today filed applications for cards at local library here without incident. Police talked with two "politely" and later contacted mother of one.

Shaw: Three Negro members of Shaw Mississippi Student Union entered town library today and successfully registered for cards. When Eddie Short, James Johnson Jr., and Willie

Wright left, they were followed by four police officers and watched by a number of bystanders.

AUG. 19: *Jackson:* Three busloads of FDP delegates and alternates to National Convention, as well as FDP staff members, left from Jackson amidst hundreds of well-wishers late this evening.

Jackson: At conclusion of 3½-day staff meeting at Tougaloo College this weekend, Dir. Robert Moses announced that Mississippi Summer Project would not end. Speaking at press conference, Moses said 200 of volunteers now in state plus 65 SNCC staff and about 30 CORE staff would stay in state throughout year. This figure does not include those who will come down for minimum stay of three months who have been applying for work during year since summer project began. Moses also noted that medical, legal, and ministerial groups have announced plans to place Mississippi operations on a permanent basis.

Natchez: Owner of house rented by SNCC workers here has indicated he does not want to rent it to civil rights workers for fear of bombing. Company holding house's insurance indicated it does not want to continue the policy on the house.

Meridian: Church burning reported in Collinsville.

McComb: Three potential Negro registrants in front of Pike Co. courthouse in Magnolia told they would be arrested if they did not move. Three sat in car for 30 minutes. Ten minutes later white volunteer Dave Gerber arrested for speeding en route from courthouse to McComb. Bond: $22.50.

Meridian: Local Negro voter registration worker Sam Brown arrested on charges of disorderly conduct and resisting arrest tonight. Released on $50 bond.

Philadelphia: Increased harassment and intimidation efforts continue at Evers Motel headquarters of Neshoba Co. mobile freedom school here. Between 8:55 and 9:15 P.M. two carloads and one truck of white men with rifles visible parked outside headquarters on outskirts of Philadelphia. Deputy Price observed smiling as one carload of whites told him, "We're gonna get the job done tonight." While carloads of whites parked or occupants milled about in front of office and other cars cruised in area, threatening phone calls received at approximate intervals of 5 minutes stating,

"Your time is up." Calls continued till 4 A.M. New office opened Aug. 14 with 11 workers, four of them staff.

Jackson: At press conference, Project Dir. Robert Moses said, "Voter registration drives will be increased across state. Campaigns will be intensified in Panola and Tallahatchie Co.'s, where recent court orders have opened new possibilities for work, and in other counties where legal relief appears imminent. Also under consideration are such new efforts as mobile libraries in rural areas, strengthening of citizens-band radio security system, development of permanent community center facilities, and an adult literacy program specially designed by SNCC for the Black Belt.

AUG. 20: *Canton:* At 1:30 A.M. pickup truck drove into driveway of Freedom House. Local Negro citizen saw "third light" inside truck, in addition to two headlights. When truck's occupants noticed all the observers, they quickly drove off, and were reportedly observed trying to put out fire in bed of truck. When witnesses got to street, they found gallon jug, broken, with oily rags sticking out at top.

Philadelphia: Neshoba Co. law enforcement has used questionable building lease to try to evict COFO workers from their newly opened office. At about 11 A.M. Deputy Cecil Price, Sheriff Rainey, and District Attorney Walter Jones presented an eviction notice, indicating that six COFO workers then in office would be arrested if they had not left premises by 1 P.M. The law officers claimed the building lease was invalid, and that old tenants still held lease. Police, both city and county, appeared frequently at office from about 1 to 3 or 4 P.M. with warrants for arrest of six on trespass charges. Former occupant of building came to office late this afternoon and agreed to terminate his hold on building and to have all his property moved out within five days. COFO workers indicated their determination to say in Philadelphia despite legal or other types of pressure. Local Negro woman told one of workers this morning: "If you leave us now, they'll kill us. They'll pile our bodies one on top of the other." Additional staff was moved into Philadelphia by late afternoon, and more will be sent as soon as needed, "to keep our pledge to the local people," a Jackson office spokesman said. Today's legal harassment followed several tense hours last night as Philadelphia office surrounded by carloads of armed whites. Following eviction notice, local Negro citizens came to office and provided "a fabulous dinner for us all."

Shaw: Herman Perry, Negro cotton farmer, elected president of the Bolivar improvement Assn. at mass meeting here Wed. night. More than 100 attended. Assn. plans to organize Negro farmers and others for community planning and improvement. With widespread Negro unemployment and poverty in area, group hopes to become eligible for federal aid. To avoid complete economic dependence, group needs some kind of industry to employ Negroes. Assn. grew out of freedom-school class in politics. Mass meeting scheduled for tomorrow evening in Shaw, to make plans for school boycott and integration of public schools here.

Clarksdale: Medical Committee for Human Rights physicians Richard Moore and Les Hoffman arrested for loitering while in their car outside Freedom House here. Released on $16 bond each; trial Aug. 21.

AUG. 21:   *Belzoni:* Police cars follow voter registration workers here continuously, surrounding them at every house at which they stop. Four to five cars of local white citizens also follow. This morning, police chief Nichols reportedly told workers to get out of town, that he was planning to bomb house. Yesterday Nichols entered house for second time without warrant. He said house is public place, and that warrant is unnecessary. House located about one block outside city limits. This evening three voter registration workers surrounded for several hours by 12 truckloads of armed whites as they sat in Wimp's Cafe here. Crowd gathered as workers stopped at filling station just inside city limits. They entered cafe to report situation to Greenwood SNCC office. Sheriff closed cafe by saying to owner, "Close that place down, nigger." Local Negro citizen reportedly hit on side of head with blackjack.

Gulfport: Local Negro Aaron Jones today was arrested while handing out leaflets here announcing performance by Caravan of Music folk singer. Jones now in Juvenile Court custody on delinquency charge.

Itta Bena: Perry's Chapel burned to ground late this evening. Wood-frame building deemed to be out of jurisdiction of Itta Bena fire department.

AUG. 22:   *McComb:* Local voter registration worker Percy McGhee arrested for "loitering" inside courthouse near here today. Being held on $60 bail. McComb police officer pulled gun on SNCC staff member Seephus Hugh, who went to post band for McGhee. Four more workers went to jail and successfully bonded out McGhee.

Jackson: As two freedom-school teachers, one white and one Negro, walked along street here today, car with two white passengers doubled back, drove by slowly, and took their picture.

Laurel: A going-away picnic given by local Negroes for three white voter registration workers was broken up today by an estimated 15 white men who beat one volunteer, reportedly with sticks and chains, and shot at two others. As group sat around private lake on Negro-owned farm near here, six white men approached and asked if group knew "Dixie." When one student began to play the song, a white man grabbed his guitar and threw it in lake. About 9 other white men came out of bushes surrounding lake site. White volunteer Willard Hayden saw at least two weapons among men: a club and a chain. Weapon brought down on his head; he and local voter registration worker Robert Morgan plunged into lake to head back to farmhouse. Shots, probably from pistol, aimed at them. White volunteer David Gelfand was severely beaten by white assailants. He sustained sprained—possibly broken—wrists, and bruises and lacerations of the back. His assailant has been tentatively identified as R. V. Lee, the man who is to stand trial Friday for beating white volunteer Anthony Lynn in front of Laurel courthouse last Monday.

AUG. 23:   *Tupelo:* Voter registration headquarters here were object of arson early this morning. Damage was moderate. Workers arrived at office today to find attic gutted, all windows in rear part of building broken, and door burned. Neighbors reported fire department had put fire out at about 3 A.M. City investigators said there was evidence of arson. Tupelo has been the scene of FDP organizing involving 20 to 30 local workers, as well as three staff workers. Office was opened six weeks ago.

McComb: Local white citizen held for 3 hours last night by five heavily armed, hooded white men. He is described by McComb SNCC spokesmen as "poor; his friends are all Negroes and he lives in Negro neighborhood."

AUG. 24:   *Columbus:* Rev. Cluke Arden and white volunteer Bruce Amundson were turned away yesterday from Lutheran Church here after being questioned at length by minister and church elders. Amundson was asked to apologize for having brought a Negro to the church last Sunday.

Greenville: Law student Len Edwards and three LCDC lawyers were refused a room after having made prior reservation at Holiday Inn here, when manager saw a Negro in their car.

Holly Springs: Local Negro sharecropper, Mr. J. T. Dean, turned off his land for no apparent reason. This is latest in series of economic actions taken against Dean since he applied to register to vote during Marshall Co. Freedom Day Aug. 15. Aug. 16 Dean's credit cut off. He was told by landowner he was no longer needed to work the land. His water supply was also cut off. Today Howard Jones, local Negro citizen who made application to register during Holly Springs Freedom Day July 24, told at courthouse that his test has not yet been graded. So far, none of more than 200 local Negro citizens who took voter registration test this summer has been notified as to whether or not he passed.

Gulfport: Local Negro voter registration worker John Handy arrested here for disturbing peace and held on $300 bond. Arrest came few hours after Handy talked with Negroes outside Henderson's store in Greenwood, which has been boycotted for more than six weeks. Owner, Greenwood police officer, dragged young, pregnant Negro woman across pavement Freedom Day. When Handy stopped outside store, Henderson told him warrant would be issued for his arrest. (Charges dropped Aug. 25.)

Gulfport: Four local Negro voter registration workers, Luther Adams, Clifton Johnson, Jonnie Campbell, and Charles Wheeler, today were refused service at Albrught and Wood Drugstore counter. They were served water, then asked to leave. Adams went back to store and asked if it were segregated; waitress replied, "You were served water, weren't you?"

Moss Pt.: Negro citizens here have decided to boycott nearby laundromat after young Negro girl arrested for attempting to wash clothes in "white section." Petition will be presented to laundry's owner tomorrow morning by boycotting citizens demanding that discrimination there be ended.

AUG. 25:   *Amory:* Three young Negro voter registration workers, Adair Howell, Andrew Moore and Essie Carr, arrested today as they canvassed for potential registrants. Trio saw police coming and went to Negro home. Police entered home and arrested workers, charging them with disturbing peace and "forcing" Negro woman to sign form. Local officials denied knowledge of whereabouts of workers after their arrest. Howell and Moore located by FBI late this evening in Amory City jail. They are being held under $100 bond each. Miss Carr released to custody of her parents.

Drew: Law student Len Edwards arrested for reckless driving after being followed by local police chief. He made U-turn at speed of 5 miles per hour.

Moss Pt.: Owner of local laundromat here refused to desegregate facilities when presented with petition by local Negro citizens. He reportedly stated that he realized Negroes constituted 80% of his business, but that whites would refuse to wash there if partition removed. He reportedly told Negroes that "Communists are behind this whole thing," and that "Negroes and whites had a good relationship in Moss Pt. until few months ago when COFO workers came in." (On Aug. 23, six Negroes arrested for urging fellow citizens not to patronize the laundromat.)

Mound Bayou: Seven young Negro members of Mississippi Student Union arrested today for allegedly chasing white salesman out of town. Man shot at students. Although the seven, Henry Martin, Wendel Ishman, Herbert Battle, Oliver Know, James McKay, Walter Ricket, and Gary Dillen, are being held in jail, no charges have been placed against them yet.

Columbus: Group of 30 Negro high-school students followed by six police cars, one containing sheriff and police dog, as they walked to voter registration meeting last night. Police remained outside meeting for over ½ hour and later returned to cafe where group had first gathered. Police entered cafe and told students who had just returned from meeting that they were to go home.

AUG. 26: *Canton:* George Johnson, registration worker, was shot at three times on his way to Freedom House early this morning. He was approximately three blocks from the house when car pulled up from behind and fired three shots from approximately 500 feet away. Johnson identified car as police car since it was equipped with searchlight and red warning light on top. Johnson, who both heard the shots and saw the flash of the bullets, ducked into nearby bushes and sought shelter in a local house. Approximately 10 min-

utes later he started back to Freedom House down another
street and stated that he saw "the same police car which
came past me at 50 or 60 miles per hour, shining its spot-
light on me." Johnson entered another local home for refuge.
Late last week, Johnson, in response to Canton CORE office
policies, registered with the police as a civil rights worker
and gave the Freedom House as his home address.

AFFIDAVITS

The following affidavits were selected to give eyewitness and first-
person accounts of specific incidents in more formal detail. In several
cases the affidavits are excerpted due to length or because more than
one affidavit has been used to describe a situation in a given location.

All affidavits included here refer to occurrences this past summer. They
are not the most atrocious statements that could have been gathered
from experiences of Mississippi Negroes in everyday life or in connection
with the movement during the past few years. It is apparent from the
Tallahatchie County and Philadelphia-Neshoba County statements that
these conditions did not begin this summer.

In most cases affidavits have been selected because they are the best
official statements describing a situation or pattern existing across the
state.

Highly publicized events such as the beating of Rabbi Arthur Lelyveld
and two volunteers in Hattiesburg, or the "reign of terror" created in
Jackson by two men one night when two separate shootings and a beating took place, have been omitted. Statements from Silas McGhee have
not been included since the—admittedly historic—FBI arrests of three
of his attackers broke that story into the nation's press.

Affidavits from Mrs. Fannie Lou Hamer, Jimmy Travis or the widow
of Louis Allen, for example, have not been included as it is assumed that
most persons who worked in Mississippi this past summer would be
familiar with their stories. And since this set of statements is restricted
to the summer of 1964 we have not attempted to insert such affidavits as
SNCC worker MacArthur Cotton's describing Parchman Penitentiary
last year where he was hung by his hands for three hours, or SNCC
worker George Greene's statements from Natchez.

It should be kept in mind that affidavits are not available for the bulk
of incidents this past summer or, more importantly, from before.

(The following analysis of violence in Mississippi is excerpted from an
analysis of affidavits submitted by plaintiffs in *COFO v. Rainey,* an

omnibus suit filed in the U.S. District Court at Meridian this past summer.)

The use of violence by white men to keep Negroes "in their place" in Mississippi did not begin, as is sometimes asserted, with the coming of the civil rights movement to that state. Violence was basic to the system of slavery, and it has never been abandoned as a means of "controlling" the Negro population. Only the forms have changed.

But there has been an amazing consistency in the forms of organization used by the white man to meet the challenge of civil rights since the freeing of the slaves. The authors of Reconstruction Legislation realized that they must meet two closely related forms of resistance: (1) One was open violence, the use of brute and indiscriminate force by private white citizens and clandestine organizations against the Negro population to ensure that it was permanently terrorized and intimidated from asserting its rights; (2) an equally serious challenge coming from the leading officials of the white community—government officials, law enforcement officers, and members of the judiciary. By their refusal to indict and prosecute those who committed acts of violence, and by their refusal to enforce the newly passed civil rights acts of the Reconstruction Period, they became accomplices in a conspiracy to "keep the Negro in his place"—a conspiracy which constantly resorted to both private and highly organized forms of violence.

. . . One hundred years later, Negroes in Mississippi and those who have come to help them . . . face [a situation] fundamentally identical to that which the legislators of 1866 faced in attempting to bring change to the South. Negroes and the civil rights workers in Mississippi today face both open violence and official negligence and complicity, just as they did in 1866 . . .

Note: All affidavits reprinted here were notarized at the time they were sworn out, or, in the event no notary public was available, were witnessed by at least two persons.

AFFIDAVIT I.   TALLAHATCHIE COUNTY

In February, 1964, Green Brewer, 29, now a resident of New Jersey, was visiting his parents in Charleston, Tallahatchie County. During this visit, he and his brother Charles went to the Huntly Grocery Store. According to Green Brewer's affidavit:

"Charles went inside the store to get soft drinks. It seemed as if it was taking a long time for him to come out. David Baskin, a friend who was with us, walked to the door, then turned around and started to walk real fast to the road. I then began to hear the sound of some licks. I ran inside the store and saw my brother Charles lying on the floor. He was bleeding. He was unconscious. Mr. Huntly had backed up against the counter, holding an axe handle. Another white man, Mr. George Little, was also holding an axe handle.

"I bent down to Charles, called him twice, and asked him, 'What's the matter? What happened?' There was no response. I then pulled him up and was getting him to the door, and by that time he was beginning to help himself. I then walked back to get the sunglasses that belonged to my brother . . . Mr. Huntly started to cuss me, saying I better 'get him out before I kill him.'

"Mr. Huntly then got his gun—and started to shake—when I got a blow from behind. I received a fractured skull, broken jawbone, broken nose and a burst eyeball, with little use of my eye. However, I was able to help my brother to the car . . . A brother, Jesse, met us and drove us to Charleston.

"Later, about a week later, the sheriff, Alex Doghan, came and asked us what happened. Another white man came later and said he was sent by the sheriff, and he interviewed us. Since then nothing has happened on our behalf."

Their mother, Mrs. Janie Brewer, said in another affidavit:

". . . A neighbor friend of mine told me that my sons had just been beaten up by white folks, and I lost my presence of mind for a while. Another son of mine, Eugene, found that my son Charles was in the Charleston Hospital, and that Green was in the Grenada Hospital. The next day I went to the Charleston Hospital and saw my son Charles. I tried to talk to him. He would cry, and then lose consciousness, in and out. He would only say: 'Where is my brother—and why?' "

In Tallahatchie County, County Registrar William Cox is currently under a court injunction to determine the qualifications of Negro registrants by the same standards as whites, not to limit Negro registrants to coming in one at a time, and not to use the Constitutional interpretation section of the registration form.

This summer marked the first attempt by SNCC to "move into" Tallahatchie County.

On August 4, 1964, four members of the Brewer family attempted to register to vote. According to some SNCC spokesmen, they were the first Negroes to try to register since Reconstruction; they were certainly the first in several decades.

The next night, according to an affidavit from Mrs. Melinda Brewer, a member of the Green Brewer family, a black pickup truck drove around past her house and the house of her brother-in-law, Jesse James Brewer. It stayed in the area 25 minutes.

On August 6, she stated, a green pickup truck drove by at about 1 or 2 A.M. and cruised around. She continued:

"As they were driving I could see them using a searchlight on the trees like they was hunting animals . . . One of the men, about 7 or 8 of them, got out of the truck and walked over towards my bedroom window. He asked me if I had seen Jesse Brewer or Earl Brewer. I said I hadn't and asked why he was looking for them. He said he just wanted to see them. He left and drove off. The man was white; I could not tell whether the rest were whites or not. I could see what I thought were guns sticking up in the back of the truck.

"Mr. Blunt is the field agent on the plantation on which I live. He said on August 6 that if anyone on Mr. Don's place went to register to vote, that person was going to get kicked off the plantation. He said no one in Tallahatchie wants any of those niggers who go to the courthouse. He said he had seen that God-damned old Jesse and Earl go at the courthouse and said they didn't have no God-damned business up there.

"I live on Mr. Don Addison's plantation. On Saturday, August 8, I went to his office to pick up my check. He told me they didn't want any of those damn niggers going down to the courthouse.

"Mrs. John Brewer, a white woman, lives right down the road from me. On August 5, she came over to talk with me. She asked what was that brown car doing down there all the time. She said if they found out we was in any way involved in civil rights they was going to put us out, and she said she would feel sorry for us losing a home. She also said that if civil rights workers lived in Jesse's house, they would get a Ku Klux Klan gang and get them out from there.

"On Saturday afternoon, August 8, several FBI agents came to see me. They asked about the incidents with the pickup trucks. I was frightened and didn't want to get my name used, so I told them I didn't see anything. I told them that the whites didn't ask for Jesse and Earl. I also said that there were no guns. I lied to them."

AFFIDAVIT II.   OFFICE HARASSMENT— CLARKSDALE

The following excerpted statement by Lafayette Surney, director of the Clarksdale COFO project, indicates the attitude of local law enforcement and authorities towards the existence of civil rights offices in the state of Mississippi. Surney, Negro, is a 22-year-old SNCC worker and a native of Ruleville.

"The first day that I arrived in Clarksdale to arrange for housing for the other workers the Chief of Police, Ben Collins, came up to me and said, 'We ain't goin' to have this shit this year.' He then asked me if I wanted to fight right then and I said that I was nonviolent . . . The next day he and other policemen sat in front of the office and took our pictures with a movie camera. Collins [a day later] said, 'I'm going to kill you if it's the last thing I do' . . . This same day Collins assigned a policeman to follow me around wherever I went. When I would go into any place, that policeman would stay outside. This same policeman would follow people from the project to try to find out what families we were living with and where we ate.

"After the Civil Rights Bill was signed, Collins went around to all the Negro restaurants and told them that if they served the project workers, either white or Negro, he would close them up . . .

"A while later an agent from the city Water and Light Department came to the office and tried to turn the lights off. He called Ben Collins, who came over and cursed us. We talked to him outside the office, he told us to get inside and instructed another policeman to 'get the damned billy clubs; we're going to have to move these niggers.' He grabbed the arm of a Negro volunteer named Doris Newman and twisted it. I called the FBI office. They asked for a statement; I said that the situation was too bad for us to go down and asked them to come over. But they wouldn't do this. The next day a Negro man came by the office . . . he told me that Ben Collins had hired some men to kill me . . . The next night . . . when I was on my way back to the Freedom House a group of white men stopped me and showed me a gun. They said, 'This has two buckshots in it and both of them have your name on them. I'm going to blow this up your ass and blow it off.' I walked off and called the chief of police; he told me to go to hell and hung up.

"About three days after the incident with the white men with the gun, I went up to the courthouse to help register some people and the sheriff and Ben Collins were there waiting for me. Collins said, 'There aren't too many white people in town who like you and I'm not one of them. If you don't want to come up like your nigger-loving friends in Philadelphia, you'd better get back to the nigger section of town.' . . . Two highway patrolmen came up and said, 'Let us show him where it is.' I was the only one standing outside so I decided to leave."

AFFIDAVIT III.   LOSS OF JOB DUE TO
VOTER REGISTRATION ATTEMPT

WILLIAMS ADAMS, being duly sworn, deposes and says:
My address is Box 118, Rt. 2, Charleston, Mississippi, and I am a Negro

citizen of the United States. I live on the Rabbit Ridge Plantation in Tallahatchie County. I and all my sons who are old enough work on this plantation.

On August 11, 1964, my son, William Ed Adams, went to the County Courthouse to register to vote. He was seen by the crowd of whites who assembled in the courthouse square. Later that afternoon, Mr. Nelson Douglas, the manager of Rabbit Ridge Plantation, told some people at the plantation store that he was going to have my son arrested because he tried to register to vote.

Mr. Riley McGee came around to my house and told me that Mr. Douglas had announced that my son would be arrested. I went over to the store and saw Mr. Douglas. I asked him, "What are you going to have him arrested for? He hasn't done anything."

Mr. Douglas replied, "He didn't have no business going down to the courthouse. He don't have no more work around here. We can't use a boy like that." I told him that I would go to Greenwood and try to talk to the SNCC people and try to get a lawyer.

I went to Greenwood. I went first to talk to Mr. J. Nolan Reed, the owner of Rabbit Ridge Plantation. He told me that nothing could be done unless my son went down to the courthouse and took his name off the rolls. He said that he would go from Greenwood to the plantation tomorrow and take my son down to the courthouse. He said that unless his name was removed, he could not work on his plantation any more . . .

(signed) Williams Adams

AFFIDAVIT IV.   INTIMIDATION TO STOP
SUMMER PROJECT (Police Brutality)

Charles McLaurin, 23, Negro, native Mississippian and field secretary for SNCC, told in an affidavit what happened to him and four other SNCC voter registration workers on June 8, 1964, in Columbus, Mississippi. McLaurin was later a summer project director in Ruleville.

On that date McLaurin and James Black, Sam Block, Willie Peacock and James Jones set out from Greenwood, Mississippi, to attend an SNCC conference in Atlanta, Ga. He said they were followed by a car all the way from Greenwood to Starkville and that after several attempts to lose their "tail," they found the car still following them outside Columbus, Miss. McLaurin stated:

"At this point, the car turned off its headlights and pulled up right behind us. There was one white man in the car. We all ducked down and pulled over to the side of the road. He passed and we continued on. We passed his car again just outside the Columbus city limits, when he pulled off on a side road.

"About five blocks after he turned off, we were stopped by a highway patrolman. At the time we were stopped we were doing nothing to break the law. In the scout car was a patrolman named Roy Elders and another man in plain clothes. Elders came to our car and said, 'You're the niggers who are going to change our way of life.' He then asked us why we were trying to run a car off the road. At no time had we done this.

"He then told us to get out of the car and we did. The sheriff of Lowndes County then drove up and said to Elders, 'What have you got there?' Elders said, 'These are the niggers who are going to change our way of life.' The sheriff asked who was driving the car: 'That little short nigger there?' Elders replied, 'No, this big, fuzzy-lipped m————— f——,' referring to James Black."

McLaurin said all of them except James Black were handcuffed and driven to the Lowndes County jail. Black was left with patrolman Elders.

"At the jail about twenty minutes later, James Black came in with Elders. Black's head was dirty; one side of his face was swollen out of shape; one of his eyes was blackened and bloodshot, and blood was running from his swollen mouth. His clothes were also torn and disarranged. He walked up to me and said, 'He beat me,' pointing to Elders. Elders said, 'This boy fell getting out of the car.' Black's physical condition made it impossible for me to believe Elders' statement that he had merely fallen."

McLaurin stated that the five were put in a cell and that shortly thereafter a white turnkey came and told Sam Block to come with him for an "interview." He said Block was taken outside, and that he could hear sounds of a beating and groans. He said Block was brought back to the cell holding his sides, his mouth swollen.

"The turnkey then said, 'Next,' and Peacock went with him. He returned a few minutes later and said he had been hit in the mouth. His mouth was swollen. . . .

"I went out next and was taken outside. Elders asked, 'Are you a Negro or a nigger?' I said, 'I am a Negro.' Jolly, another highway patrolman, hit me across the face with his forearm. Elders repeated the question, and my answer was the same. I was then punched hard in my left ear by Elders and knocked to the ground. The highway patrolmen helped me up and one of them said, 'Boy, can't you stand on your own two feet?' They stood me up against the wall and repeated the question. This time I answered, 'I am a nigger.' They then lectured me and told me nobody wanted me in town and I should leave. Elders said, 'If I ever catch you here again I'll kill you.'

"They took me upstairs to my cell. James Jones was taken out and came back with a swollen lip, saying he had been hit in the mouth. The next day James Black was charged with reckless driving and running a stop sign. He was not, to the best of my knowledge, guilty of either. He was fined $28 and we were released."

James Jones said in an affidavit that when he was beaten, Elder "kept calling me a black nigger and said he would put me on the county farm for twenty years and that if he ever saw me after that he would kill me. Elder asked me if I had been born in Mississippi. I said yes. He asked me whether I'd ever been in a position where the niggers didn't help me but the white did. I told him I'd been poor all my life . . .

"I spent the night in jail with the rest of the fellows. We were all in pain. At no time was I informed of the charges against me or allowed to make phone calls. The next morning [June 9], we were all finger-printed and photographed. I asked the sheriff what we were charged with, and he said reckless driving and possession of illegal literature."

Samuel Block, in his affidavit, quoted the jailer as saying, "The river is just right; let's carry them out and rifle them right now."

"Elder hit me on the cheek with his fist. I staggered and fell back to the window, and he grabbed me and hit me in the groin with his fist very hard. I fell down and he kicked me hard in the shin . . . He asked if any white person has mistreated me in Mississippi. I answered, 'Yes, you are mistreating me now.' He hit me again with his fist and knocked me back. When it was over, I could just barely make it back upstairs to the cell. I fell to the concrete floor and blacked out and lay there for about 20 minutes."

Block said Judge R. V. Whittaker questioned him about himself and James Black. Block said he did not answer any questions about Black, and that the judge replied, "You can sit there and act a damn m——f—— fool if you want to, but we are trying to help this 17-year-old boy whom we have charges on."

Block said a man he believed to be the prosecuting attorney told him that if the traffic charges against James Black were not appealed, the other charges against the five would be dropped—and that if there was an appeal, the other charges would remain.

Willie Peacock described his beating in another affidavit:

"Elder hit me twice with his fist. He asked me how old I was and I told him. He said, 'Nigger, you just want to die young. I'd just as soon shoot you now as to look at you. Do you believe it?' I said yes. He said, 'Nigger, I'm gonna erase that bit of doubt out of your mind.

And if you come back here again, I'm going to roll you out as thin as
cigarette paper.' "

AFFIDAVIT V.   POLICE COLLABORATION
(with Arsonists in Community Center Burning)

The following statement describes the actions of local law enforcement officers in relation to the burning of a community center about
six miles from Vicksburg. The building, which was constructed more
than ten years ago, was last used for organized civil rights activity
during the COFO mock Freedom Ballot gubernatorial campaign in
November, 1963. Many, perhaps most, of the twenty-one churches burned
from the start of the Mississippi Summer Project through August 24
had no record of civil rights involvement. Arson has been used as a
general form of intimidating the Negro community of Mississippi. In
this case, however, it is rumored in the Negro section of Bovina that
passers-by may have observed a car with Ohio license tags at a July 6
meeting and thought that it belonged to a COFO summer volunteer.
One member of the community center had come to that meeting in a
relative's car which had the out-of-state plates.

DAVID RILEY, being duly sworn, deposes and says:

In my capacity as reasearch man for the Vicksburg COFO project,
I have talked with several [five] leaders of the Bovina community . . .
about the burning of the Bovina Community Center on Tuesday night,
July 7, 1964, between 10:30 and 11:30. The building was completely
destroyed; no one was in the building at the time; no one was injured.

A small group of people gathered around the burning building between
10:45 and 11:45 on Tuesday night. Many were Negro leaders of the
Bovina community; some were whites from Bovina; others were police
officers, including Warren County Sheriff Vernon O. Luckett. At least
three Negroes present—two of whom I spoke to—saw firemen pull a
torch out from under the front part of the building. The torch, still
blazing when the firemen pulled it out, was a three-foot-long pole with
rags wrapped around the end and wire wrapped around the rags, according to an eyewitness. Also, according to the eyewitnesses, policemen took
several pictures of the burning building and the torch. One man who
saw the torch on Tuesday night said it was not there when he stopped
by on his way to work the next morning at 5:00 A.M. Another woman
who also saw the torch said she did not see it when she returned to
the burned building late Wednesday morning.

Wednesday's Vicksburg *Evening Post* carried a short article on the
burning. There were no direct quotes, but one paragraph read: "Sheriff

Vernon O. Luckett said the preliminary investigation showed no indications that arson might be involved." The article went on to say that since there was "a mild wind" and since the "fire did start in the rear of the building," it was likely that burning rubbish in a trash can eight feet behind the building started the fire, according to Sheriff Luckett.

This is in complete contradiction to what the Sheriff later told one man . . . He said that he did *not* believe the fire was set by the burning rubbish, and "no doubt it was set" by someone deliberately.

It is also in contradiction to my personal examination of the ruins of the building. The floor beams at the front of the building were completely destroyed, while several charred ones remained at the rear; one beam, directly opposite the trash can from which the fire supposedly was started, even had a completely uncharred portion of wood on it. The trash can itself was about one-quarter full of rusted and somewhat charred cans; one can still had paper on it, and there was more unburnt paper only slightly below the surface trash which had been burnt. The trash barrel did not have holes in the bottom to allow a draft to build up a large fire. So it seems extremely unlikely that a fire in the trash can could have been or was large enough to set a whole building on fire, especially a building more completely destroyed on the front and one covered on the outside with inflammable asphalt shingles. I have photographs of all this evidence at the ruins of the building.

The Sheriff's account of the fire in the newspaper article of July 8 is further contradicted by the fact that no one from the Bovina Community Center had been burning trash in the barrel either on Tuesday, July 7, the day of the fire, or for several weeks before the fire. The last time trash had been burnt in the barrel was in the beginning of June, according to officials of the Bovina Community Center. Again, according to officials of the Center, the last time a party had been held in the Center was in the third week of June. On Monday night, July 6, a routine meeting was held at the Center, but only Cokes and cookies were served; so there was no trash that needed to be burned after the meeting.

What has Sheriff Luckett done to investigate the information recorded here? He had photographs taken of the torch, but there was no mention of either the torch or the photographs in the newspaper article. No official of the Bovina Center has seen the photographs. Sheriff Luckett never contacted the president of the Bovina Center; he did not speak with her the night of the fire although she was there at the burning; he has not spoken with her or contacted her in any way in the three weeks that have passed since the burning. Nor had any of his deputies contacted her. Two deputies did visit Bovina about two weeks after the fire and talked with some officials of the Center, but that is apparently the only effort county officials have made to find out who burned down the Bovina Community Center.

(Signed)   David Riley

AFFIDAVIT . VI.   VIOLENCE BY POLICE
(Canton)

Sections of three affidavits from people who met with the Canton, Mississippi, police force are given below. They could as well have come from any of the scores of Mississippi communities in which the legally constituted authorities are themselves the lawless.

The first event is told through the affidavits of Steven Smith of Marion, Iowa, and Eric Morton of New York City, both volunteers then working in voter registration, when four workers were driving a truck of voter registration materials from Jackson to Greenwood and Greenville on Wednesday, July 15. They decided to drive by way of Canton.

Morton's statement reads: "As we were entering highway 51 [in Jackson] we were stopped by two Jackson city policemen. They asked Steve where we were going and he told them Canton. They looked through the truck and saw the voter registration material we were carrying. They then gave Steve a ticket for driving without a commercial license . . . We proceeded on toward Canton. Along the way we were worried that the Jackson police might call ahead to the highway patrol to have us stopped . . . About five miles out of Canton we saw one car that was definitely following us. The car was unmarked and there was no indication that it was a police car . . . It just remained behind us, blinking its lights. As we reached Gluckstadt, the car pulled up close to us and began blinking a red light. We then pulled over. It was about 10:30 P.M. at this time. The doors and windows of our truck were locked."

Smith's affidavit states: "I pulled over and stopped, even though I heard no siren and had no definite knowledge that the following car contained police . . . and waited until the man in the car arrived. He came up to the truck and told me to get out. I asked for identification. He didn't show me anything, but told me to get out of the truck. I got out . . . and he and I walked to his car. Eric also got out and we received a . . . lecture while he was writing a ticket for speeding . . . A highway patrol car arrived . . . A third car then pulled up which was unmarked and contained one man not in uniform. We could tell he had been drinking because of his actions and because we could smell the liquor . . .

"After a short interchange between him and the first man, the first man left and the third man took me back to the car of the highway patrolman. He opened the car and told me to get inside. I got inside and sat on the back seat. He told me to move over and got in. All the doors and windows were shut. He said, 'I can't kill you, but you know what I'm going to do to you.' I answered, 'No, sir.' At this time he pulled his gun out of his holster and started to hit me on the head with the gun butt. I put my hands up to protect my head and rolled into a ball on the seat. Over a period of about a minute he hit me about four times on the head and about eight to ten times on the left hand. He also hit me about three time on the left leg, twice on my right hand, and once on my left shoulder. All of this was with the gun butt . . . Three of them then went up to Eric. They had a conversation with Eric which I could not hear and one of the men raised a gun and struck Eric, knocking him down. He got up and was knocked down again. I had been sitting in the car through all of this. I felt the blood on my face and on my arm. The man who had beaten me then came back to the car and sat down in the back seat. He picked up a flashlight and hit me across the mouth with it. I then rolled into a ball again and he put the gun to my temple and cocked it. He said, 'If you move, I'll blow your brains out.' "

They went to the Canton police station and then to the jail. According to Morton's affidavit, the other two workers in the truck were let out on the road and told to "run back to Jackson." They were told, Morton says, to "quit working for COFO or COFO would get them killed." The two of them started down the highway on foot.

During this time Morton was told that they had no charges against him and that he was free to go. "I was afraid they would come after me if I tried to go," Morton reported, "so I refused." His affidavit reported that two of the men suggested that Morton should be driven to Philadelphia [Miss.] and made reference to the then-missing three COFO workers. "They continued to make comments until we arrived at the Madison County jail in Canton." (Morton and Smith were taken to Canton in separate cars.)

Morton's statement continues: "At the jail they locked me up until the next morning. The next morning, after four requests, I was allowed to make a phone call by the jailer's wife. I had also asked to make a phone call the night before when I was first taken to the jail . . . I called COFO in Jackson and spoke to Bob Moses . . . I was taken to the home of a judge in Madison. Court was held in his garage and two lawyers from COFO were there . . . I heard the man who had beaten me referred to as Sheriff Holly . . . I was then charged with interfering with Steve's arrest and with resisting arrest. Bail was set at $150 . . ."

Smith reported that he was placed in a cell with three white men and was questioned the following morning in the jailer's office by the three men who had stopped him the night before. They threatened to shoot him if he ever returned to Madison County, he stated. During questioning a college newspaper in Iowa City called and he was allowed to speak over the phone. However, "Before I got on the phone they asked me if I was willing to accept it as my one phone call without telling me where it was from. I thought the call was coming from the COFO office in Jackson and said yes. I was not allowed to make a phone call of my own either before or after that . . . In the evening I was released on bond and given back my wallet. When my wallet was returned, the ticket I had been given the night before was missing and so was my driver's license."

In the same city of Canton the events sworn to in the following affidavit excerpts took place when a local Negro called upon city police to investigate a bombing at the COFO Freedom House.

Mr. George Washington, Sr., a well-known Negro store proprietor and adamant supporter of the movement, who is in his late fifties, rented a house to COFO for use as a Freedom House. Early in the morning of June 8, 1964, about 1:30 A.M., a bomb was thrown at the Freedom House. As little damage resulted, the police were not immediately notified, although the FBI was called. After rising in the morning, Mr. Washington's wife called the police. Mr. Washington described his treatment:

"When the police came, they used abusive language in talking to me. Mr. Cooks and Mr. John Chance told me to get in the car, they were going to send me to the penitentiary for failing to report the bombing incident the preceding night. I asked if they could take me in without a warrant. They said they didn't need one, and they shoved me into the car . . .

"When we got to the jailhouse, Mr. Cooks was opening the door. While he was doing so, as I began to go in the door, Mr. Chance struck me over the eye—the blow struck me over the eye because I attempted to duck the blow when I saw it coming—otherwise he would have hit me right in the eye . . . They began to question me, if I had any idea about who had thrown the bomb at the Freedom House. I told them I didn't know who had thrown the bomb. Then Mr. Chance said I was lying again and came up and hit me on top of the head . . . Then he said he 'just hates me and despises me and it makes him sick just to look at me . . . I feel like taking my pistol and beating your face flat so your wife won't even recognize you.' He said he thought that I was all right, but now that I wouldn't cooperate and put those out of the house so they have to get out of the town, he didn't think so any more.

"About 8:00 Chief Dan Thompson came in and asked me what had they held me for and Mayor Stanley Matthew and City Atty. Bob Goza also came in and they talked much nicer to me than Chance had, didn't use any more abusive language and asked me many questions about selective buying campaigns and the boycott. He told me I'd lose my reputation with my white friends in town. The question went on until about 11:00 when they let me go.

"My right eye didn't swell up right away [but] the next day, Tuesday, it began to hurt and swell up very badly . . . I've had to see the specialist about three times a week, and he said I have to have an operation on my right eye . . ."

AFFIDAVIT VII.
HARASSMENT UNPROVOKED BY
POLITICAL ACTIVITY
(Jackson)

Of the many affidavits available on general treatment of Negroes in Mississippi, the following is one example of both unprovoked police hostility and what may be called the "semantics of race." It is worth noting that the event described took place in the largest and most cosmopolitan city in the state.

WILLIE FUNCHES, being duly sworn, deposes and says:

On July 5, 1964, at about midnight, I was walking from Farish Street to the COFO office on Lynch Street with Harry Lowe and Jimmy Lee Wilcox. At the corner of Poindexter and Lynch we were passing a police car which was parked there. This police car had a cross on the side and a red light on the top, an "accident car." As we passed by, one of the two policemen in the car said, "Hey, nigger, were you throwing stones?" I said, "No, sir." Jimmy Lee Wilcox said, "No, we weren't." The policeman said, "Can't you say 'yes, sir' to me, nigger? That's one of them smart niggers standing in the middle there [referring to Jimmy]." He then said, "Don't you lie to me, nigger, or I'll make your face blacker than his [referring to Jimmy]."

They called in and told headquarters that they had the black SOB's who had thrown the bricks—they had the little nigger in the red shirt. My shirt was red. Two other police cars came up. The policeman in the first car said that he would take off his belt and beat my rump if I was identified. Another car came up and one of the two policemen in that car said, "Yeah, I want that little nigger with the red shirt especially." The policeman who had said this snatched me out of the car and put me in the other car. Then he hit me in the stomach four times. Then he asked me where I lived. He asked me if I had been throwing rocks and when I said no he called me a "goddamned liar." Then he told me to get "your goddamned ass on the ground out there with the rest of the niggers." The other cop had brought Jimmy back and we were all sitting on the ground next to the car. The policeman who had been

talking to Jimmy then said, "I ought to kick all three of your teeth in."
He said, "Get up, nigger, and if I catch any of you three in any of the
demonstrations I'll shoot all of you niggers and smoke my cigar on top
of you and think nothing about it." Then he said, "You niggers go home
and let's run." We ran and I met my boss, who told me to come to the
COFO office and tell you about it.

(Signed)   Willie Funches

Compiled by:
Communications Section
MISSISSIPPI PROJECT
1017 Lynch Street
Jackson, Miss.
601-352-9605

AFFIDAVIT VIII.
PHILADELPHIA—NESHOBA COUNTY

Junior Roosevelt Cole, 58, lay leader of Mt. Zion Methodist Church
in rural Neshoba County, Mississippi, told, in a statement signed in
the presence of two witnesses, of his beating near the church on June
16, 1964. Later that night the church, site of a mass meeting on May 31
at which Michael Schwerner and James Chaney had spoken, was burned
to the ground. Cole said a leaders and stewards meeting at the church
had broken up about 10 P.M. that night and they got into their cars and
pickup trucks to drive home. His statement said:

"We saw two cars and a truck driving up, and the people in them
wasn't our color, but we didn't bother about it. Me and my wife got in our
car and drove off. About 50 yards from the churchyard we were forced
to stop. The lights in those cars was out. A man said to me, 'What are
you doing? What you got those guards out there for?' I said we didn't
have any guards. He said, 'You're a liar.' They jerked me out of the
car and let me have it with a heavy instrument, on the jaw, the head, the
neck, the back, and when I was lying there, they kicked me. Then I
was unconscious.

"None of them where I was had any masks on, but Mrs. Georgia Rush
and her son, John T., who were stopped down the road, said there were
men with hoods on where she was. As far as I know there was only three
of us beaten: myself, Mrs. Rush and her son. The men had many, many
guns.

"I was treated at Dr. Charles Moore's clinic in Philadelphia. I don't
think my jaw is broken, but it's out of line a bit.

"About 12:30 or 1 A.M. that night I saw a big light in the sky over where the church was, but I didn't think anything of it. Later, in the morning, I saw it was the church burned. The FBI's came by the following Friday."

His wife, Beatrice, said in her statement:

"There was at least 20 of them there. One of them pulled my husband out of the car and beat him, I couldn't see what with, but it looked like an iron object. Then they kicked him while he was lying on the ground. Then they said to him, 'Better say something or we'll kill you.' I said, 'He can't say nothing; he's unconscious.'

"Then I began to pray, a little prayer. They told me to shut my mouth. But I said, 'Let me pray.' I stretched out my hands and said, 'Father, I stretch out my hand to thee; no other help I know; if thou withdrew thyself from me; Oh Lord, whither shall I go?'

"That struck the hearts of those men. The Lord was there, because then the man said, 'Let her alone,' and he looked kinda sick about it.

"I think my husband's jaw is broken, because his teeth don't sit right in his mouth. But he doesn't think it is, and I can't get him to go down to the clinic again."

Mrs. Dona Richards Moses told in an affidavit of harassment by three highway patrolmen while returning from an attempted private investigation of the disappearance of the three civil rights workers in Neshoba County. She said she was riding in a car driven by Matteo Suarez, in the company of Preston Ponder, Gwen Gillon and David Welsh, when they were stopped.

"The patrolman asked us why we had been in Neshoba. Mr. Suarez answered that we had wanted to investigate the situation of the missing men. The policeman then answered, 'There is nothing to investigate.' He began asking us questions about our work. He looked through all our belongings and the literature we had in the car, pulling them out in the rain to read them. He read a personal letter that Gwen Gillon had, which mentioned an SNCC worker in Batesville. He made mention of the SNCC worker and asked who he was.

"When I answered 'uh-huh' to the question 'Are you from New York?' this policeman said, 'You'd better say 'yes, sir' to me, little nigger.' . . .

"We were allowed to leave. It was then that we realized that during the whole interrogation there had never been mention of our violating the law in any way. We were surprised to find this attitude in the police since we had been led to understand by the Justice Department that there was federal presence in the area and local police were cooperating in the search for the missing men. Otherwise such treatment is the rule in

Mississippi by the police, particularly of civil rights workers, and we are always afraid when we are stopped by the police."

Daniel Pearlman, a law student, and David Welsh, a free-lance reporter, told in affidavits of their beating by civilians in the middle of a summer afternoon in downtown Philadelphia, Miss., on July 17, 1964. The pair were investigating the disappearance of the 3 civil rights workers and preparing a newspaper article.

Pearlman stated they had just left the office of a local attorney when they were stopped near the street corner by a man who asked what business they had in town.

"When Dave identified himself as a reporter, two men came out of the shadows and stood alongside of me. Another man approached from the opposite end of the street . . . The man who first stopped us threw a hard punch to Dave's eye. I was hit over the head by the man standing next to me. I ran and turned to face him. He was chasing me with a link chain hanging from his raised right hand. The doctor said that my wound cannot have been inflicted from a fist alone. I therefore assume that I was hit with the link chain I saw hanging from his hand . . .

"I was then chased by two men and ran to the sheriff's office . . . The sheriff sent Deputy Cecil Price to the scene. Price leisurely strolled to the corner. When we got there he said that he didn't see my friend. I pointed to a crowd on the street corner and said, 'They know . . . He strolled toward the crowd."

Welsh said in his affidavit: "The first man struck me in the jaw hard with his fist. The other man then hit me several times, and additional men appeared to be closing in at the scene. I could not see Pearlman. I ran toward the courthouse, where two more men intercepted and struck me. So I turned around again and ran back to retrieve my sunglasses. As I did so, I was kicked in the ribs—one rib was cracked, according to X rays taken in Jackson at the office of Dr. McIlwain—and absorbed a few more blows in the face. One of them gave me a symbolic kick in the pants and advised me to leave town. I ran to my car and drove back to the site of the initial attack. A crowd was gathering; in the center were Price and Pearlman, his head and shirt were bloody. The mood of the crowd was less than friendly. After explaining what happened to Price, we left town."

APPENDIX III

LEGAL CO-ORDINATION

NATIONAL LAWYERS GUILD
Detroit, Michigan

July 14, 1964

Honorable Lyndon B. Johnson
President of the United States
The White House
Washington, D.C.

Honorable Sir:

Recent events in the State of Mississippi have led to calls for Federal intervention in that State for the protection of those who are attempting to assist Negro citizens in the exercise of their Constitutional right to vote. The Attorney General of the United States has responed by expressing his opinion publicly to the effect that the Federal Government lacks the power to take preventive police action in Mississippi.

The National Lawyers Guild has, in such circumstances, referred the question of the powers of the Federal Government to a Committee headed by Mr. Laurent Frantz, a member of the Alabama and Tennessee Bars, who is an authority on Constitutional Law in the area of civil rights. Our Committee has studied the legal questions involved and the applicable law. Its Memorandum of Law is annexed.

We respectfully submit that the Memorandum establishes that the Federal Government does have explicit and adequate powers by which it can protect the voting rights of the Negro citizens of Mississippi, or any other State, through the use of whatever Federal agencies it deems necessary to overcome systematic resistance to the execution of Federal law or the exercise of Federally protected rights.

We believe it is appropriate and necessary that such powers be used with all possible speed in order to bring to an end the intimidation of voters in Mississippi and those who would assist them in voting.

In our view, the best way to reduce the necessity for employing massive Federal power, possibly including the use of Federal troops to take over the administration of the State of Mississippi, is to employ without delay the full measure of Federal power through the less drastic measures described in the attached Memorandum. Following this course will place Federal-State relationships upon the footing intended by our Constitutional system rather than serving to impair those relationships.

We further suggest the immediate àssignment to Mississippi of additional visiting United States District Judges who are needed to preside over the many proceedings which will be initiated as the voter registration campaign progresses and the new Federal Civil Rights Law is implemented. The present complement of *three* District Judges is obviously inadequate for present and future needs in this large State.

The future of our country as a nation founded on law depends on the speed and forthrightness of our nation's leaders' action in this time of crisis. We pledge our support for such leadership.

> Respectfully submitted,
> National Lawyers Guild
> (Signed)   Ernest Goodman,
>   President
> (Signed)   Herman B. Gerringer,
>   Secretary

COUNCIL OF FEDERATED ORGANIZATIONS LEGAL GUIDE

We cannot hope to provide a complete guide to the law, your rights, or what you should do. However, COFO has worked out certain guidelines which should apply to almost every situation. There are now in the state attorneys from the NAACP Legal Defense and Educational Fund, Inc., the National Lawyers Guild, the Lawyers Constitutional Defense Committee, and the Lawyers Committee for Civil Rights Under Law. In addition, there is a group of law students available to us through the Law Students Civil Rights Research Council. The students are to clerk for whatever lawyers are in the area working on COFO cases, help work up evidence for suits, and be the local channel for legal problems. *No suits are to be signed or brought or lawyers retained except through the Jackson legal office.* When arrests occur in an area having a COFO volunteer attorney, he would normally be assigned to the case, but the Jackson office must still be requested to make the assignment. This can be done when the call is made informing us of the arrest.

ARRESTS AND POLICE

1. Don't give out local people's names, addresses or phones. Beware of "friendly" conversations with police. They might well be trying to get some information against someone or against the project and trying to trick us. Be guarded but always polite.

2. Registering with the police. Some people have registered—including having their pictures and fingerprints taken—feeling that the local police would offer protection. Others have just given their names and COFO address. Others refuse to go down to the police station unless arrested.

3. Make full reports of all harassments, arrests, beatings, suspicious cars (license plates, make, year, model, and color) to the local police, sheriff, highway patrol, FBI, Justice Department and, most important, to Jackson COFO.

4. Don't go anywhere with a policeman unless you are under arrest.

5. If you are under arrest, you have a right to know what law you have violated and what the charge is.

6. Be sure to ask for receipts itemized for every item taken by the police.

7. Ask to make a phone call for obtaining legal aid upon arrival at the police station. You don't have to tell anyone who that might be. Call your local COFO office, or, if that can't be done, call Mr. Jonathan Smith at 352-9478, collect.

8. Don't worry if a lawyer doesn't immediately come. We are working on your case and many others.

9. Remember to get exact descriptions of the police, and names.

10. *To local project office:* Call Jackson COFO staff phone, 352-9478. Report names, ages, race, organizational affiliation, home address, project phone and address, date, time and place of incident, the circumstances leading up to the arrests, police descriptions, jail location, charges, likelihood of danger, hearing or trial dates, whether affidavits were taken, what contacts with officials have been made, and the bond information as indicated below.

BAIL BONDS

1. Give full bond details when calling Jackson COFO the first time. What is the *total* amount needed (in cash and in property) to get the person out of jail? Who with the local project is handling the bond situation (preferably the project director or the law student)? What is his name, address and phone number?

2. List the name, age, etc., of each summer volunteer requiring bond money to be sent from his parents or contacts. Each project should have a complete list of summer volunteers, staff and local people working with the project, including names, ages, birth dates, home addresses and phones.

3. When only a few people are arrested, the local project will obtain the bail bonds. (Try to set up a local bonding committee of local residents who will sign as sureties on property bonds.) Call collect to the bond contacts or parents of the summer volunteers when they need bailing out.

When larger numbers of people get arrested, call Greenwood SNCC (453-4995). Notify Greenwood when planning Freedom Days and when any bond problem arises.

4. The parents or bail contacts for the summer volunteers will wire the money to whoever and to what address the local project designates and in whatever form specified. The project bond person must obtain a receipt for each bond and send a copy of that, including the bail receipt number, to: 1017 Lynch St., Jackson; 708 Ave. N., Greenwood; and 8½ Raymond St., N.W., Atlanta, Ga. 30314. Each bail bond sender or donor needs to be sent that information, along with the trial dates and charges for each defendant.

TRIALS AND HEARINGS

1. REFUSE TO PARTICIPATE IN ANY HEARING WITHOUT A LAWYER. Request a continuance until you have had a reasonable chance to get a lawyer of your own choosing. This right to counsel includes the right to an attorney who will raise all the relevant Constitutional issues, including segregated courtroom, exclusion of Negroes from the juries, discriminatory references to Negroes in the courtroom, etc. Therefore, do not accept a court-appointed lawyer, since in most cases he'll not help.

2. If the judge tries you without a lawyer, stand mute, which means that you are not to make any plea of any sort. Do not plead guilty, *nolo contendere,* or not guilty. Refuse to plead.

3. *Nolo contendere* pleas are discouraged.

4. Be cautious in your first hearing. What you say in the Justice of Peace, Police, or Municipal Court will most probably be used to strengthen the case against you in the trial *de novo* in the county court.

5. Ask the judge to inform you of your rights.

REPORTS

Fully report all harassments, intimidations, arrests, trials, etc., including difficulty in obtaining or using the telephones so that proper legal aid and/or protests can be made. Each project should keep a chronological log with details (names, days, dates, times, places, etc.). Copies to Jackson, Greenwood, and Atlanta. In addition, the U.S. Commission on Civil Rights is required to investigate every signed voting complaint (Washington, D.C.).

CARS

1. Must have state license plates (and as soon as have plates *must* have an inspection sticker) within 30 days and operator's license within 60 days of entering state. *One can be validly arrested if one has Mississippi tags but not an inspection sticker.*

2. Insurance. SNCC and COFO require every car to be insured. At present, we have no means to own or insure cars. Therefore, all cars must be owned and insured by individuals themselves. We hope that soon SNCC's Sojourner Motor Fleet will be able to own and insure those cars SNCC agrees to own. Contact Atlanta SNCC, Mrs. S. D. Johnson, about this.

3. Drivers. Always have automobile registration in glove compartment. Only the owner or duly authorized person can drive the car. The latter must have written and preferably notarized authorization.

4. COFO requires all cars used by us to be registered with this office. Copy the car's registration form, including the date entered the state, the license plate number, operator's license number, and complete insurance information.

5. In case of accident. First aid the injured. Call an ambulance if necessary. Get the license plate numbers, the make and year of all cars involved and names, addresses, and insurance companies of all drivers. Call the police, but don't discuss who was at fault. Be sure to file the complete report with the Mississippi Highway Patrol within 24 hours.

SECURITY

1. Lock all COFO buildings at night and have the front door closed, if possible, during the day. Don't allow a policeman to enter, unless he has a valid search warrant. Consent or failure to object at the time waives one's rights. Search warrants are illegal if: they are for the "premises," they vary from the affidavit, have no return date, person in charge of the premises isn't given a copy of it prior to the search, or if it is a "John Doe" warrant. Treat automobiles as buildings, except that they are much less secure. In arrests, searches can be made of the immediate vicinity, but subsequently warrants are necessary.

2. Don't allow anyone to wander about your office or freedom house. Be strict about checking credentials and control visitors. Accept no additional workers unless they have been assigned by COFO. Call Jackson about any special problems.

LAWYERS

Attorneys are sent out upon request given to the Legal Coordinator in Jackson. No suits are to be filed or trial work done without our O.K. and assignment.

COFO AND THE CIVIL RIGHTS BILL

1. *Public Accommodations.* Concentrating on political rights such as voting, education and eliminating violence, COFO is not at this time sponsoring demonstrations for desegregation of public accommodations. However, certain rights of citizens are more clearly defined now.

In this regard, when noncompliance with the public accommodations section of the new law is found, suits can be considered. Send the Legal Coordinator a statement of the facts, affidavits or signed statements of people refused service, and signed varifications, which will be supplied by your law student or this office.

2. *Voting.* A form (based on the CR Bill) to request from the Registrar a copy of the test taken by applicant, together with his answers, is shown below. We request every Project to duplicate this form for each county in which they work. Prospective registrants (or re-registrants) should submit this form to the Registrar together with self-addressed, stamped envelope.

When reproducing this form for your own county, please be sure that the name of *your* county and the name of *your* registrar appear. The only blanks on the form should be for name, signature, dates, address.

To: Registrar of Sunflower County
Re: Request for Copy of Registration Test and Answers

I, _____, pursuant to the provisions of Title I of the 1964 Civil Rights Bill, do hereby request Cecil C. Campbell, Registrar of Sunflower County, Mississippi, or anyone acting in such capacity, to furnish this applicant with a certified copy of the registration test and of this applicant's answers to this test within 25 days of receipt of this request. I took this test on _____, 196__.

_____
Applicant's Signature

Submitted to the registrar this _____ day of _____, 196__.
Attached: Self-addressed, stamped envelope
Name _____
Address _____

ATTORNEY'S PROJECT

Some attorneys have pointed out that there are times when it would be useful to have some contact with local whites in the power structure or law enforcement agencies. At the discretion of the local Project Director, lawyers can help set up such a line of communication.

PROTECT LOCAL PEOPLE

Do not take any statements or affidavits from local people, or ask them to serve as plaintiffs in any action, unless they know exactly what is happening. Every party to an action must fully realize the nature of what he is getting into and the risks involved. This does not preclude us from encouraging people to fight for their rights.

THIS IS THE LAW OF THE LAND

Title 18, U.S. Code, Section 241, CONSPIRACY AGAINST RIGHTS OF CITIZENS

If two or more persons conspire to injure, oppress, threaten, or intimidate any citizen in the free exercise or enjoyment of any right or privilege secured to him by the Constitution or laws of the United States, or because of his having so exercised the same . . .

They shall be fined not more than $5,000 or imprisoned not more than ten years, or both.

ATTORNEYS AND LEGAL SECRETARIES WHO SERVED IN THE 1964 SUMMER PROGRAM

LAWYERS CONSTITUTIONAL DEFENSE COMMITTEE, INC.
NEW YORK, N.Y.

JACKSON OFFICE

Paul Chevigny, Esq. 6/20-7/5   1 Wall St., NYC

Robert W. Lentz, Esq. 6/21-7/4   34 E. Market St., West Chester, Pa.

Alan Nevas, Esq. 6/21-7/4   256 E. State St., Westport, Conn.

Daniel H. Blatt, Esq. 6/21-7/4   51 Chambers St., NYC

Marvin Braiterman, Esq. 7/3-7/18   506 Tower Bldg., Baltimore, Md.

Ann Cooper, 7/3-7/17   % Herrick, Smith, Farley & Ketchum, 294 Washington St., Boston Mass.

Peter Marcuse, Esq. 7/3-7/18   49 Leavenworth St., Waterbury, Conn.

Donald Elliott, Esq. 7/3-7/18   1 Rockefeller Plaza, NYC

Alan Richenaker, Esq. 7/16-7/31   152 Market St., Paterson, N.J.

John W. Herz, Esq. 7/16-7/31   270 Madison Ave., NYC

Ellis L. Bert, Esq. 7/16-7/31   138-20 31st Road, Flushing 54, NY

George Constantikes, Esq. 7/16-7/31   256 E. State St., Westport, Conn.

Charles Arensberg, Esq. 7/29-8/13   1404 1st Nat'l Bank Bldg., Pittsburgh, Pa.

Jesse Brenner, Esq. 7/29-8/13   157 West 79th St., NYC

Bernard Jackson, Esq. 7/29-8/13   401 Broadway, NYC

C. A. Frerichs, Esq. 8/12-8/26   703 1st Nat'l Bank Bldg., Waterloo, Iowa

William J. Rooney, Esq. 8/11-8/26   651 Grand Concourse, Bronx, N.Y.

James B. Wilson, Esq. 8/16-8/30   3505 E. Olive, Seattle, Wash.

Frank E. G. Weill, Esq. 8/24-9/8   301 "G" St., S.W., Wash., D.C.
Neil J. Toman, Esq. 8/24-9/8   122 E. Main St., Madison, Wisconsin
Melvin Margolies, Esq. 8/30-9/12   175 W. 13th St., NYC
Mary Ann Glendon, 8/23-9/8   % Mayer, Friedlich, Spiess, Tierney,
    Brown & Platt, 231 S. LaSalle St., Chicago, Ill.
David Goldstick, Esq. 7/29-8/13   204 W. 34th St., NYC
William P. Streng, Esq. 8/2-8/16   27 Central Ave., Dayton, Ohio
Philip Hilsenrad, Esq. 7/23-8/4   96 Main St., Ridgefield, Conn.
Henry J. Stern, Esq. 8/15-8/29   2045 Municipal Bldg., NYC
Edward Koch, Esq. 8/15-8/29   52 Wall St., NYC
Ralph Lockwood, Esq. 7/3-7/17   1115 Main St., Bridgeport, Conn.
Jack Oppenheim, Esq. 7/15-7/30   312 W. 73rd St., NYC
Martin Berger, Esq. 8/17-8/31   377 Broadway, N.Y. 13, N.Y.
Dickinson R. Debevoise, Esq. 7/18-7/25   744 Broad St., Newark, N.J.
Joseph S. Lobenthal, Jr., Esq. 7/30-8/14   150 Nassau St., NYC
Harvey Klaris, Esq. 7/30-8/14   1 Clark St., Brooklyn, N.Y.
Robert B. Bourne, Esq. 8/22-9/1   382 Springfield Ave., Summit, N.J.
Kenneth Griswold, Esq. 8/15-8/29   1001 N.Y. Bldg., St. Paul, Minn.
Miss Sandra Nystrom (Sec'y) 8/22-9/5   Church World Service, 475
    Riverside Drive, N.Y. 27, N.Y.

MEMPHIS OFFICE
Henry M. Aronson, Esq. 8/1-8/29   151 Farmington Ave., Hartford,
    Conn.
Robert Feldt, Esq. 6/21-7/5   1909 Amsterdam Ave., NYC
Benjamin Greshin, Esq. 6/21-7/5   14 Carl Ave., Smithtown, N.Y.
Thomas Seymour, Esq. 6/21-7/5   1115 Main St., Bridgeport, Conn.
Erwin Cherovsky, Esq. 7/3-7/18   445 Park Ave., NYC
Joseph Halper, Esq. 7/3-7/19   18 E. 41st St., NYC
George Nims Raybin, Esq. 7/2-7/18   1367 Sheridan Ave., Bronx, N.Y.
Bertram Perkel, Esq. 7/16-7/31   39 Broadway, NYC
Catherine Roraback, 7/16-7/30   185 Church St., New Haven, Conn.
Jeremiah Gutman, Esq. 7/29-8/13   363 7th Ave., NYC
George Zeidenstein, Esq. 7/29-8/13   63 Wall St., NYC
Abe Weitzman, Esq. 7/29-8/13   100 N. Wood Ave., Linden, N.J.
Faith Seidenberg 8/11-8/26   217A State Tower Bldg., Syracuse, N.Y.
Pierre Tonachel, Esq. 8/11-8/26   63 Wall St., NYC
Martin Weinraub, Esq. 8/24-9/8   41 E. 42nd St., NYC
Philip Feiring, Esq. 7/9-7/23   205 W. 34th St., NYC
William Reynolds, Esq. 8/12-8/26   510 E. 85th St., NY 28, NY
Robert Shulman, Esq. 7/16-7/29   290 Old Country Road, Mineola,
    N.Y.
Gilbert Bond, Esq. 7/15-7/30   683 Macon St., Brooklyn, N.Y.

Elsbeth Levy 7/28-8/12   41 W. Preston St., Baltimore, Md.
Haskell Kassler, Esq. 7/28-8/12   1 State St., Boston, Mass.
Robert P. Schulman, Esq. 7/3-7/17   30 E. 42nd St., N.Y. 17, N.Y.
Thomas J. Connelly, Esq. 8/8-8/29   188 Weeks Rd., N. Babylon, N.Y.
David Hoffman, Esq. 7/16-7/31   500 S. Center St., Orange, N.J.
James Sobieski, Esq. 8/11-8/26   634 S. Spring St., Los Angeles, Calif.

NEW ORLEANS OFFICE

George Hinckley, Esq. 7/21-7/31   34-10 94th St., Jackson Hts. 72, N.Y.
Jack Brian, Esq. 7/21-8/4   209 McClatchey Bldg., Upper Darby, Pa.
Paul Haskell, Esq. 6/20-7/4   5119 Allan Terrace, Wash. 16, D.C.
Arthur Berger, Esq. 6/21-7/5   Box 432, Harrisburg, Pa.
Richard Floum, Esq. 7/3-7/18   9720 Wilshire Blvd., Beverly Hills, Calif.
Hal Witt, Esq. 7/1-7/16   600 "F" St., N.W., Wash. 4, D.C.
Lewis Stern, Esq. 7/7-7/22   120 Broadway, NYC
Norman Zalkind, Esq. 8/3-8/21   % Morris Michelson, Esq., 18 Tremont St., Boston 8, Mass.
Laurence Weisman, Esq. 7/3-7/18   % Cohen & Wolf, 955 Main St., Bridgeport, Conn.
Arthur Greenberg, Esq. 7/16-7/31   Jefferson Bldg., Peoria, Ill.
Carol Weisbrod, 7/13-7/27   15 East 84th St., NYC
John Burnett, Esq. 7/16-7/31   146 N. Grant St., Manteca, Calif.
Myron Nadler, Esq. 7/16-7/31   3215 Third Ave., Bronx, N.Y.
Melvin Warshaw, Esq. 7/16-7/30   % N.Y. State Labor Relations Board, 270 Broadway, NYC
Leo Kuperschmid, Esq. 7/29-8/13   10 East 40th St., NYC
Donald Landis, Esq. 7/29-8/13   270 Madison Ave., NYC
Jay Greenfield, Esq. 8/11-8/26   575 Madison Ave., NYC
Joe Meyers, 8/11-8/26   123 W. 74th St., NYC
Esther Frankel, 8/11-8/26   262 Main St., Paterson, N.J.
Eleonore Beth, 8/24-9/8   501 Fifth Ave., NYC
Ralph Werner, Esq. 7/23-8/7   521 Fifth Ave., NYC
Joseph Goldberg, Esq. 8/1-8/16   635 Madison Ave., NYC
Thelma Gregory, 7/29-8/13   155 Ridge St., NYC
Leslie Finch, 7/21-8/4   7 Tappan Ave., Belleville, N.J.
Muriel Finch, 7/21-8/4   7 Tappan Ave., Belleville, N.J.
Anthony LoFrisco, Esq. 8/10-8/25   104 E. 40th St., NYC
Eugene N. Sosnoff, Esq. 8/1-8/16   655 Madison Ave., NYC
Bradlee M. Backman, Esq. 8/14-8/29   31 Exchange St., Lynn, Mass.
Howard Stern, Esq. 8/24-9/8   152 Market St., Paterson, N.J.
Charles Paolillo, Esq. 8/29-9/15   26 Broadway, NYC
Alan H. Levine, Esq. 8/1-9/15   44 Gramercy Park, NYC

LIST OF GUILD ATTORNEYS
PARTICIPATING IN
THE MISSISSIPPI PROJECT—1964

NAME	HOME	ASSIGN- MENT STATION	WEEK OF
1. Anglin, Frank	Chicago	Jackson- Greenwood	July 20th
2. Brown, Nelson F.	Chicago	Jackson	August 10th
3. Buhai, Harriet	San Diego	Hattiesburg	July 27th
4. Brocato, Justin	Kalamazoo	Biloxi	July 6th
5. Baker, Oscar W.	Bay City	Hattiesburg	July 13th
6. Carey, Thomas	Kalamazoo	Greenwood	July 6th
7. Culver, William	Kalamazoo	Jackson	July 6th
8. Craig, Roger	Detroit	Greenwood	August 3rd
9. Crane, Eugene	Chicago	Hattiesburg	August 10th
10. Cohn, Fred	Chicago	Meridian	August 10th
11. Diggs, Anna	Detroit	Meridian- Philadelphia	June 22nd
12. Dunnings, Stuart J.	Lansing	Meridian	August 3rd
13. Dunaway, Jack	Hollywood	Hattiesburg	August 17th
14. Enslen, Richard	Kalamazoo	Jackson	July 6th
15. Epstein, Pauline	Los Angeles	Greenwood	August 17th
16. Finkel, David	Los Angeles	Meridian- Columbus	June 22nd
17. Fieger, Bernard	Detroit	Meridian	July 13th
18. Francher, Samuel	Spokane	Meridian	July 13th
19. Faulkner, Stanley	New York City	Hattiesburg	August 3rd
20. Feldman, Howard	New York City	Meridian	August 10th
21. Gostin, Irwin	San Diego	Hattiesburg- Laurel	July 20th
22. Hoffman, David	Chicago	Hattiesburg	August 10th
23. Howard, Norman	Berkeley	Meridian	August 10th

NAME	HOME	ASSIGN-MENT STATION	WEEK OF
24. Katz, Sanford	New York City	Greenwood-Meridian	June 29th
25. Kessler, Marvin	New York City	Meridian	July 6th
26. Kievits, Elsa	Beverly Hills	Meridian	July 27th
27. Kozupsky, Harold	New York City	Meridian	July 27th
28. Kennon, Lawrence	Chicago	Greenwood	August 10th
29. Loria, Donald	Detroit	Meridian-Vicksburg	June 15th
30. Lynch, William	Spokane	Jackson	July 13th
31. Laster, Clarence	Detroit	Meridian	August 3rd
32. Lore, Harry	Philadelphia	Greenwood	August 17th
33. Langford, Anna R.	Chicago	Meridian	August 17th
34. Lake, Leonard M.	New York City	(Contributed for Substitute Attorney)	
35. Markels, Charles	Chicago	Meridian-Vicksburg	June 15th
36. Maki, D. Wm.	Detroit	Jackson	June 29th
37. McGee, Henry, Jr.	Chicago	Columbus	June 29th
38. Maxey, Carl	Spokane	Jackson	July 13th
39. Moore, Warfield	Detroit	Meridian	July 20th
40. McCloskey, Jerry	Muskegon	Greenwood	July 20th
41. Miller, Irving	Philadelphia	Greenwood	August 17th
42. Nier, Harry	Denver	Greenwood	August 10th
43. Omerberg, Maynard	Hollywood	Greenwood	July 13th
44. Perdix, George	Kalamazoo	Biloxi	July 6th
45. Pestana, Frank	Hollywood	Greenwood	July 13th
46. Pontikes, George	Chicago	Hattiesburg	July 27th
47. Piel, Eleanor	New York City	Hattiesburg	August 17th
48. Porter, John W.	San Diego	(Contributed for Substitute Attorney)	
49. Rossmore, William	Newark	Greenwood	July 20th

NAME	HOME	ASSIGN-MENT STATION	WEEK OF
50. Shropshire, Claudia	Detroit	Greenwood-Jackson	June 22nd
51. Shapiro, Ralph	New York City	Columbus	June 29th
52. Stein, Robert	Detroit	Greenwood	July 27th
53. Sowell, Myzell	Detroit	Meridian	August 3rd
54. Smith, Wm. G.	Los Angeles	Hattiesburg-Greenwood	August 3rd
55. Soroka, Walter	Chicago	Greenwood	August 10th
56. Stender, Fay	San Francisco	Jackson	August 10th
57. Standard, William	New York City	(Contributed for Substitute Attorney)	
58. Warren, Lawrence	Detroit	Greenwood-Jackson	Duration
59. Wechsler, Burton	Chicago-Gary	Meridian	July 20th
60. Wysocker, Jack	Perth Amboy	Greenwood	August 10th
61. Zemmol, Allen	Detroit	Greenwood	August 3rd
*62. Brock, Robert	Hollywood	Hattiesburg-Laurel	July 20th
63. Danelski, David	Seattle		August 24th
64. Caughlan, John	Seattle		August 24th
65. Hood, David	Seattle		August 24th
66. Tuckel, Irving	Detroit		August 24th
67. Krandle, Richard	Detroit		August 24th
68. Smith, Benjamin E.	New Orleans		
69. Crockett, George W. Jr.	Detroit		Duration

TOTALS BY STATES:

Michigan—23	New Jersey—2	Women Participants—8
California—13	Pennsylvania—2	
Illinois—12	Colorado—1	Negro Participants—14
New York—9	Louisiana—1	
Washington—6		Non-Guild Members—12

* Out of order

APPENDIX IV

THE MISSISSIPPI LEGISLATURE, 1964

COFO
Jackson, Miss. June 2, 1964

This report concerns the composition and activities of the Mississippi Legislature in 1964. The report seemed necessary because of the large number of anti-civil rights bills and other bills of a racial character dealt with by the 1964 Legislative Session.

The body of the report lists and explains the key bills introduced and passed in this session. Only the most important sections of the bills are quoted in full; other portions are explained in the text. Where relevant, selections from floor debate are given, as well as biographical notes on legislators associated with specific measures. These notes make clear the racial aspects of the legislation.

Please note that *only* those bills starred with an asterisk have actually been signed into law, as of June 2, 1964. Several other bills which have been passed in either or in both houses will probably become law before adjournment of the current session, expected in late June or early July.

The Table of Contents and the Introduction, taken together, serve as a summary of the full report.

TABLE OF CONTENTS

—A bill to allow unlimited deputy sheriffs "to cope with emergencies."

—page 7

*6. BILL TO "RESTRAIN MOVEMENTS OF INDIVIDUALS UNDER CERTAIN CIRCUMSTANCES"—THE CURFEW LAW— House Bill No. 64 (Passed in Both Houses and Signed)—This bill would allow police to restrict freedom of movement of individuals and groups and to establish curfews without formally declaring martial law.

—page 7

7. BILL "TO PROVIDE FOR APPOINTMENT OF SECURITY AND PATROL PERSONNEL FOR STATE INSTITUTIONS"— House Bill No. 617 (Passed in House and Sent to Senate)—This bill provides for "security patrol officers" to be appointed at all State institutions by the Public Safety Commissioner. —page 7

8. BILL TO AUTHORIZE A COMPLETE RADIO STATION FOR POLICE IN ANY COUNTY—House Bill No. 101 (Passed in Both Houses). —page 8

*9. THE "MUNICIPAL AGREEMENT" ACT—Senate Bill No. 1526 (Passed by Both Houses and Signed)—A bill to allow municipalities to share police force and firefighting equipment during "riots and civil disturbances." page 9

10. THE "REFUSAL TO COMPLY WITH CERTAIN REQUESTS" BILL—House Bill No. 777 (Passed in Both Houses)—A bill to outlaw passive resistance in civil rights demonstrations. —page 9

*11. THE HIGHWAY PATROL ACT—House Bill 564 (Passed in Both Houses and Signed)—An omnibus bill enlarging the Highway Patrol and expanding its powers, and allowing the Governor to order the Patrol into local situations without the request of local authorities.

—page 11

12. ANTI-FREEDOM SCHOOL BILL NO. 1—Senate Bill No. 2136 (Still in Judiciary Committee)—This bill makes illegal the Freedom Schools and Community Centers planned by COFO for the coming summer. —page 13

13. ANTI-FREEDOM SCHOOL BILL NO. 2—Senate Bill No. 1969 (Still in Education Committee)—This is an earlier attempt to ban the Freedom Schools. —page 15

14. A BILL TO RAISE QUALIFICATIONS FOR MEMBERS OF COUNTY BOARDS OF EDUCATION—Senate Bill No. 1702 (Released from Education Committee)—Among other things, this bill would require Board members to be high-school graduates. The bill has had trouble in the Senate. —page 15

15. A BILL TO PERMIT SEGREGATION OF PUBLIC SCHOOLS BY SEXES—(Approved by the House Education Committee)—The bill is to be used in the event Mississippi schools are forced to integrate racially. —page 16

16. BILLS TO ALLOW STATE SUPPORT OF PRIVATE SCHOOLS —(Introduced into the Senate)—This is a series of bills to allow state funds to be used in support of private schools if public schools are closed to avoid integration. —page 16

17. BILL TO REVOKE THE CHARTER OF TOUGALOO COL-LEGE—Senate Bill No. 1672 (Still in Judiciary Committee)—This bill was introduced in retaliation for civil rights activities of students and faculty at integrated Tougaloo College. —page 16

18. BILL TO END ACCREDITATION OF TOUGALOO COLLEGE —Senate Bill No. 2043 (Passed in Both Houses)—This bill would change the accreditation system in the state so that Tougaloo could be dropped from accreditation. —page 17

19. INVESTIGATION OF UNIVERSITY OF MISSISSIPPI PROFES-SOR CRITICAL OF THE STATE—Concurrent resolution introduced in the House—An attack by legislators against a critical university professor. —page 18

20. ANTI-SUMMER PROJECT BILL—TO PROHIBIT ENTRY INTO THE STATE—House Bill No. 870 (Still in Judiciary "A" Committee)—This bill attempts to prohibit entry into the state of volunteers for the Mississippi Summer Project on the grounds that their purpose is "willful violation of the laws of the state." —page 18

21. THE "CRIMINAL SYNDICALISM" BILL—Senate Bill No. 2027 (Passed in Senate, Reported Out Favorably by House Committee)—This bill makes illegal any association which advocates or practices crime or violence. It is aimed both at white extremist groups and at civil rights organizations. —page 19

22. BILL TO PROHIBIT THE CAUSING OF CRIME FROM OUT-SIDE THE STATE—Senate Bill No. 2026 (Passed in Senate, Reported Out Favorably by House Committee)—This bill, like the Criminal Syndicalism bill, could be applied to both white extremists and civil rights workers. —page 20

23. AN ACT TO PROHIBIT "ENTICEMENT" OF A CHILD TO VIOLATE THE LAWS AND ORDINANCES OF THE STATE—

House Bill No. 786 (Still in Judiciary "A" Committee)—This bill attempts to keep minors from participating in civil rights activites by punishing teachers, parents, and civil rights workers.   —page 21

24. BILL PROVIDING FOR COURTS TO TREAT JUVENILES ARRESTED IN CIVIL RIGHTS CASES AS ADULTS—House Bill No. 960 (Passed by House, Now in Senate)—This bill removes from Youth Court jurisdiction minors under 21 years of age charged under those laws most often used for arrest of civil rights workers.   —page 22

*25. APPROPRIATION FOR THE STATE SOVEREIGNTY COMMISSION—$50,000—Senate Bill No. 1896 (Passed in Both Houses and Signed)—An emergency $50,000 appropriation to the State Sovereignty Commission, the official watchdog of segregation in Mississippi, to fight the Civil Rights Bill now pending before Congress.   —page 22

26. SUPPORT FOR GOVERNOR WALLACE—Concurrent Resolution in the House (Passed by the House)—A Resolution commending Wallace for his Wisconsin "victory."   —page 24

27. BILL TO PAY COSTS OF COUNTY REGISTRARS AND CIRCUIT CLERKS CONVICTED UNDER THE 1957 and 1960 CIVIL RIGHTS ACTS—Senate Bill No. 1880 (Passed in Senate, Now in House)—This bill would allow the State to actively support county officials who refuse to comply with Federal Court orders to register Negroes on an equal basis with whites.   —page 24

28. THE "LIBERTY AMENDMENT" TO OUTLAW FEDERAL AGENCIES AND THE INCOME TAX—House Concurrent Resolution No. 16 (Passed in Both Houses, Now in Joint Committee)—This proposed amendment to the U.S. Constitution would require the U.S. Government to dissolve or sell all agencies which might compete with private enterprise. The personal income tax would also be ended.

—page 24

29. BILL TO END URBAN RENEWAL—House Bill——(Passed in House, Sent to Senate)—A bill ending urban renewal in Mississippi to avoid "federal encroachment."

*30. BILL TO INVALIDATE THE 24TH AMENDMENT, WHICH BANS THE POLL TAX—Senate Bill No. 1783 (Passed in Both Houses and Signed)—This bill appears to comply with the 24th Amendment, which bans the poll tax in Federal elections. But the bill in fact provides for a similar form of registration which would have the same exclusive effects as the poll tax itself.   —page 27

31. BILL TO REDUCE THE NUMBER OF NEGROES ON MISSISSIPPI JURY LISTS—House Bill No. 937 (Passed in House, Sent to

Senate)—This bill attempts to reduce the number of Negroes on Mississippi jury lists by changing the qualifications for jury members.

—page 29

*32 BILL TO PROVIDE PRISON TERMS OR STERILIZATION FOR PARENTS OF ILLEGITIMATE CHILDREN—House Bill No. 180 (Passed by House, Revised Version Passed by Senate, Senate Version Finally Approved by Both Houses and Signed)—This bill in its original House form gave parents of a second illegitimate child the choice between three to five years in the State Penitentiary and sexual sterilization. A Senate version, striking the sterilization clause and reducing the penalty to a misdemeanor, was finally approved and signed.

—page 29

33. BILL TO PROVIDE STERILIZATION FOR THOSE CONVICTED OF A THIRD FELONY—House Bill No. 788 (Still in Judiciary En Banc Committee)—A bill to provide mandatory sterilization of those convicted of a third felony.

—page 31

34. BILL TO REDUCE THE PENALTY FOR RAPE—House Bill No. 145 (Defeated in the House)—A defeated bill which would have reduced the penalty for rape. The present penalty is either death or life imprisonment.

—page 32

*35. BILLS TO ALLOW ARRESTED CIVIL RIGHTS WORKERS TO BE TRANSFERRED TO PARCHMAN PENITENTIARY—House Bills No. 321 and 322 (Passed in Both Houses and Signed)—These bills provide that city and county officials may transfer prisoners to the State Penitentiary in the event of "crowded or inadequate" facilities.

—page 33

36. BILL TO ALLOW DISCLOSURE OF JUVENILE COURT RECORDS TO STATE AGENCIES—Senate Bill No. 2016 (Passed in Senate, Amended Version Passed in House)—This bill would allow disclosures from records of juvenile offenders to any office or agency of the State, at the discretion of the Youth Court Judge. The purpose of the bill is to allow the Board of Trustees of the University of Mississippi to consider the civil rights arrest records of Negro applicants.

—page 34

*37. BILL TO REFORM PARCHMAN PENITENTIARY—House Bill No. 227 (Passed in House, Revised Bill Passed in Senate, House Version Finally Passed in Both Houses and Signed)—A "reform" bill for Parchman Penitentiary which, however, allows continued use of the lash on prisoners. The bill centralizes control of the Penitentiary under the Governor.

—page 34

APPENDIX V

FEDERAL LAW IN MISSISSIPPI

INTRODUCTION

Nowhere is the corruption and hypocrisy of Mississippi's white community more apparent than in the composition and activity of the State Legislature. In the past few months, spurred on by the success of civil rights work in the state and by COFO's plans for the coming summer, the Legislature has worked feverishly to produce legislation restricting civil rights and liberties for those who would change the Mississippi "way of life."

Lawmakers in floor debate have constantly talked of the coming "invasion" of the state, and their attitude has helped to create near-hysteria in sections of the white community. The Ku Klux Klan and other white vigilante groups have revived, and citizens are being advised to arm to meet the pending crisis.

The Legislature has done its own share to make of Mississippi an armed and authoritarian state. Two hundred men have been added to the Highway Patrol and the Governor has been given the power to order the Patrol into local racial "emergencies," even if local authorities do not request his aid. The state penitentiary has also been opened for the use of municipal and county police. Picketing of public facilities, organizing boycotts, and leafleting have been made illegal; and bills have been introduced to outlaw COFO's Freedom Schools, Community Centers, and libraries.

All this has been done in the name of meeting the "crisis" to Mississippi presented by civil rights activities. The legislators seem genuinely frightened that civil rights successes are undermining the racist power structure of the state.

Their fear is understandable, given the composition of the Mississippi Legislature. Even more than in most states, the Legislature of Mississippi is an elitist group, representing the dominant political and economic powers of the state, pledged to white supremacy and the one-party system.

In 1956 the Legislature created the State Sovereignty Commission, an executive body which plans the state's battle against civil rights. This year, in addition to regular budget allotments, the Legislature voted the

Sovereignty Commission $50,000 in tax money to fight the Civil Rights Bill.

The racism of the Mississippi legislators also shows up through their involvement with the White Citizens Councils, the semiofficial watchdogs of segregation in the state. Known Citizens Council members hold key positions in both houses of the Legislature. But even those who are not known as members usually have close ties to Council members and share the same views.

The connections of some members of the Legislature with the Citizens Councils and the State Sovereignty Commission are documented below:

(1) The President of the Senate is automatically a member of the Sovereignty Commission. In addition, Sen. Herman DeCell and Sen. Earl Evans were appointed to the 1960–64 Commission (Evans has since been replaced).

(2) At least 10 of the 53 members of the Senate are members of the Citizens Councils. Sen. James Edgar Lee is President of the Citizens Council of Jefferson Davis County. Sen. George Yarbrough of Red Banks, President Pro Tempore of the Senate, is listed as a Citizens Council member in the Mississippi Legislative Handbook and is on the present State Executive Committee of the Citizens Councils.

(3) Citizens Council and Sovereignty Commission members sit as both Chairman and Vice-chairman on the Constitution and the Oil and Gas Committees of the Senate. They also hold Chairmanships of the Transportation, County Affairs, Claims, Temperance (Mississippi is a dry state with an open bootleg market), Contingent Expense, and Interstate- and Federal-Cooperation Committees.

Sen. Yarbrough, who heads the last two committees, is also Vice-chairman of the powerful Rules Committee. Other Citizens Council or Sovereignty Commission members are Vice-chairman of Fees and Salaries, Finance, Forestry, and Corporations Committees.

(4) The Speaker of the House (presently Rep. Walter Sillers) is automatically a member of the State Sovereignty Commission. Rep. W. H. Johnson, Jr., and Rep. Wilber Hooker have both been appointed to the 1960–64 Commission. Both are also members of the State Executive Committee of the Citizens Council.

(5) In the House, known Citizens Council members number 19 out of 122. Two of these, Rep. Hooker and Rep. Fred Jones of Sunflower County, were members of the State Executive Committee of the Citizens Council in 1956. In addition to Hooker and W. H. Johnson, Jr., Rep. Horace Harned of Starkville is also on the present Executive Committee.

Rep. Charles Blackwell of Laurel is past president of the Oxford

Citizens Council. Walter Sillers, Speaker of the House, was Master of Ceremonies at a recent Boliver County Citizens Council meeting.

(6) Citizens Council and Sovereignty Commission members are both Chairman and Vice-chairman of the Labor, County Affairs, and Insurance Committees of the House. They also chair the Constitution, Federal Relations, Public Utilities, Corporations, Levees, Conservation, University and Colleges, and Census and Apportionment Committees. They are Vice-chairman of the Insurance, Penitentiary, and Education Committees of the House and on the Joint House-Senate Library Committee.

The significance of the role of Citizens Council members in the Legislature is clear from the 5-point Action Program of the Citizens Councils:

(1) Prevent Race Mixing. Racial integrity is essential to civilization and liberty. . . .

(2) Avoid Violence. Experience has proved that where integration occurs, violence becomes inevitable.

(3) Maintain and Restore Legal Segregation. . . .

(4) Defend States' Rights. The states are the sources of all governmental power, local and Federal. . . .

(5) Reverse the "Black Monday" Decision. The Supreme Court's school integration decision of May 17, 1954, is a patent perversion of the Constitution, based on false "science." If it stands, social segregation and laws against racial intermarriage will be subject to judicial condemnation. Such a prospect is intolerable!

Such are the views of the President Pro Tempore of the Senate, the Speaker of the House, and other key figures in the Mississippi Legislature. With such a background, it is not surprising that the 1964 Session has had an anti-civil rights and civil liberties orientation.

Many of the laws dealt with in this report are clearly unconstitutional. But Mississippi's legislators, most of whom are opposed to the decisions of the "Warren Court," have little concern for the ultimate constitutionality of the legislative activities. They are concerned instead with providing the state with emergency powers to combat civil rights within the next few months.

Because of this, the 1964 Legislative Session has often seemed like an episode out of *Alice in Wonderland*. The Legislature has even violated the very principles which the state's representatives claim to uphold on the national level. In Congress, Mississippi's representatives have consistently attacked the Civil Rights Bill as a violation of State's Rights and have deplored the use of Federal troops in racial crises. But at the same time, the Mississippi Legislature has centralized control of the Highway

Patrol and the Penitentiary under the Governor and given him the power to use the Patrol to intervene in local affairs.

No matter how otherworldly the Mississippi Legislature may seem, however, it cannot be taken lightly. The final effect of the laws proposed and passed in the Legislature this session would be to turn Mississippi into a totalitarian state, for white and black alike. As AFL-CIO Labor Council President Claude Ramsey has already warned, "Legislation enacted by the Mississippi Legislature under the guise of 'segregation maneuvers' could, in reality, be used against the labor movement. . . ." (Jackson *Daily News,* May 25, 1964). It must be remembered, in reading through the following pages, that preservation of "Racial Integrity" has been the traditional excuse by which Southern white politicians have maintained the Closed Society, in which all whites as well as all Negroes must suffer from fear and loss of freedom.

POWER OF THE DEPARTMENT OF JUSTICE TO TAKE PREVENTIVE ACTION NOW TO PROTECT THE RIGHT TO VOTE IN MISSISSIPPI

The Constitution, Art. I, Sec. 2, adopts as the qualifications necessary to vote for a Representative from Mississippi in Congress whatever valid qualifications are laid down by Mississippi law for voting for the most numerous branch of the State Legislature. The Seventeenth Amendment adopts the same qualifications with respect to Senators.

Negro citizens of the United States residing in Mississippi who, in fact, possess these qualifications (whether or not any state official has recognized that they possess them) therefore have a right to register and vote in federal elections. That right is not conferred on them by state law, but by the Constitution of the United States. Ex parte Yarbrough, 110 U.S. 651; United States v. Classic, 313 U.S. 299. Accordingly, it cannot be conferred or withheld by any state official.

It is both common and official knowledge that widespread combinations to frustrate and defeat this right and to prevent its assertion by threats and intimidation have long been in existence in Mississippi. See 1961 Voting Report of the United States Commission on Civil Rights. Under the Yarbrough and Classic decisions, supra, such combinations are a violation of 18 U.S.C. Sec. 241 and a federal felony.

Such combinations have been successful in preventing the registration of all but a very minute proportion of those eligible. See 1963 Report of the Civil Rights Commission, p. 34. This fact has made necessary the efforts of those who are currently seeking to aid and encourage Mississippi

Negroes to assert and vindicate their voting rights under the federal Constitution and laws.

Efforts to harass and intimidate such persons and thereby prevent them from bringing such aid are clearly efforts to continue and implement the existing conspiracy, and to make its fruits more secure, and are, therefore, also subject to prosecution under 18 U.S.C. Sec. 241.

Section 241 also protects the right to sue in the federal courts, United States v. Lancaster, 44 Fed. 883, 891, and the right to inform the federal government of a violation of its laws, in re Quarles, 158 U.S. 532, 536. It seems clear, therefore, that other violations of Section 241 are also occurring in the form of pressures to refrain from bringing test cases and to refrain from making complaints of civil rights violations.

Reportedly, Mississippi officers are engaging frequently in the following acts which have been held to be federal crimes under 18 U.S.C. Sec. 242: harassment arrests, Brown v. United States, 204 F2d 247; mistreatment of persons in custody, Screws v. United States, 325 U.S. 91, Williams v. United States, 341 U.S. 97, Lynch v. United States, 189 F2d 476; denying equal protection to persons whose skin color or activities they disapprove by refusing to protect them from private violence, Lynch v. United States, 189 F2d 476, Catlette v. United States, 132 F2d 902.

Nothing in the Constitution requires the United States to stand idly by waiting for violations of its laws to take place and be reported to it through official channels, but making no effort to interfere with them at the time they occur or to prevent their occurrence.

The Attorney General, under existing statutes, can authorize the appointment of additional deputy marshals, 28 U.S.C. Sec. 542, and can supervise and direct them in the performance of their duties, 28 U.S.C. Sec. 547 (c).

Deputy marshals may arrest without warrant for federal offenses committed in their presence, or on reasonable grounds to believe that a federal felony has been or is being committed. 18 U.S.C. Sec. 3053.

They are authorized to exercise the same power in executing federal laws that the sheriff would have in executing the laws of the state. 28 U.S.C. Sec. 549.

It is, therefore, obvious that, under existing law, federal deputy marshals could be assigned to be present whenever a voter registration activity is about to take place, with orders to arrest any person who attempts to interfere with such activity or to injure or threaten those engaged in it.

Under 10 U.S.C. Sections 332, 333, the President has full power to use troops or such other means as he deems necessary to overcome massive resistance to the execution of federal law. There should be no hesitation to invoke this authority if the supremacy of the federal Constitution and laws cannot be otherwise vindicated.

It would seem clear that the best way to reduce the probability that it will prove necessary would be for the Department of Justice to make vigorous, thorough and determined use of the less drastic powers to which reference has already been made.

The Supreme Court has never repudiated the following declaration which it made in 1880:

"It is argued that the preservation of peace and good order in society is not within the powers confided to the Government of the United States, but belongs exclusively to the States. Here, again, we are met with the theory that the Government of the United States does not rest upon the soil and territory of the country. We think that this theory is founded on an entire misconception of the nature and powers of that government. We hold it to be an incontrovertible principle that the Government of the United States may, by means of physical force, exercised through its official agents, execute on every foot of American soil the powers and functions that belong to it. This, necessarily, involves the power to command obedience to its laws, and hence the power to keep the peace to that extent."

Ex parte Siebold, 100 U.S. 371, 394-395.

> Respectfully submitted,
> National Lawyers Guild
> Special Committee on Legal
> Protection for Voting Rights
> (Signed) Laurent B. Frantz, Chairman
> (Member of the Alabama and
> Tennessee Bars)

BRIEF MEMORANDUM ON FEDERAL CIVIL RIGHTS AUTHORITY

(Note: Statutes which are cited in this memorandum are found in the Appendix which is attached in chronological order as they appear in the U.S. Code.)

I. LEGAL AUTHORITY OF THE FEDERAL GOVERNMENT IN CIVIL RIGHTS MATTERS

The principal area in which the federal government is authorized to go into court to protect civil rights is that of the vote. The main law is section 1971 of Title 42 of the U.S. Code. This section was amended by the Civil Rights Act of 1957 and further amended by the Civil Rights Act of 1960. As the section now stands, the federal government can ask

the federal court for injunctions to prevent intimidation of people attempting to register to vote or to do any other act in connection with the
right to vote, request the appointment of voting referees to register persons denied the right to vote, and ask for whatever orders are necessary
to fully guarantee the right to vote. Suits under this section may also be
brought by private persons—however, there is some doubt as to the court's
power to appoint voting referees when the suit is so initiated; the better
view of the law would appear to be that the court has such inherent
power in any case. The most dramatic use of Section 1971 was in a
recent suit of a month or so ago in North Carolina, where private
parties requested and received extremely far-reaching relief. The Federal
District judge apparently ordered the registrar to (1) hire additional
deputy registrars; (2) process the applications for registration at the rate
of no less than one every five minutes; (3) directed the FBI to observe
the registration process and report back to the Court; (4) directed the federal marshals to protect prospective registrants; and (5) ordered the
federal district attorney and the Justice Department to come into the
case. The relief granted in this suit by private parties apparently exceeds
that achieved by the Justice Department in any of its numerous cases.
(However, the Justice Department's Civil Rights Division was successful
in securing rather far-reaching relief in the Panola County, Mississippi,
case, *U.S. v. Duke,* a few days ago.) The referee procedure can be
enormously effective if properly done. (See remarks of the Honorable
James Corman, page 1593, *Congressional Record,* February 1, 1964.)

Another key provision of law protecting the right to vote is, of course,
the 15th Amendment to the Constitution. This may be useful in some
cases.

In any case, voting or otherwise, in which a person interferes with or
otherwise obstructs the effectiveness of a Federal Court order he may
be fined up to $1,000 and imprisoned for no more than one year. This
provision was added by the Civil Rights Act of 1960. (Section 1509,
Title 10, U.S. Code.) That same act also made it a Federal crime to flee
across state lines to avoid persecution for attempting to or damaging or
destroying any building, dwelling, house, church, or educational institution or in connection with any such crime. More importantly, anyone
having any connection whatsoever with the use of any explosive material
in connection with damaging or destroying any such buildings commits
a Federal crime. *Also of great importance is the section which makes it
a crime to threaten in any way whatsoever the damage or destruction
in any manner of such buildings.* (Sections 837 and 1074, Title 18, U.S.
code.)

Section 1987 of Title 42 of the U.S. Code requires all federal judicial
officials such as U.S. Attorneys, Marshals, and Commissioners to arrest

and prosecute all persons violating any of the older civil rights statutes. This section has largely been ignored by the Justice Department and other federal officials. Under Section 1992, the President has the power to order the judge, marshal, and U.S. District Attorney of any judicial district to go immediately to any place in their district and to arrest and try any person violating any of the older civil rights laws. (The older civil rights laws include Sections 241 and 242 of Title 18, which are the statutes making it a crime to deprive any person of his Constitutional rights.)

Section 241 of Title 18 of the U.S. Code makes it a crime for two or more persons to conspire to deprive or intimidate any person in the enjoyment of his Constitutional rights or rights secured by the laws of the United States. Section 242, of Title 18, makes it a crime for any person, one or more, under color of law, to deprive any other person of rights secured by the Constitution or laws of the United States. Section 243 makes it a crime for any person in any manner to be a party to discrimination on account of race in the selection of any jury, state or federal. Although 241 and 242 have been restrictively interpreted by the courts, they still have not begun to be used by the Justice Department to the extent that their validity merits in police brutality cases. The Justice Departments' Civil Rights Division has repeatedly taken the position that since Southern juries will not convict, almost no prosecutions will be brought under Section 242 of Title 18.

It also should be noted that there are many suits and types of action that cannot be brought by the U.S. Government, but can only be brought by private persons. Such actions, for example, are school integration suits. In these cases when a court order is obtained, it may then be necessary for the federal government to become a party to the suit in order to insure the enforcement of the court order. This was true in the Meredith case.

II. AUTHORITY FOR THE USE OF FORCE BY THE FEDERAL GOVERNMENT IN CIVIL RIGHTS MATTERS

A. *Authority for the Use of Marshals and the FBI*

The Federal marshal and his deputies, in executing the laws of the United States within a state, have the same powers that a sheriff of that state has in enforcing the state laws. (Section 549, Title 20, U.S. Code.) Both U.S. marshals and agents of the FBI are authorized to (1) carry firearms; (2) serve warrants and subpoenas; (3) *make arrests without warrants and on the spot for any offense against the United States committed in their presence;* and (4) *arrest for any felony under the laws of the United States if they have reasonable grounds to believe that the per-*

son to be arrested has committed or is committing such felony. (Sections 3052 and 3053, Title 18, U.S. Code.) (It should be noted that after the Communist espionage case of Judith Coplon, the Congress amended Section 3052 by the Act of January 10, 1951, to allow FBI agents to make arrests without warrant for any offense against the United States committed in their presence. Apparently, the lack of such a provision in the Coplon case had resulted in a reversal by the Court of Appeals, so Congress acted specifically to give the FBI this power. Apparently, this power has almost never been used in even the most blatant violations of the U.S. Civil Rights criminal statutes.)

B. *Authority for the Use of Troops or Whatever Force Is Necessary*
The Federal Government, through the person of the President, has more than ample authority to make sure that the Constitution and the laws of the United States relating to the civil rights of all its citizens are enforced and scrupulously adhered to. Section 332 of Title 10 of the U.S. Code provides as follows:

Use of militia and armed forces to enforce Federal authority.

Whenever the President considers that unlawful obstructions, combinations, or assemblages, or rebellion against the authority of the United States, makes it impracticable to enforce the laws of the United States in any State or Territory by the ordinary course of judicial proceedings, he may call into Federal service such of the militia of any State, and use such of the armed forces, as he considers necessary to enforce those laws or to suppress the rebellion. (Aug. 10, 1956, ch. 1041, 70A Stat. 15.)

It is to be noted that this section is one of enormous power, since the President may use troops to enforce the laws even though it is only *"impracticable* to enforce the laws of the United States in any state or territory *by the ordinary course of Judicial proceedings."* Such conditions clearly exist today and have existed for many years in many Southern states such as Mississippi and Alabama. The statute plainly says that when effective enforcement of the laws of the United States is not obtained through the courts, then troops may be used.

Another, more specific, section is Section 333 of Title 10 of the U.S. Code:

Interference with State and Federal law.

The President, by using the militia or the armed forces, or both, or by any other means, shall take such measures as he considers necessary to suppress, in a State, any insurrection, domestic violence, unlawful combination, or conspiracy, if it—

(1) so hinders the execution of the laws of that State, and of the

United States within the State, that any part or class of its people is deprived of a right, privilege, immunity, or protection named in the Constitution and secured by law, and the constituted authorities of that State are unable, fail, or refuse to protect that right, privilege, or immunity, or to give that protection; or

(2) opposes or obstructs the execution of the laws of the United States or impedes the course of justice under those laws.

In any situation covered by clause (1), the State shall be considered to have denied the equal protection of the laws secured by the Constitution. (Aug. 10, 1956, ch. 1041, 70A Stat. 15.)

Section 333 is of considerable power and is normally invoked together with Section 332 to send in troops in racial situations such as the Little Rock and Oxford crises. However, the important point is that both of these sections are far, far broader than those limited situations; and the sections fully authorize much more extensive use of troops to rectify the existing conditions in such states as Mississippi and Alabama.

It is to be noted, however, that immediately prior to invoking either Section 332 or 333, the President, pursuant to Section 334, must issue a proclamation ordering those persons blocking the execution of the laws to cease such action. (Frequently, this requirement is complied with by simply signing the proclamation paper a few minutes prior to the 332 and 333 papers.)

A further point should be made that, under the Republican Form of Government Clause of the Constitution (Article IV, Section IV), the President initially and the Congress ultimately have the power of recognizing the legitimate government of a state. It could well happen this summer that an insurgent government be set up in Mississippi seeking recognition as the lawful government of that state. In such a case, the Supreme Court has held (*Luther v. Borden; Texas v. White*) that first the President and ultimately the Congress have the power to decide which is the legitimate government of a state under the Republican Form of Government Clause and that this decision is not subject to review in the Courts. Such a condition occurred (1) during Dorr's Rebellion in 1848 in Rhode Island based upon the denial of the right to vote of a substantial part of the population (as exists today in Mississippi) and (2) in Texas and other Southern states immediately after the Civil War when various rival governments were seeking recognition by the President and the Congress. (Title 10, Section 331, U.S. Code; U.S. Constitution, Article IV, Section IV.)

Prepared for the Council of Federated
Organizations
by William Higgs, Esq.

FEDERAL DIRECTIVES ON CIVIL RIGHTS LAWS

Section 331, Title 10, U.S. CODE (1958 edition). *Federal aid for state governments.*

Whenever there is an insurrection in any State against its government, the President may, upon the request of its legislature or of its governor if the legislature cannot be convened, call into Federal service such of the militia of the other States, in the number requested by that State, and use such of the armed forces, as he considers necessary to suppress the insurrection. (Aug. 10, 1956, ch. 1041, 70A Stat. 15.)

Section 332, Title 10, U.S. CODE (1958 edition). *Use of militia and armed forces to enforce federal authority.*

Whenever the President considers that unlawful obstructions, combinations, or assemblages, or rebellion against the authority of the United States, make it *impracticable to enforce the laws of the United States in any State or Territory by the ordinary course of judicial proceedings,* he may call into Federal service such of the militia of any State, and use such of the armed forces, as he considers necessary to enforce those laws or to suppress the rebellion. (Aug. 10, 1956, ch. 1041, 70A Stat. 15.)

Section 332, Title 10, U.S. CODE (1959-1962 supplement).

Ex. Ord. No. 11053. ASSISTANCE FOR REMOVAL OF UNLAW-FUL OBSTRUCTIONS OF JUSTICE IN THE STATE OF MISSISSIPPI.

Ex. Ord. No. 11053, Sept. 30, 1962, 27 F.R. 9681, provided:

WHEREAS on September 30, 1962, I issued Proclamation No. 3479 (set out as a note under section 334 of this title) reading in part as follows:

"WHEREAS the Governor of the State of Mississippi and certain law enforcement officers and other officials of that State, and other persons, individually and in unlawful assemblies, combinations and conspiracies, have been and are willfully opposing and obstructing the enforcement of orders entered by the United States District Court for the Southern District of Mississippi and the United States Court of Appeals for the Fifth Circuit; and

"WHEREAS such unlawful assemblies, combinations and conspiracies oppose and obstruct the execution of the laws of the United States, impede the course of justice under those laws and make it impracticable to enforce those laws in the State of Mississippi by the ordinary course of judicial proceedings; and

"WHEREAS I have expressly called the attention of the Governor of Mississippi to the perilous situation that exists and to his duties in the premises, and have requested but have not received from him adequate assurances that the orders of the courts of the United States will be obeyed and that law and order will be maintained;

"NOW, THEREFORE, I, JOHN F. KENNEDY, President of the United States, under and by virtue of the authority vested in me by the Constitution and laws of the United States, including Chapter 15 of Title 10 of the United States Code (this chapter) particularly sections 332, 333, and 334 thereof (this section and sections 333, 334 of this title) do command all persons engaged in such obstructions of justice to cease and desist therefrom and to disperse and retire peaceably forthwith;" and

WHEREAS the commands contained in that proclamation have not been obeyed and obstruction of enforcement of those court orders still exists and threatens to continue;

NOW, THEREFORE, by virtue of the authority vested in me by the Constitution and laws of the United States, including Chapter 15 of Title 10 (this chapter) particularly Sections 332, 333 and 334 thereof (this section and sections 333, 334 of this title), and Section 301 of Title 3 of the United States Code (section 301 of Title 3, The President), it is hereby ordered as follows:

SECTION 1. The Secretary of Defense is authorized and directed to take all appropriate steps to enforce all orders of the United States District Court for the Southern District of Mississippi and the United States Court of Appeals for the Fifth Circuit and to remove all obstructions of justice in the State of Mississippi.

SECTION 2. In furtherance of the enforcement of the aforementioned orders of the United States District Court for the Southern District of Mississippi and the United States Court of Appeals for the Fifth Circuit, the Secretary of Defense is authorized to use such of the armed forces of the United States as he may deem necessary.

SECTION 3. I hereby authorize the Secretary of Defense to call into the active military service of the United States, as he may deem appropriate to carry out the purposes of this order, any or all of the units of the Army National Guard and of the Air National Guard of the State of Mississippi to serve in the active military service of the United States for an indefinite period and until relieved by appropriate orders. In carrying out the provisions of Section 1, the Secretary of Defense is authorized to use the units, and members thereof, ordered into the active military service of the United States pursuant to this section.

SECTION 4. The Secretary of Defense is authorized to delegate to

the Secretary of the Army or the Secretary of the Air Force, or both, any
of the authority conferred upon him by this order.

JOHN F. KENNEDY

Section 333, Title 10, U.S. CODE (1958 edition). *Interference with the
state and federal law.*

The President, by using the militia or the armed forces, or both, or by
any other means, shall take such measures as he considers necessary to
suppress, in a State, any insurrection, domestic violence, unlawful combination, or conspiracy, if it—

(1) so hinders the execution of the laws of that State, and of the
United States within the State, that any part or class of its people is deprived of a right, privilege, immunity, or protection named in the Constitution and secured by law, and the constituted authorities of that State
are unable, fail, or refuse to protect that right, privilege, or immunity,
or to give that protection; or

(2) opposes or obstructs the execution of the laws of the United States
or impedes the course of justice under those laws.

In any situation covered by clause (1), the State shall be considered to
have denied the equal protection of the laws secured by the Constitution.
(Aug. 10, 1956, ch. 1041, 70A Stat. 15.)

Section 334, Title 10, U.S. CODE (1958 edition). *Proclamation to
disperse.*

Whenever the President considers it necessary to use the militia or the
armed forces under this chapter, he shall, by proclamation, immediately
order the insurgents to disperse and retire peaceably to their abodes
within a limited time. (Aug. 10, 1956, ch. 1041, 70A Stat. 16.)

Section 334, Title 10, (1959-62 supplement).

Proc. No. 3497. OBSTRUCTION OF JUSTICE IN THE STATE
OF MISSISSIPPI.

Proc. No. 3497, Sept. 30, 1962, 27 F.R. 9681, provided:

WHEREAS the Governor of the State of Mississippi and certain law
enforcement officers and other officials of that State, and other persons,
individually and in unlawful assemblies, combinations and conspiracies,
have been and are willfully opposing and obstructing the enforcement
of orders entered by the United States District Court for the Southern
District of Mississippi and the United States Court of Appeals for the
Fifth Circuit; and

WHEREAS such unlawful assemblies, combinations and conspiracies
oppose and obstruct the execution of the laws of the United States,
impede the course of justice under those laws and make it impracticable

to enforce those laws in the State of Mississippi by the ordinary course of judicial proceedings: and

WHEREAS I have expressly called the attention of the Governor of Mississippi to the perilous situation that exists and to his duties in the premises, and have requested but have not received from him adequate assurances that the orders of the courts of the United States will be obeyed and that law and order will be maintained;

NOW, THEREFORE, I, JOHN F. KENNEDY, President of the United States, under and by virtue of the authority vested in me by the Constitution and laws of the United States, including Chapter 15 of Title 10 of the United States Code (this chapter), particularly sections 332, 333 and 334 thereof (this section and sections 333, 334 of this title), do command all persons engaged in such obstructions of justice to cease and desist therefrom and to disperse and retire peaceably forthwith.

JOHN F. KENNEDY

Section 241, Title 18, U.S. CODE (1958 edition). *Conspiracy against rights of citizens.*

If two or more persons conspire to injure, oppress, threaten, or intimidate any citizen in the free exercise or enjoyment of any right or privilege secured to him by the Constitution or laws of the United States, or because of his having so exercised the same; or

If two or more persons go in disguise on the highway, or on the premises of another, with intent to prevent or hinder his free exercise or enjoyment of any right or privilege so secured—

They shall be fined not more than $5,000 or imprisoned not more than ten years, or both. (June 25, 1948, ch. 645, 62 Stat. 696.)

Section 242, Title 18, U.S. CODE (1958 edition). *Deprivation of rights under color of law.*

Whoever, under color of any law, statute, ordinance, regulation, or custom, willfully subjects any inhabitant of any State, Territory, or District to the deprivation of any rights, privileges, or immunities secured or protected by the Constitution or laws of the United States, or to different punishments, pains, or penalties, on account of such inhabitant being an alien, or by reason of his color, or race, than are prescribed for the punishment of citizens, shall be fined not more than $1,000 or imprisoned not more than one year, or both. (June 25, 1948, ch. 645, 62 Stat. 696.)

Section 243, Title 18, U.S. CODE (1958 edition). *Exclusion of jurors on account of race or color.*

No citizen possessing all other qualifications which are or may be prescribed by law shall be disqualified for service as grand or petit juror in any court of the United States, or of any State on account of race, color, or previous condition of servitude; and whoever, being an officer or other person charged with any duty in the selection or summoning of jurors, excludes or fails to summon any citizen for such cause shall be fined not more than $5,000. (June 25, 1948, ch. 645, 62 Stat. 696.)

Section 837, Title 18, U.S. CODE (1959-62 supplement). *Explosives; illegal use or possession; and, threats or false information concerning attempts to damage or destroy real or personal property by fire or explosives.*

(a) As used in this section—

"commerce" means commerce between any State, Territory, Commonwealth, District, or possession of the United States, and any place outside thereof; or between points within the same State, Territory, or possession, or the District of Columbia, but through any place outside thereof; or within any Territory, or possession of the United States, or the District of Columbia;

"explosive" means gunpowders, powders used for blasting, all forms of high explosives, blasting materials, fuses (other than electric circuit breakers), detonators, and other detonating agents, smokeless powders, and any chemical compounds or mechanical mixture that contains any oxidizing and combustible units, or other ingredients, in such proportions, quantities, or packing that ignition by fire, by friction, by concussion, by percussion, or by detonation of the compound or mixture or any part thereof may cause an explosion.

(b) Whoever transports or aids and abets another in transporting in interstate or foreign commerce any explosive, with the knowledge or intent that it will be used to damage or destroy any building or other real or personal property for the purpose of interfering with its use for educational, religious, charitable, residential, business, or civic objectives or of intimidating any person pursuing such objectives, shall be subject to imprisonment for not more than one year, or a fine of not more than $1,000, or both; and if personal injury results shall be subject to imprisonment for not more than ten years or a fine of not more than $10,000, or both; and if death results shall be subject to imprisonment for any term of years or for life, but the court may impose the death penalty if the jury so recommends.

(c) The possession of an explosive in such a manner as to evince an intent to use, or the use of, such explosive, to damage or destroy any building or other real or personal property used for educational, religious, charitable, residential, business, or civic objectives or to intimidate any persons pursuing such objectives, creates rebuttable presumptions that the explosive was transported in interstate or foreign commerce or caused to be transported in interstate or foreign commerce by the person so possessing or using it, or by a person aiding or abetting the person so possessing or using it: *Provided, however,* That no person may be convicted under this section unless there is evidence independent of the presumptions that this section has been violated.

(d) Whoever, through the use of the mail, telephone, telegraph, or other instrument of commerce, willfully imparts or conveys, or causes to be imparted or conveyed, any threat, or false information knowing the same to be false, concerning an attempt or alleged attempt being made, or to be made, to damage or destroy any building or other real or personal property for the purpose of interfering with its use for educational, religious, charitable, residential, business, or civic objectives, or of intimidating any person pursuing such objectives, shall be subject to imprisonment for not more than one year or a fine of not more than $1,000, or both.

(e) This section shall not be construed as indicating an intent on the part of Congress to occupy the field in which this section operates to the exclusion of a law of any State, Territory, Commonwealth, or possession of the United States, and no law of any State, Territory, Commonwealth, or possession of the United States which would be valid in the absence of the section shall be declared invalid, and no local authorities shall be deprived of any jurisdiction over any offense over which they would have jurisdiction in the absence of this section. (Added Pub. L. 86-449, title II, Section 203, May 6, 1960, 74 Stat. 87.)

Section 1074, Title 18, U.S. CODE (1959-62 supplement). *Flight to avoid prosecution for damaging or destroying any building or other real property or personal property.*

(a) Whoever moves or travels in interstate or foreign commerce with intent either (1) to avoid prosecution, or custody, or confinement after conviction, under the laws of the place from which he flees, for willfully attempting to or damaging or destroying by fire or explosive any building, structure, facility, vehicle, dwelling house, synagogue, church, religious center or educational institution, public or private, or (2) to avoid giving testimony in any criminal proceeding relating to any such offensive shall be fined not more than $5,000 or imprisoned not more than five years, or both.

(b) Violations of this section may be prosecuted in the Federal judicial district in which the original crime was alleged to have been committed or in which the person was held in custody or confinement: *Provided, however,* That this section shall not be construed as indicating an intent on the part of Congress to prevent any State, Territory, Commonwealth, or possession of the United States of any jurisdiction over any offense over which they would have jurisdiction in the absence of such section. (Added Pub. L. 86-449, title II, Section 201, May 6, 1960, 74 Stat. 86.)

Section 1509, Title 18, U.S. CODE (1959-62 supplement). *Obstruction of court orders.*

Whoever, by threats or force, willfully prevents, obstructs, impedes, or interferes with, or willfully attempts to prevent, obstruct, impede, or interfere with, the due exercise of rights or the performance of duties under any order, judgment or decree of a court of the United States, shall be fined not more than $1,000 or imprisoned not more than one year, or both.

No injunctive or other civil relief against the conduct made criminal by this section shall be denied on the ground that such conduct is a crime. (Added Pub. L. 86-449, title I, Section 101, May 6, 1960, 74 Stat. 86.)

Section 3052, Title 18, U.S. CODE (1958 edition). *Powers of Federal Bureau of Investigation.*

The Director, Associate Director, Assistant to the Director, Assistant Directors, inspectors, and agents of the Federal Bureau of Investigation of the Department of Justice may carry firearms, serve warrants and subpoenas issued under the authority of the United States and make arrests without warrant for any offense against the United States committed in their presence, or for any felony cognizable under the laws of the United States if they have reasonable grounds to believe that the person to be arrested has committed or is committing such felony. (June 25, 1948, ch. 645, 62 Stat. 817; Jan. 10, 1951, ch. 1221, Section 1, 64 Stat. 1239.)

Section 3053, Title 18, U.S. CODE (1958 edition). *Powers of marshals and deputies.*

United States marshals and their deputies may carry firearms and may make arrests without warrant for any offense against the United States committed in their presence, or for any felony cognizable under the laws of the United States if they have reasonable grounds to believe that the person to be arrested has committed or is committing such felony. (June 25, 1948, ch. 645, 62 Stat. 817.)

Section 549, Title 28, U.S. CODE (1958 edition). *Power as sheriff.*

A United States marshal and his deputies, in executing the laws of the United States within a state, may exercise the same powers which a sheriff of such state may exercise in executing the laws thereof. (June 25, 1948, ch. 646, 62 Stat. 912.)

Section 1971, Title 42, U.S. CODE (1958 edition plus 1963 supplement). *VOTING RIGHTS*

(a) Race, color, or previous condition not to affect right to vote.

All citizens of the United States who are otherwise qualified by law to vote at any election by the people in any State, Territory, district, county, city, parish, township, school district, municipality, or other territorial subdivision, shall be entitled and allowed to vote at all such elections, without distinction of race, custom, usage, or regulation of any State or Territory, or by or under its authority, to the contrary notwithstanding.

(b) Intimidation, threats, or coercion.

No person, whether acting under color of law or otherwise, shall intimidate, threaten, or coerce any other person for the purpose of interfering with the right of such other person to vote or to vote as he may choose, or of causing such other person to vote for, or not to vote for, any candidate for the office of President, Vice-President, presidential elector, Member of the Senate, or Member of the House of Representatives, Delegates or Commissioners from the Territories or possessions, at any general, special, or primary election held solely or in part for the purpose of selecting or electing any such candidate.

(c) Preventative relief; injunction; costs; State as party defendant.

Whenever any person has engaged or there are reasonable grounds to believe that any person is about to engage in any act or practice which would deprive any other person of any right or privilege secured by subsection (a) or (b) of this section, the Attorney General may institute for the United States, or in the name of the United States, a civil action or other proper proceeding for preventive relief, including an application for a permanent or temporary injunction, restraining order, or other order. In any proceeding hereunder the United States shall be liable for sists the same as a private person.

Whenever, in a proceeding instituted under this subsection any official of a State or subdivision thereof is alleged to have committed any act or practice constituting a deprivation of any right or privilege secured by subsection (a) of this section, the act or practice shall also be deemed that of the State and the State may be joined as a party defendant and, if, prior to the institution of such proceeding, such official has resigned or has been relieved of his office and no successor has assumed such office, the proceeding may be instituted against the State.

(d) Jurisdiction; exhaustion of other remedies.

The district courts of the United States shall have jurisdiction of proceedings instituted pursuant to this section and shall exercise the same without regard to whether the party aggrieved shall have exhausted any administrative or other remedies that may be provided by law.

(e) Order qualifying person to vote; application; hearing; voting referees; transmittal of report and order; certificate of qualification; definitions.

In any proceeding instituted pursuant to subsection (c) of this section in the event the court finds that any person has been deprived on account of race or color of any right or privilege secured by subsection (a) of this section, the court shall upon request of the Attorney General and after each party has been given notice and the opportunity to be heard make a finding whether such deprivation was or is pursuant to a pattern or practice. If the court finds such pattern or practice, any person of such race or color resident within the affected area shall, for one year and thereafter until the court subsequently finds that such pattern or practice has ceased, be entitled, upon his application therefor, to an order declaring him qualified to vote, upon proof that at any election or elections (1) he is qualified under State law to vote, and (2) he has since such finding by the court been (a) deprived of or denied under color of law the opportunity to register to vote or otherwise to qualify to vote, or (b) found not qualified to vote by any person acting under color law. Such order shall be effective as to any election held within the longest period for which such applicant could have been registered or otherwise qualified under State law at which the applicant's qualifications would under State law entitle him to vote.

Notwithstanding any inconsistent provision of State law or the action of any State officer or court, an applicant so declared qualified to vote shall be permitted to vote in any such election. The Attorney General shall cause to be transmitted certified copies of such order to the appropriate election officers. The refusal by any such officer with notice of such order to permit any person so declared qualified to vote at an appropriate election shall constitute contempt of court.

An application for an order pursuant to this subsection shall be heard within ten days, and the execution of any order disposing of such application shall not be stayed if the effect of such stay would be to delay the effectiveness of the order beyond the date of any election which the applicant would otherwise be enabled to vote.

The Court may appoint one or more persons who are qualified voters in the judicial district, to be known as voting referees, who shall subscribe to the oath of office required by section 16 of Title 5, to serve for such period as the court shall determine, to receive such applications and to take evidence and report to the court findings as to whether or not at any election or elections (1) any such applicant is qualified under State law to vote, and (2) he has since the finding by the court heretofore specified been (a) deprived of or denied under color of law the opportunity to register to vote or otherwise to qualify to vote, or (b) found not qualified to vote by any person acting under color of law. In a proceeding before a voting referee, the applicant shall be heard ex parte at such times and places as the court shall direct. His statement under oath shall be prima facie evidence as to his age, residence, and his prior efforts to register or otherwise qualify to vote. Where proof of literacy or an understanding of other subjects is required by valid provisions of State law, the answer of the applicant, if written, shall be included in such report to the court; if oral, it shall be taken down stenographically and a transcription included in such report to the court.

Upon receipt of such report, the court shall cause the Attorney General to transmit a copy thereof to the State attorney general and to each party to such proceeding together with an order to show cause within ten days, or such shorter time as the court may fix, why an order of the court should not be entered in accordance with such report. Upon the expiration of such period, such order shall be entered unless prior to that time there has been filed with the court and served upon all parties a statement of exceptions to such report. Exceptions as to matters of fact shall be considered only if supported by a duly verified copy of a public record or by affidavit of persons having personal knowledge of such facts or by statements or matters contained in such report; those relating to matters of law shall be supported by an appropriate memorandum of law. The issues of fact and law raised by such exceptions shall be determined by the court, or, if the due and speedy administration of justice requires, they may be referred to the voting referee to determine in accordance with procedures prescribed by the court. A hearing as to an issue of fact shall be held only in the event that the proof in support of the exception discloses the existence of a genuine issue of material fact. The applicant's literacy and understanding of other subjects shall be determined solely on the basis of answers included in the report of the voting referee.

The court, or at its direction the voting referee, shall issue to each applicant so declared qualified a certificate identifying the holder thereof as a person so qualified.

Any voting referee appointed by the court pursuant to this subsection shall to the extent not inconsistent herewith have all the powers conferred upon a master by rule 53(c) of the Federal Rules of Civil Procedure. The compensation to be allowed to any persons appointed by the court pursuant to this subsection shall be fixed by the court and shall be payable by the United States.

Applications pursuant to this subsection shall be determined expeditiously. In the case of any application filed twenty or more days prior to an election which is undetermined by the time of such election, the court shall issue an order authorizing the applicant to vote provisionally: *Provided, however,* That such applicant shall be qualified to vote under State law. In the case of an application filed within twenty days prior to an election, the court, in its discretion, may make such an order. In either case the order shall make appropriate provision for the impounding of the applicant's ballot pending determination of the application. The court may take any other action, and may authorize such referee or such other person as it may designate to take any other action, appropriate or necessary to carry out the provisions of this subsection and to enforce its decrees. This subsection shall in no way be construed as a limitation upon the existing powers of the court.

When used in the subsection, the word "vote" includes all action necessary to make a vote effective including, but not limited to, registration or other action required by State law prerequisite to voting, casting a ballot, and having such ballot counted and included in the appropriate totals of votes cast with respect to candidates for public office and propositions for which votes are received in an election; the words "affected area" shall mean any subdivision of the State in which the laws of the State relating to voting are or have been to any extent administered by a person found in the proceeding to have violated subsection (a) of this section; and the words "qualified under State law" shall mean qualified according to the laws, customs, or usages of the State, and shall not, in any event, imply qualifications more stringent than those used by the persons found in the proceeding to have violated subsection (a) in qualifying persons other than those of the race or color against which the pattern or practice of discrimination was found to exist.

(f) Contempt; assignment of counsel; witnesses.

Any person cited for an alleged contempt under this Act shall be allowed to make his full defense by counsel learned in the law; and the court before which he is cited or tried, or some judge thereof, shall immediately, upon his request, assign to him such counsel, not exceeding two, as he may desire, who shall have free access to him at all reasonable hours. He shall be allowed, in his defense, to make any proof that he can produce by lawful witnesses, and shall have the like process of the court to compel his witnesses to appear at his trial or hearing, as is usually granted to compel witnesses to appear on behalf of the prosecution. If such person shall be found by the court to be financially unable to provide for such counsel, it shall be the duty of the court to provide such counsel. (As amended May 6, 1960, Pub. L. 86-449, title VI, Section 601, 74 Stat. 90.)

Section 1987, Title 42, U.S. CODE (1958 edition). *Prosecution of violation of certain laws.*

The United States attorneys, marshals, and deputy marshals, the commissioners appointed by the district and territorial courts, with power to arrest, imprison, or bail offenders, and every other officer who is especially empowered by the President, are authorized and required, at the expense of the United States, to institute prosecutions against all persons violating any of the provisions of section 1990 of this title or of sections 5506-5516 and 5518-5532 of the Revised Statutes, and to cause such persons to be arrested, and imprisoned or bailed, for trial before the court of the United States or the territorial court having cognizance of the offense. (R.S. Section 1982; June 25, 1948, ch. 646, Section 1, 62 Stat. 909.)

Section 1992, Title 42, U.S. CODE (1958 edition). *Speedy trial.*

Whenever the President has reason to believe that offenses have been, or are likely to be, committed against the provisions of section 1990 of this title or of sections 5506-5516 and 5518-5532 of the Revised Statutes, within any judicial district, it shall be lawful for him, in his discretion, to direct the judge, marshal, and United States attorney of such district to attend at such place within the district, and for such time as he may designate, for the purpose of the more speedy arrest and trial of persons so charged, and it shall be the duty of every judge or other officer, when any such requisition is received by him to attend at the place and for the time therein designated. (R.S. Section 1988; June 25, 1948, ch. 646, Section 1, 62 Stat. 909.)

Article IV, Section IV, *United States Constitution.*

The United States shall guarantee to every State in this Union a Republican Form of Government, and shall protect each of them against Invasion; and on Application of the Legislature, or of the Executive (when the Legislature cannot be convened), against domestic Violence.

Article XV, *United States Constitution.*

SECTION 1. The right of citizens of the United States to vote shall not be denied or abridged by the United States or by any State on account of race, color, or previous condition of servitude.

SECTION 2. The Congress shall have power to enforce this article by appropriate legislation.

APPENDIX VI

SUPPORTING ORGANIZATIONS

HARVARD'S RESPONSIBILITY IN MISSISSIPPI

The Harvard Crimson
Cambridge, Mass.

Dear Editor,

The April 30 and May 5, 1964, issues of the *Crimson* carry a debate on what might happen in Mississippi this summer and who holds responsibility for the outcome.

We maintain that the President and Fellows of Harvard University, and Harvard University as an institution, must bear heavy responsibility for what has happened and will happen in Mississippi.

Harvard University, through its holdings, plays an important role in the dominant economic, social and political institutions of Mississippi. Let's see how.

According to reports filed with the Securities and Exchange Commission, for 1961, the President and Fellows of Harvard College are the largest stockholder in Middle South Utilities, Inc. Furthermore, Paul C. Cabot, Treasurer of the University, is Chairman of the State Street Investment Corp., which is the third largest stockholder in Middle South, according to the same report. Again, Thomas D. Cabot, Overseer of the University, is a member of the Advisory Board of Massachusetts Investors Trust, which is the second largest stockholder in Middle South. These three entities control 4.5 per cent of the outstanding stock of Middle South. In a corporation with outstanding shares amounting to almost 19 million, this is a formidable voting block. What is Middle South Utilities? It is a holding company.

Among the operating companies wholly-owned by Middle South is the Mississippi Power and Light Company, which sells electric power to the Western half of Mississippi. Thus, Harvard University as an institution, and through at least two members of its ruling body, is intimately involved in the economy of Mississippi. What does that involvement imply?

We can show that Harvard University, through Mississippi Power and Light, is closely connected to the largest banks, the White Citizens'

Council, and the Democratic Party of Mississippi, which are the dominant economic, social and political institutions of Mississippi.

Electric power and finance capital form the keystone of industrialization, with which Mississippi is most concerned today. Mississippi Power and Light is the largest producer of electric power in Mississippi. Electric power is fundamental to commerce and industry. Deposit Guaranty Bank and Trust Company of Jackson and the First National Bank of Jackson are the two largest banks in the State of Mississippi. You cannot do business in the state without dealing, directly or indirectly, with one of the two banks. Therefore, Harvard's connections with Mississippi electric power and finance capital will reveal its strong hand in the Mississippi Way of Life.

The White Citizens' Council, through its connections in political and economic structures, dominates the prevailing social policies throughout the state. We will show that electric power and finance capital play a leading role in the White Citizens' Council of Mississippi. Harvard is involved in the White Citizens' Council's work through its connections with Mississippi electric power and finance capital.

The overwhelmingly dominant political machinery in Mississippi is the Mississippi Democratic Party. We will show that electric power, finance capital and the White Citizens' Council dominate the Democratic Party. Harvard plays an important role in Mississippi politics through its ties with Mississippi electric power, finance capital and the White Citizens' Council.

We will try to show that because of Harvard University's important role in Mississippi affairs, the University must bear part of the responsibility for the way of life there. The University must face the fact that it has an important say in the future of Mississippi and will bear responsibility for how that future unfolds.

Now let's look at Harvard's connections in Mississippi.

First, R. B. Wilson of Jackson, Miss., is a member of the Board of Directors of Middle South Utilities, whose largest stockholder is Harvard University. Mr. Wilson is also President and a member of the Board of Directors of Mississippi Power and Light, which is wholly-owned by Middle South Utilities. In addition, Mr. Wilson is a member of the Board of Directors of the Deposit Guaranty Bank and Trust Company of Jackson, the largest bank in the state of Mississippi.

Then there is Wm. P. McMullan, who is a Director of Mississippi Power and Light. Mr. McMullan is also Chairman, Chief Executive Officer, a Director and important stockholder of Deposit Guaranty Bank and Trust Company. Furthermore, Mr. McMullan occupies a seat on the Board of Directors of the Jackson White Citizens' Council.

Another member of the Board of Directors of Mississippi Power and

Light is Robert M. Hearin, who is President, Director and member of the Advisory Committee of the First National Bank of Jackson, and controls the second largest percentage of outstanding stock of First National Bank. Mr. Hearin is a past president of the Jackson Chamber of Commerce and now a Director of the United States Chamber of Commerce. In addition he is a colonel on the official staff of Mississippi Governor Paul B. Johnson.

The Vice-President and Secretary of Mississippi Power and Light is Alex Rogers, who was also appointed by Governor Johnson as a colonel on his official staff.

The Public Information Director for Mississippi Power and Light is Alex McKeigny, who holds a seat on the Board of Directors of the Jackson Citizens' Council.

Thus, we can see already Harvard's connections with electric power, finance capital, the White Citizens' Council and the Mississippi Democratic Party.

Let's explore this further.

A scoreboard of Directors of Deposit Guaranty Bank and Trust Company would read the following way. On the Deposit Guaranty Board there is one member who sits on the Board of Middle South Utilities (principal stockholder, Harvard University). There are two Deposit Guaranty Board members who sit on the Board of Mississippi Power and Light (wholly-owned by Middle South Utilities). There are five Deposit Guaranty Board members who sit on the Board of Directors of the Jackson White Citizens' Council. And there are two Deposit Guaranty Board members who are colonels on Governor Johnson's staff.

A similar scoreboard for the First National Bank would read this way. One First National Board member is on the Board of the Jackson White Citizens' Council. And four First National Board members are colonels on the Governor's staff.

We have seen above that Harvard has important connections with the White Citizens' Council and the Mississippi Democratic Party through the Board of Mississippi Power and Light. It's important to understand what the White Citizens' Council and Democratic Party of Mississippi believe and stand for.

In the North, White Citizens' Council supporters may talk about States Rights and Constitutional government. But in Mississippi it sounds much different. And its main purposes are to prevent Negroes from voting, to maintain white supremacy and racial segregation in all phases of life, and to squash any semblance of Negro or Negro and white organization which is concerned with making changes in the Mississippi pattern of life. The White Citizens' Councils' principal techniques are economic intimidation and political control of the state.

Following is a statement from Mississippi Governor Vardaman in 1907, which the White Citizens' Council includes in its standard literature packet available from the Greenwood headquarters of the Council:

"The Negro should never have been trusted with the ballot. He is different from the white man. He is congenitally unqualified to exercise the most responsible duty of citizenship. He is physically, mentally, morally, racially and eternally the white man's inferior. There is nothing in the history of his race, nothing in his individual character, nothing in his achievements of the past nor his promise for the future which entitles him to stand side by side with the white man at the ballot box . . .

"We must repeal the Fifteenth and modify the Fourteenth Amendment to the Constitution of the United States. Then we shall be able in our legislation to recognize the Negro's racial peculiarities, and make laws to fit them. This would leave the matter precisely as was intended by the father of the Republic."

At a Harrison County White Citizens' Council banquet on May 2, 1964, Master of Ceremonies Raymond Butler ended his remarks with the following statement: "Throughout the pages of history there is only one third-class race which has been treated like a second-class race and complained about it— and that race is the American Nigger."

Mr. Butler introduced several important Mississippians who had attended the banquet. Most prominent among them was the Chairman of the State Democratic Executive Committee, Bidwell Adam. Mr. Adam is also Chairman of the Harrison County Democratic Executive Committee.

Mr. Butler also introduced the Sheriff of Harrison County, the President of the Gulfport Port Authority and state representative Jim True, a Council member.

The guest speaker at the banquet was Gen. Edwin A. Walker, who was introduced by Medford Evans. Mr. Evans, who holds a Ph.D. from Yale University, is a Consultant to the Citizens' Councils of Texas, Louisiana, Mississippi, Tennessee, Georgia, South Carolina and North Carolina. Mr. Evans is Secretary of the Louisiana States Rights Party, Coordinator of the John Birch Society and was Consultant to General Edwin A. Walker at the Senate Preparedness Sub-Committee hearings when Gen. Walker was recalled from Germany.

Mr. Evans said of the White Citizens' Councils:

"It is the only organization which recognizes . . . that the key to world revolution, in which we are involved against the revolutionaries, is the racial issue. People are increasingly aware of this due to the racial extremists and our Ambassador of Intelligence in the North: Governor Wallace."

Of General Walker, Evans said:

"The most important individual in the United States is Gen. Edwin A. Walker."

During his speech, Gen. Walker noted that half the proceeds of the banquet would be sent to Governor Wallace's Presidential primary campaigns.

How does the Citizens' Council operate?

A voter registration drive and boycott of white merchants in Canton this year was met with large numbers of arrests of civil rights workers and local citizens and with economic reprisals against Canton's Negro residents. The State Senator and two State Representatives from Madison County (in which Canton is located) are White Citizens' Council members. They sponsored bills making the distribution of literature concerning the boycott a crime. The white political and economic domination should be contrasted with the population figures: Madison County has 9,267 whites and 23,630 Negroes, according to the 1960 U.S. Census.

The Canton Citizens' Council distributed an open letter to whites in Canton, calling for their support against Negro efforts to change their way of life.

Here are excerpts from that letter:

"Dear Fellow White Citizens:

". . . THE WHITE CITIZENS OF CANTON MUST BE UNIFIED IN ORDER TO SAVE CANTON FROM MASS CONFUSION LEADING TO RACE MIXING. Organization is the key to victory!

"The Canton Citizens Council is the gathering place for those white men and women who are determined to keep the white people in all governmental positions and in complete control of our way of life . . .

"Thank you for your support and continued effort to keep Canton, Madison County and Mississippi in the hands of white men and women.

> "Sincerely,
> Our Noble President"

We have seen some of the approaches of the White Citizens' Councils with which Harvard University is involved. Now let's look at the position of the Mississippi Democratic Party with which Harvard University is involved.

The Mississippi Democratic Party dominates the politics of Mississippi. The Republicans have only one member in the State Legislature and none in the Executive branch or among the Congressional and Senatorial delegations. And the White Citizens' Councils dominate the Mississippi Democratic Party.

First, let's look at the platform of the Mississippi Democratic Party, adopted in Convention, June 30, 1960:

"We believe in the segregation of the races and are unalterably opposed to repeal or modification of the segregation laws of this State, and we condemn integration and the practice of non-segregation. We unalterably oppose any and all efforts to repeal the miscegenation laws. We believe in the doctrine of interposition as defined in the appropriate resolution adopted by the Legislature of the State of Mississippi at its regular session of 1956 . . .

"We believe in the separation of the races in the universities and colleges, in the public schools, in public transportation, in public parks, in public playgrounds, and in all spheres of activity where experience has shown that it is for the best interest of both races that such separation be observed."

August 16, 1960, the State Democratic Party, meeting in Jackson, adopted the following measures in response to the 1960 National Democratic Convention held in Los Angeles, California:

"That we reject and oppose the platforms of both National parties and their candidates. That we reaffirm and readopt the Platform and principles of the Democratic Party of Mississippi adopted in Convention Assembled in the City of Jackson, Mississippi, on the 30th day of June, 1960."

Another important measure of the Mississippi Democratic Party is the campaign literature of Paul Johnson's 1963 race for Governor. Johnson's campaign themes focused on maintaining white supremacy through a one-party system, segregation in Mississippi forever, and bury the Republican Party once and for all.

Here is an excerpt from the standard leaflet which could be obtained from Johnson headquarters during the campaign:

"A DIVISION OF CONSERVATIVE MISSISSIPPIANS INTO TWO POLITICAL CAMPS . . . WOULD GIVE THE BALANCE OF POWER TO OUR MINORITY GROUP. This would be the end of our way of life in Mississippi and the peace, tranquillity, law and order we now enjoy in all of our communities would soon come to an awesome end.

"To have Mississippi Democratic nominees and Republican nominees running for every public office . . . municipal, county and state . . . every four years . . . would constitute an unnecessary nuisance and would bring to Mississippi the same political evils and dangers that now beset such states as Illinois, New York, Michigan, Pennsylvania and California . . .

"If you've already had enough of politics for 1963, then help stamp out Republicanism on November 5. Let's bury these Republican 'upstarts' so deep under good, solid Mississippi Democratic votes that it will be the year 2000 before you hear of Republican candidates for Mississippi offices again!

"We do not have to belong to and participate in an integrated national party, which tolerates in its ranks radical leftists like Governor Nelson Rockefeller and Senator Jacob Javits of New York and 'Black Monday' Earl Warren, in order to cast Mississippi's electoral votes for a true conservative. We do not have to make an 'accommodation' with liberals, and we do not have to compromise our principles, in order to make our electoral votes count for freedom.

"Let's . . . bury forever these 'overnight' Republicans who would like to divide our State and hand it over to a minority group."

So we can see the themes of one-party rule and white supremacy coming through Johnson's campaign. And we can see the overlap of principles between the Mississippi Democratic Party and the White Citizens' Councils.

Now let's look at how the White Citizens' Council exerts control over the State Legislature, which is strictly a Democratic Party affair.

Of the 122 members of the House of Representatives in the 1964-68 Legislature, at least 20 are known to belong to the White Citizens' Councils, including House Speaker Walter Sillers. Six of the 20 are on the State Executive Committee of the White Citizens' Council.

In the Senate at least 10 of the 53 members are known to belong to the White Citizens' Councils, including President pro-tem George Yarbrough, who is on the Citizens' Councils' State Executive Committee.

In the 1960-64 Legislature the line-up was slightly different. There were 140 members of the House and 22 of them were known to be Citizens' Council members. And there were 49 Senators, of whom 12 were Citizens' Council members.

Another measure of Citizens' Council legislative strength is placement of Council members on committees which control key legislation.

Of the seven members on the very important Senate Rules Committee, three are known to belong to the Citizens' Councils. Of the 14 members of the House Rules Committee, four are known to be members of the Council.

On the House Ways and Means Committee, nine of the 33 members are known to be Council members. In the Senate, Council members hold at least four of the 13 seats on the Oil and Gas Committee, including Chairman and Vice-Chairman. In the comparable House committee, called Conservation of Minerals and Natural Resources, eight of the 29 members are Council members, including the chairman.

Another measure of Citizens' Council importance in the Mississippi Democratic Party is Executive appointments. We've already mentioned the Governor's official staff of colonels. Colonels receive their appointments because of their support for the gubernatorial candidate during the campaign. Therefore, an analysis of the colonel staff should give some indication of where Johnson's support came from and to whom he owed political debts.

We find that Paul Johnson appointed fourteen members of the Jackson White Citizens' Council (13 of them Board members) to his colonel staff. He also appointed eight members of the State Executive Committee of the White Citizens' Councils to his colonel staff.

The State Sovereignty Commission is another place where Executive appointments are very important. The Commission, which is supported by state tax money, has been the official segregation watchdog agency of the State since 1956. Its body for the 1964-68 session has not yet been chosen, but we know that at least seven of its 13 members for the 1960-64 session were members of the White Citizens' Councils.

Until the fight on the civil rights bill began last summer, the Commission had been channeling state funds every year to the Citizens' Councils in Mississippi. Now the money is used to fight the civil rights bill. The State Legislature, which had donated more than 10 thousand dollars to the Washington anti-civil rights lobby, recently appropriated another fifty thousand dollars of state funds for the same purpose.

So we can see how the White Citizens' Council dominates the Executive and Legislative branches of the State Government of Mississippi. And we have seen what the White Citizens' Councils believe and stand for.

We have seen how the two leading banks and the leading electric power company, which are crucial to commerce and industry, play major roles in the Citizens' Council.

We have seen the major role electric power, finance capital and the White Citizens' Council play in the Mississippi Democratic Party.

And we started off by showing the important place Harvard University, through Middle South and Mississippi Power and Light, has in the electric power-finance capital-Citizens' Council-Democratic Party setup.

Harvard must see its responsibility. Negroes are killed, beaten and run out of the state for being Negroes. Negroes have no recourse at the polls, in court, at the police station or in the classrooms.

Harvard cannot disclaim responsibility for the "goings-on down there." With its political, economic and social roots in the state, it could wield tremendous pressure to change Mississippi. The economic and political structures could not last long if Harvard applied its weight against their foundations.

But Mississippi is a profitable business enterprise. We wonder whether education is only incidental to the Board of Trustees of Harvard University.

There is much to be done. And time is running out.

(Student Nonviolent Coordinating Committee—5/30/64)

APPENDIX VII

FREEDOM SCHOOLS

FREEDOM SCHOOL DATA

a) *Background on Freedom Schools:* The Freedom Schools were proposed late in 1963 by Charles Cobb, a Howard University student until he joined the SNCC staff and "a gifted creative writer," according to Freedom School Director Professor Staughton Lynd. That "help from outside Mississippi is needed if the Negro youngster were to have any chance of access to a larger world" was an obvious fact, according to Lynd, after preliminary studies of the Mississippi educational system. In *Mississippi: The Closed Society,* James Silver noted that the per capita expenditure of the Mississippi local school boards for the white child is almost four times the figure for the Negro child. More than the statistics, the limited subject matter available for study to Mississippi Negro students, the fear of dismissal that restrains their teachers from exploring controversial topics demonstrated that if Mississippi's Negroes were to take part in an academic process it would have to be in a context supplemental to the schooling available through the state.

b) *Freedom Schools in Operation:* As of July 26, there were 41 functioning Freedom Schools in twenty communities across the state with an enrollment of 2,135 students—twice the figure projected in planning for the summer. There are approximately 175 teaching full-time in the Freedom Schools, with recruitment of 50 to 100 more in process.

The typical Freedom School has an enrollment of 25 to 100 and a staff of five to six teachers, and is held in a church basement or sometimes the church itself, often using the outdoor area as well. Typically, the morning will be taken up with a "core curriculum" built around Negro History and citizenship. The late morning or afternoon is taken up with special classes (such as French or typing— both very popular) or projects (such as drama or the school newspaper). In the evening classes are held for adults or teen-agers who work during the day.

The idea of the school is centered on discussion of the group. One suggested guide distributed by COFO to Freedom School teachers noted, "In the matter of classroom procedure, questioning is the vital tool. It is meaningless to flood the student with information he cannot understand; questioning is the path to enlightenment. It requires a great deal of skill and tact to pose the question that will stimulate but not offend, lead to unself-consciousness and the desire to express thought. . . . The value of the Freedom Schools will derive mainly from what the teachers are able to elicit from the students in terms of comprehension and expression of their experiences."

At a time when the nation's educators have become concerned—and stymied—by bringing to children of the non-verbal "culturally deprived" community the ability to formulate questions and articulate perceptions, the daily pedagogical revolutions that are the basis of any success in a Freedom School classroom become overwhelming upon considering that the students are Mississippi Negroes—possibly the single most deprived group in the nation—and the teachers are the culturally alien products of the much-maligned liberal arts undergraduate education. An indication of what is happening among the students and their young teachers in the Freedom Schools is given by a single line of COFO advice given to the teachers: "The formal classroom approach is to be avoided; the teacher is encouraged to use all the resources of his imagination."

According to Director Lynd, the Freedom Schools may be dealt with in the context of three general situations: a) rural areas; b) urban areas where the civil rights movement has been strong; c) urban areas where the movement has been weak. "In the first and third situations," analyzes Lynd, "the Freedom Schools have been most successful, not just in numbers, but in what is going on there."

In the rural areas where there is little recreation or diversion available to the Negro community, the Freedom School becomes the center of teen-age social activities, according to Lynd. Lynd draws upon the Holmes County and Carthage Freedom Schools as examples of this rural success. When the Freedom School staff arrived in Carthage, the entire Negro community was assembled at the church to greet them; when, two days later, the staff was evicted from its school, the community again appeared with pickup trucks to help move the library to a new school site. As this is being written, the Carthage community, with the help of summer volunteers and a National Council of Churches minister, is building its own community center which will be staffed by civil rights workers and local volunteers.

An example of the second situation, the urban success, is the Hattiesburg Freedom School system, which Lynd refers to as the "Mecca of the Freedom School world." In Hattiesburg there are more than 600 students in five schools. Each teacher has been told to find a person from the community to be trained to take over his teaching job at the end of the summer. Much of the second session in Hattiesburg will be devoted to the training of local Freedom School teachers. "Here, as in Canton," states Lynd, "there can be no doubt that the success of the schools stemmed from the intensive civil rights campaign in the community during the months of late winter and spring."

In Gulfport and Greenville, urban environments with alternative attractions, the movement has not been strong enough in the past to counteract traditional time-passing activities. Lynd notes, however, that the generalization has exceptions. Holly Springs, an urban area in which the movement has not been strong in the past, has a highly successful Freedom School.

It should also be noted that in Holly Springs, Carthage, and Shaw, the Freedom Schools are competing against the regular public schools which are currently in session as public schools close in early spring to allow students to chop cotton.

In Mississippi's stronghold of organized terror, the Southwest, the McComb Freedom School has proven the political value of the schools as an instrument for building confidence in the Negro community when canvassing is impractical. Lynd cites the instance of Miss Joyce Brown's poem concerning the Freedom School held at a bombed home which moved the community to provide a meeting place for the school. "Thus," notes Lynd, "the presence of a Freedom School helped to loosen the hard knot of fear and to organize the Negro community." There are 108 students at the McComb Freedom School.

c) *The Future of the Freedom Schools:* The Freedom Schools will continue beyond the end of the Summer Project in August. Freedom Schools in several areas are already running jointly with the regular public school session. The Freedom Schools offer subjects—such as foreign languages—not offered in the regular schools, and students are attracted to the informal questioning spirit of the Freedom Schools and academics based around their experiences as Mississippi Negroes. In situations like McComb, the Freedom School has proven its value to the over-all COFO political program as an organizing instrument. Also, among the various COFO programs, the Freedom School project is the one which holds out a particular hope of communication with the white community. In at least two situations, Vicksburg and Holly Springs, white children have attended for short periods. Another factor in the decision to continue the Freedom Schools is the possibility-turned-probability that the Mississippi legislature will offer private school legislation designed to sidestep public school integration (already ordered for the fall of 1964 in Jackson, Biloxi, and Leake County). One is faced by situations such as that in Issaquena County, where there are no Negro public schools and children must be transported into other counties. The backwardness of Mississippi's educational system in the context of racial discrimination is demonstrated by the fact that in many areas the impact of the 1954 Supreme Court decision that separate cannot be equal was to have separate schools erected for the first time; the step previous to school segregation is concluding that Negro children should be educated. The rural hard-core area of Issaquena County is an example of a prolonged holdout. A final but not secondary factor is the "widespread apprehension among Mississippi Negroes as to what will happen to them when the Summer Project volunteers leave." Staughton Lynd adds, "We want to be able to tell them that the program will *not* end, that momentum cumulated during the summer months will not be permitted to slack off."

The long-range Freedom School program will be carried on through evening classes in local community centers. "Already in many communities Freedom School and Community Center programs are combined and often in the same building," according to Lynd. One source of teachers for the continuing Freedom School program will be volunteers who decide to stay beyond the summer; if only one in five stayed, fifty teachers would remain in the state. Another source would be Southern Negro students coming in under the work-study program which provides them with a one-year scholarship to Tougaloo College after one year's full-time work for SNCC. Other teachers would come through the local communities, under programs of training such as that which has already begun in Hattiesburg. Teachers could also be provided from the ranks of full-time SNCC staff members; in areas such as McComb where the movement can't register American citizens as voters, civil rights workers can teach in Freedom Schools. There is no doubt but that, in Professor Lynd's words, "It is a political decision for any parent to let his child come to a Freedom School."

The Freedom School program can develop as an aid in enabling Mississippi Negro students to make the transition from a Mississippi Negro high school to higher education. Standardized tests will be administered to the most promising Freedom School students under the direction of the College Entrance Examination Board (CEEB) in mid-August. Evaluation of these scores and other data by the National Scholarship Service Fund for Negro Students will lead some of the Freedom School students to a program involving a) a transitional educational experience during the summer after high school, b) a reduced load during the freshman year at college, and c) financial aid. Others can be helped by the already-existing work-study program.

d) *Free Southern Theater:* As the second Freedom School session (August 3–21) begins, a tour of the Freedom Schools throughout the state is scheduled for the Free Southern theater production of *In White America.* The Free Southern Theater was organized early this year by SNCC with the assistance of COFO and Tougaloo College as an attempt to "stimulate thought and a new awareness among Negroes in the deep South," and "will work toward the establishment of permanent stock and repertory companies, with mobile touring units, in major population centers throughout the South, staging plays that reflect the struggles of the American Negro . . . before Negro and, in time, integrated audiences," according to a Free Southern Theater prospectus. An apprenticeship program is planned which will send a number of promising participants to New York for more intensive study. The company will include both professional and amateur participants.

The development of the Free Southern Theater was sparked by the "cultural desert" resulting from the closed society's restriction of the patterns of reflective and creative thought.

Each performance of *In White America* will be accompanied by theater workshops in the Freedom Schools designed to introduce students to the experience of theater through participation. As the classroom methods of the Freedom School are revolutionary in the context of traditional American patterns of education, so the Free Southern theater brings a new concept of drama to these Mississippi students. Dr. Lynd comments that the aim of the Theater "is the creation of a fresh theatrical style which will combine the highest standards of craftsmanship with a more intimate audience rapport than modern theater usually achieves."

Segregated schools, controlled textbooks, lack of discussion of controversial topics, the nature of the mass media in Mississippi demand the development of a cultural program, to be viewed in the context of education, among an entire people.

Among the objectives listed for the Free Southern Theater by its originators are "to acquaint Southern peoples with a breadth of experience with the theater and related art forms; to liberate and explore the creative talent and potential that is here as well as to promote the production of art; to bring in artists from outside the state as well as to provide the opportunity for local people with creative ability to have experience with the theater; to emphasize the universality of the problems of the Negro people; to strengthen communication between Southern Negroes; to assert that self-knowledge and creativity are the foundations of human dignity."

Among the sponsors of the Free Southern Theater are singer Harry Belafonte, authors James Baldwin and Langston Hughes, performers Ossie Davis, Ruby Dee, and Theodore Bikel, and Lincoln Kirstein, general director of the New York City Ballet.

The proposal for the Free Southern Theater originated with SNCC workers Doris Derby, Gilbert Moses, and John O'Neal, and Tougaloo drama instructor William Hutchinson.

e) (This section dealt with the Mississippi Summer Caravan of Music.)

f) *Excerpts from Freedom School Newspapers:* The first ones to insist upon connecting the Freedom Schools to the opening of the closed society of segregated Mississippi are the young students of the Freedom Schools. The average author of a Freedom School newspaper article is between 13 and 15 years of age.

The cover of the first issue of the McComb Freedom School's "Freedom Journal" depicts a Negro in chains with a scroll below him reading, "Am I not a man and a brother?" One girl, in the same paper, remarks, ". . . too long others have done our speaking for us. . . ." Her mother is a domestic who fears for what will happen to the family due to her child's attendance at the Freedom School. One 15-year-old student there remarked that the Freedom School "enables me to know that I can get along with the whites and they can get along with me without feeling inferior to each other."

Two young students in the Holly Springs Freedom School describe their home town: "The working conditions are bad. The wages are very low. The amount paid for plowing a tractor all day is three dollars. . . . The white man buys most of the supplies used for the annual crops, but the Negro contributes all the labor. In the fall of the year when the crop is harvested and the cotton is sold to market, the white man gives the Negro what he thinks he needs, without showing the Negro a record of the income the white man has collected for the year. This process of farming has become a custom. This way of livelihood is not much different from slavery."

A student describes her life in the "Benton County Freedom Train:" "We work eight to nine hours each day and are paid daily after work is over. We get only $3.00 per day . . . and . . . chop cotton 8½ hours to 9 hours each day. . . . The man whom we worked for is responsible for having fresh cold water handy in the field for the workers to drink. The whites also fail to take us to the store in time to eat dinner. . . . When it's harvest Negroes pick cotton by hand at $2.00 for a hundred pounds and some places $3.00 per hundred."

In the Mt. Zion Freedom School's "Freedom Press," a girl states she comes to the Freedom School because "I want to become a part of history also."

Joyce Brown, the 15-year-old author of "The House of Liberty" . . . will be a senior next year at McComb's Negro Burgland High School. When she was 12 years of age she was doing voter registration canvassing when Bob Moses, director of the Mississippi Summer Project, first began voter activities in Mississippi for SNCC in 1961.

DECLARATION OF INDEPENDENCE

by the
Freedom School Students of
St. John's Methodist Church,
Palmer's Crossing, Hattiesburg, Miss.

In this course of human events, it has become necessary for the Negro people to break away from the customs which have made it very difficult for the Negro to get his God-given rights. We, as citizens of Mississippi, do hereby state that all people should have the right to petition, to assemble, and to use public places. We also have the right to life, liberty, and to seek happiness.

The government has no right to make or to change laws without the consent of the people. No government has the right to take the law into its own hands. All people as citizens have the right to impeach the government when their rights are being taken away.

All voters elect persons to the government. Everyone must vote to elect the person of his choice; so we hereby state that all persons of twenty-one years of age, whether black, white, or yellow, have the right to elect the persons of their choice; and if these persons do not carry out the will of the people, they have the right to alter or abolish the government.

The Negro does not have the right to petition the government for a redress of these grievances:

For equal opportunity.
For better schools and equipment.
For better recreation facilities.
For more public libraries.
For schools for the mentally ill.
For more and better senior colleges.
For better roads in Negro communities.
For training schools in the State of Mississippi.
For more Negro policemen.
For more guarantee of a fair circuit clerk.
For integration in colleges and schools.

The government has made it possible for the white man to have a mock trial in the case of a Negro's death.
The government has refused to make laws for the public good.
The government has used police brutality.
The government has imposed taxes upon us without representation.
The government has refused to give Negroes the right to go into public places.

The government has marked our registration forms unfairly.

We, therefore, the Negroes of Mississippi assembled, appeal to the government of the state, that no man is free until all men are free. We do hereby declare independence from the unjust laws of Mississippi which conflict with the United States Constitution.

NOTES ON TEACHING IN MISSISSIPPI
COFO, Jackson, Mississippi

INTRODUCTION TO THE SUMMER—Jane Stembridge

This is the situation: You will be teaching young people who have lived in Mississippi all their lives. That means that they have been deprived of decent education, from the first grade through high school. It means that they have been denied free expression and free thought. Most of all—it means that they have been denied the right to question.

The purpose of the Freedom Schools is to help them begin to question.

What will they be like? They will all be different—but they will have in common the scars of the system. Some will be cynical. Some will be distrustful. All of them will have a serious lack of preparation both with regard to academic subjects and contemporary issues—but all of them will have a knowledge far beyond their years. This knowledge is the knowledge of how to survive in a society that is out to destroy you . . . and the knowledge of the extent of evil in the world.

Because these young people possess such knowledge, they will be ahead of you in many ways. But this knowledge is purely negative; it is only *half* of the picture and, so far as the Negro is concerned, it is the first half. It has, in a sense, already been lived through. The old institutions are crumbling and there is great reason to hope for the first time. You will help them to see this hope and inspire them to go after it.

What will they demand of you? They will demand that you be honest. Honesty is an attitude toward life which is communicated by everything you do. Since you, too, will be in a learning situation— honesty means that you will *ask* questions as well as answer them. It means that if you don't know something you will say so. It means that you will not "act" a part in the attempt to compensate for all they've endured in Mississippi. You can't compensate for that, and they don't want you to try. It would not be *real,* and the greatest contribution that you can make to them is to be real.

Remember this: These young people have been taught by the system not to trust. You have to be trust-*worthy*. It's that simple. Secondly, there is very little if anything that you can teach them about prejudice and segregation. They know. What you can and must do is help them develop ideas and associations and tools with which they can do something *about* segregation and prejudice.

How? We can say that the key to your teaching will be honesty and creativity. We can prepare materials for you and suggest teaching methods. Beyond that, it is your classroom. We will be happy to assist whenever we can.

How? You will discover the way—because that is why you have come.

THIS IS THE SITUATION—Charlie Cobb

Repression is the law; oppression, a way of life—regimented by the judicial and executive branches of the state government, rigidly enforced by state police machinery, with veering from the path of "our way of life" not tolerated at all. Here, an idea of your own is a subversion that must be squelched; for each bit of intellectual initiative represents the threat of a probe into the why of denial. Learning here means only learning to stay in your place. Your place is to be satisfied—a "good nigger."

They have learned the learning necessary for immediate survival: that silence is safest, so volunteer nothing; that the teacher is the state, and tell them only what they want to hear; that the law and learning are white man's law and learning.

There is hope and there is dissatisfaction—feebly articulated—both born out of the desperation of needed alternatives not given. This is the generation that has silently made the vow of no more raped mothers— no more castrated fathers; that looks for an alternative to a lifetime of bent, burnt, and broken backs, minds, and souls. Where creativity must be molded from the rhythm of a muttered "white son-of-a-bitch"; from the roar of a hunger-bloated belly; and from the stench of rain and mud-washed shacks.

There is the waiting, not to be taught, but to reach out and meet and join together, and to change. The tiredness of being told it must be, 'cause that's white folks' business, must be met with the insistence that it's their business. They know that anyway. It's because their parents didn't make it their business that they're being so systematically destroyed. What they must see is the link between a rotting shack and a rotting America.

PROBLEMS OF FREEDOM SCHOOL TEACHING
—Mendy Samstein

The Freedom Schools will not operate out of schoolhouses. There will rarely be classrooms, certainly no bells, and blackboards only if they can be scrounged. Freedom Schools in Mississippi will be a low-cost operation since funds will be very limited. Furthermore, the community will have little to offer in the way of resources. In many places, particularly in rural towns, there are no really suitable facilities available either in the white or in the Negro communities. As a result, most Freedom Schools will have to be held in church basements, homes, back yards, etc.

In some towns in the state, the students are waiting with great excitement in anticipation of the Freedom Schools. In other areas, however, special interest will have to be created—the teachers themselves will have to recruit students before the Freedom Schools begin. In these places, you will find that you are almost the first civil rights workers to be there, and if you are white, you will almost certainly be the first white civil rights workers to come to the town to stay. You will need to deal with the problem of your novelty as well as with the educational challenge.

There will be some advantages which will, we hope, overcome some of the material shortcomings. If you go to a town where COFO has had an active project for some time, you will probably be greeted warmly because there is a great deal of support for the Freedom School program. However, even if you go to a relatively new place, you can count on some things: In no community will there be a Freedom School unless the people of that community have expressed a desire for one, have shown their support by finding housing for staff at low cost (typically $10 a week for room and board), and have scouted out a place for a Freedom School.

The greatest advantage, however, will be the students and, we hope, your approach. In the final analysis, the effectiveness of the Freedom Schools this summer will depend upon the resourcefulness and honesty of the individual teachers—on their ability to relate sympathetically to the students, to discover their needs, and to create an exciting "learning" atmosphere. The informal surroundings, the lack of formal "school" trappings, will probably benefit the creation of this atmosphere more than the shortage of expensive equipment will discourage it. Attendance will not be required, so if the teacher is to have regular attendance from his students, he must offer them a program which continues to attract; this means that he must be a human and interesting person.

It is important to recognize that these communities are in the process of rapid social change and our Freedom School program, along with the rest of the summer activities, will be in the middle of this ferment. The students will be involved in a number of political activities which will be relatively new in Negro communities in Mississippi. They will be encouraging people to register to vote, organizing political rallies, campaigning for Negro candidates for high public offices, and preparing to challenge the Mississippi Democratic Party. These activities will be a large part of the experience which the students will bring to your classes. In most instances, we believe that this will help the Freedom School program and you should capitalize on these experiences by relating it to classroom work. You will need to know something about these experiences, so you will have the opportunity to share them by canvassing, campaigning, distributing leaflets, etc., with the students. You will define your role more precisely when you arrive by consulting with COFO voter registration people in the area. It will probably be important to the students that you show willingness to work with them but you will have to balance this against your own need to prepare for classes, recreation and tutoring.

In some communities, however, the situation may go beyond this. The community may embark upon more direct kinds of protest, resulting in mass demonstrations, jail, and any number of eventualities. We have no specific suggestions to make if this situation arises. You will have to play it by ear. We can only say that if you are teaching in a Freedom School in Mississippi, you *must* keep a sensitive ear to the ground so that if this should happen, you will be aware of what is happening in the community. You will have to decide if a continuing educational program is possible, and, if it is not, what modification of the program you can arrange to make this summer as constructive a period for the community as possible.

REMARKS TO THE FREEDOM SCHOOL TEACHERS ABOUT METHOD—Noel Day
TEACHING TECHNIQUES AND METHOD: The curriculum is flexible enough to provide for the use of a wide range of methods in transmitting the material. The basic suggested method is discussion (both as a class and in small groups) because of the opportunities this method provides for:
1. Encouraging expression.
2. Exposing feelings (bringing them into the open where they may be dealt with productively).
3. Permitting the participation of students on various levels.
4. Developing group loyalties and responsibility.
5. Permitting the sharing of strengths and weaknesses of individual group members.
However, presentation lectures, reading aloud (by students), the use of drama, art, and singing can be utilized in many sections of the curriculum. We recommend, however, that discussion be used as a follow-up in each instance in order to make certain that the material has been learned.

TEACHING HINTS:
1. Material should be related whenever possible to the experience of students.
2. No expression of feelings (hostility, aggression, submission, etc.) should ever be passed over, no matter how uncomfortable the subject

or the situation is. Both the students and the teacher can learn something about themselves and each other if it is dealt with honestly and with compassion.

3. The classroom atmosphere should not be formal (it is not a public school). Ways of accomplishing an informal atmosphere might be arrangement of seats in a circle, discussions with individuals or small groups before and after sessions, use of first names between teachers and students, shared field-work experiences, letting students lead occasionally, etc.

4. Prepare ahead of time for each session.

5. When using visual materials, make certain they are easily visible to all students and large enough to be seen. (When smaller materials must be used, pass them around after pointing out significant details.)

6. Let students help develop visual materials wherever possible (perhaps after class for the next session).

7. At the end of each session, summarize what has been covered and indicate briefly what will be done in the next session.

8. At the beginning of each session, summarize the material that was covered the day before (or ask a student to do it).

9. Keep language simple.

10. Don't be too critical at first; hold criticism until a sound rapport has been established. Praise accomplishments wherever possible.

11. Give individual help to small groups, or when students are reading aloud or drawing.

12. A limit of one hour (an hour and a half at most) is probably desirable for any one session. This limit can be extended, however, by changing activities and methods within a session.

DISCUSSION-LEADING TECHNIQUES

1. The leader must always be aware of his role: that he is, on the one hand, only the leader and not the dominant participant, and, on the other hand, that he is in fact the leader and responsible for providing direction and keeping the discussion going.

2. The use of questions is probably the best way to start and keep a discussion going. The questions should be:
   a. simple and clearly phrased.
   b. in language understood by the discussants.
   c. not answerable by "yes" or "no."

3. The best types of questions fall into three categories:
   a. Those investigating emotional response (e.g., how did you feel when? or how would you feel if?)
   b. Those investigating motivation (e.g., why did you feel that way? why would you do that? why do you think that?—etc.)

    c. Those in response to others' reactions (e.g., what do you think about what Bob said?)

4. The physical arrangements can affect the quality of discussion. The best arrangement has everyone in view of everyone else. The leader then stands to introduce a visual aid so that it is visible to all.

5. The leader should be careful to be adroit at keeping the discussion on the track.

6. The leader should occasionally summarize what has been said:
    a. to provide continued direction.
    b. to provide smooth transitions from one major topic to another.
    c. to emphasize important points (and by exclusion to de-emphasize irrelevant points).
    d. to re-stimulate the group if discussion has lagged.

7. The leader should encourage participation by everyone. Some techniques for this are:
    a. direct questions to silent participants (do not press if they continue to be reticent).
    b. use of small groups with the usually silent members as reporters.
    c. praise when the usually-silent members participate.
    d. relating topics to their personal interests and experiences.
    e. restating inarticulate statements for them (e.g., Do you mean? —etc.).

8. The leader should be sensitive to lagging interests and overextended attention spans. (The form of activity can be changed after a brief summary of the discussion to that point. A change of activity form is often restful—particularly when it requires some physical movement, such as breaking one large group into smaller groups scattered throughout the room, or putting review in the form of a TV quiz game, or asking that a particular point be dramatized, or a picture drawn, etc.)

9. The leader should have all resource materials, visual aids, etc., at hand.

10. The leader should always leave time for the students to ask him questions.

11. The leader should be willing to share his experiences and feelings, too.

12. The leader should not insist that words be pronounced in any particular way. Respect regional variations (e.g., Southern pronunciation of "bomb" is typically "bum"). The basic point is communication— if it gets the idea across it is good.

13. The leader should not be critical—particularly at the start. For many of the students, JUST BEING ABLE TO VERBALIZE IN THIS

SITUATION IS PROGRESS that can easily be inhibited by a dis-
approving remark or facial expression.

14. Learn the students' slang. It can often be used to ease tensions or to
express tones of feeling and certain meanings more succinctly than
more academic language.

15. Protect students from each other's verbal attacks and downgrading
(ranking, etc.)—particularly the slower or less articulate students.

USING DRAMA: Probably the best way of using the dramatic method is
the extemporaneous approach. In this approach, learning lines in a
formal way is avoided. A story is told, or a "Let us suppose that"
or a "Pretend that . . ." situation is structured, and then parts assigned.
The actors are encouraged to use their own language to interpret the
story or situation and some participants are assigned to act the part of
nonhuman objects as well (e.g., trees, a table, a mirror, the wind, the
sun, etc.). Each actor is asked to demonstrate how he thinks the character
he is portraying looks, what expression, what kind of voice, how he
walks, what body posture, etc. As soon as each actor has determined
the characteristics of his part, the story outlined is reviewed again, and
then dramatized. This method can permit the expression of a wide range
of feelings by the students, involve their total selves, stimulate creativity,
provide the teacher with insights about the students, and, at the same
time, get across the content material.

USING SPECIAL RESOURCE PEOPLE: There will be many talented
people in Mississippi this summer. Some of them will be attached to
projects in voter registration, community centers and freedom schools
(you). There will be other professional people who will not be staying
long enough to follow one project through from beginning to end, but
they are eager to make what contribution they can. Included in this
category are physicians, attorneys, ministers, and, most notably, entertainers. In the group of entertainers will be some very eminent folk
singers and comedians. (Folk singers are being recruited on a formal
basis. Lawyers are too. Physicians and ministers may or may not be
attached to specific programs.) Whatever their formal status, these
people will represent a great advantage to your program. You, however
will have to make the best use of them. You should try to make their
contribution as great, and as well-coordinated with the regular program,
as you and they can make it. This will require creative thinking and
prior planning for both the guests and the freedom school personnel.

FREEDOM SCHOOLS IN MISSISSIPPI, 1964

From the carbon copies of the spring's letters and reports I see what
real apprehensions, as well as hopes, the people who dreamed of Freedom

SECURITY CHECK-OUT FORM   (Give to Wats operator)

Date: _____

1. List driver and all passengers: _____

_____

_____

_____

2. Describe car: Make: _____ Model _____ Color: _____

Year: _____ Licence No.: _____ State: _____

Registered in name of : _____

3. Destination: _____
   (Name, address, and phone no. of contact if not regular office.)

_____

Time leaving: _____ Estimated Time arriving: _____ Route: _____

(Do not write below this line.)
Checked in by: _____ Time: _____

Schools had. Out of Charlie Cobb's idea of a situation in which there would be questioning, release from rigid squelching of initiative and expression—from Charlie Cobb's bitterness about the way the Negro has had to be silent in order to survive in white America, and his vision of the kids' articulateness and reaching for change, meaningful change, in Mississippi—out of his seeing that the kids are ready to see "the link between a rotting shack and a rotting America"—came the original plan for Freedom Schools in Mississippi. That it could be an idea that people working desperately on voter registration and on keeping alive in the state could take seriously is perhaps evidence of the validity of Charlie Cobb's dream: Mississippi needed more, needs more, than that all Negroes 21 and over shall have the right to vote. The staff in Mississippi understood what Charlie was dreaming because they, too, were daring to dream that what could be done in Mississippi could be deeper, more fundamental, more far-reaching, more revolutionary than voter registration alone: more personal, and in a sense more transforming, than a political program.

The decision to have Freedom Schools in Mississippi, then, seems to have been a decision to enter into every phase of the lives of the people of Mississippi. It seems to have been a decision to set the people free for politics in the only way that people really can become free, and that is totally. It was an important decision for the staff to be making, and so it is not surprising that the curriculum for the proposed schools become everyone's concern. I understand that Lois Chaffee, Dona Moses, Mendy Samstein, and Casey Hayden as well as Noel Day, Jane Stembridge, and Jack Minnis worked on and argued about what should be taught, and what the realities of Mississippi are, and how those realities affect the kids, and how to get the kids to discover themselves as human beings. And then, I understand, Staughton Lynd came into impose a kind of beautiful order on the torment that the curriculum was becoming —torment because it was not just curriculum: it was each person on the staff in Mississippi painfully analyzing what the realities of his world were, and asking himself, with what pain I can only sense, what right he had to let the kids of Mississippi know the truth, and what right he had had to keep it from them until now. And because of these sessions, the whole concept of what could be done in Mississippi must have changed.

In a way, the Freedom Schools began to operate in those planning sessions. A section of the curriculum called "Poor whites, poor Negroes and their fears," for example, considers the unity of experience between whites and Negroes, as well as the psychological and political barriers. And out of the discussions that produced this part of the curriculum came, perhaps, the idea of a "White Folks' Project," and the intense economic orientation of what was begun in Research, and Federal Programs, also new projects. And out of work with the people day after day in the Freedom Schools emerged medical concerns, and farm league ideas, and the community building of community centers. It was because the people trying to change Mississippi were asking themselves the real questions about what is wrong with Mississippi that the Summer Project in effect touched every aspect of the lives of the Negroes in Mississippi, and started to touch the lives of the whites.

It was the asking of questions, as I see it, that made the Mississippi Summer Project different from other voter registration projects and other civil rights activities everywhere else in the South. And so it is reasonable that the transformations that occurred—and transformations did occur— out of the Freedom School experience occurred because for the first time in their lives kids were asking questions.

The way the curriculum finally came out was that it was based on the asking of certain questions, questions which kept being asked through the summer, in connection with the kids' interest in their Freedom School teachers (mostly northern, mostly white, mostly still in college), in connection with Negro History, in connection with African culture, in connection even with the academic subjects, as well as in connection with the study of the realities of Mississippi in the light of Nazi Germany, 1935. The so-called "Citizenship Curriculum" set up two sets of questions. The primary set was: 1. why are we (teachers and students) in Freedom Schools? 2. what is the Freedom Movement? 3. what alternatives does the Freedom Movement offer us? what was called the secondary set of questions, but what seemed to me the more important, because more personal, set was: 1. what does the majority culture have that we want? 2. what does the majority culture have that we don't want? 3. what do we have that we want to keep?

The answering of these questions, and the continual raising of them in many contexts, may be said perhaps to be what the Freedom Schools were about. This was so because in order to answer anything out of what these questions suggest, it is necessary for the student to confront the question of who he is, and what his world is like, and how he fits into it or is alienated from it.

It was out of the experience of asking these questions that the transformations occurred. At the beginning of the summer, with rare amazing exceptions, the kids who were tentatively exploring us and the Freedom Schools were willing to express about themselves only one thing with honesty and passion, without the characteristic saying of the thing they think the white man wants to hear: that thing was that as soon as they could gather enough money for a ticket they were going off to Chicago, or to California! To leave the state was their ambition, and about it they were certain, even though they had not thought any further than that, even in terms of where the money was to come from, and certainly not in terms of what they would find there and what they would do there. Some sense of "go home to my Lord and be free"—some vague hope of a paradise beyond—seemed to inform their passion for the north, their programless passion.

But by the end of the summer almost all of these kids were planning to stay in Mississippi.

Within the flexible structure of the Freedom School it was natural that a confession of—an insistence on—the desire to race northward lead to a discussion of the condition of the Negro in the North, about which most of the teachers could tell specifically. And then came the news stories about Harlem, and Rochester, and Medford, Massachusetts, and the kids were interested, and worried. But it was not just because the truth about the North began to shatter their dream of it as a paradise that the kids changed their minds. The yearning for the North was, of course, the expression of a need to escape the intolerability of the situation in Mississippi. But the nature of their need to escape was that they really did not know what it was about Mississippi that they hated— or, rather, they felt that what was intolerable for them had somehow to do with the white man, somehow to do with getting only $3.00 a day for 10 hours' work chopping a white man's cotton, somehow to do with the police—but they had not yet articulated, if they knew, the connections among all these things. And they had not, as well, articulated the connections of those things with their experiences of repression at home and in school. And so the very amorphous nature of the enemy was threatening to them.

The experience in the Freedom School was that patterns began to be seen, and patterns were real and could be dealt with. So the kids began to see two things at once: that the North was no real escape, and the South was not some vague white monster doomed irrationally to crush them. Simultaneously, they began to discover that they themselves could take action against the injustices—the specific injustices and the condition of injustice—which kept them unhappy and impotent.

Through the study of Negro History they began to have a sense of themselves as a people who could produce heroes. They saw in the story of Joseph Cinque of the Amisted a parallel to the kinds of revolts that the Movement, as they began to learn about it, represented. They saw that Joseph Cinque, in leading a mutiny on that slave ship instead of asserting his will to freedom by jumping off the ship into the shark-waiting waters, was saying that freedom is something that belongs to life, not to death, and that a man has responsibility for bringing all his people to freedom, not just for his own escaping. Connections between then and now kept being made—at first by the teachers, very soon by the students: who do you know that is like Joseph Cinque? How is Bob Moses like Moses in the Bible? How is he different? Why did Harriet Tubman go back into the South after she had gotten herself free into the North—and why so many times? And why doesn't Mrs. Hamer stay in the North once she gets there to speak, since she doesn't have a job on that man's plantation any more, and since her life is in so much danger? And what do you think about Fredrick Douglass's talking so straight to the President of the United States? And how does the picture of Jim Forman in the Emancipation Proclamation issue of *Ebony* suggest that same kind of straight talking? And who do you think the Movement is proving right—Booker T. Washington or W. E. B. duBois? And what comment on your own upbringing is made by the fact that you all knew about Booker T. Washington but most of you had never heard of W. E. B. duBois? And why are the changes of gospel songs into Freedom Songs significant? What does "We Shall Overcome" really mean in terms of what we are doing, and what we can do?

Beginning to sense the real potency of organized Negroes in Mississippi, the kids in the Freedom Schools found an immediate area of concern in the Negro schools they attended or had dropped out of: the so-called "public" schools. They had grievances, but had, until drawn into the question-asking, only been able to whine, or to accept passively, or to lash out by dropping out of school or getting themselves expelled. Within the Freedom Schools, especially by comparing the Freedom Schools with the regular schools, they began to become articulate about what was wrong, and the way things should be instead: Why don't they do this at our school? was the first question asked, and then there began to be answers, which led to further questions, such as, Why don't our teachers register to vote, if they presume to teach us about citizenship? And why can't our principal make his own decisions instead of having to follow the orders of the white superintendent? And why do we have no student government, or why doesn't the administration take the existing student government seriously?

This was the main question, which came also out of why there are no art classes, no language classes, why there is no equipment in the science labs, why the library is inadequate and inaccessible, why the classes are overcrowded. The main question was WHY ARE WE NOT TAKEN SERIOUSLY?—which is of course the question that the adults were asking about the city and county and state, and the question the Freedom Democratic Party asked—and for which the Party demanded an answer—at the Convention.

The students were taken seriously in the Freedom Schools. They were encouraged to talk, and their talking was listened to. They were assigned to write, and their writing was read with attention to idea and style as well as to grammar. They were encouraged to sing, to dance, to draw, to play, to laugh. They were encouraged to think. And all of this was painful as well as releasing because to be taken seriously requires that one take himself seriously, believe in himself, and that requires confrontation. And so Freedom School was painful for the kids who grew the most.

Tangibly, what was set in motion out of this experience of joy and pain was the thing the Mississippi staff had hoped could happen in Mississippi, but could not totally form. In the spring before the summer, SNCC in Mississippi had tried to organize a Mississippi Student Union, bringing together kids from all over the state. And there was good response, but not on the scale the MSU was soon to achieve out of the Freedom Schools. This summer the kids began to talk boycott of the schools, but to be able to discipline their thinking about boycott so that their action would not just be acting out their frustrations but careful, considered, programed, revolutionary meaningful action along the lines of the Montgomery bus boycott and African revolutionary action. The kids were able to come together in the middle of the summer, in Meridian, and draw up a series of resolutions which said with terrible clarity what they felt about their world: what a house should be, what a school should be, what a job should be, what a city should be—even what the federal government should be. And they were able to ask why it was that the people did not have a voice, and to assert that their voices would be heard. The seriousness of their concern for a voice is reflected in the final statement of the list of grievances drawn up by the McComb Freedom School:

We are 12 Pike Couty high-school students. Until we are assured our parents will not suffer reprisals, until we are sure this list of grievances is met with serious consideration and good will, we will remain anonymous.

The McComb students are sounding this list of grievances to the school officials, the senators and the newspapers and the city officials and the President of the United States. Out into the world: look at me—I am no longer an invisible man.

And back again into themselves. Whoever the Freedom Schools touched they activated into confrontation, with themselves and with the world and back again. On one level, it was the white teacher saying to the Negro girl that nappy hair vs. "good hair" is not a valid distinction: that it is a white man's distinction, and that the queens in Africa—in Senegal, Mali, Ghana—in Ethiopia—had nappy short hair!

On another level, it was the Northern Negro student-teacher saying to the kids yearning Northward that he himself had gone to an almost completely (or completely) segregated school, and that his home was in a ghetto. On another, it was a senior, suspended from the split-session summer school for participating in the movement and taking Freedom School academic courses (fully parallel) instead, saying of Robert Frost's "The Road Not Taken" that the man took the road that needed him more: "because it was grassy/and wanted wear/. . . . and that has made all the difference." On another level, it was the white and Negro Freedom School teachers sitting with the adults in the evening classes talking about what kids want and what kids deserve, and hearing the adults express some of their concern for their kids in the forming of a parents' group to support the kids' action against the schools. On still another, it was the junior-high-school kids in the community coming over in the evening to sit with the adults who were learning their alphabets, one kid to one adult, and both, and the staffs, crying with awe for the beauty and strangeness and naturalness of it. And on all levels, it was the whites, the northerners, listening to the Mississippi Negroes, reading what they wrote, taking them seriously, and learning from them.

Visible results of the Freedom Summer include the kids' drawings on the walls of Freedom Schools and COFO offices all over the state, as well as kids' applications for scholarships (National Scholarship Service and Fund for Negro Students) and even more applications for the Tougaloo Work-Study program, which commits them to staying to work in Mississippi. In addition, there is the real probability that the Negro teachers in the regular schools—the teachers who have to sign an oath not to participate in civil rights activities or try to vote—have, this first week of school, begun to experience for the first time in their lives the challenge from a student that is not adolescent testing or insolent acting out but serious demanding that in truth there is freedom and that he will have the truth!

Most significantly, the result of the summer's Freedom Schools is seen in the continuation of the Freedom Schools into the fall, winter, spring, summer plans of the Mississippi Project. Some project directors, who had been in Mississippi since 1961 during the slow, sometimes depressing, always dangerous, serious, tiring work of voter registration, first thought of the Freedom Schools as a frill, detrimental to the basic effort. At best, they were a front for the real activity. But Freedom Schools were not just, as the same project directors came to concede, a place where kids could be inducted into the Movement, a convenient source of canvassers. They were something else, and in realizing this the dubious project directors were themselves transformed by the Freedom

Schools. They were, instead of anything superficial, and will go on to be, the experience—not the place—in which people, because we needed them, emerged as discussion leaders, as teachers, as organizers, as speakers, as friends, as people. I know this is so because in leaving the Freedom School in Indianola, the county seat of Sunflower County where the Movement had been resisted for three years, and where, when we came in, the people did not know how to cross arm over arm to sing "We Shall Overcome," I learned for the first time in my life that with kids you love to disconnect is to suffer. So the teachers were transformed, too.

The transformation of Mississippi is possible because the transformation of people has begun. And if it can happen in Mississippi, it can happen all over the South. The original hope of the Freedom School plan was that there would be about *1,000* students in the state coming to the informal discussion groups and other sessions. It turned out that by the end of the summer the number was closer to 3,000, and that the original age expectation of 16-17-18-year-olds had to be revised to include preschool children and all the way up to 70-year-old people, all anxious to learn about how to be Free. The subjects ranged from the originally anticipated Negro History, Mississippi Now, and black-white relations to include typing, foreign languages, and other forms of tutoring. In fact, these aspects of the program were so successful that the continuation of the Freedom Schools into the regular academic year will involve a full-scale program of tutorials and independent study as well as exploration in greater intensity of the problems raised in the summer sessions, and longer range work with art, music, and drama.

To think of kids in Mississippi expressing emotion on paper with crayons and in abstract shapes rather than taking knives to each other; to think of their writing and performing plays about the Negro experience in America rather than just sitting in despairing lethargy within that experience; to think of their organizing and running all by themselves a Mississippi Student Union, whose program is not dances and fund-raising but direct action to alleviate serious grievances; to think, even, of their being willing to come to school *after school*, day after day, when their whole association with school had been at least uncomfortable and dull and at worst tragically crippling—to think of these things is to think that a total transformation of the young people in an under-developed country can take place, and to dare to dream that it can happen all over the South. There are programs now, as well as dreams, and materials, and results to learn from. And it may well be that the very staffs of the Freedom Schools in Louisiana and Georgia, etc., will be the kids who were just this past summer students themselves in the Freedom Schools in Mississippi, and discovered themselves there.

                    Liz Fusco, Coordinator, COFO Freedom Schools

APPENDIX VIII

MISSISSIPPI FREEDOM DEMOCRATIC PARTY

MISSISSIPPI FREEDOM DEMOCRATIC PARTY DELEGATION:

National Committeewoman: Mrs. Victoria Gray
National Committeeman: Rev. Edwin King
Chairman of the Delegation: Dr. Aaron Henry
Vice-chairman of the Delegation: Mrs. Fannie Lou Hamer
Secretary: Mrs. Annie Devine

Delegates	*Alternates*
Mrs. Helen Anderson	Mr. C. R. Darden
Dr. A. D. Beittel	Mrs. Ruby Evans
Mrs. Elizabeth Blackwell	Mr. Oscar Giles
Mrs. Marie Blalock	Mr. Charlie Graves
Mr. Sylvester Bowens	Mrs. Pinkie Hall
Mr. J. W. Brown	Mr. George Haper
Mr. Charles Bryant	Mrs. Macy Hardaway
Mr. James Carr	Mr. Andrew Hawkins
Miss Lois Chaffee	Mr. William Jackson
Mr. Chois Collier	Mrs. Alta Lloyd
Mr. J. C. Fairley	Rev. J. F. McRae
Mr. Dewey Green	Rev. W. G. Middleton
Mr. Laurence Guyot	Mr. Joe Newton
Mrs. Winston Hudson	Mrs. M. A. Phelps
Mr. Willie Ervin	Mrs. Beverly Polk
Mr. N. L. Kirkland	Mr. Henry Reaves
Miss Mary Lane	Mr. Harold Roby
Rev. Merrill W. Lindsay	Mrs. Emma Sander
Mr. Eddie Mack	Mrs. Cora Smith
Mrs. Annie Matthews	Rev. R. L. T. Smith
Mrs. Yvonne MacGowan	Mrs. Elmira Tyson
Mr. Charles McLaurin	Mr. L. H. Waborn
Mr. Leslie McLemore	
Mr. Robert Miles	

Delegates   *Alternates*

Mr. Otis Millsaps
Mrs. Hattie Palmer
Rev. R. S. Porter
Mr. Willie Scott
Mr. Henry Sias
Mr. Robert Lee Slinson
Mr. Slate Stallworth
Mr. E. W. Steptoe
Mr. Joseph Stone
Mr. Eddie Thomas
Mr. James Travis
Mr. Hartman Turnbow
Mr. Abraham Washington
Mr. Clifton R. Whitley
Mr. Robert W. Williams
Mr. J. Walter Wright

FREEDOM PRIMER
NO. 1

The Convention Challenge

and

The Freedom Vote

THE CHALLENGE AT THE DEMOCRATIC NATIONAL CONVENTION

What Was the Democratic National Convention?

The Democratic National Convention was a big meeting held by the National Democratic Party at Atlantic City in August. People who represent the Party came to the Convention from every state in the country. They came to decide who would be the candidates of the Democratic Party for President and Vice-President of the United States in the election this year on November 3rd. They also came to decide what the Platform of the National Democratic Party would be. The Platform is a paper that says what the Party thinks should be done about things like Housing, Education, Welfare, and Civil Rights.

Why Did the Freedom Democratic Party Go to the Convention?

The Freedom Democratic Party (FDP) sent a delegation of 68 people to the Convention. These people wanted to represent you at the Convention. They said that they should be seated at the Convention instead of the people sent by the Regular Democratic Party of Mississippi. The Regular Democratic Party of Mississippi only has white people in it. But the Freedom Democratic Party is open to all people—black and white. So the delegates from the Freedom Democratic Party told the Convention *it* was the real representative of *all* the people of Mississippi.

How Was the Regular Democratic Party Delegation Chosen?

The Regular Democratic Party of Mississippi also sent 68 people to the Convention in Atlantic City. But these people were not chosen by all the people of Mississippi. Negroes were not allowed to attend the precinct, county, district, and state meetings where these delegates were chosen. Members of the Freedom Democratic Party tried to go to these meetings, but they were turned away from the door because these meetings were for white people only. But even most white people could not go to these meetings. The Regular Democratic Party of Mississippi is not controlled by all the white people, but only by a few powerful people—like James Eastland in Sunflower County and Billy and Gus Noble in Canton. They do not want to share their power. So they do not let most of the white people come to the meetings of the Regular Democratic Party either.

How Was the Freedom Democratic Party Delegation Chosen?

When the Regular Democratic Party of Mississippi told Negroes they could not come to its meetings, the Negroes held their own meetings. They called their party the Freedom Democratic Party. They held precinct, county, district, and state meetings just like the Regular Demo-

cratic Party. But the Freedom Democratic Party meetings were open
to anyone, black or white. At their meetings the Freedom Democratic
Party also chose delegates to the National Convention in Atlantic City.
Most of the delegates were Negroes. But some white people were chosen
too.

Who Decided If the Freedom Democratic Party Could Sit at Atlantic City?

At Atlantic City the delegates from the Freedom Democratic Party
went to a Committee that decided who could sit and vote in the Convention. This Committee was made up of two delegates from each state.
The Regular Democratic Party asked the Committee to let them sit and
vote in the seats for Mississippi. But the Freedom Democratic Party said
that they should be allowed to sit and vote for Mississippi. People like
Mrs. Fannie Lou Hamer and Dr. Aaron Henry told about the things
that happened to them in Mississippi, how they had been arrested and
beaten and how their homes had been shot into. They told how badly
all the Negro people in Mississippi are treated. And they told how they
had tried to go to the meetings of the Regular Democratic Party. They
told too how they had held meetings open to everyone to choose the
Freedom Democratic Party Delegation to Atlantic City. They were on
television, and many people everywhere in America saw them. Many
people in Mississippi saw them too.

What Did the Committee Decide?

The Committee made its decision by a vote. It voted that the Regular
Democratic Party in Mississippi should represent Mississippi at the Convention. This means that the Regular Democratic Party would sit in
the Mississippi seats at the Convention and cast all the votes for Mississippi. The Committee said that the Freedom Democratic Party could
not represent Mississippi at the Convention. The Committee said that
only Dr. Aaron Henry and Rev. Edwin King from the Freedom Democratic Party could sit and vote in the Convention. But Dr. Henry and
Rev. King would not be allowed to sit in the Mississippi seats or cast
the votes for Mississippi. The Committee did not say who Dr. Henry
and Rev. King would represent. The Committee also said that the members of the Regular Democratic Party of Mississippi would have to
promise to support President Johnson and his vice-president in the election November 3. If the delegates from the Regular Democratic Party
refused to promise this, they would not be allowed to sit and vote in the
Convention.

Why Did the Committee Make This Decision?

Many members of the Committee were afraid. Many of them wanted
to support the Freedom Democratic Party. But they were afraid they

would lose their jobs in Washington or back home in the state where they lived. In other parts of the United States it is often just like in Mississippi. You can lose your job if you stand up and say what you believe in.

President Johnson supported the all-white Regular Democratic Party. He wanted the Regular Party to be the only official party back here in Mississippi. President Johnson was afraid, too. Freedom Democratic Party delegate Hartman Turnbow of Holmes County said the President was afraid he would lose his job too if he stood up and said what he believed in.

Lyndon Johnson wants to be elected President again this November. He wants to get as many votes as possible in as many states as possible. President Johnson was afraid that if he supported the Freedom Democratic Party, the Republican candidate Barry Goldwater would get most of the votes in the Southern states and then President Johnson would lose his job as President.

President Johnson knows that in the Southern States there are many, many Negroes. But very, very few of them are allowed to vote. So most of the voters in the Southern states are whites. The President knew that if he supported the Freedom Democratic Party he might lose white friends in the South, and then he would not win the election in the Southern states. President Johnson was also afraid of the Regular Democratic Party of Mississippi. He knows that they do not like Civil Rights, or Aid to Education, or more Medical Care. He is afraid that the white politicians from Mississippi like James Eastland, Jamie Whitten and John Bell Williams will stop these programs in Washington. So President Johnson is afraid of these men.

But President Johnson had a lot of power at the Convention. He could tell many of the members of that Committee how to vote. The President can make many people judges or put them in other important positions. Since many members of the Committee want to be judges or important officials, when the President told them to vote against the Freedom Democratic Party, that is what they did.

What Did the Freedom Democratic Party Do?

The Freedom Democratic Party did not accept the decision of the Committee. They said that all the people at the Convention should be able to vote on who should have the seats for Mississippi. They knew that most of the delegates at the Convention, and people all over the country, believed what the Freedom Democratic Party said about Mississippi. They knew these people wanted to vote at the Convention, just as Negroes from Mississippi wanted to vote at the Convention.

The President did not want all the delegates to vote at the Convention. He knew that if all the delegates voted he might lose, and the

Freedom Democratic Party would be seated. He wanted to tell the delegates what to do.

But the Freedom Democratic Party stood together. And when people stand together they become strong. When you are strong you have some power, too. So President Johnson was not the only one at the Convention with power. The Freedom Democratic Party's power came from standing up and talking about what it believed in. People believed what Mrs. Hamer and Dr. Henry said, and they wanted to support the Freedom Democratic Party. For three days, the Freedom Democratic Party and its friends were strong enough to keep the President of the United States from doing what he wanted. But the President used all the pressure that he could, and finally he was able to stop all the delegates from voting about Mississippi.

Why Did the Freedom Democratic Party Reject the Committee's Decision?

The Committee offered two token seats to the Freedom Democratic Party. And the Committee chose the two people to sit in them, Dr. Henry and Rev. King. The Committee said this offer was the best they could do.

The Freedom Democratic Party delegation also voted. They voted whether or not to accept the decision of the Committee. They voted NOT to accept the decision of the Committee. The Freedom Democratic Party delegation said the offer was not good enough. They insisted that the Committee had to do better.

The Freedom Democratic Party said it was tired of tokens. It wanted 68 votes, not two votes. It wanted to vote for Mississippi. And it wanted to choose its own leaders—it did not want the Committee to say who could vote from the Freedom Democratic Party. The Freedom Democratic Party wanted its delegation to sit and vote with Democrats from all the other states in the country.

So the Freedom Democratic Party delegation said "No!" to the Committee. The delegation talked about the offer for many hours and voted several times. Each time the delegation said "No!" President Johnson and Hubert Humphrey could not understand why the Freedom Democratic Party would not give in. And many of our Negro and white friends could not understand either. Very few people in the country understand what it means to say "No!" to what is wrong and to say "Yes!" to what you believe in.

Most people think that you have to give in at some point so that other people will not be mad. They think that you are supposed to accept what you are offered by powerful people because that is the way things are done in this country. That is the way things have been done in Mississippi, too, for a long time.

It takes courage to stand up for what you believe in. That is why the Freedom Democratic Party was started. So that people could stand up for what they believe in in Mississippi. But because the Freedom Democratic Party stood up for what it believed in in Mississippi, it knew it had to do this everywhere. So when the President and the Committee said "No!" to the Freedom Democratic Party in Atlantic City, the Freedom Party continued to say "Yes!" to what it believed in.

What Did the Regular Party of Mississippi Do?

The Regular Party of Mississippi did not like the Committee's decision either. They were mad because Dr. Henry and Rev. King had been able to get seats in the Convention. They were mad too because they did not want to promise that they would work for President Johnson and Hubert Humphrey in the election. So Gov. Johnson of Mississippi told the Regular Democratic Party delegation to come home. And that is what they did, all except four of them who said they would support President Johnson and Hubert Humphrey.

What Happened to the Mississippi Seats at the Convention?

The four delegates from the Regular Democratic Party of Mississippi who promised to support President Johnson took their seats at the Convention. But the Freedom Democratic Party delegation also tried to take the Mississippi seats. When the Freedom delegates walked in, the four delegates from the Regular Democratic Party walked out. Then they went home too. So the Freedom Democratic Party delegation sat in some of the seats from Mississippi. For four days they kept coming to the Convention. In this way they showed that they felt they should be a part of the Convention, and that they wanted to support the national Democratic Party.

THE FREEDOM VOTE

What Will the Freedom Democratic Party Do Next?

The Freedom Democratic Party will keep working and spreading all over Mississippi. It wants more and more Negroes in Mississippi to take part in politics. It wants to grow and grow until it is stronger than the Regular Democratic Party of Mississippi.

The Freedom Democratic Party will also campaign for President Johnson and Hubert Humphrey in the November election. The Freedom Democratic Party is supporting Johnson and Humphrey even though Johnson and Humphrey supported the Regular Democratic Party of Mississippi at Atlantic City. The reason is that the Regular Democratic Party is fighting hard to get the Republican candidate Barry Goldwater and his conservative program into the White House. To support Johnson in Mississippi, therefore, is to help fight the Regular Democratic Party of Mississippi and the conservative program it supports.

The Freedom Democratic Party will also support other candidates in November. Dr. Aaron Henry is running for Senator from Mississippi,

and Mrs. Fannie Lou Hamer, Mrs. Victoria Gray, and Mrs. Annie
Devine are running for the House of Representatives. They are running
as Independents, but they will have the support of the Freedom Democratic Party. The Freedom Democratic Party wants everyone who is
registered to vote for Lyndon Johnson, Hubert Humphrey, Mrs. Hamer,
Mrs. Gray, and Mrs. Devine in November. But for those people who are
not registered there will be another vote—the FREEDOM VOTE.

What Is the Freedom Vote?

The Freedom Vote is a special vote for *all* people, Negro or white,
who are at least 21 years old and live in Mississippi. This year the Freedom Vote will be October 30 and 31 and November 1 and 2. The same
candidates will be on the Freedom Vote as are in the Regular Election
on November 3. People can FREEDOM REGISTER any time to vote
in the Freedom Vote.

The Freedom Democratic Party will try to get more votes in the
Freedom Vote than there are in the regular election. This will show that
Negroes want to vote and would vote if they were allowed to. It will
also show that if Negroes were allowed to vote in Mississippi, there
would be different people representing Mississippi.

The Regular Democratic Party does not like the Freedom Vote. But
the Negroes of Mississippi want to stand up and be counted. They know
that if they vote in the Freedom Vote their voices will be heard. And
they know that if they vote for President Johnson, he will have to listen.

Release 1200.4   1 January, 1965

MISSISSIPPI FREEDOM DEMOCRATIC PARTY
Washington, D. C.

TO: ALL MEDIA, FOR IMMEDIATE RELEASE
RE: THE STATUS OF MRS. HAMER, MRS. DEVINE
AND MRS. GRAY AS CONTESTANTS FOR
THE SEATS IN THE 2ND, 4TH, AND
5TH CONGRESSIONAL DISTRICTS
OF MISSISSIPPI

FROM: Executive Committee, Mississippi Freedom Democratic Party

There has been considerable discussion, confusion, and misrepresenta-
tion of the MFDP's posture in the challenge to the unlawfully elected
congressmen from Mississippi. In the challenges filed against the repre-
sentatives-elect, Messrs Whitten, Walker, and Colmer, three Negro ladies

from Mississippi are contesting the seats for which Messrs Walker Whitten, and Colmer now hold credentials by the State of Mississippi.

The MFDP contestants, as you know, have filed notices of challenge under Title 2, U.S. Code 201, et seq.

Persons have called into question the availability of this statute to the three MFDP contestants for the reason that they were not included on the official ballot on November 3. This argument could not be raised had they been on the ballot.

The fact is, however, that their exclusion from that ballot was illegal in that they had complied with all state statutes regulating their appearance on the ballot only to be unlawfully excluded therefrom by officials of the State of Mississippi.

Inasmuch as this is so, under precedents already established they will seek access to the Floor of the House of Representatives on January 4, not declaring their right to replace the Mississippi congressmen-elect in the seats which are being contested, but as contestants who wish to avail themselves of the business of the Congress during the period of contest so that in the event that contest is decided in their favor they will have sufficient background about the current session of Congress so that they might function effectively.

This right, they claim, is granted to the principals in contested elections, both by precedent and House of Representatives Rule XXXII governing access to the Floor of the House during the pendency of the cases before the House.

They are also seeking access to the Floor in order that they might, themselves, assist in the preparation and presentation of their contest.

TEXT OF THE FAIRNESS RESOLUTION TO BE INTRODUCED BY CONGRESSMAN WILLIAM F. RYAN

WHEREAS Article 1, Section 5 of the Constitution of the United States provides that "each House shall be the judge of the elections, returns and qualifications of its own members;" and

WHEREAS the Fourteenth and Fifteenth Amendments to the Constitution forbid the denial of the right of citizens to vote on account of race or color; and

WHEREAS between ninety and ninety-five per cent of all Negroes 21 years of age and resident in the State of Mississippi are not registered to vote and did not vote in November, 1964, election for members of congress from Mississippi due in at least substantial measure to violence, terror, discriminatory testing, economic reprisal, and similar measures,

WHEREAS the House in the Act of February 23, 1870, warned the

State of Mississippi that wholesale denial of the vote to her Negro citizens would result in a loss of her representation in this body,

WHEREAS, relying upon the foregoing, the validity of the election of Messrs. Abernathy, Whitten, Williams, Walker and Colmer, respectively, from the First, Second, Third, Fourth and Fifth Districts of Mississippi, is hereby challenged,

RESOLVED that the question of the right of Messrs. Abernathy, Whitten, Williams, Walker, and Colmer to be seated in the 89th Congress shall be referred to the Committee on House Administration when elected and said Committee shall have the power to send for persons and papers and examine witnesses under oath in relation to the subject matter of this Resolution; and be it further

RESOLVED that in view of the prima facie case of widespread violations of the Fourteenth and Fifteenth Amendments resulting from the fact that between ninety and ninety-five per cent of all Negroes 21 years of age and resident in the State of Mississippi are not registered to vote and did not vote in the November, 1964, election, Messrs. Abernathy, Whitten, Williams, Walker and Colmer shall not be sworn at this time and the question of their being sworn shall be held in abeyance until the House shall finally decide the question of the right of each said Messrs. to be seated in the 89th Congress; and be it further

RESOLVED that the Committee on House Administration shall make its report to the House of Representatives not later than 260 days following adoption of this Resolution, and be it finally

RESOLVED that this Challenge is separate from, but not in derogation of, whatever rights flow from the Challenge of the Mississippi Freedom Democratic Party under Title 2 of the U.S. Code, Section 201, et seq.

WASHINGTON MFDP NEWSLETTER TO ALL MFDP SUPPORT GROUPS

To: All MFDP Support Groups

From: Washington MFDP

December 31, 1964

At a meeting of the Washington Leadership Conference on Civil Rights yesterday the members of the Conference listed below resolved to support the Ryan Fairness Resolution.

As most of you know, Congressman William F. Ryan plans to object to the swearing-in of the Mississippians. Then, after the other Members have been sworn in, Ryan intends to introduce his resolution. According to the House parliamentarian, each Member has an absolute privilege to object to the swearing-in of any other Member. This means that Ryan is assured of the opportunity to make the objection. But whether or not he is able to introduce the resolution depends solely upon Speaker McCormack's recognizing him for that purpose. Ryan has been in touch with McCormack, but it remains uncertain just what position McCormack has taken about recognizing Ryan on Jan. 4 for introduction of the resolution.

At a meeting with several of the Conference people on Dec. 31, McCormack informed them that he would recognize Carl Albert, House Majority Leader, for the introduction of a motion to seat the Mississippians. He said that the precedents were all in favor of the priority of a motion to seat over a motion to unseat and that he felt constrained to follow the precedents.

MFDP's position is that all supporters should make every effort to commit Congressmen to support of the Ryan resolution and against any motion or resolution by anyone which would seat the illegally-elected Mississippians.

But whatever happens to the Ryan resolution the MFDP will be continuing with the statutory proceedings. Already there are 25 lawyers who have volunteered to head up teams to go into the state and collect evidence. Under the statute we have the right to subpoena testimony from all persons having relevant information and to submit this information to the Clerk of the House.

It is equally important now that all MFDP groups begin recruiting lawyers to assist in the taking of depositions during the 40 days following Jan. 4th in Mississippi. All lawyers willing to go to Mississippi during some or all of this period should be told to get in touch with Morton Stavis, Esq., 744 Broad St., Newark, N.J. (phone: 201-622-3790), or the Washington MFDP Office at 1353 U Street, N.W. (phone: 202-332-7732).

COUNCIL MEMBERS SUPPORTING RYAN
FAIRNESS RESOLUTION

American Jewish Congress
American Veterans Committee
Americans for Democratic Action
Anti-Defamation League of B'nai B'rith
Catholic Interracial Council
Commission on Religion & Race, NCC
CORE
Council for Christian Social Action, United Church of Christ
International Union of Electrical Workers

Jewish War Veterans of the U.S.
NAACP
National Catholic Conference for Interracial Justice
National Council of Catholic Women
National Student Association
Presbyterian Interracial Council
SCLC
SNCC
Urban League

Other DACAPO

ENCYCLOPEDIA OF
BLACK
AMERICA

SPIRITUALS
JAMES WELDON JOHNSON
& J. ROSAMOND JOHNSON
TWO VOLUMES IN ONE

323.1196 Holt, Len.
H
    The summer that
     didn't end.
        A18856

$14.95

323.1196 Holt, Len.
H
    The summer that
     didn't end.
       A18856

$14.95

DATE	BORROWER'S NAME	